THE CAMBRIDGE COMPANION TO AMERICAN LITERATURE AND EMPIRE

The story of American literature and empire goes beyond the broad historical periodization of empire to reimagine that history. The central terms *American* and *literature* have always been tied up in US empire as well as other empires in the Americas. The word "America," itself the product of interimperial intellectual rivalry, claims the name of an entire hemisphere for one country therein. To understand the full history of American literature and empire is to recognize its deep, strategically obscure, and often disavowed imperial contexts that in turn require differentially transatlantic, hemispheric, and global frameworks of analysis. This collection thus takes a skeptical stance toward its own geographical referent. Literature has a long and continuing imperial history as empire's proxy. These chapters cover canonical authors such as Cooper, Melville, Whitman, and Baldwin as well as lesser-known writers, including emergent artists focused on world-making with a reparative, speculative attention to the future.

ANNA BRICKHOUSE teaches English and American studies at the University of Virginia. Her books include *Earthquake and the Invention of America* (Oxford University Press, 2025), supported by a Guggenheim Fellowship, *The Unsettlement of America* (Oxford University Press, 2014), awarded the Modern Language Association's James Russell Lowell Prize, and *Transamerican Literary Relations and the Nineteenth-Century Public Sphere* (Cambridge University Press, 2004).

SUSAN GILLMAN teaches in the Literature Department at the University of California–Santa Cruz. Her books, published by the University of Chicago Press, include *Dark Twins: Imposture and Identity in Mark Twain's America* (1989), *Blood Talk: American Race Melodrama and the Culture of the Occult* (2003), which received honorable mention for the MLA's William Sanders Scraborough Prize, and *American Mediterraneans: A Study in Geography, History, and Race* (2022).

A complete list of books in the series is at the back of the book.

THE CAMBRIDGE COMPANION TO AMERICAN LITERATURE AND EMPIRE

EDITED BY

ANNA BRICKHOUSE

University of Virginia

SUSAN GILLMAN

University of California–Santa Cruz

CAMBRIDGE
UNIVERSITY PRESS

Shaftesbury Road, Cambridge CB2 8EA, United Kingdom

One Liberty Plaza, 20th Floor, New York, NY 10006, USA

477 Williamstown Road, Port Melbourne, VIC 3207, Australia

314–321, 3rd Floor, Plot 3, Splendor Forum, Jasola District Centre,
New Delhi – 110025, India

Cambridge University Press is part of Cambridge University Press & Assessment,
a department of the University of Cambridge.

We share the University's mission to contribute to society through the pursuit of
education, learning and research at the highest international levels of excellence.

www.cambridge.org
Information on this title: www.cambridge.org/9781009739436

DOI: 10.1017/9781009739467

First published 2026

A catalogue record for this publication is available from the British Library

A Cataloging-in-Publication data record for this book is available from the Library of Congress

ISBN 978-1-009-73943-6 Hardback
ISBN 978-1-009-73942-9 Paperback

Cambridge University Press & Assessment has no responsibility for the persistence
or accuracy of URLs for external or third-party internet websites referred to in this
publication and does not guarantee that any content on such websites is, or will remain,
accurate or appropriate.

For EU product safety concerns, contact us at Calle de José Abascal, 56, 1°, 28003 Madrid, Spain,
or email eugpsr@cambridge.org

Dedicated to the memory and work of Amy Kaplan

Contents

Figures

Contributors

MONIQUE ALLEWAERT is Professor of English and an affiliate of the Center for Culture, History, and Environment at University of Wisconsin–Madison. A specialist in eighteenth- and nineteenth-century American literatures and cultures, colonialism, and environmentalism, Allewaert is the author and editor of two books, numerous articles, and is completing a book about the connections between science, nature, and literature in the early Caribbean.

RALPH BAUER is a professor of English and comparative literature at the University of Maryland specializing in colonial American literatures, hemispheric studies, as well as literature and science in the early modern Atlantic world. His most recent publications include *The Alchemy of Conquest: Science, Religion, and the Secrets of the New World* (University of Virginia Press, 2019); (with Jaime Marroquín Arredondo) *Translating Nature: Cross-Cultural Histories of Early Modern Science* (University of Pennsylvania Press, 2019); and (with Alex Mazzaferro) *The Epistemological Turn in Early American Literary Studies* (a special issue of *American Literature* 97 (2025)).

ANNA BRICKHOUSE is Linden Kent Memorial Professor of English and American Studies at the University of Virginia. Her books include *Earthquake and the Invention of America* (Oxford University Press, 2024), *The Unsettlement of America* (Oxford University Press, 2014), and *Transamerican Literary Relations and the Nineteenth-Century Public Sphere* (Cambridge University Press, 2004). She is currently working on a transatlantic study of vulnerability, sovereignty, and literary style.

STEPHANIE J. FITZGERALD is an associate professor of American Indian studies at Arizona State University where she teaches American Indian and Indigenous literatures, American Indian studies, and Indigenous media. Her books include *Native Women and Land: Narratives of Dispossession and*

Resurgence (University of New Mexico Press, 2015), and with Jaye T. Darby, *Keepers of the Morning Star: An Anthology of Native Women's Theater* (UCLA American Indian Studies Center, 2003) and other articles and book chapters. Her current project examines the relationship between Red Power–era activism and contemporary Indigenous literatures.

SUSAN GILLMAN is Distinguished Professor of Literature at the University of California–Santa Cruz. She is the author of three University of Chicago Press books, *Dark Twins: Imposture and Identity in Mark Twain's America* (1989), *Blood Talk: American Race Melodrama and the Culture of the Occult* (2003), and *American Mediterraneans: A Study in Geography, History, and Race* (2022). She has worked collaboratively on several essay collections, including with coeditor Alys Eve Weinbaum, *Next to the Color Line: Gender, Sexuality and W. E. B. Du Bois* (University of Minnesota Press, 2007), with coeditor Russ Castronovo, *States of Emergency: The Object of American Studies* (University of North Carolina Press, 2009), and, most recently, with coeditor Christopher Castiglia, *Neither the Time nor the Place: Today's Nineteenth Century* (University of Pennsylvania Press, 2022).

EMILIO IRIGOYEN is Professor of Modern Literature at the Universidad de la República in Uruguay. He has published a book on the transatlantic afterlives of neoclassicism and essays on comparative literature and theater, with a focus on Modernism and the 1920s avant-gardes. In English, he has published an essay on Melville's *Israel Potter* in *Leviathan* (2018) and has coedited a special issue of the same journal on "Melville and Spanish America" (2021), as well as contributed a chapter to *A New Companion to Herman Melville* (Wiley, 2022). He currently codirects the Montevideana research group – active since 2003 – whose conference series and book collection propose (re)thinking Euro-American literature and culture from Latin American perspectives.

RODRIGO LAZO is a scholar of American literature broadly conceived across the Americas, with specialties in the nineteenth century, print culture, and archival studies. He is a professor of literature at University of California–Santa Cruz, where he is also an affiliate of the Latin American and Latino Studies Department. His books include *Letters from Filadelfia: Early Latino Literature and the Trans-American Elite* (University of Virginia Press, 2020), which won the best book in Early American Literature in 2022; *Writing to Cuba: Filibustering and Cuban Exiles in the United States* (University of North Carolina Press, 2005); and *The Latino Nineteenth Century*, coedited with Jesse Alemán (New York

University Press, 2016). He has published more than thirty academic articles and is a general editor of *The Broadview Anthology of American Literature*.

JEEHYUN LIM is Associate Professor of English and core faculty in Asian American studies at the University of Texas at Austin. She is currently working on a book project that explores the cultural legacies of the Korean War in American literature and visual culture. Parts of this work have been published in *American Quarterly* and *positions: asia critique*. She is the author of *Bilingual Brokers: Race, Literature, and the Language of Human Capital* (Modern Language Initiative, 2017) and coeditor of *Looking Back on the Vietnam War: Twenty-First-Century Perspectives* (Rutgers University Press, 2016).

ALEX LUBIN is Professor of African American Studies and History at Penn State University. His research and teaching focus on Black internationalism and diaspora, with a particular focus on the Middle East and North Africa. The author of *Geographies of Liberation: The Making of an Afro-Arab Political Imaginary* (University of North Carolina Press, 2014). Lubin is currently working on a new monograph about the African American expatriate community in Cairo, Egypt in the era of the Third World Movement titled, *Third World Ensemble: African Americans in Cairo Between the Suez and Six-Day Wars* (forthcoming from University of California Press).

GESA MACKENTHUN is Professor of American Studies at Rostock University, Germany. She has published widely on early modern colonial discourse, the disarticulation of the transatlantic slave trade in classic US literature, colonial and transcultural constructions of American antiquity, and the cultural discourse on plant cultivation. Her books include *Metaphors of Dispossession: American Beginnings and the Translation of Empire* (University of Oklahoma Press, 1997), *Embattled Excavations: Colonial and Transcultural Constructions of the American Deep Past* (Waxmann, 2021), and *Decolonizing "Prehistory": Deep Time and Indigenous Knowledges in North America*, coedited with Christen Mucher (University of Arizona Press, 2021). Her current research deals with representations of the transatlantic history of enclosures, evictions, and ecocide.

NADIA NURHUSSEIN is a professor in English and Africana studies, specializing in African American literature and culture. She is the author of *Black Land: Imperial Ethiopianism and African America* (Princeton University Press, 2019) and *Rhetorics of Literacy: The Cultivation of*

American Dialect Poetry (The Ohio State University Press, 2013), and editor of a new edition of *The Pedro Gorino* by Harry Foster Dean and Sterling North (Broadview, 2024). Her contribution comes from a chapter of her forthcoming monograph, which examines writing by Black sailors and sea captains about the liberatory potential of the sea.

JAK PEAKE, Senior Lecturer in Literature at the University of Essex, is a scholar of Caribbean and African American writing. His first book, *Between the Bocas: A Literary Geography of Western Trinidad* (Liverpool University Press, 2017), examines writing of and about Trinidad from the nineteenth to the twenty-first century, placing works by well-known authors such as V. S. Naipaul and Samuel Selvon alongside writing by Michel Maxwell Philip, Marcella Fanny Wilkins, Earl Lovelace, Monique Roffey, and Yseult Bridges. His current research focuses on US and Caribbean writing in the 1910–40 period. In spring 2024 he was the Stuart Hall Fellow at the Hutchins Center for African & African-American Research at Harvard University. He is also coauthor with professors Peter Hulme and Susan Gillman of a monograph, *The Tropics in New York: Race and Empire in Print Culture, 1919–1928*, which has been accepted for publication by University of Massachusetts Press.

CATHERINE S. RAMÍREZ, Professor of Latin American and Latino Studies at the University of California–Santa Cruz, is a scholar of Latinx literature, history, visual culture, and performance. Her expertise includes immigration and assimilation, historical memory and erasure, Mexican American women's history, zoot suits and style politics, and Latinxfuturism. She is the author of *Assimilation: An Alternative History* (University of California Press, 2020), *The Woman in the Zoot Suit: Gender, Nationalism, and the Cultural Politics of Memory* (Duke University Press, 2009), and more than a dozen essays about Latinx science fiction. She is a coeditor of *Precarity and Belonging: Labor, Migration, and Noncitizenship* (Rutgers University Press, 2021), and she has written for *The New York Times*, *The Atlantic*, and *The Washington Post*.

MARÍA JOSEFINA SALDAÑA-PORTILLO is Director of the Center for Latin American and Caribbean Studies at New York University and a professor in the Department of Social & Cultural Analysis. Her book *Indian Given: Racial Geographies across Mexico and the United States* (Duke University Press, 2016), received the 2019 Casa de Las Americas Literary Prize in Latino Studies; the 2017 ASA John Hope Franklin Book Prize; and the 2017 NACCS Book Award. Her title *The Revolutionary Imagination in the Americas and the Age of Development* (Duke University Press, 2003) is still her favorite. She has written over thirty articles on revolution, subaltern politics, Indigenous history, racial formation, migration, narco-economies, and Latin American and Latinx cultural studies: her most recent include "The Crisis for Asylum Victims is Gender Based Violence" coauthored with Laura Briggs (Public Books, 2021); and "What Does Mestizaje Name?" coauthored with Simón Trujillo (*Aztlán* 2021). A board member of the Coalición Mexicana, an immigrants' rights organization, she is also an expert witness for Central American asylum cases.

RAFAEL WALKER is Associate Professor of English at Baruch College. He specializes in American and African American literature, theory of the novel, and gender and sexuality studies. He is the author of *Realism after the Individual: Women, Desire, and the Modern American Novel* (University of Chicago Press, 2025). He is working on another book, "Biraciality in American Literature and Culture." His essays have appeared or will appear soon in several journals, including *ELH, J19, Twentieth-Century Literature, Studies in the Novel*, and *MELUS*. He is the editor of two critical editions – *The Awakening and Selected Stories* (Warbler Classics, 2021) and Nella Larsen's 1929 novel *Passing* (Broadview Press, 2023). He writes often about issues in higher education, mostly for the *Chronicle of Higher Education*.

MEG WESLING is Associate Professor of US Literatures at University of California–San Diego, and an affiliate of the Critical Gender Studies Program. She is past faculty director of University of California Education Abroad Program in France (2013–15). She earned her doctorate from Cornell University (English) and her bachelor's degree from Indiana University (French and women's studies). She is the past recipient of a year-long faculty fellowship at the Society for the Humanities at Cornell University, and of the Hellman and other faculty research fellowships at University of California–San Diego. Dr. Wesling's monograph, *Empire's Proxy: American Literature and US Imperialism in the Philippines*, was published by New York University Press in 2011. She is also the author of numerous essays on American literature, sexuality studies, and feminist theory, published in *American Quarterly, MELUS, Mosaic, GLQ, American Literature*, and *Feminist Review*, among others.

HILARY E. WYSS is the Allan K. Smith and Gwendolyn Miles Smith Professor of English at Trinity College in Hartford, Connecticut, where she teaches early American literature, American studies, and Indigenous literatures. Her books include *English Letters and Indian Literacies: Reading, Writing, and New England Missionary Schools, 1750–1830* (University of Pennsylvania Press, 2012); *Writing Indians: Literacy, Christianity, and Native Community in Early America* (University of Massachusetts Press, 2000); and with Kristina Bross, *Early Native Literacies in New England: A Documentary and Critical Anthology* (University of Massachusetts Press, 2008). She is currently working on a transatlantic study of intersecting eighteenth-century rhetorics of race, benevolence, and childhood and the rise of institutions through which to manage children throughout the British Empire.

Acknowledgments

Our volume reaped the practical benefits of a strong team: huge thanks to Rachel Haines for careful reading and copyediting; to Biju Singh for submission and production assistance; and to Ray Ryan for inviting us to take on this project.

Working on this collection was from the beginning a labor of love, reflected in the dedication to Amy Kaplan. We thank our wonderful contributors for honoring her, sharing their work with us, and teaching us so much. It was a privilege to think in this company. Finally, we are endlessly grateful for Amy herself; it is in her memory and with the aim of carrying on her work that we first agreed to edit this volume. We hope it may bring new readers to her field-defining work and new afterlives to her vision.

Timeline of Texts and Events

Early 1400s	Ptolemy's *Geography*, which presented a spherical earth in a geometrical grid, is rediscovered in Europe.
1469	The Spanish kingdom of Castille and Leon is united with the Crown of Áragon through the marriage of Queen Isabella and King Ferdinand.
1492	October: Christopher Columbus's landfall in the Bahamas.
1493	Pope Alexander VI promulgates the *Inter caetera* bulls, assigning monopolies of access to the newly discovered territories west and east of a vertical geographical line of demarcation in the Atlantic Ocean 100 leagues (ca. 350 miles) west of the Azores between Spain and Portugal respectively.
1494	Treaty of Tordesillas between Spain and Portugal: reaffirms Pope Alexander's line of demarcation but moves it 270 leagues (ca. 950 miles) to the west, placing the eastern tip of South America (what would become Brazil) under Portuguese dominion.
1497	John Cabot's first voyage to North America on behalf of the English crown.
1498	Vasco de Gama, sailing for Portugal, lands in Calicut, India. Columbus reaches the Orinoco Delta on his third voyage.
1500	Pedro Álvares Cabral lands in Brazil near present-day Río de Janeiro on route to India.
1503	First publication of *Mundus Novus*, a tract attributed to Amerigo Vespucci claiming that the newly

1552	Bartolomé de Las Casas publishes *A Short Account of the Destruction of the Indies*.
1555	Founding of "Antarctic France," a French Huguenot colony in present-day Río de Janeiro by Nicolas Durand de Villegaignon (destroyed by the Portuguese in 1567).
1557	Hans Staden publishes his *True History: An Account of Cannibal Captivity in Brazil*.
1564	René Goulaine de Laudonnière establishes a French military and trading outpost Fort Caroline (near present-day Jacksonville, Florida).
1565	Founding of St. Augustine, south of present-day Jacksonville, Florida, by Don Pedro Menéndez de Avilés; destruction of Fort Caroline by Menéndez de Avilés.
1570s	Offices of the Inquisitions are established in Mexico and Peru.
1578	Jean de Léry publishes *History of a Voyage to the Land of Brazil, also called America*, about his stay in Antarctic France, in Brazil.
1585	Establishment of the first English colony at Roanoke (in present-day North Carolina) under the governorship of Ralph Lane with a patent and sponsorship by Sir Walter Raleigh but abandoned the following year.
1590	Theodor de Bry publishes the first volume of his popular *America* series, an illustrated re-edition of Thomas Harriot's *A True and Brief Report of the Newfound Land of Virginia* (about the 1585 colonial venture at Roanoke in present-day North Carolina), in a coastal area then called "Virginia" by English colonists.
1593	John Dee's *The Limits of the British Empire*.
1595	Sir Walter Raleigh's expedition to Guiana, in South America.
1605	Founding of Port Royal in Acadia by Samuel de Champlain.
1607	First permanent English colony is established at Jamestown (in modern-day Virginia).

1758	Antoine-Simon Le Page du Pratz publishes *History of Louisiana*.
1763	End of Seven Years' War in North America (1756–63). France loses territories in Canada.
1765–8	Samson Occom embarks on a multiyear fundraising mission to Great Britain for Moor's Charity School.
1767	Expulsion of Jesuits from the Spanish American Empire.
1769	Dartmouth College is founded in New Hampshire by Wheelock to replace Moor's Charity School, much to the dismay of Samson Occom.
1776	Founding of the Viceroyalty of La Plata. Abigail Adams pens the famous letter to her husband, John Adams, now remembered by the shorthand title "Remember the Ladies," in which she paves the way toward the repeal of coverture in the USA – a system, undergirded by the law, stipulating that women could not own property because they were themselves property, of either their fathers or their husbands. In this same year – which, of course, includes American independence – Jemima Wilkinson (self-styled as "The Friend" or "The Public Universal Friend") emerges from an illness declaring themself genderless. Wilkinson, a preacher, developed a following dubbed the Society of Universal Friends.
1776–83	Anglo-American War of Independence.
1780	Thomas Jefferson writes letter envisioning an "Empire of Liberty" to follow the Revolutionary War.
1784	Charles Hérard-Dumesle born in Les Cayes, Haiti.
1785	Thomas Jefferson publishes *Notes on the State of Virginia*, his scientific survey of his home state. Written in response to an inquiry of the French politician François-Barbé Marbois, Jefferson here formulates foundational ideas about agriculture, slavery, and territorial conquest. Samson Occom writes petitions for the Montaukett Tribe to the State of New York and the Brothertown community to the United States Congress.

1786	"Poet of the Revolution" Philip Freneau publishes revised, post-Revolution version of "The Rising Glory of America."
1787	US Constitution ratified.
1791–1804	Haitian Revolution.
1792	The Sierra Leone Company, established by British abolitionists, founds a colony in West Africa for Black Britons and Canadians who were Loyalists during the Revolutionary War.
	Olaudah Equiano was a significant advocate of this early repatriation movement, having been involved as early as the first failed attempt to found a British settlement there several years earlier.
1803	Louisiana Purchase. United States acquires vast territories west of the Mississippi from France.
1804	Haiti gains independence from France.
1807–19	Haitian Civil War.
1815–16	Paul Cuffe, a Black mariner from Massachusetts, sails to Sierra Leone with Black families from the United States who intend to settle in the colony; he had discussed the colony with President James Madison during a meeting at the White House.
1819	Herman Melville is born in New York.
1821	Mexican independence.
1823	President James Monroe argues that the Americas are the USA's exclusive sphere of influence, which will become a key tenet of US long-term foreign policy, known as the "Monroe Doctrine."
1824	Hérard-Dumesle publishes *Voyage dans le Nord d'Hayti*.
1827	James Fenimore Cooper publishes *The Pioneers*.
1830	Indian Removal Act of 1830 is signed into law by President Andrew Jackson, beginning the process of forcibly removing Indigenous people from their homelands east of the Mississippi River to the Indian Territory west of the Mississippi River. The act is part of Jackson's policy of eradicating the Indigenous presence and culminates in the Trail of Tears in 1838 and the forcible displacement of

60,000 Native Americans over the following two
decades.

1837   *Fisher* v. *Allen* is decided in Mississippi, dealing
a crippling blow to coverture in the USA, creating
the conditions for women to live independently
from men – and with other women if they wished.

1839–45   Anti-Rent War. A peasant revolt in upstate
New York to fight the quasi-feudalist property
structures and rent system of the landed gentry of
the Hudson River Valley.

1841   Melville sails from New Bedford in January as part
of the crew of the whaler *Acushnet*. He will spend
almost four years overseas, mostly in Polynesia and
the South American Pacific.

In the Northeast USA, E. E. Barclay begins publishing and selling sensational fiction about murders
and kidnappings, a nineteenth-century print form
of violence as entertainment.

1843–4   Melville serves for fourteen months on the frigate
United States, mostly patrolling the South American
Pacific.

1844–55   The period of the California Gold Rush, an historical event in which a preponderance of single men
was drawn to California. In the absence of women
in the wild, wild west, many of these male adventurers formed same-sex relationships in a time and
place unusually hospitable to such arrangements.

1845   John L. O'Sullivan coins the phrase "Manifest
Destiny" in *The United States Magazine and
Democratic Review* to advocate for the annexation
of Texas and the Oregon Country and, more
broadly, to describe the belief that the USA was
divinely ordained to expand its territory across
North America.

The Republic of Texas, proclaimed in 1836 by US
Immigrants in Mexico territory, is annexed by
the USA.

1845–6   Publication of James Fenimore Cooper's Littlepage
trilogy, consisting of the novels *Satanstoe* (1845), *The
Chainbearer* (1845), and *The Redskins* (1846).

1846   Melville's first novel, *Typee*, portrays European and
            US imperialism in Polynesia.

1846–8   United States military invasions of Mexico; aka the
            US-Mexican War. The war results in the USA
            annexing nearly half of Mexico's national territory.

1847   A settlement in West Africa named Liberia, estab-
            lished by the American Colonization Society and
            intended for formerly enslaved Black Americans,
            becomes an independent republic.

1848   Treaty of Guadalupe-Hidalgo; Mexico loses half its
            national territory. Treaty establishes *all* Mexicans in
            annexed territory will be treated as full US citizens;
            in practice, the USA refuses to recognize tens of
            thousands of Indigenous and Afro-mestizos within
            the annexed territories, who are actively excluded
            from citizenship, ushering in an era of dispossession
            and disenfranchisement, which will ultimately
            impact white Mexicans as well.
            James Fenimore Cooper publishes *The Crater*.
            US President James Polk attempts to purchase
            Cuba.

1849   Following the discovery of gold in California,
            Chinese laborers arrive in California to work the
            mines and railroads.

1850   *White-Jacket*, a novel inspired by Melville's time in
            the US Navy, is published in New York.

1851   Narciso López, supported by US southerners, leads
            pro-annexationist uprisings in Cuba.
            Moby-Dick is published in London and New York.
            Barclay publishes the sensationalist novel,
            *A Thrilling and Exciting Account of the Sufferings and
            Horrible Tortures Inflicted on Mortimer Bowers and
            Miss Sophia Delaplain by the Spanish Authorities, for
            a Supposed Participation with General Lopez in the
            Invasion of Cuba.*

1854   US President Franklin Pierce attempts to purchase
            Cuba.

1855   Walt Whitman publishes the first edition of his
            poetry collection, *Leaves of Grass*, now considered

a landmark work in gay history and in the history of modern poetry.

1858   Hérard-Dumesle dies in Jamaica.

1861–5 US Civil War.

1864   The Sand Creek Massacre is a bloody massacre of inhabitants of a Cheyenne and Arapahoe village by the US Army in present day Colorado.
Harry Foster Dean is born.

1869   US President Grant proposes the annexation of Santo Domingo (today the Dominican Republic) with the promise of eventual statehood. The attempted treaty fails.

1870   Bayard Taylor publishes *Joseph and His Friend*, widely considered the first gay novel published in the USA.

1873   Comstock Act, named for anti-vice crusader Anthony Comstock, prohibited the mailing of "obscene" material, including any material related to education about sex, contraception, and abortion. This law has significant effects on the availability of contraception through the twentieth century; it was invalidated by the Supreme Court Decision *Griswold* v. *Connecticut* (1965).

1875   The Page Act bans Chinese women from entering the USA to prevent family settlement.

1879   The Carlisle Indian Industrial School is founded in Carlisle, Pennsylvania under the leadership of Captain Richard Henry Pratt, with the mission of "kill the Indian, save the man."

1882   Chinese Exclusion Act, prohibits further immigration from China while denying the right to naturalization to Chinese immigrants already in the USA.

1887   General Allotment Act, also known as the Dawes Act, authorizes the US government to divide tribal lands into parcels of 160 acres per head of household to be distributed to those Native Americans who are willing to become US citizens. The act converted tribal lands into private property and sold off "surplus" land to white settlers, leading to extensive tribal land losses: the loss of 90 million acres of

	Indian land. The act also inscribes Native Americans on the tribal rolls of the Office of Indian Affairs.
	Marcus Garvey is born.
1889	Mark Twain publishes his anti-imperialist *A Connecticut Yankee in King Authur's Court* with Charles Webster & Co.
1893	US-backed overthrow of Queen Lili'uokalani results in the provisional government with Sanford B. Dole as president. Dole was instrumental in the annexation of Hawaii.
1897	Sexologist and eugenicist Havelock Ellis publishes *Studies in the Psychology of Sex*.
1898	The Spanish-American War marks the beginning of US overseas imperial expansion; the USA acquires the territories of (that is, takes neocolonial control over) Puerto Rico, Guam, and the Philippines.
1898–1945	The era of Pan-African Congresses begins, launched in London by Sylvester Williams and revised after World War I by W. E. B. Du Bois. The Pan-African Congresses were attempts to discuss anticolonialism by Africans and global members of the diaspora in the context of evolving national liberation movements across Africa and during the formation of a liberal internationalist world order. W. E. B. Du Bois's 1928 *Dark Princess* is a record of the making of a Pan-African consciousness.
1899	The Philippine-American War begins when the USA refuses to recognize the First Philippine Republic.
	Melville dies in New York.
1899–1902	Following the Spanish-American War, the USA occupies Cuba, establishing a military government until Cuba's formal independence in 1902.
1900	The first Pan-African Conference is held in London.
1901	Mark Twain, "To the Person Sitting in Darkness," *North American Review* Vol. 172, No. 531 (February 1901).
1903	Hay-Bunau-Varilla Treaty grants the USA the right to "use, occupation and control" of the land and

	water for the Panama Canal's construction and operation.
1903(–14)	US President Theodore Roosevelt supports Panamanian independence from Colombia. In return, Panama grants the USA rights to build and control the Panama Canal Zone. Construction of the canal (1903–14) depends heavily on Black West Indian laborers, particularly from Barbados, Jamaica, Grenada, Martinique, and Trinidad.
1904	The USA occupies the Panama Canal Zone until 1999.
1906	Edward Prime-Stevenson privately publishes *Imre: A Memorandum*, the first gay novel an American author published with a happy ending for the same-sex couple.
1906–9	After the collapse of President Tomás Estrada Palma's government in Cuba, President Theodore Roosevelt orders an invasion of Cuba to protect US interests, which leads to what is often termed the "second occupation of Cuba."
1912–33	The USA occupies Nicaragua, backing conservative regimes and suppressing liberal uprisings. This long-term intervention, part of the broader "Banana Wars," includes military conflict with nationalist leader Augusto César Sandino, who leads a guerrilla resistance against US forces between 1927 and 1933.
1915	Charlotte Perkins Gilman publishes *Herland* as monthly installments in *The Forerunner*; about a feminist utopia engineered through "negative eugenics" for the elimination of "unattractive" or "unproductive" members of society.
1915–34	The US occupation of Haiti begins after the assassination of the Haitian President Vilbrun Guillaume Sam; in the 1920s, the US occupation becomes a focal point of anti-imperial critique in Black and leftist US periodicals.
1916	The USA invades the Dominican Republic with US Marines, occupying it for eight years.

1916–24	The USA occupies the Dominican Republic; during this occupation, US forces dissolved the Dominican Congress, impose military rule, and build infrastructure to serve American strategic interests – prompting resistance from Dominican nationalists.
1917	The USA purchases the Danish West Indies from Denmark for $25 million, renaming them the US Virgin Islands. The acquisition, driven by strategic concerns during World War I – particularly fears of German encroachment in the Caribbean – expands US territorial control in the region and reinforces its naval presence near the Panama Canal, further consolidating US interests and influence across the Caribbean.
1917–22	In what is often termed the "third occupation of Cuba," the USA deployed Marines to Cuba to safeguard its economic interests, particularly in the sugar industry. This period saw heightened US intervention in Cuban domestic affairs, marked by the suppression of strikes and the protection of US-owned property and infrastructure.
1919	Marcus Garvey's Black Star Line is incorporated; its first ship, the SS *Yarmouth*, is purchased, with plans to rename it the *Frederick Douglass*. Although the ship was not in good shape, it makes stops throughout the Caribbean during its first major trip to considerable fanfare.
1920	James Weldon Johnson's "Self-Determining Haiti" is published in *The Nation*, a four-part exposé of the US occupation of Haiti.
	Eugene O'Neill's *The Emperor Jones* premiers on November 1 at the Provincetown Playhouse in Greenwich Village. A landmark in US theatre history, it is widely regarded as the first Broadway play to feature a racially integrated cast and to star a Black actor in a leading role. Charles Gilpin, who played the title character Brutus Jones, earns widespread acclaim for his performance.
1921	The musical of *Shuffle Along* debuts on Broadway. Composed by Eubie Blake, with lyrics by Noble

Sissle, and performances by comedy duo Flournoy Miller and Aubrey Lyles, *Shuffle Along* broke ground as an all-Black hit on Broadway. The show, which ran for just over a year, also introduces Paul Robeson and Josephine Baker to Broadway.

The first full-length biography of Melville is published, contributing to a renewal of interest in his work that will become known as the "Melville revival."

1922   Marcus Garvey is arrested and imprisoned for mail fraud.

1925   In March, a special issue of the *Survey Graphic* "Harlem: Mecca of the New Negro," edited by Alain Locke is published. The issue is devoted to the New Negro and sells 40,000 copies in two weeks – a record unmatched until the 1940s. In December, Albert and Charles Boni publish the anthology *The New Negro: An Interpretation*, an expanded version of the March *Survey Graphic* Harlem issue in book form.

Harry Foster Dean's Habashi Nautical College is incorporated in Alameda, California.

1926   W. E. B. Du Bois organizes a symposium on Black representation in art in *The Crisis*: "The Negro in Art: How Shall He Be Portrayed?"

Carl Van Vechten's *Nigger Heaven* is published by Knopf.

Langston Hughes's debut poetry collection, *The Weary Blues*, is published by Knopf.

Eric Walrond's short story collection, *Tropic Death*, is published by Boni and Liveright.

Opportunity: A Journal of Negro Life, edited by Charles S. Johnson, devotes a special issue to the Caribbean, highlighting the region's literary, cultural, and political significance.

1928   Claude McKay's *Home to Harlem* is published by Harper and is widely compared to Van Vechten's novel *Nigger Heaven*. McKay's novel centers on Harlem's nightlife while also incorporating Caribbean themes, including the Haitian character

	Ray, a counterpart to the African American protagonist Jake.
1929	William Seabrook publishes *The Magic Island*, a sensationalist travel account of Haiti during US occupation.

Carl Van Doren declares in *Wings* magazine that Americans are now "citizens of an empire," reflecting an increasing awareness that the USA played an imperial role in the world.

Harry Foster Dean's memoir, *The Pedro Gorino: The Adventures of a Negro Sea-Captain in Africa and on the Seven Seas in his Attempts to Found an Ethiopian Empire, An Autobiographical Narrative*, is published by Houghton Mifflin.

1930   Coup de'état overthrows President Horacio Vásquez of the Dominican Republic; installation of US-backed General Rafael Trujillo as dictator; his brutal regime stays in power for thirty-one years until he is assassinated.

1935   Harry Foster Dean dies.

1940   Marcus Garvey dies.

1941   F. O. Matthiessen's *American Renaissance: Art and Expression in the Age of Emerson and Whitman* is published, which is influential in establishing Melville at the core of a US literary canon – one described as fundamentally democratic and distinctly national.

1943   The USA and Mexico sign the "Bracero Agreement" which allows Mexican workers to enter the United States for agricultural work during planting and harvesting seasons; agreement stays in place until 1964.

1945   World War II ends; American "rise to globalism" and Pax Americana begin. The front known as the Pacific War ends with Japanese surrender to the United States, and Korea is partitioned along the 38th parallel line with the Japanese soldiers north of the 38th parallel surrendering to the Soviet Union and south of the line surrendering to the United States.

1947	Democratic People's Republic of Korea is proclaimed in North Korea with Kim Il-Sung as the supreme leader.
1948	Republic of Korea is formed in South Korea with the US-backed Syngman Rhee as president.
	President Harry Truman issues Executive Order to end segregation in the Armed Services, a landmark beginning of the modern Civil Rights struggle to end racial discrimination and establish equal rights under the law.
	James Baldwin moves to Paris.
1950	The Korean War breaks out when the North Korean army crosses the 38th parallel into South Korea.
1952	The McCarran–Walter Act, or the Immigration and Nationality Act of 1952, repeals measures of Asian exclusion and allows the naturalization of Asians as American citizens.
	Trinidadian critic C. L. R. James detained by immigration officials and removed to Ellis Island, where he remains confined for the next six months under the McCarran–Walter Act as a "foreign subversive." He begins writing *Mariners, Renegades and Castaways: The Story of Herman Melville and the World We Live In*.
1952 (and 1956)	The Indian Relocation Act results in the removal of more than 100,000 Indians from reservations to selected urban centers such as Chicago, Seattle, Los Angeles, and Phoenix.
1952–67	Egypt wins independence from Britain, and Gamal Abdel Nasser becomes an Arab and African leader of an African anti-colonial movement. Cairo becomes a hub of Third World politics following Nasser's participation in the 1955 Bandung, Indonesia conference that launched the Third World project, and following the 1956 formation of the Afro-Asian People's Solidarity Organization (AAPSO) in Cairo. During this period, Cairo hosted anti-colonial leaders across the Afro-Asian world, and this is one of the draws for African American expats,

some of whom had lived in Ghana, to travel and reside in Cairo. Among the African American expats in Cairo during this Third World era were Shirley Graham Du Bois, David Graham Du Bois, Maya Angelou, and dozens of African Americans Muslims studying Sunni Islam at Al-Azhar University.

1953   The Termination Act of 1953 ends the special relationship between tribal nations and the federal government, leading to 109 tribes losing their federal recognition status.

The Korean Armistice Agreement is signed at Panmunjom with representatives from the USA, the United Nations Command, North Korea, and the People's Republic of Korea being present; South Korea does not sign the armistice.

Executive Order 10450, signed by President Eisenhower, bars homosexuals from federal employment.

1954   French troops are defeated by Viet Minh troops led by Ho Chi Minh at Dien Bien Phu, and Geneva Accords brings about a ceasefire in Vietnam while dividing the country at the 17th parallel.

US-backed overthrow of democratically elected President Jacabo Árbenz Guzmán in Guatemala leads to thirty-six years of civil war and the assassination of over 200,000 Indigenous Guatemalans by the CIA-trained Guatemalan National Guard.

Algerian War of Independence begins. The FLN (National Liberation Front) fights French colonial forces for Algeria's independence.

1955   Two-decade Vietnam War (1955–75) begins. The USA backs Ngo Dinh Diem as leader of South Vietnam; Ho Chi Minh leads North Vietnam.

Juan Rulfo publishes *Pedro Páramo* with Fondo de Cultura Economica.

1956   First International Congress of Black Writers and Artists in Paris, France.

1960   In South Korea the April Revolution (referred to in South Korea as 4.19) – mass protests led by students and intellectuals – puts an end to Syngman Rhee's monopoly on power.

1961   Park Chunghee seizes power through a military coup d'état (referred to in South Korea as 5.16), and the country is placed under martial law.

1963   Ngo Dinh Diem is assassinated in a military coup backed by the USA; John F. Kennedy is assassinated in Dallas, Texas.

1965   The Hart–Celler Act, or the Immigration and Nationality Act of 1965, opens the door to Asian immigration to the USA.

1967–80 In the USA the Black Power movement has grown out of the mainstream Civil Rights movement and articulates solidarity with the Third World movement. Various political organizations articulate a vision for Black power, including the Student Nonviolent Coordinating Committee (SNCC), the League of Revolutionary Black Workers, and the Black Panther Party, among others. David Graham Du Bois helps translate the politics of Third World-ism in Cairo (where he was a newspaper editor) to the United States, as he becomes the editor of the Black Panther Party's newspaper in 1971. Du Bois's experiences in Cairo allow him to articulate a politics of "intercommunalism" within the Black Panther Party that becomes one of the hallmarks of the Panthers' internationalism, anti-imperialism, and solidarity with Afro-Asian movements.

1968   The Tet Offensive becomes a turning point in the waning of American public support for the Vietnam war; between 400 and 500 civilians are massacred in My Lai and My Khe by US troops.
         N. Scott Momaday publishes *House Made of Dawn*.

1971   Quentin Anderson publishes *The Imperial Self: An Essay in American Literary and Cultural History*.

1975   Saigon, the South Vietnamese capital, falls to North Vietnamese forces.

1977   Leslie Marmon Silko publishes *Ceremony*.

1978   The Indian Child Welfare Act establishes guidelines and set minimum standards for handling child abuse and neglect and adoptions involving Indian children.

Gerald Vizenor writes "Custer on the Slipstream."

Edward Said publishes *Orientalism*.

1979   The socialist Sandinista National Liberation Front overthrows Nicaraguan president and US ally Anastasio Somoza Debayle, thereby ending a familial dynasty that had been in power since 1937. Military officials in El Salvador fear that Salvadoran president Carlos Humberto Romero's government will fall to left-wing guerillas backed by the Sandinistas. With the support of the United States, members of the Salvadoran military launch a coup d'état, sending Romero into exile and igniting the Salvadoran civil war.

1980   Farabundo Martí Popular Liberation Front (FMLN), a political party made up of leftist organizations, is founded in El Salvador.

Assassination of Óscar Arnulfo Romero y Galdámez, Auxiliary Bishop of the Archdiocese of San Salvador and a vocal critic of the military government. No one was convicted, but the United Nations Truth Commission for El Salvador maintained that Romero's murder was ordered by Roberto D'Aubuisson Arrieta, a Salvadoran military officer trained at the Western Hemisphere Institute for Security Cooperation (formerly the School of the Americas), a US Department of Defense school that has trained tens of thousands of soldiers and police, primarily from Latin America.

1981   D'Aubuisson establishes the right-wing Nationalist Republican Alliance (ARENA) political party.

1984   Louise Erdrich publishes *Love Medicine*.

1986   The Supreme Court rules in *Bowers* v. *Hardwick* that the 14th Amendment's Due Process clause does not prohibit the state from criminalizing private sexual conduct involving same-sex adults.

1988   Louise Erdrich publishes *Tracks*.

1989	The United States invades Panama, primarily to depose General Manuel Noriega, who was wanted in the USA for drug trafficking and racketeering; the military action is dubbed Operation Just Cause.
1990	Javier Zamora is born in San Luis La Herradura, El Salvador.
1991	Zamora's father, the head of a leftist co-op, flees El Salvador, migrates without authorization to the United States, and settles in the San Francisco Bay Area.
1992	Brokered by the United Nations, the Chapultepec Peace Accords end the Salvadoran civil war, recognize FMLN as a political party, and establish the Truth Commission for El Salvador.
	Alejandro Morales publishes *The Rag Doll Plagues* with Arte Publico Press.
	Guillermo del Toro directs and releases *Cronos*.
1994	ARENA candidate Armando Calderón Sol is elected president of El Salvador and Zamora's mother migrates without authorization to the USA. She crosses the US–Mexico border near San Diego, California, epicenter of Operation Gatekeeper, a US Border Patrol initiative launched in 1994 that sought to curb unauthorized migration via Prevention through Deterrence, a policy that diverts migrants from high-traffic entry points to more remote and, therefore, more dangerous areas, such as the Sonoran Desert in southern Arizona.
	The North American Free Trade Accord goes into effect leading to the displacement of four million primarily Indigenous farmers from their lands in Mexico, most of whom migrate to the United States in search of work.
	Amy Kaplan publishes "'Left Alone with America': The Absence of Empire in the Study of American Culture" in *Cultures of United States Imperialism*, coedited with Donald Pease.
1996	Illegal Immigration Reform and Immigration Responsibility Act.
1998	Centenary of Spanish-American-Cuban War.

	Jan Radway "What's in a Name?" Presidential Address to the American Studies Association, November 20.

Jan Radway "What's in a Name?" Presidential Address to the American Studies Association, November 20.

Amy Kaplan publishes landmark essay "Manifest Domesticity."

1999   Zamora migrates from El Salvador to the United States via Guatemala, Mexico, and the Sonoran Desert. He departs San Luis La Herradura on June 6 and reunites with his parents in Tucson, Arizona, on June 11. For seven weeks during this nine-week journey, he is unable to communicate with his family and they do not know his whereabouts.

2000   Michael Hardt and Antonio Negri publish *Empire*, arguing that US imperialism has yielded to a "new global form of sovereignty."

2001   September 11 terrorist attacks.
President George W. Bush announces "Global War on Terror."
USA leads multinational invasion of Taliban-ruled Afghanistan; the two-decade War in Afghanistan begins.
The US television show *24*, featuring a federal agent who uses torture to extract information from terrorists, begins airing. The series runs until 2014.

2002   President George W. Bush establishes a prison camp at Guantánamo naval base to hold suspected terrorists and what his administration called "illegal enemy combatants."
Amy Kaplan publishes *The Anarchy of Empire in the Making of US Culture*.

2003   US-led invasion of Iraq; Iraq War begins.
Amnesty International publishes reports of US military human rights abuses at Abu Ghraib prison and other detention centers in Iraq.
Amy Kaplan delivers American Studies Association Presidential Address, "Violent Belongings and the Question of Empire Today."
The Supreme Court ruling in *Lawrence* v. *Texas* invalidates sodomy law across the USA, making

	same-sex sexual activity legal in every US state and territory.
2004	Photos of torture and mistreatment of prisoners by US military personnel at Abu Ghraib prison made public.
2004–18	US drone strikes in Pakistan.
2006	George W. Bush acknowledges the US use of "black sites" or secret prisons operated by the CIA during the "War on Terror."
2007	Sherman Alexie publishes *Flight* with Black Cat Press.
2008	Alex Rivera directs and releases *Sleep Dealer* with Likely Story and This is That Productions.
2011	Osama Bin Laden, founder of al-Qaeda and organizer of the September 11 terrorist attacks, killed by US Navy Seals in Operation Neptune Spear.
	Homeland, an American espionage thriller series about the CIA, begins airing. It features torture scenes as a routine element in the representation of violence. The show airs until 2020.
2012	Junot Díaz publishes "Monstro" in *The New Yorker*.
	Zamora graduates with a bachelor's degree in Latin American history, with a minor in creative writing, from the University of California, Berkeley.
	Publication of *Walking the Clouds: An Anthology of Indigenous Science Fiction*, edited by Grace Dillon.
	The film *Zero Dark Thirty* features explicit torture scenes in a fictional retelling of the search for Osama bin Laden.
2013	Video game *Grand Theft Auto* (*GTA*) 5 – featuring torture as entertainment – is released.
2014	US media sources announce a "child migrant crisis" due to an increase in the number of unaccompanied minors, many from Honduras, Guatemala, and El Salvador, apprehended at the US-Mexico border.
	The Senate Intelligence Committee Report on Torture concludes that "The CIA's use of its enhanced interrogation techniques was not an effective means of acquiring intelligence or gaining cooperation from detainees."

2015	Nilüfer Demir's photographs of two-year-old Alan Kurdi's lifeless body lying on a beach near Bodrum, Turkey, go viral. Along with his mother and brother, Kurdi, a refugee fleeing the Syrian civil war, drowned in the Mediterranean Sea trying to reach Europe.
	Along with Marcelo Hernandez Castillo and Christopher Soto, Zamora cofounds the Undocupoets Campaign, a group protesting the US citizenship requirement for many literary contests and awards.
	The Supreme Court holds in *Obergefell* v. *Hodges* that state bans on same-sex marriage are unconstitutional under the due process and equal protection clauses of the 14th Amendment.
	Viet Thanh Nguyen's *The Sympathizer* features a torture scene in a novel that raises questions about how filmmakers depict violence against Vietnamese people for entertainment.
	Raza Ali Hasan publishes "On Imperialism" in *Sorrows of the Warrior Class*.
2016	Donald Trump is elected 45th President of the United States on a right-wing, anti-immigrant platform.
	US superhero film *Deadpool* features a super-hero whose strength is the result of prolonged torture.
2017	Louise Erdrich publishes *Future Home of the Living God*; Cherie Dimaline publishes *The Marrow Thieves*.
	Copper Canyon Press publishes Zamora's poetry collection *Unaccompanied*.
2018	Tommy Orange publishes *There There*.
	Images and sounds of hundreds of child migrants locked in cages at the Central Processing Center, a detention center run by US Customs and Border Protection in McAllen, Texas, spark global outrage.
	Nearly twenty years after his departure, Zamora returns to El Salvador to apply for a visa from the United States. US Citizenship and Immigration Services grants him an EB-1 ("Einstein") visa.

2019	Joy Harjo named 23rd US Poet Laureate.
2020	The World Health Organization announces the COVID-19 pandemic and the Trump administration activates Title 42, a 1944 public health law that restricts immigration in the name of protecting public health, thereby preventing numerous people from seeking asylum.
	Publication of *Latinx Rising: An Anthology of Latinx Science Fiction and Fantasy*, edited by Matthew David Goodwin.
	Love After The End: An Anthology of Two-Spirit and Indigiqueer Speculative Fiction, edited by Joshua Whitehead.
2022	Hogarth publishes *Solito*, Zamora's memoir about his journey from El Salvador to the United States at the age of nine years.
	Silvia Moreno-García publishes *Mexican Gothic* with Penguin Random House.
	Jayro Bustamante directs and releases *La Llorona* with The Criterion Collection.
	Florida's notorious "Don't Say Gay" law (HB 1557) is signed into law, prohibiting classroom discussion of sexual orientation and gender identity.
2023	HB 1069 is signed into law in Florida, expanding HB 1557, while prohibiting the use of pronouns consistent with the use of a student's gender identity and expanding book banning procedures. Similar laws are proposed in other states.
	Samson Occom's papers repatriated to the Mohegan Nation by Dartmouth College.
2025	In January, President-elect Donald Trump discusses the acquisition of Greenland, the return of the Panama Canal, the annexation of Canada as a 51st state, an invasion of sovereign Mexican territory, and renaming of the Gulf of Mexico as the "Gulf of America."

Introduction
American Literary Studies as Empire Studies
Anna Brickhouse and Susan Gillman

The story of American literature and empire is vast and complex, its boundaries as hard to draw and as continuously disputed as the historical borders of the US nation-state itself. Historians of US empire tend to periodize their field into three broad eras of imperial formation: (1) continental expansion under the aegis of Manifest Destiny in the nineteenth century; (2) the emergence of overseas empire with the Spanish-American War in 1898, when the US first acquired formal territories abroad; and (3) the rise to globalism after World War II, when US military policing in the interests of global capitalism created an empire of military bases around the world while rebranding US imperialism and neocolonialism as embodiments of democracy and freedom, in part through a series of "endless" wars spanning the Cold War through the post-9/11 War on Terror. But for literary scholars, this broad historical periodization of empire loses coherence in the face of literature's persistent ability to reimagine history, to make counterfactual claims, to invent new worlds, to change the experience of time, and to speculate and counter-speculate about the grounds of reality. Furthermore, empire's relationship with what we call "American literature" fluctuates once the central terms themselves are brought under scrutiny. The definitions of *American* and *literature* have always been tied up in the existence of US empire as well as other empires in the Americas.

The word "America" is itself the product of interimperial intellectual rivalry, of course, borne of the Italian explorer Amerigo Vespucci's voyage and his subsequent understanding that Columbus, who had claimed to reach the East Indies for the Spanish Crown, was wrong. The term's current use in designating the USA – as in the case of this volume – casts its own imperial shadow. As Latin Americans have always known, and as Jan Radway argued in her 1998 American Studies Association (ASA) address, the "American" adjective modifying the phrase "American literature" represents a linguistic annexation, claiming the name of an entire hemisphere for one country therein – and thereby ignoring Canada while reiterating a long history of US imperial relations to the southern half of the hemisphere.[1] As a volume exploring American literature and empire, this companion thus takes a necessarily skeptical stance toward its own major geographical referent. This skepticism means recognizing *American* as "a term of consolidation, homogenization, and unification," as Kirsten Silva Gruesz has observed, that both records and obscures the imperial contexts that produced it and continue to sustain it.[2] To understand the full history of the term "American," then, is to recognize its deep, strategically obscure, and often disavowed imperial contexts – differing contexts that in turn require differentially transatlantic, hemispheric, and global frameworks of analysis.

   The concept of "literature," too, bears close analysis for those interested in the connections between American literary history and empire. Empire went hand in hand with the invention of the printing press as new writing about the Americas justified violence, lured European participants and investors, and brought new knowledge commodities – drawn from new worlds and valued alongside more traditional sources of wealth – to European readers. If European-authored literature of the Americas served imperial interests, so too did early American writing by Euro-American creole elites across the hemisphere. As scholars such as Ralph Bauer and José Antonio Mazzotti have shown, these Euro-Americans wrote in part to shore up settler claims both to land and to the right of domination over its original inhabitants as well as those enslaved to excavate its mines and harvest its plantations.[3]

   Moreover, while literature has been understood since classical Western antiquity as a hallmark of civilization and a bearer of imperial values across conquered territories and peoples, the nature of alphabetic writing became ideological in a new way once Europe dubbed the American hemisphere as a New World it had purportedly discovered. Written literature was reconceived as a sign of humanity precisely as humanness was being invented in this "Age of Discovery" that inaugurated the conquest of Indigenous peoples and the seizing of African captives for the transatlantic slave trade. The "Age of Revolution" cemented the equation between writing and the human through written constitutions. Yet a written constitution did not guarantee the new nation of Haiti rights in the eyes of Europe or in the settler polities of the Americas, nor did they confer a place for the Haitian Revolution – which remained until the late twentieth century "unthinkable" in the West – in conventional scholarship on the Age of Revolutions.[4]

If literature and alphabetic writing have a storied place in imperial history, so too has translation served a "poetics of imperialism" across the centuries; Columbus's kidnapping of Amerindians to serve as interpreters was the "primal crime in the New World ... committed in the interest of language."[5] This interest of language has a long and continuing imperial history, as the chapters collected here make clear. By the aftermath of the Spanish-American War and the US occupation of the Philippines – and just as the field was being codified as a discipline – American literature emerged as "empire's proxy," in Meg Wesling's helpful phrase, deeply intertwined with the process of colonial management abroad.[6]

If literature has been empire's proxy, it has also been an imaginative resource for contestation. Thus, while the myth of America has from Columbus's first landfall overwritten and displaced Indigenous peoples, histories, and geographies, Indigenous critiques of empire have been forcefully advanced in writing across the centuries since European invasion. So too has a broadly conceived Black literary history critically engaged various forms of empire, including the extraction of human labor from Africa and the continued devaluation of Black lives throughout the African diaspora. Indigenous Studies and African American and African Diaspora Studies emerged as fields during the often conjoined Civil Rights and anti-imperial struggles of the 1960s, and together archive a deep and growing US intellectual history of empire as well as a specifically literary apprehension of its workings. The formation known as Asian American literature coincided with the emergence of ethnic studies departments in the 1960s in response to student protests against war in Vietnam, bringing to light the extraction of Asian labor in the making of US capitalism, from its eighteenth-century beginnings to its consolidation during the post–Civil War importation of Asian and South Asian indentured workers as substitutes for enslaved Black labor to the long series of incursions and US wars in Asia throughout the so-called American Century. This long history culminated in the creation of the "foreigner-within," Lisa Lowe's term for the Asian American subject perpetually misrecognized, regardless of birthplace, as an immigrant.[7]

The field of Latinx literature, too, might be productively understood as a countervailing force to "empire's proxy" in the emergence of American literature as a disciplinary field in the early twentieth century. Since the rise of an epistolary-political culture of Spanish-American letters centered in Philadelphia in the late eighteenth century, Latino/a/x writers have negotiated the boundaries of multiple modern empires – Spanish, British, Portuguese, and French – while also appealing to the histories and cosmologies of the African diaspora as well as the vast Indigenous empires that preceded European invasion.[8] But the US empire represents, for now, the final crucible of the "cruel modernity," in Jean Franco's phrase, out of which Latinx history emerges.[9] US imperial relation to Latin America and the Caribbean begins with the annexation of nearly half of sovereign Mexico, the acquisition of Puerto Rico as a colonial territory, and the various occupations of and attempts to annex Cuba, Nicaragua, the Dominican Republic, Panama – and, crucially, Haiti, the second modern republic in the Americas (after the US) to claim independence from imperial Europe and the only one to found its new state on the abolition of slavery and the stated principle of an equal *noir* or Black identity among its citizens.

The study of American literature's relation to empire is vitally enriched by such recognitions of what Aníbal Quijano has called the "coloniality of power" – a framework for understanding how the legacies of European imperialism and the ongoing practices of colonialism in the Americas have structured not just an unequal social order and distribution of wealth but the very forms of domination that underlie knowledge and the production of scholarship.[10] Drawing on this and related concepts, our volume aims to offer a more robust conception of American literature's relation to empire by widening the temporal and geographical frame of analysis.

The chapters in the first part of the volume examine in various ways the European race for empire in the Americas starting in the late fifteenth century to help underscore that "empire" should not be understood as a single, coherent monolith but as a set of related, sometimes overlapping forms that shape what we call "American literature," and that are particularly relevant to the history of "early America," which was of course far broader than just the original thirteen English colonies. We thus aim to offer in Part I a nuanced understanding of the multiple forms and meanings of empire across the hemisphere. This wider context of the early Americas necessarily opens the later national US field featured in Part II to the postcolonial and decolonial scholarship of Latinx, Latin Americanist and Caribbeanist scholarship as well as to new ways of understanding the different periods and literary cultures of American empire.

Part III of this volume resonates with the insights of Michael Hardt and Antonio Negri, who have argued that US imperialism – like all prior nation-based imperialisms – is in many ways over. The US may have briefly inherited the mantle of European imperialism during the twentieth century, in their view, but imperialism per se has since yielded to what they term Empire, a "new global form of sovereignty" that exceeds nation-states and has no territorial center of power. Even in Hardt and Negri's estimation, however, US imperial "interventions" – to use the sanitized language of the Pax Americana for military occupations and wars – continue to play a key role in what they define as Empire's "mixed constitution."[11] Their contextualization of empire in the neoliberal, postmodern, and globalist era since the late twentieth century has invited us to expand the earlier "New Americanist" focus on empire in the narrower context of aggressive nineteenth- and early twentieth-century US military expansionism and overseas empire. More generally, the widened and varied temporal, geographic, and theoretical frame of the entire volume has allowed for a collectively told story about empire and American letters that also points to some of the most exciting new directions in literary studies more broadly.

Before turning to the individual chapters, however, we want to dwell briefly on the received story of empire and American literature that was once centered on the elite men in the North American colonies who wrote in celebration of their own role as imperial subjects of the English Crown. These early American writers understood themselves to be participating in a noble *translatio imperii* from ancient world empires, to classical Rome, to seventeenth-century Britain, to a monumental British imperial future in the American hemisphere: the "rising glory of this western world," as Philip Freneau put it in an eighteenth-century poem of the same name, which prophesied "the day when Britain's sons shall spread/Dominion to the north and south and west/Far from th' Atlantic to Pacific shores." The poet thus predicted a glorious future British empire on both American continents, of which "we too shall boast/Our Alexanders, Pompeys, heroes, kings/That in the womb of time yet dormant lye."[12] With the coming of the American Revolution, such encomiums to British empire naturally fell out of literary favor, but the "poetics" of empire did not.

A major strand of early US literature augured what Thomas Jefferson famously called an "empire of liberty": an American empire moving progressively away from British imperial guilt toward a putatively shining and innocent future.[13] Popular public memory since then holds persistently to the myth of America as a nation fundamentally opposed to empire, a modern republic founded in a heroic act of *anti*-imperialism: wrenching itself free from the powerful British empire so it could one day, as President Woodrow Wilson put it upon entering World War I, make the world "safe for democracy" by taking on a European imperial foe once again.[14] Even the most blatantly imperial exercises of US power have always been cast by the state as anti-imperial, as simply bringing light "To the Person Sitting in Darkness," as Mark Twain once put it satirically in an essay under this title.[15]

The genealogy of criticism attending to the relationship between empire and what was once called "classic American literature" is also worth revisiting, if in necessarily abbreviated form. In 1971, during the US-in-Vietnam years, Quentin Anderson published a landmark study founded on the idea that a specifically American version of Western individualism emerged in the national US imagination early in the nineteenth century and became a nexus of ideology that he termed the "imperial self." For Anderson, Emerson was the prophet and greatest theological exponent of this imperial American self, which absolved itself of responsibilities to the social world and then devoured everything else (even God and Nature), relocating the universe and all cosmology within a great drama of internal consciousness. The emergence of this imperial self – which rapidly banished any "communally shared sense of goal, or indeed of being" – had profound and detrimental political and social effects, as Anderson saw it; writing at the height of the Vietnam War, and in the wake of a quarter century of decolonization movements in Asia and Africa that the US had actively undermined, Anderson surfaced the often disavowed inextricability between literary and cultural imagination, on the one hand, and geopolitics on the other. The prior generation of literary critics had been "culturally irresponsible" – not just for overlooking the evidence of these connections, but for developing a mode of scholarship that reinforced them and gave them cover by conjuring the mystique of the imperial imagination as the only true form of liberation possible from an inherently constraining social world. "Our dreams of empire" in the geopolitical world, he speculated, emerged with and through the imperial selves dreamed into being by American writers: Emerson, Whitman, Henry James.[16]

Anderson's attempt to link the imperial self to the nation's "dreams of empire" was mournful and oblique. But two decades later, Wai Chee Dimock's *Empire for Liberty: Melville and the Poetics of Individualism* (1989) reprised Jefferson's supposedly paradoxical phrase and showed that "empire" and "liberty" were not opposed terms at all but in fact "instrumentally conjoined," with the former protecting the latter and the latter authorizing the former. Examining Melville's corpus in the context of Jacksonian America, Dimock postulated an individualism not just in flight from the social but as a form of market-driven Lockean self-possession – a personification of the laboring self within market relations. If liberal self-possession buttressed the institution of slavery as a means of possessing and trading the labor of the enslaved, it also required Jacksonian imperialism in the form of continental expansion and Indigenous dispossession to "fashion a 'destiny' out of temporality" and thereby "impose a 'manifest' harmony on what might otherwise appear naked conflict." An acute observer of the "controlling 'logic of culture'" in his era, Melville developed what Dimock called a "controlling logic of form" that expressed "the sovereignty of both self and nation – both the freedom of the former and the domination of the latter – to bring forth a new sovereign, an authorial variety, a figure whose literary individualism is always imperially articulated." Dimock thus showed that in the nineteenth-century US, "literature," the "author," "selfhood," and the "individual" were all historically constituted by empire, and she did so at a time, the 1980s, when the absence of empire in US cultural studies was still pronounced.[17] But as Toni Morrison put it in her 1989 essay, "Unspeakable Things Unspoken," published the same year as Dimock's *Empire for Liberty*, "invisible things are not necessarily 'not-there'; a void may be empty but it is not a vacuum."[18] Within a few years, Amy Kaplan would teach the next generation of Americanists that the field of American Studies – "conceived on the banks of the Congo," as she memorably put it – was birthed out of an enduring, seemingly unending denial of the US imperial past and present.[19]

By the time this proposed volume comes to print, over three decades will have passed since the publication of that field-defining essay in *Cultures of US Imperialism* (1993), edited by Kaplan and Donald Pease, which inaugurated more than a generation's worth of Americanist scholarship on the subject. As ASA president Matthew Frye Jacobson observed at the annual conference in 2013 – using his address as an occasion, in part, to honor the collection's twentieth anniversary – the "cultural analyses of empire . . . have been the hallmark and the signal contribution of American studies scholarship in recent decades."[20] This 2013 moment at the ASA also recalled Kaplan's own 2003 presidential address, "Violent Belongings and the Question of Empire Today," setting up a timeline of empire's increasingly visible role in American literary and historical studies.[21] Jacobson was issuing his own charge in this talk, asking the field to keep its eyes on the ball of empire – not to look away just when the so-called "decline of American empire" was being loudly announced in other disciplines. Countering the Hardt and Negri narrative of US imperialism's decline and disappearance, Jacobson reminded listeners that the contemporary neoliberal regime – even on occasions where the US nation-state takes a backseat to the power of multinational corporations – is itself a form of empire in which the United States continues to play an outsized role. Jacobson took into explicit account Hardt and Negri's insights regarding globalizing capital and the changed "ontology" of postmodern imperial domination. Yet he nevertheless called forcefully for a reinvigorated Americanist study of US imperialism, an interdisciplinary scholarship that would reflect both what the field has learned since the early 1990s and where it might be going. The present volume aims to answer that call, supplementing Jacobson's contention that "empire *is* US history" – and Kaplan's enduring analysis of empire as "a way of life" in the United States – with its own interdisciplinary and yet discipline-specific charge: a collective effort toward a renewed American *literary* studies as empire studies.[22]

This volume fashions a provisional temporality out of the contradictions of the field. We hope to foreground both the conventional periodization of American empire – as an aberration occurring after the Spanish-American War, a flicker of imperialist occupations that quickly died down – and the revisionist chronologies of US imperialism that tell another story altogether and that often emanate from American literary history itself. This literary history has been shaped by the critical return to elided and forgotten imperial times and places through the recovery of key texts in key historical moments: for example, the Trinidadian critic C. L. R. James interpreting Melville's *Moby-Dick* as a prophecy of Cold War America during his detention in Ellis Island as he fought deportation procedures in 1952; or the recovery of James's 1938 history *The Black Jacobins* (and 1934 stage play of the same title) by the anthropologist David Scott during the early years of the US wars in Afghanistan and Iraq.[23] As these examples remind us, "empire" was the central term of postcolonial studies long before it was taken up by American literary studies, and any project on American literature and empire must recognize its intellectual debt to that groundbreaking tradition of postcolonial scholarship. The fit between the two fields has not always been an easy one given that the US is a settler colonial nation rather than a postcolonial one: that is, US national independence from imperial Britain did not end the original invasion of Native lands nor did it stop the colonial extraction of labor and life from enslaved Africans and their descendants. And all kinds of colonialism, as many scholars have shown, have their own neos: their own afterlives, their own forms of open-endedness, that invite reciprocal consideration.

Yet some of the most enduring Americanist scholarship of the last thirty years, especially in the 1990s – the decade following the centennial of the renamed Spanish-American-Cuban War – might be said to co-articulate, or to move in implicit dialogue with, postcolonial studies. Toni Morrison's 1989 conception of "Africanism" in American literature, for example, brilliantly reprised Edward Said's 1978 "Orientalism" to make the study of race central to American literary studies.[24] What Gayatri Chakravorty Spivak termed "feminist individualism in the age of imperialism" in 1985 finds an Americanist analogue in Amy Kaplan's 1998 essay, "Manifest Domesticity," which brought to light other foundational text-networks of US empire, including nineteenth-century women's domestic and sensation fiction.[25] Both postcolonial studies and studies of US empire have long insisted that categories of gender and sexuality are central to the formation and maintenance of imperial power – and must therefore be central to the continuing analysis of empire and to ongoing efforts to decolonize scholarship and the production of knowledge.

The Cambridge Companion to American Literature and Empire explores and responds to these and other critical interventions, and particularly those of the intervening decades since *Cultures of US Imperialism* and Kaplan's subsequent monograph *The Anarchy of Empire in the Making of US Culture* (2002). In telling the story of American literature and empire across its fourteen chapters, this volume also highlights the potential liberatory role of literature in making visible and creating alternative spaces for what Native literary scholars have called "survivance" in the face of "empire's detritus," the "ruins and ruination" of its long catastrophe, in Ann Laura Stoler's words.[26] If the volume makes an argument for American literary studies as empire studies, a field that examines literature's relation to past, present, and ongoing forms of empire, it also reflects on literature's potential role in the non-inevitability of this unfolding of history. Moving beyond the literary capacity for exposure – the ability to help us see and discern – many of these chapters elaborate the dynamics of literature's vital place in imagining alternative futures, unfinished pasts, and the creation of what have been called the "otherwise worlds" made possible by collective critical work in this vein.[27]

Part I of this volume, "Reimagining 'Early American' Literature," approaches its subject from the perspective of empire studies. Here, "early American" is not Anglo-American or North American, and the Haitian Revolution rather than the American Revolution is the key event in the story of empire and American literature fleshed out by these essays. The volume begins with Ralph Bauer's "Reimagining the Early Americas: Empire and the Hemisphere," which presents a detailed contextualization of empire in the early Americas. Modern European empire in the American hemisphere was distinct from Europe's prior imperial formations, whether the medieval Holy Roman Empire or the Ancient Roman one, with what Bauer calls its "singular fusion of religious, political, and economic object-ives." To read the literary history of the early Americas produced by Europeans beginning in the late fifteenth century is to glimpse modernity's emergence, from the origins of modern totalitarianism to the US form of "neo-colonial hegemony over the hemisphere that is still with us today." This early literary history was always by definition concerned with some aspect of empire – its legitimacy, its future, and its potential enemies – even as European imperialism in the Americas also took on multiple and distinct forms in different periods as well as across the national boundaries (Spanish, Portuguese, French, British, Dutch) of the hemisphere. Bauer's chapter introduces readers to the key texts and writers of empire in the early Americas, showing how they reflected and helped to produce varied imperial ideologies and ontologies, beginning with those underpinning the name "America" itself.

The resistance of enslaved Amerindians and later Africans and their descendants was a constant across the hemisphere from the outset of empire. The Haitian Revolution of 1804 marks a flashpoint in this history because it culminated in the first nation of the Americas to enshrine the abolition of slavery in the new constitution, the first Black republic in the modern world, and the first successful overthrow of European empire led by the enslaved. Chapter 2, Monique Allewaert's "Against Imperial Nature: Hérard-Dumesle and the Making of Haitian Eloquence," turns to the early nineteenth-century Haitian poet, politician, and naturalist Charles Hérard-Dumesle to consider his challenge to a particular Western genre that had long served the interests of European empire: natural history. Taking up this genre himself in his *Voyage dans le Nord de Haïti* (1824), Hérard-Dumesle sought to remake natural history by explicitly naming its deadly racializing project: its desire "to prove the inferiority of a great portion of the human race." To work within and against this imperial genre required Hérard-Dumesle to invent a new kind of revolutionary eloquence, forged in a generic mixture of the descriptive discourse of natural history with poetry, politics, and the other-than-human forces of Amerindian and Afro-diasporic naturalisms. The resulting work, as Allewaert argues, both witnessed and created "nature" as a potentially planetary anti-imperial force.

The final essay in Part I turns to the North American land now known as the United States to introduce a long Native American literary and cultural history that runs from the eighteenth through the twenty-first centuries. In "Empire, Apocalypse, and Native American Literature, from Samson

Occom to the Contemporary Moment," Stephanie Fitzgerald and Hilary E. Wyss emphasize the repetitions, echoes, and circularities of imperial history across centuries, and show how, from the earliest accounts through to the most recent speculative fiction, Indigenous intellectuals have characterized the arrival and ongoing settler colonial iteration of empire as an apocalypse. With its close attention to the links between empire and ecological devastation, the chapter illuminates the critiques of and alternatives to imperial thought that Native American literature and culture always offer, opening transformative, participatory, and "world rebuilding" possibilities for diverse audiences.

Part II, "Imperial Nation," explores a selection of canonical nineteenth-century US authors, including James Fenimore Cooper, Walt Whitman, and Herman Melville, to grasp their diverse meditations on the intertwinement of national and imperial history. But the story emerging around this overwhelmingly white and all male group of authors is an unexpectedly diverse and original one. Gesa Mackenthun's chapter, "Conquest and Compost: James Fenimore Cooper and the Literature of Ecological Empire," further develops the connections between empire and ecological devastation registered by Fitzgerald and Wyss. Working at the intersection of the environmental humanities and the critical field of settler colonial studies, Mackenthun identifies "ecological-agrarian imperialism" as a mode of empire rooted in "the intersections between soil depletion, food scarcity, biodiversity reduction, and colonial capitalism" – one that is assuming "a global, life-threatening dimension" today. Cooper's novels offer a rich analytical lens onto the nineteenth-century culture of ecological-agrarian imperialism and its dark, ecocidal impulses while also introducing a utopian ecological strain taken up by later US writers, from Nathaniel Hawthorne, William Dean Howells, and Charlotte Perkins Gilman to Ursula Le Guin, Ernest Callenbach, Octavia Butler, and Kim Stanley Robinson.

Rafael Walker's "Manifestly Queer Domesticity: Empire and Nineteenth-Century Queer Fiction" revisits Amy Kaplan's famous formulation "manifest domesticity," itself a reworking of the nineteenth-century imperial concept of the nation's so-called "manifest destiny" to expand its territory westward and southward until reigning over the full hemisphere. Kaplan's analysis of nineteenth-century literature and popular culture showed how the cult of true womanhood and its seemingly private sphere of domesticity were inseparable from the political and military culture of empire. Updating this analysis, Walker's essay recovers an archive of nineteenth-century queer fiction – from Whitman's little-known short story of 1841, "The Child's

Champion," to works by Bret Harte, William Dean Howells, Mary E. Wilkins Freeman, and Sarah Orne Jewett – to show that many writers "used the affordances of this apparently heterosexual imperial paradigm to carve out space for lives and desires otherwise considered deviant or unspeakable." In their improvisations with imperial-domestic discourse, Walker argues, these writers "exceed the ideological standpoints that most cultural historians of empire recognize" while also writing queer lives into the literary record.

While Walker's chapter brings attention to a Whitman text long overlooked by critics, Emilio Irigoyen turns our eye toward Melville and the role critics themselves have played in the long story of US empire. Irigoyen's "Herman, or the Ambiguities: Melville, US Imperialism, and the Participant Critic" plays on the titular ambiguities of Melville's autofictional novel *Pierre*, arguing that equivocation is central to the author's relation to empire. For this reason, the critical tradition on Melville has produced both imperial and anti-imperial versions of the author, depending on the changing politics of scholarly discourse in the US. Irigoyen – contributing to this volume from Montevideo, Uruguay – is well positioned to illuminate both Melville's complex engagement with US imperialism and the equally complicated story about the potential myopia of a US-centric critical tradition. Melville was not just an author-commentator on multiple empires (Spanish, French, British, US), Irigoyen reminds us, but a direct participant in US intervention in the Americas. This biographical-historical truth must be taken into consideration when grasping the rhetorical and ideological ambiguities of his most explicit commentary on US empire. Turning in conclusion to José Martí's landmark anti-imperial essay "Nuestra América," this chapter argues for Melville's place in a continental American critical tradition – a tradition that can help us to better see ourselves not only as readers and critics but, like Melville, as participants in a long imperial history.

The final chapter in Part II, Rodrigo Lazo's "Cultures of US Torture," bolsters the hemispheric argument advanced in Irigoyen's essay. Like the final chapter by Fitzgerald and Wyss in Part I, this chapter also performs a double critical movement between two distinct historical-imperial moments by exploring the presence of torture in US popular culture of the nineteenth century and our own post-9/11 era. Torture supposedly disappeared from public view in late eighteenth-century Europe, introducing a new liberal moment. Today torture as public spectacle has again become central to contemporary popular culture in the spectacularized images of post-9/11 film, television, and video games. How do we interpret this reemergence of torture as public spectacle in its current mediated popular forms? To answer this question, Lazo juxtaposes two texts with explicit depictions of torture from very different moments in the history of US empire: the film *Zero Dark Thirty* (2012), about the hunt for Osama bin Laden, and a sensational dime novel, *A Thrilling and Exciting Account of the Sufferings and Horrible Tortures Inflicted on Mortimer Bowers and Miss Sophia Delaplain* ... (1851), set during the age of US filibustering expeditions to gain political control of Cuba in the 1840s. The comparison yields what Lazo calls "torturetainment" as a heretofore unidentified genre of US literary imperialism – a genre that turns to torture as entertainment while disavowing this function in part by appealing to political urgency. If the nineteenth-century novel marks the practice of torture as colonial and Cuban – inimical to US liberal values – *Zero Dark Thirty* implies that torture is necessary to defending those values in the "war on terror." Amy Kaplan observed in 2004 that public self-definition of the US had come to embrace rather than deny the term "empire." In this historical moment, Lazo shows that "torturetainment" must be understood as central to that dramatic and ongoing redefinition while also showing how torture itself, as a defining element of the Black Legend of Spanish colonization, was always part of US self-imagining. In this sense, Lazo's chapter thus also takes up a thread in Bauer's commentary on the comparative literary production of imperial ideology in the early Americas.

Part III, "Ongoing Empire and Speculative Worlds," brings the volume into the twentieth and twenty-first centuries. The first three chapters in this section take up Black anti-imperial literary traditions, beginning with Alex Lubin's "The Du Bois Genealogy: Three Worlds and Three Writers on Black Anti-Imperialism." Reading across the work of W. E. B. Du Bois, his wife Shirley Graham Du Bois, and his stepson David Graham Du Bois, the chapter introduces readers to Pan-Africanism, its literary front, and its crucial analysis of what W. E. B. Du Bois called the "anarchy of empire": the self-perpetuating circuit of US imperial expansion abroad and domestic anti-Blackness at home. Lubin's analysis of this Du Bois genealogy offers a global overview of empire across the twentieth century: from the interwar years and W. E. B. Du Bois's 1928 anti-imperial novel, *Dark Princess*, to Shirley Graham Du Bois's journalistic essays and biographies confronting empire at the height of the Cold War, to David Graham Du Bois's novel, *And Bid Him Sing*, responding to the Afro-Asian movement in Cairo, Egypt as well as his work as an editor for the Black Panther Party newspaper in the US. The Du Bois genealogy, Lubin argues, invites a planetary approach to the story of empire and US literature.

Nadia Nurhussein's "Black Transnationalism as Anti-Imperialist Empire" takes an equally expansive and more speculative view of the anarchy of empire, focusing on the little-known figure of Harry Foster Dean, who wrote a forgotten memoir about the failed founding of a Black empire in Africa. The chapter offers a brief comparative history of sea-captain Dean, whose ship "The Pedro Gorino" also inspired the title of his memoir about his dream of establishing an improbable, transnational Black empire in the maritime nation of Liberia. Nurhussein's chapter explores both the commercial ambitions of Dean to establish a shipping line, adapting Garvey's Caribbean Black Star Line to a California-Liberia route, and his pedagogical project of promoting an interdisciplinary nautical science at a college in Alameda, California. Lubin's planetary approach to Black empire thus becomes Nurhussein's oceanic history of Dean's alternative – restorative and reparative – Afrocentric empire that never was. The long geographical reach of this comparative history, from Liberia to California, reflects the rich body of scholarship on oceans in Black studies as well as the absence of Dean from that work. In embracing Dean, this chapter weaves together a literary lost past and possible Africanist future in a speculative line of thinking that recalls Lazo's double critical movement between two distinct historical-imperial moments.

Jak Peake's chapter, "Elusive 'Sun-Bright Hardness': The Caribbean Horizons of Black Renaissance Fiction in an Age of Rising US Empire," explores how and why the Caribbean became a problem space of self-contradiction in 1920s Black literature, political writing, and literary criticism. Why, Peake asks, was a writer such as W. E. B. Du Bois able to write cogently about US empire in his nonfiction essays yet unable to transport this knowledge to his critical appraisals of Harlem Renaissance literature that engaged Caribbean horizons? The problem was by no means Du Bois's alone. Peake charts how disagreements about the relationship between art, politics, and propaganda – a term associated with Du Bois's famous pronouncement on the role of propaganda in Black art – dominated the coverage in magazine book reviews of Black Renaissance fiction in the late 1910s and 1920s in ways that continually occluded empire. The rise of US empire coincided with a rising vogue for blackness, as Peake observes, and yet the illusory logo map of the United States that dominated then and still prevails today created conceptual problems for readers and critics in apprehending the geography of US empire and understanding how it related to some of the most vital new modernist fiction and its oblique Caribbean historical and political register. Introducing readers to four key literary fictions from the period – Eugene O'Neill's *The Emperor Jones*, Carl Van Vechten's *Nigger Heaven*, Claude

McKay's *Home to Harlem*, and Eric Walrond's *Tropic Death* – along with the rich cultural conversation surrounding each, Peake shows what happens in even the best literary reviewing when our conceptual maps hide what has been there all along.

Meg Wesling's chapter, "What We Know We Don't Know," picks up in some ways where Rafael Walker's leaves off by taking up a particular strand of queer fiction, running from the early twentieth century through the contemporary moment, that raises new questions about the role of literature in the imperial work of establishing racial and sexual normativity. Through her readings of three novels – Nella Larsen's *Passing* (1929), James Baldwin's *Giovanni's Room* (1956), and Ocean Vuong's *On Earth We're Briefly Gorgeous* (2019) – Wesling introduces some of the key insights of recent scholarship on sexuality and its always racialized relation to empire. At the same time, the chapter invites us to consider the unpredictability of literature in the hands of its discrepant readers – and what this can teach us about how all desire emerges in relation to the political and social world, including the world of ongoing empire.

Jeehyun Lim addresses another unpredictable cluster of empire literature, three Korean-American works that engage with the rise of militarized modernity during the second half of the twentieth century, when the US consolidated its reach as a global superpower. Focusing on the legacies of the Korean War and its lasting effects on sociopolitical relations in postwar South Korea, these writers write in English for a primarily English-speaking audience, positioning their work right on the borders of Korean and American literatures. Lim explores what she calls "pacific entanglements" or the web of relations and ongoing back-and-forth flows between South Korea and the US that register both US imperialism and the ambiguous, changing status of South Korea transitioning from protectorate, to occupied country, to ally, and finally sub-empire. Tuning into the Americanness of militarized modernity in these three immigrant texts reveals an under-studied dimension of the cultures of US imperialism as it took shape in and through Cold War Asia.

Catherine S. Ramírez turns to the figure and story of the child migrant that marked the simultaneous global emergence of migrant "crises" from the Darién Gap to the Mediterranean Sea, from Ukraine to Gaza in the late 2010s. The essay works with Javier Zamora's 2022 memoir *Solito*, written primarily in English, part of a twenty-first-century boom in life writing by once-undocumented immigrants as well as of the burgeoning scholarship on the "necropolitics of migration" at the Mexico-US border. A detailed close reading of the memoir's descriptions of the body and language of its

Salvadoran child narrator-protagonist demonstrates the spatial-physical, linguistic, and temporal dimensions of his personal story that are identified with what Ramírez calls "undocutime" and the bioprecarity this state produces. The chapter concludes with a meditation on the politics of border militarization and the specific role as well as the value of youth in the contemporary coloniality of migration in the Americas.

Finally, María Josefina Saldaña-Portillo's chapter on contemporary speculative fiction as anti-colonial theory assembles a deep storehouse of Latinx and Indigenous authors and directors of science fiction, neo-gothic, time-travel adventure and dystopic/utopic genres. Defining speculative fiction expansively (and the term 'American' hemispherically), her sources include Mexican, Central American, US and Canadian literature and film, and adduce the complex legacies and ongoing practices of colonialism, neocolonialism, dispossession, and extractivism as well as reparative visions of future worlds yet to come. These speculative forms provide alternative Indigenous theories of liberation for the land itself, known by Indigenous and decolonial nomenclatures, from "Abya Yala" or "living land," to "Turtle Island." As Saldaña argues here, the relation between Indigenous and Latinx history is itself constituted by multiple, sequential, and over-lapping imperial projects and racial regimes. At the same time, Saldaña explores the range of speculative genres in this expanded archive – ghost, neogothic, sci-fi, fantasy, and the weird – as corrective forms that put racial reasoning in its place as the fantastical product of seemingly rational Enlightenment thinking, both cause and effect of colonialism. Her chapter bolsters this volume's collective vision regarding the capacity of literature to reimagine the past while helping to make and sustain the possible worlds of the present and future.

Notes

1. Janice Radway, "What's in a Name?" Presidential Address to the American Studies Association, November 20, 1998, in *American Quarterly* 51.1 (1999): 1–32.
2. Kirsten Silva Gruesz, "America," in *Keywords for American Cultural Studies*, eds. Bruce Burgett and Glen Hendler (New York: New York University Press, 2007).
3. Ralph Bauer and José Antonio Mazzotti, *Creole Subjects in the Colonial Americas: Empires, Texts, Identities*, Omohundro Institute (Chapel Hill: University of North Carolina Press, 2009).
4. Michel-Rolph Trouillot, *Silencing the Past: Power and the Production of History* (Boston: Beacon Press, 1995).

5. Eric Cheyfitz, *The Poetics of Imperialism: Translation and Colonization, from The Tempest to Tarzan* (New York: Oxford University Press, 1991) and Stephen Greenblatt, *Learning to Curse: Essays in Early Modern Culture* (New York: Routledge, 1990), 17.

6. Meg Wesling, *Empire's Proxy: American Literature and US Imperialism in the Philippines* (New York: New York University Press, 2011).

7. Lisa Lowe, *Immigrant Acts: On Asian American Cultural Politics* (Durham: Duke University Press, 1996) 5.

8. On the epistolary-political culture of Spanish-American letters centered in Philadelphia in the late eighteenth and early nineteenth century, see Rodrigo Lazo, *Letters from Filadelfia: Early Latino Literature and the Trans-American Elite* (Charlottesville: University of Virginia Press, 2020).

9. Jean Franco, *Cruel Modernity* (Durham: Duke University Press, 2013). See also María Josefina Saldaña-Portillo, "Cruel Coloniality; or, The Ruse of Sovereignty," *PMLA* 131.3 (2016): 722–30.

10. Aníbal Quijano and Michael Ennis, "Coloniality of Power, Eurocentrism, and Latin America," *Nepantla: Views from South* 1.3 (2000): 533–80.

11. Michael Hardt and Antonio Negri, *Empire* (Cambridge: Harvard University Press, 2001).

12. Philip Freneau, "The Rising Glory of America" (1772, 1786). Hugh Henry Brackenridge is sometimes also listed as a coauthor of the poem.

13. Jefferson developed the theme of an "empire of liberty" over the course of his career and also used the specific phrase in his writings. See especially Robert W. Tucker and David C. Hendrickson, *Empire of Liberty: The Statecraft of Thomas Jefferson* (Oxford: Oxford University Press, 1992).

14. Address of President Wilson to Joint Session of Congress, April 2, 1917. Sixty-Fifth Congress, 1 Session, Senate Document No. 5.

15. Mark Twain, "To the Person Sitting in Darkness," *North American Review* 172.531 (February 1901): 161–76.

16. Quentin Anderson, *The Imperial Self: An Essay in American Literary and Cultural History* (New York: Knopf, 1971), 18, 8.

17. Wai-chee Dimock, *Empire for Liberty: Melville and the Poetics of Individualism* (Princeton: Princeton University Press, 1989) 9, 20, 7–8.

18. Toni Morrison, "Unspeakable Things Unspoken: The Afro-American Presence in American Literature," *Michigan Quarterly Review* 28 (1989): 11.

19. Amy Kaplan, "'Left Alone with America': The Absence of Empire in the Study of American Culture," in Amy Kaplan and Donald E. Pease, eds., *Cultures of United States Imperialism* (Durham: Duke University Press, 1994), 3.

20. Matthew Frye Jacobson, "Where We Stand: US Empire at Street Level and in the Archive," *American Quarterly* 65.2 (2013): 265–90, 283.

21. Kaplan, "Violent Belongings and the Question of Empire Today," *American Quarterly* 56.1 (2004): 1–18.

22. Jacobson, "Where We Stand," 275–6, 274, 265 and Kaplan, "'Left Alone with America'," 14.

23. C. L. R. James, *Mariners, Renegades and Castaways: The Story of Herman Melville and the World We Live In* (Chicago: University of Chicago Press, 2001 [1953]); David Scott, *Conscripts of Modernity: The Tragedy of Colonial Enlightenment* (Durham: Duke University Press, 2004).

24. Toni Morrison, *Playing in the Dark: Whiteness and the Literary Imagination* (Cambridge: Harvard University Press, 2001) and Edward W. Said, *Orientalism* (New York: Pantheon, 1978).

25. Gayatri Chakravorty Spivak, "Three Women's Texts and a Critique of Imperialism," *Critical Inquiry* 12 (1985): 243–61, 244; and Amy Kaplan, "Manifest Domesticity," *American Literature*. Special issue, No More Separate Spheres! 70.3 (1998): 581–606. This essay was revised as chapter 1 of *The Anarchy of Empire in the Making of US Culture* (Cambridge: Harvard University Press, 2002).

26. Anishinaabe scholar and theorist Gerald Vizenor first developed the term "survivance" in *Manifest Manners: Narratives on Postindian Survivance* (Lincoln: University of Nebraska Press, 1999); see also his edited collection *Survivance: Narratives of Native Presence* (Lincoln: University of Nebraska Press, 2008). On imperial detritus, ruins, and ruination, see chapter 10 of Ann Laura Stoler, *Duress: Imperial Durabilities in Our Times* (Durham: Duke University Press, 2016).

27. See the foundational collection *Otherwise Worlds: Against Settler Colonialism and Anti-Blackness*, eds. Tiffany Lethabo King, Jenell Navarro, and Andrea Smith (Durham: Duke University Press, 2020).

PART I

Reimagining "Early American" Literature

CHAPTER I

Reimagining the Early Americas: Empire and the Hemisphere

Ralph Bauer

The field of early American literary studies has seen significant changes in the last thirty years or so. The proto-nationalist geographic focus on Puritan New England and other areas that would later become the United States has been supplemented with various comparatist, hemispheric, transatlantic, and even transpacific approaches.[1] Chronologically, the period that once defined "early America" as beginning in approximately 1620 (the arrival of the Pilgrims at Plymouth) or 1607 (the founding of Jamestown) and ending in approximately 1800 (the end of the Federalist era) has been extended into the sixteenth century (and even the pre-Columbian era) as well as into the first three decades of the nineteenth century. The traditional emphasis on theology and Revolutionary politics of the colonial elites has been complemented by the exploration of diverse identities along lines of race and gender in colonial and imperial contexts. And the linguistic focus on texts originally written in English has been expanded to include texts written in other European languages, including Spanish, Portuguese, French, Dutch, and German, as well as Native American languages. As one prominent literary historian announced during the 1990s, early American literature would no longer be understood merely as the precursor to the national literature of the United States but would more broadly be redefined as a "New World of Words" – as all writing that attempts, linguistically and mentally, to "make room" for the very idea of America across multiple languages since the late fifteenth century.[2]

When reimagining the early Americas from a more global or hemispheric perspective, however, it is important to recognize that "America" did not emerge in literary history as a mere cognitive or semantic consequence of the "hard fact" of a new scientific discovery – the so-called Discovery of America by Europe. Rather, the beginnings and the development of early American writing across multiple languages were inscribed in

distinct imperial contexts that shaped its content and form and that
competed with one another for hegemony throughout their histories in
the hemisphere. All too often, the hemispheric context still in view
during the so-called Age of Exploration of the sixteenth century disappears
from the historiography of early American literature once Jamestown is
founded. Texts that straddle early modern and modern national boundaries such as Álvar Núñez Cabeza de Vaca's *Relación*, which describes
a journey through regions that today form part of the southern United
States but were in the northern frontier of the Viceroyalty of New Spain
when it was written, are seen as early examples of a (proto-)ethnic literature
of the United States, rather than as writings of the Spanish Empire in
North America. While this chapter cannot pretend to offer
a comprehensive treatment of these multiple imperial contexts from the
sixteenth to the nineteenth century – an enormous topic – it will attempt
to sketch the most salient features of early modern European imperialism
in the Americas in terms of its singular fusion of religious, political, and
economic objectives while also attending to some of the geographic,
economic, political variations.

Religion and Empire

America was bound up with empire even before it was so named. During
his first transatlantic voyage in search of a western sea route to India,
Christopher Columbus had made landfall in certain islands that we
today call the Bahamas but that he, according to his letters and diary,
believed to be somewhere in Asia.[3] After Columbus's return to Spain, Pope
Alexander VI issued, in the spring and summer of 1493, the famous bulls
Inter Caetera. These bulls donated to Spain all the islands that had been
newly discovered and the lands that would still be discovered if they lay
west of a meridian drawn on a world map, pole to pole, 100 leagues (ca. 350
miles) west of the Azores, which had already been claimed by Portugal
earlier in the fifteenth century. Portugal, however, was not mentioned in
Alexander's bulls, even though it had been conducting its own Atlantic
voyages down the African coast in search of a sea route to India. Displeased
with this omission, King Joao II of Portugal renegotiated the line of
demarcation directly with the Spanish monarchs in the Treaty of
Tordesillas (1494), in which he agreed in principle to honor Alexander's
donation of the lands discovered by Columbus, provided that the line of
demarcation was moved 270 leagues (ca. 950 miles) further to the west and
that Spain would, in turn, honor Portugal's claim to all newly discovered

lands to its east. While, under this treaty, most of the Americas would later fall under the dominion of Spain, only the eastern extremity of South America – what is now part of Brazil – would fall to Portugal. However, King Joao II was then primarily concerned with protecting Portugal's interest in Africa and Asia. Indeed, Portugal "won" the race to India when, in 1498, Vasco da Gama landed in Calicut after having successfully circumnavigated Africa. When later a similar interimperial conflict of territorial interest between the two maritime powers emerged over the Moluccas (the "Spice Islands"), the line of demarcation dividing the Atlantic world established at Tordesillas was extended across the Pacific in the Treaty of Saragossa of 1529.

The idea of a global line of demarcation dividing the world between expanding empires introduced by the *Inter Caetera* bulls was inspired by the classical tradition of the geographic grid, which had been revived during the Renaissance after the rediscovery of Ptolemy's *Geography* during the early fifteenth century. Applying Ptolemy's mathematical method of cosmography to international law, the global line of demarcation drawn by Pope Alexander in 1493, revised at Tordesillas and completed at Saragossa in 1529, laid the foundation of modern imperialist geography, which divided newly "discovered" territories outside Europe among competing European empires. Later, this new imperialist geography would also include the so-called amity lines that began to appear in the sixteenth century in treaties of truce between nonbelligerent European rival powers, especially Protestants and Catholics, competing for territory in the New World. While these treaties of amity obtained in Europe, they did not in the New World, which became an extralegal zone in international law in which raids and skirmishes occurred outside the context of formal war between two European colonial powers.[4]

But even the invention of the very name "America" by European geographers was intimately bound up with the history of imperialism. As is well known, the name originated with the German humanist cartographers Martin Waldseemüller and Matthias Ringmann, who, in an attempt to update Ptolemy's world map in light of the new discoveries, published in 1507 the first world map to depict South America as a landmass separate from Asia (see Figures 1.1 and 1.2). Although Waldseemüller and Ringmann acknowledged that the Portuguese navigator Pedro Álvares Cabral had landed there on his way to India already in 1500, they named this land "America" in honor of the Italian banker Amerigo Vespucci after having read a French translation of the tract *Mundus Novus* (*A New World*), an account of a voyage to Brazil in 1502

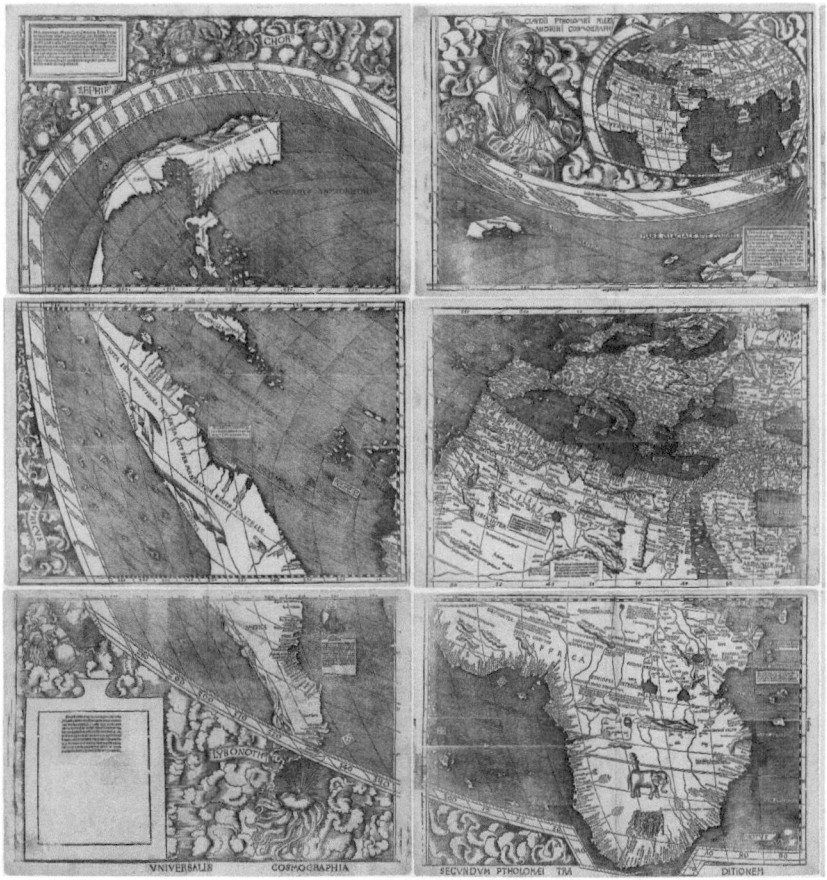

1.1 Martin Waldseemüller, *Universalis Cosmographia* (1507). Courtesy of the Library
of Congress.

in service of the crown of Portugal that had been published under
Vespucci's name and that had first hypothesized that this land was not
part of Asia but another, hitherto unknown, "fourth part" of the world.[5] In
their annotations, Waldseemüller and Ringmann also acknowledged the
discoveries of Columbus but presented the islands that he had discovered
further north as part of Asia. Later, they quietly replaced the name
"America" with "Terra Incognita" (Unknown Land) and "Terra Nova"
(New Land) in reference to South America in subsequent editions of their

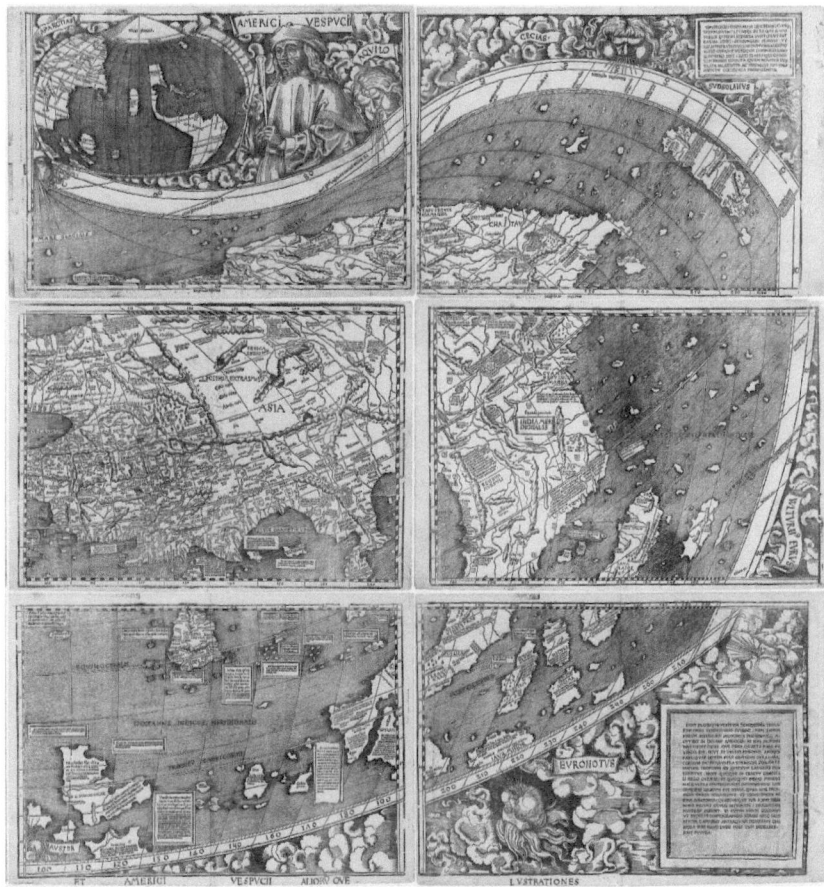

1.1 (cont.)

world map – perhaps after having realized that Columbus had also reached the South American mainland already in 1498, four years before Vespucci, though Columbus himself had believed it to be the earthly Paradise of the Old Testament, rather than a new continent.[6]

Nevertheless, the name "America" stuck – at least in (mainly Protestant) northern Europe – and was there, by the end of the sixteenth century, frequently used in reference not only to South America (to which it had initially referred) but also to North America, including territories that would later become the nation state that inherited this name – the United States of

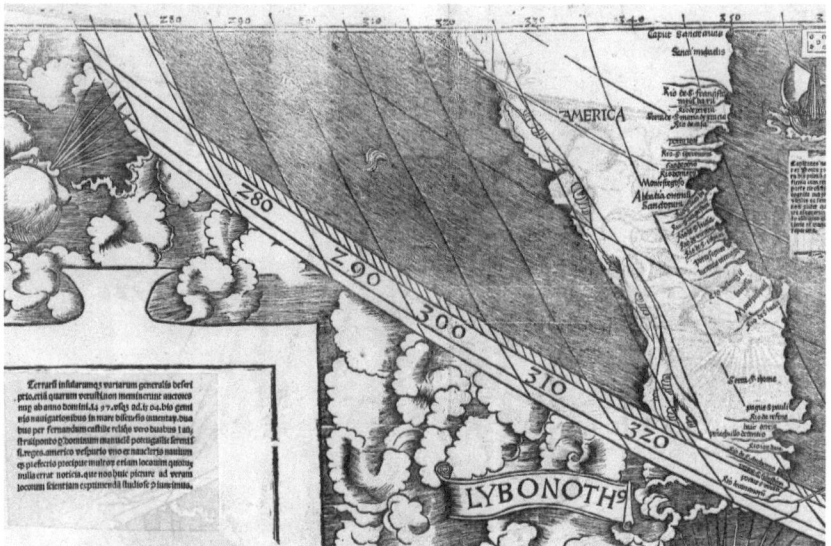

1.2 Martin Waldseemüller, *Universalis Cosmographia* (1507), detail. Courtesy of the
Library of Congress.

America. Spanish cosmographers, by contrast, continued to refer to all the
newly discovered lands in the western Atlantic Ocean as the "Indies" and
presented them as more or less continuous with Asia at least through to the
end of the seventeenth century.[7] Thus, as surprising as it may seem to us
today, when the Spanish Augustinian friar Juan González de Mendoza
published in 1585 one of the earliest Spanish accounts about China, he
included chapters not only about China, Japan, the Moluccas, and the
Philippines but also about New Mexico and what is today the Southwest of
the United States – which were, for Mendoza, part of "las Indias
Occidentales" (the Indies of the West).[8] While we today consider North
and South America as one continent connected with one another through the
Panamanian Isthmus and disconnected from Asia since the submersion of the
Bering land bridge some 13,000 years ago, Europeans during the sixteenth and
seventeenth centuries had a rather vague knowledge of North American
geography, and its actual relationship to Asia was far from clear or certain.
In the absence of empirical geographic information, the contested ontological
status of the newly discovered lands – a discrete, hitherto unknown continent
(or part) called "America" or a series of islands on the way to Asia (las Indias) –
assumed distinctly ideological implications: for, if the land discovered by
Vespucci in service of the Portuguese crown was "new" and separate from

the "Indies" discovered by Columbus on his way to Asia, it may not have been implied in Alexander's donation of the Indies to Spain. Thus, the emergence of the very ontology of "America" as a new continent separate from Asia (las Indias) was part of an ideological process that is deeply implicated in Protestant northern Europe's interimperial rivalry with Catholic Spain for the rights of dominion in the Americas. It is a rivalry for European imperial dominance that began in 1493 and did not end until 1898, when Cuba and Puerto Rico gained their independence from Spain. By then, the United States had become the dominant imperial power in the Americas and began to exert the neocolonial hegemony over the hemisphere that is still with us today.

If America's ontology was still contested in the sixteenth and seventeenth centuries – in what we call the "early modern period" – another question concerned the nature of Pope Alexander's papal "donation." On the face of it, it seems to have been primarily intended as a monopoly of access for the purpose of trade and proselytization. During the fifteenth century, various popes had been making similar donations in Africa and the eastern Atlantic to Portugal. However, while those donations usually referred to specific places or kingdoms, Alexander's donation in *Inter Caetera* was distinguished within this tradition by its sheer open-endedness and purely mathematical rationale. In 1508, Pope Julius II, expanding on Alexander's bulls *Inter Caetera*, issued a new bull granting the Spanish monarchs the authority to name bishops and other religious officials in the Americas – a right that came to be known as the *patronato real*, which in effect conferred to Spain's temporal rulers the spiritual dominion over the New World. This fusion of temporal and spiritual authority assumed its most extreme expression with the establishment of the Inquisition in the core areas of Spanish America, Mexico, and Peru during the 1570s, which ultimately reported not to Rome but rather to Madrid – a development that some historians have interpreted as the beginning of modern totalitarianism.[9] And while the fusion of temporal and spiritual authority was most pronounced in Spanish America resulting from the *patronato real*, the prominent role that religion would play in underwriting early modern European expansionism was, to varying degrees, *the* defining feature of early modern empires throughout the Americas. Thus, virtually all colonizing expeditions were in part rationalized in terms of spreading the Christian faith and included missionaries who collaborated in the project of imperial conquest more or less directly. Even in Protestant nations such as England, where the authority of the pope was not generally accepted but where the monarch presided over both state and church, some of the most outspoken promoters of empire were ministers and theologians, including Richard Hakluyt, who cited the propagation of "reformed religion" as the first reason why Great Britain must engage in "Western Planting" in America.[10] This strong nexus between the spread of the Christian religion and European expansionism distinguished early modern empires in America not only from their medieval precedent – the Holy Roman Empire, where the temporal authority of the emperor was always counterbalanced by the spiritual authority of the pope[11] – but also from their classical pagan model, despite the frequent invocation of Ancient Rome by early modern theorists of empire in reference to their colonial expansionist projects in the Americas.[12]

Contested Empires

Yet, empire was not a monolith – in the colonial Americas or elsewhere – but had multiple forms and historical developments in various national contexts. And even within the paradigmatic Spanish context, "empire" was a contested concept that generated much debate and controversy during the sixteenth century. Although Castile and León had been united with the crown of Áragon through the marriage of Queen Isabella and King Ferdinand in 1469, the American territories were under the exclusive jurisdiction of Castile. Due in large part to the extraction of enormous mineral wealth from its colonial possessions in America, Castile emerged as the most powerful state in Europe, with a distinctly modern administrative structure that historians have seen as paradigmatic in the rise of early modern absolutism in Europe.[13] And while the history of the Spanish Empire in America briefly intersected with that of the multinational Holy Roman Empire that had been the dominant power on the European continent for some 700 years when Charles I of Spain was crowned as Emperor Charles V in 1519, the unprecedented reach of the Spanish Empire overseas, as well as its acquisition by conquest and quasi-colonial structure, raised unprecedented questions that would transform the traditional framework of the law of nations (*ius gentium*), governing relations between people in one Christian republic (under the dual authority of emperor and pope), into modern international law, governing relations between sovereign nation states.

   Although Alexander's original donation and the *patronato real* had not sanctioned conquest and the appropriation of land and property, Spanish jurists soon devised ingenious legal instruments by which violent conquest, including the taking of the vanquished population's property and even their enslavement, could be justified. Thus, the infamous law known as the *requerimiento* (Requirement) of 1513, authored by the Spanish jurist Juan López de Palacios Rubios, stipulated that Spanish soldiers were justified in making war on pagan communities that did not voluntarily submit to

Christian rule after having been read (in Latin) a declaration explaining the papal donation and Spain's divinely ordained mission to spread the faith. The lands and property taken in such a violent conquest would lawfully become the property of the conqueror. Jurists in Spain allied with the interests of the conquerors offered a number of rationales by which the Spanish conquest and dominion in America could be justified. Besides pointing to Canon Law and the *Inter Caetera* bulls, they also looked to philosophy, in particular to the ideas of Aristotle, whose legacy had gradually been gaining in prominence since the thirteenth century in the Latin West and seen a veritable revival with the rise of Christian Humanism in the sixteenth century. In his *Politics*, Aristotle had posited that men fall into one of two categories – natural lords and natural slaves. Natural slaves were "barbarians" who were constitutionally ("by nature") incapable of ruling themselves except by tyranny and who were therefore better off being ruled by others, such as the Greeks, who were favored by nature (including a temperate climate) to become natural lords. Thus, some Spanish humanists such as Juan Ginés de Sepúlveda poured over the accounts and descriptions of Native Americans by European travelers and conquerors to find evidence for their argument that the American Indians were specimens of Aristotle's natural slaves, barbarians who required the rule of the Spanish civilized Christians for their own benefit.[14]

When looking for evidence supporting their allegations of Native Americans' natural servitude, the apologists of the Spanish Conquest and of unbridled European imperial expansionism in the Americas could turn to a vast literary archive of proto- (and often pseudo-)scientific travel literature and natural histories that was accumulating during the sixteenth century. As early as the letters of Christopher Columbus, there were reports that the Indigenous inhabitants of America were not only pagans but also savages who engaged in abominable violations of natural law, such as cannibalism.[15] One of the first Europeans who claimed to have witnessed such practices first hand was none other than the author of the aforementioned *Mundus Novus* (attributed to Vespucci), which was replete with sensationalist proto-ethnographic descriptions of Brazilian cultural mores that Europeans would have associated with barbarism and savagery, including not only cannibalism but also sexual licentiousness.[16] The obsessive focus on Native American cannibalism became a mainstay in sixteenth-century European writing about America in virtually all languages and media, from Jean de Léry's (French) and Hans Staden's (German) sixteenth-century accounts of Brazil to the enormously influential copperplate prints produced by the publishing house of the Flemish Huguenot printer Theodor de Bry working in Frankfurt during the 1590s (see Figure 1.3).

1.3 Theodor de Bry, from *America*. Courtesy of the Library of Congress.

Some writers and publicists, including the de Brys as well as the Spanish conqueror of Mexico Bernal Díaz del Castillo, the Spanish Jesuit natural historian José de Acosta, the early seventeenth-century

English colonist and propagandist John Smith, and the late seventeenth-century New England theologian Cotton Mather even alleged that the Native Americans were not only recalcitrant pagans and cannibals but also idolaters and Satanists, intent on defending the dominion of the Devil in the New World against the advances of Christianity brought by the Europeans. The rise of a proto-scientific discourse that I have elsewhere called "ethno-demonology" in texts written about America in European languages during the sixteenth century forms the nexus in which early American literary history and the history of empire coalesce most directly not only across linguistic and national boundaries but also across the centuries of Euro-American colonialism in America.[17]

At the same time, however, the legal justifications of military conquest were already being challenged during the first part of the sixteenth century by several influential theologians and missionaries in imperial Spain, especially among the friars of the Dominican Order, who had themselves long been versed in Scholastic (i.e. medieval) Aristotelianism, especially as mediated by Thomas Aquinas (1225–74). In 1538, the influential Dominican theologian at the University of Salamanca delivered a famous lecture, "De indis" ("On the American Indian"), in which he rejected all the reasons that had been advanced in justification of the Spanish conquest. While he acknowledged the Spaniards' rights to travel to America for the purpose of peaceful proselytization and trade, neither natural law nor the papal donation gave them the right to take anyone's land or property by force. Those who argued that European titles to the New World were founded on the so-called Rights of Discovery (*iure inventionis*) derived from Roman Law were also mistaken, he explained, because that law only pertained to newly found lands and things without an owner (*terra/res nullius*). Since the Americas already had an owner – the American Indians – Roman Law, Vitoria concluded, "provides no support for possession of these lands, any more than it would if they [the Indians] had discovered us."[18]

Perhaps the most prominent critic of the Spanish conquest was the Dominican bishop of Chiapas, Bartolomé de Las Casas, who not only set out to refute Sepúlveda's allegation of the Native Americans' natural servitude in a famous debate at Valladolid (1550–1) but also published scathing critiques of the cruelty and barbarity of the Spanish conquerors and their descendants, who had illegitimately set themselves up as the overlords of the Indians, holding them in *encomienda* (the obligation to render tribute and service) and even slavery. In his early influential tract

Brevíssima Relación de la Destrucción de las Indias (*A Short Account of the Destruction of the Indies*, 1552), Las Casas had only challenged the titles of the Spanish conquerors and their descendants while upholding the Spanish monarchy's supreme sovereignty to rule over the Americas. However, in his later years he grew increasingly radical, to the point of arguing, in his *Tratado de las doce dudas* (*Treaties of the Twelve Doubts*, 1563–5), that the only legitimate rulers of America were the American Indians.[19] While the legal and administrative questions regarding Spanish titles to the New World was never completely settled, the Spanish crown insisted on its political sovereignty over the Americas, dividing up its enormous empire into several territorial viceroyalties, each of which were divided into two separate "republics" of free imperial subjects – the republic of Spaniards and the republic of Indians. Although the crown recognized existing *encomiendas* and *haciendas* (private land holdings), it granted new titles to individuals only for mining mineral resources, such as gold and silver, which could be said to have remained hidden in the earth and, thus, undiscovered by the American Indians.[20]

Much of the narrative literature produced in colonial Spanish America during the sixteenth century was preoccupied with the questions raised by the conquest and its aftermath – about the justness of military force in carrying out Spain's evangelical mission; about the division of the spoils of conquest; and about the viceregal legal and political structure implemented by the crown for the administration of a trans-oceanic empire of unprecedented territorial proportions. Collectively, the body of narrative literature in which this "polemics of possession" was being negotiated is known as the *crónicas de Indias* (chronicles of the Indies), which offered historical accounts of the conquest from various political and social perspectives.[21] The crown's own perspective was officially represented by the *cronista mayor* (royal chronicler), a position established in 1520 with the appointment of its first incumbent, the Italian humanist Peter Martyr of Angleria (1456–1526), as part of the newly created Council of the Indies in Seville, the clearing house for all information about the Spanish American empire. The *cronista mayor* collected and synthesized letters, reports, and accounts written by persons with first-hand knowledge of the events on the ground in America and sent across the ocean on board the annual fleets.

Within the patrimonialist bureaucracy of this transatlantic knowledge production about the Spanish Empire in America, the paradigmatic genre was the *relación de méritos y servicios* (account of merits and services). The discursive designation of the *relación* (account) had originally derived from forensic or notarial rhetoric, in which an eye-witness gave testimony before a judge in a court of law.[22] Similarly, in the American *relación de méritos*, a participant, witness, or direct stake-holder in the historical events of the Conquest addressed a reader typically positioned at a higher level in the administrative order in one of the centers of imperial power (the seat of the vice-royalty, the *Casa* in Seville, or the royal court in Madrid) in order to make an appeal for grants of favors, privileges, or imperial office based on services rendered to the crown, either by the author himself (and in one famous case, herself) or by his ancestors.[23] From Hernando Cortés's letters to Charles V to Las Casas's resounding indictments of the cruelties of the conquerors and the petitions written by the Native Andean noblemen, such as Felipe Guaman Poma de Ayala, who had become conversant with the Latin script and Spanish linguistic and rhetorical conventions, authors of *relaciones* availed themselves of the ethos of the eye-witness in making their cases in the courts of imperial authority.[24] Only a fraction of the thousands of *relaciones* that were sent from the Americas to Seville were printed for a wider public audience at the time when they were written. While the crown initially intervened into the public dissemination of knowledge about the Americas only indirectly – by granting a sort of copyright known as the *privilegio* (privilege) to publications it viewed favorably – after the 1550s, it required that all writings about the Americas be inspected, possibly censored, and licensed by the Council of the Indies before they could be published in the Spanish Empire. Authors wishing to publish and sell books that were not approved for a license had to find printers abroad.

The Black Legend and the Challenge of Empire

The publication history of Las Casas's works is a prominent case in point. Initially, his arguments were favorably received by royal officials under the reign of Charles V, while Sepúlveda's writings justifying the Spanish conquest were banned from circulation in Spain. The reason for this was in part that Las Casas's arguments were initially helpful to the crown's efforts to reign in the neo-feudal pretensions and power of the new conqueror caste in America. Thus, several measures designed to this effect, such as the abrogation of the inheritability of the encomienda after the original conqueror's death stipulated under the New Laws of 1542, were ostensibly introduced for the protection of the Indians.[25] Later, however, Las Casas's writings were suppressed under the reign of Charles's son, King

Philip II. The reason for this was (in addition to Las Casas' increasing radicalism) that his scathing critiques of the Spanish conquest, especially his *Brevísima relación*, were being translated into other European languages and were used by other nations to cast doubt on the legitimacy of the Spanish rule over America and its theological foundation in the papal bulls of donation.[26] Already during the 1540s, King Francis I of France, having commissioned Jacques Cartier to explore and settle in North America, reportedly remarked (in reference to *Inter Caetera*) that "The sun shines for me as it does for others. I would very much like to see the clause of Adam's will by which I should be denied my share of the world."[27] King Francis questioned the legal notion that "mere discovery" gave Spain and Portugal exclusive title to territory in America, but as a Catholic, it was difficult for him to defy outrightly Pope Alexander's donation. It is therefore no coincidence that some of the earliest French endeavors to gain colonial toeholds in the Americas were undertaken (with royal sanction or even support) by French Protestant Huguenots, who looked for a refuge from persecution during the sectarian wars that ravaged France in the sixteenth century. However, the French were latecomers in the race for empire in America and therefore initially focused on areas that either had not yet been occupied by the Iberian powers or where they thought the Iberian hold was too weak to be effectively defended.

Nevertheless, many of the early French attempts to gain colonial toeholds ended in disaster. Thus, in 1564 the French Huguenot René Goulaine de Laudonnière was commissioned by King Charles IX to establish a military and trading outpost in Florida near modern-day Jacksonville, named Fort Caroline. Although the enterprise produced an interesting narrative account of the colony written by Laudonnière as well as influential watercolor paintings of Floridian flora, fauna, and Native culture by the artist Jacques le Moyne that were later publicized by the de Brys in Frankfurt,[28] it came to an abrupt end when it was wiped out by a Spanish army stationed to the south at St. Augustine under the leadership of Pedro Menéndez de Avilés. Likewise, in Brazil the French colony that Nicolas Durand de Villegaignon had founded near present-day Rio de Janeiro in 1555 named *France Antarctique* (Antarctic France) produced two important narrative accounts, both written by participants in the colonial expedition who focused their descriptions on Native Brazilian practices of cannibalism among the Tupinamba, though from divergent sectarian viewpoints: *Les singularitez de la France Antarctique* (1557; Engl. *The New Found World, or Antarctike*) by the Franciscan friar André Thevet (1516–90) and *Histoire d'un voyage fait en la terre de Brésil* (1578) by the French Calvinist Jean de Léry (1536–1613), who compared Tupinamba cannibalism favorably to the savagery of French Catholics in the religious wars in France. However, like Fort Caroline, France's colonial venture in Brazil was also short-lived, being destroyed by the Portuguese in 1567.[29]

Similar to France, England was a latecomer in the race to empire in the Americas; and like their French counterparts, English promoters of empire challenged the legitimacy of the papal donation on which the exclusive Iberian claims to dominion in the New World had rested. During the early seventeenth century, the Anglican minister and collector of travel literature Samuel Purchas invoked "[Bartolomé de las] Casas, a Spanish Bishop in those parts" to ask "what right then had the Pope" to donate America to Spain in his bull? Instead of converting the American "Ethnikes" to Christianity, the Spanish conquerors had acted like "Wolves amongst Sheepe." It is therefore "no marvell," he concluded, "that this Bull hath begotten such brutish Christians in America."[30] Thus, what had begun as an internal debate among Spanish theologians, jurists, and politicians about the legal and religious foundations of empire became an international polemic culminating in Protestant nations with the formation of the so-called Black Legend – the notion of the unusual cruelty of the Spanish Conquest of America and the degeneracy of Catholic Spain more generally – which became one of the ideological cornerstones of Protestant imperialism in America and of Western modernity.[31]

But when rationalizing their imperial designs on America, British writers did not have to challenge the legitimacy of the papal bulls outrightly; they also searched for legal arguments limiting Spanish claims to the New World under the regime set up by *Inter Caetera*. Thus, the Elizabethan mathematician, alchemist, and magician John Dee – who is credited with coining the phrase "British Empire" – had elaborated what he called "this Brytish discovery and recovery enterprise" by explaining why British claims to North America were not in conflict with either the Alexandrine bulls of donation or the law of nations. The argument hinged on a mythology he had constructed surrounding the medieval exploits of "British" rulers starting with King Arthur's sixth-century conquests in the northern Atlantic and culminating with those of Prince Madoc of Wales in the twelfth century, which Dee located in America: "Circa Anno 1170," Dee claimed, Prince Madoc had founded a colony in the "province then named *Iaquaza* (but of late *Florida*) or into some of the provinces and territories neere ther aboutes, as in *Apalchen, Mocosa,* or *Norembega,* eache of these 4 beinge notable portions of the ancient *Atlantjs,* not longe synce nowe named *America*."[32] In his *The Limits of the British Empire* (1593) and several other works, Dee spelled out the implications for the British rights of dominion in North America, citing the stipulation in the *Inter Caetera* bulls that the papal donation on account of Columbus's discovery only pertained to lands "which were not yet in the actual possession of any other Christian king or prince before the beginning of Anno Domini 1493."[33] Even though the first modern voyages of discovery in North America on behalf of the English crown – led by John and Sebastian Cabot in 1494 and 1497 – did not take place until after 1493, Dee argued, Prince Madoc's discovery in the twelfth century long predated that of Columbus.[34] Ultimately, however, Dee argued, "actual possession" does not automatically derive from "mere discovery" but is completed only through occupation. While Spain can be said to be in actual possession of many of the southern parts of the New World in this sense, the "northern portion," which had first been discovered by Madoc, the "*Spaniard* occupieth not" and therefore presents "a due tytle for clayme" to those who first occupy it.[35]

While it could be argued that in imperial Spain there had been a "struggle for justice" for the rights of Native Americans to a certain extent,[36] few British promoters and theorists of empire questioned their right to take Native American land and property. Indeed, the fact that land not yet occupied by Spaniards was still *Native* land was hereby either ignored or dismissed: Native Americans may have occupied the land, but they did not truly own it because they had not been cultivating it – at least not using European-style agriculture. Even though the documentary record of the failed attempt in the 1580s to establish the first English colony at Roanoke in present-day North Carolina under a patent granted to Sir Walter Raleigh includes watercolor paintings by the English artist John White clearly showing evidence of Native American agriculture (see Figure 1.4), Thomas Harriot (whose account of the Roanoke colony was published in 1588 and republished in 1590 by de Bry with engravings based on White's watercolors) named the land "Virginia" – after the "Virgin Queen" (Elizabeth I) – because it had not yet been occupied by Spain. Even though Harriot also briefly discussed Algonquin agricultural practices, he suggested that the land had retained its "virginal" character because the Indians "neuer fatten [the ground] with mucke, dounge or any other thing; neither plow nor digge it as we in England."[37] Similarly, in his *The Discoverie of the Large, Rich and Bewtiful Empyre of Guiana* (1596), Raleigh attempted to persuade his Queen that an English invasion of the north-eastern part of South America would be both feasible and justified because Guiana is still saving herself for her

1.4 "The Tovvne of Secota." Theodor de Bry, from *America*, pt. 1. Courtesy of the Library of Congress.

legitimate English husband, having so far escaped the "rape" by cruel Spanish Catholics:

> *Guiana* is a country that hath yet her maidenhead, never sacked, turned, nor wrought; the face of the earth hath not been torn, nor the virtue and salt of the soil spent by manurance. The graves have not been opened for gold, the mines not broken with sledges, nor their images pulled down out of their temples. It hath never been entered by any army of strength, and never conquered or possessed by any Christian prince.[38]

What's more, Raleigh argued that somewhere in Guiana was the secret location of the city of Manoa, home to the fabulous Native ruler known as "El Dorado" (the Golden One), who, he speculated, must have been the last descendant of the "Inga" (Inca) dynasty deposed by the Spaniards in Peru but surviving in their Guianese exile, eagerly awaiting the ally from "Inglatierra" who would help him overthrow the Spanish usurpers of his throne in a joint invasion of Peru and restore him as legitimate ruler over his empire.[39] While Raleigh's early colonial ventures in both North and South America, like those of the French, ended in failure, the literature that these ventures produced, written by him and others, laid the ideological groundwork for an incipient British empire in North America, leading to the first permanent English colony at Jamestown in 1607.

Economy and the Proliferation of Empire

If Raleigh was still enchanted by the Spanish model of the conquest of Native American empires, exploits in gold and silver, and the subjugation of vast Indigenous populations laboring in the imperial economy, the failure of this model in much of the Americas outside of the Spanish American core regions of Mexico and Peru inspired the search not only for alternative modalities of colonial exploitation but also for new defin-itions of the rights of dominion – and ultimately divergent forms of empire. As a result, each European nation with imperial ambitions in the Americas during the early modern period pursued particular economic and geopolitical interests that help explain not only the distinctive relations they established with Native Americans but also the colonial societies they created. This had been evident from the beginning in the example of the Portuguese, whose primary economic interest remained in the African slave trade and in the Indian spice trade throughout the early modern era and who had established a maritime empire that consisted of a diasporic network of migrants, traders, artisans, mariners, servants, and slaves.[40] The Portuguese founded their first American colony at Rio de Janeiro primarily as a maritime landing station almost by accident when, in 1500, Pedro Álvares Cabral's expedition to set up a *feitoria* or trading station in Calicut, India, sailed so far west in the route around Africa that they made landfall in Brazil. The expedition's scribe, Pero Vaz de Caminha wrote a *Carta* (letter) to King Dom Manuel that offers the earliest descriptions of the Indigenous peoples as well as the flora and fauna of Brazil.[41] In its early stage, the Portuguese *feitoria* focused on trading (sometimes forcibly) Brazil wood (*Paubrasilia echinate*), from which the region's name derives.

Later in the sixteenth century, the economic focus shifted to sugar production in large plantations based on African slave labor and then mining of gold and silver with both Indigenous and African slaves, especially in the eastern province of Minas Gerais. Also, in the 1550s, the first Governor General of Brazil, Tomé de Sousa, had invited the Jesuits, who set up missions among the Tupinamba and Guaraní.[42] Throughout much of the colonial period, Brazil's colonial economy was subject to the boom-and-bust cycles governed by the larger interimperial development of the Atlantic economy, especially during the seventeenth century after the introduction of sugar plantations in the Spanish Caribbean as well as on the islands that the British and French had conquered from Spain, including Jamaica, Barbados, and a part of Hispaniola (Haiti).[43] Unlike Spanish America, where the European conquerors had subjugated large and complex societies that were integrated into the imperial order of the Spanish viceroyalties, Brazil remained a frontier society during much of its colonial period, with settlements consisting of European colonists, as well as African and Indigenous slaves concentrated along the Atlantic coast that were closely tied to the global maritime networks of the Portuguese mercantile empire centered in Lisbon.

Meanwhile, the French had set up a network of small trading outposts along the vast waterways of North America since Cartier's early explorations in 1534–35. While no permanent settlements were established during the sixteenth century, French merchants followed Cartier's route up the St. Lawrence River and established a lucrative fur trading network that provided the economic basis for the first permanent French colonial settlements during the seventeenth century. The founding of Port Royal in Acadia in 1605 and Quebec City in 1608 marked the beginnings of what would become the vast viceroyalty of New France. The central actor in (and writer of) the early history of New France was Samuel de Champlain, who had come to Canada as Royal Geographer accompanying a fur trading expedition. After the founding of Quebec, Champlain arranged for French settlers to be brought to Canada and forged an alliance with the Wyandot (Hurons) in their rivalry against the Haudenosaunee (Iroquois) Confederacy. This early alliance had long-lasting consequences for imperial diplomacy in North America that were still felt over 150 years later, as the Iroquois, in turn, allied themselves with the English in their rivalry with the French for hegemony in North America. Champlain told of these events in several of his earlier works,[44] but his magnum opus, *Les Voyages de la Nouvelle France Occidentale* (1632), was written in captivity in England following the English capture of Quebec City in the Anglo-French War

(1627–29). When Quebec was restored to France after the war, Champlain returned to Canada once more and, in 1634, sent Jean Nicolet to explore the western parts of New France as far as the modern state of Wisconsin. Meanwhile, in 1611, the Jesuits had arrived also in Canada and set up their evangelical missions among the Wyandot. The collected annual reports about their activities they sent to Rome during the seventeenth and eighteenth century – including accounts of some proselytizing successes but many more of missionary martyrdoms – add up to more than seventy volumes published in the late nineteenth century.[45] Due to the active interest that the colonial American authors writing in French had in Native Americans – either as partners in trade or as potential Christian converts – both the secular and the missionary literature of colonial New France is exceptionally rich in detailed ethnographic information about Northeastern America's indigenous cultures.

By the end of the seventeenth century, the territory claimed by the French as part of New France encompassed not only modern-day Quebec but also all the territory from the Great Lakes region down to the Gulf of Mexico, and from the Appalachian region to the Rocky Mountains – a vast area called (French) Louisiana. One of the most important historical accounts of Louisiana was written during the early eighteenth century by Antoine-Simon Le Page du Pratz, who had come to America in 1718 after having received some training in engineering, architecture, and astronomy, as well as enough wealth to obtain a concession near Natchez, in the present state of Mississippi. In 1758, he published a historical account of the territory under the title of *Histoire de la Louisiane*, which was partially translated into English in 1763 as *The History of Louisiana, or of the Western Parts of Virginia and Carolina* and which contains a mix of ethnographic description and colonial history, beginning with the sixteenth-century Spanish and French explorers to the establishment of the French settlements along the Mississippi.

However, while France claimed the vast territory of Louisiana from the Appalachian to the Rocky Mountains, it actually controlled very little of it, as most of it was inhabited by Native American nations who had not agreed (or were unaware) that they were subjects of the French crown. After having lost the interimperial Seven Years' War in North America (1756–63), France was forced to cede the northern part of New France (in modern-day Canada) to victorious Great Britain and the western part (French Louisiana) to Spain, which received the territory as a compensation for its own loss of Florida to Britain in the Anglo Spanish War (1762–3). France temporarily regained control of Louisiana in 1800, when Napoleon Bonaparte attempted to rebuild France's empire in America and traded Louisiana for Tuscany to Spain. However, when France, preoccupied with Napoleon's wars in Europe, was unable to suppress the ongoing slave rebellion in Haiti, which ended in the first creation of an independent nation state by former slaves in 1804, Napoleon sold Louisiana to the United States. But since much of the territory that was transferred with the Louisiana Purchase of 1803 was actually still controlled by Native American nations, the United States in effect acquired from France only the future preemptive right to obtain Indian lands by treaty or by conquest, to the exclusion of other colonial powers. With the sale of Louisiana and the eventual loss of Haiti, which had been France's most valuable colony in America due to its lucrative sugar plantations, the French empire in America was reduced to a few remaining Caribbean islands, mainly Guadeloupe and Martinique at the beginning of the nineteenth century.[46]

As in New France, in Protestant British America, the encounters with the more decentralized Native cultures in North America, as well as the failure to find large quantities of silver and gold, necessitated a redefinition of the objectives of empire. But whereas the French had initially focused on trade and the acquisition of American natural resources (from Brazil wood to beaver pelts) and only later established large-scale plantation monocultures with the use of African slave labor in the Caribbean, the first British colonial ventures were conceived as plantations of European settlers from the beginning. In this British colonial scheme, the primary interest was vested in Native American land, not in the products of Native American labor or in Native American souls. As we have already seen, English theorists of empire therefore frequently compared their own invasions of American land to an act of "husbandry" in which virgin American soil was tilled (or penetrated) by its rightful English "husband." With regard to conceivable Native American claims to Virginia, Samuel Purchas seems to have fully adopted the arguments by sixteenth-century Spanish apologists of conquest such as Sepúlveda when he suggested in the early seventeenth century that Native possession of the land would have amounted to a rape ("ravishment") by "savages," rather than true marriage to English husbands.

> But looke upon Virginia; view her lovely looks (howsoever like a modest Virgin she is now vailed with wild Coverts and shadie Woods, expecting rather ravishment then Mariage from her Native Savages) survey her Heavens, Elements, Situation; her divisions by armes of Bayes and Rivers into so goodly and well proportioned limmes and members; her Virgin portion nothing empaired, nay not yet improved, in Natures best Legacies; the neighbouring Regions and Seas so commodious and obsequious; her

opportunities for offence and defence; and in all these you shall see, that she
is worth the wooing and loves of the best Husband.[47]

By the time Purchas penned these lines in 1625, England's first permanent
colony at Jamestown had barely survived the first five years after its
founding in 1607 but found its footing with the cultivation of tobacco,
which had been introduced in 1612. In 1620, a second English colony had
been established further north at Cape Cod by Puritan Separatists without
any official charters or titles, Plymouth Plantation. Five years later, a third
colony would be established at Boston, Massachusetts Bay, also by (non-
Separatist) Puritans. With the lone exception of the Puritan minister Roger
Williams, the founder of Rhode Island, none of the seventeenth-century
English founders of colonies questioned their right to occupy Native lands.
For them, American territory not yet occupied by another European power
was a "virgin land," a "terra nullius" (a land without an owner) that is there
for the taking. By the end of the seventeenth century, English philosophers
such as John Locke, in his *Second Treatise of Government* (1689), argued
that America before the arrival of Europeans had consisted of "wild woods
and uncultivated waste . . . left to nature without any improvement, tillage
or husbandry." For Locke, only labor – and in particular, European-style
agricultural labor—could transform the fruits of the earth from the non-
proprietary state of nature into private property. Since the economic life of
American Indians was not (according to Locke) based on agricultural
labor, America was like a *vacuum domicilium* (an empty dwelling place),
that could lawfully be appropriated by English colonists.[48]

However, the British model of empire in America, based as it was on
plantations of European settlers, required long-term investment without
the promise of a quick return of profits through trade or mineral extraction. The English crown, though liberal in granting patents and charters to
individuals or companies willing to invest, was reluctant to take on the
financial and geopolitical risks of underwriting colonial adventures (especially in light of Spanish maritime power). The exorbitant expenses
involved in establishing and supporting a plantation consumed and out-
stripped the means of wealthy aristocrats such as Raleigh, while the trading
companies that had existed in England since the sixteenth century, such as
the Muscovy Company, were not prepared to underwrite colonial adventures without foreseeable returns on investments. Thus, much of the
literature of the early British American colonies is promotional in purpose.
Addressed to both potential investors and settlers enlisted by the newly
forming corporations for the promotion of colonial planting, these

"promotion tracts" extolled the economic potential of colonial development in America.

Like their Spanish American counterparts, many of the colonial British American authors also invoked their ethos as eye-witnesses when writing first-hand "accounts" of the events and things on the ground. However, their rhetorical situation was fundamentally different from that of most of the colonial writers in Spanish America. We might say that, while the majority of the sixteenth-century writers of colonial Spanish American narratives were inscribed in a "vertical" rhetorical situation when addressing readers who were placed in a higher and more central position of power in the imperial hierarchy, colonial British American were typically inscribed in a "horizontal" rhetorical situation when addressing potential investors and settlers in the general public. In this regard, Walter Raleigh was still a transitional figure: when publishing his *The Discoverie of the Large, Rich and Bewtiful Empyre of Guiana* (1596), he wrote not one but two prefaces – one addressed to a courtly audience imploring the Queen to outfit a military expedition of conquest and another one to a general reader promising financial gain on investment in colonial ventures. By contrast, Thomas Harriot's account about Virginia (1588) was already exclusively addressed to potential investors and settlers in the general public, presenting long lists and descriptions of "commodities" to be had or planted in Virginia. Significantly, his account was not entitled "account" or "relation" but rather "report" – *A briefe and true report of the new found land of Virginia* – a generic designation that can be seen, as has recently been argued, as an early modern prototype of the modern IPO (Initial Public Offering), enticing financial speculators (called "adventurers" in early modern England) to invest in a capitalist colonial enterprise.[49]

In conclusion, while during the late fifteenth and early sixteenth centuries, the Iberian empires derived the justification of their expansionism primarily from the papal donation and Canon Law, during the second part of the sixteenth century, apologists of the Spanish Conquest increasingly invoked natural law as derived by Aristotelian philosophy, according to which natural slaves who do not voluntarily subject to the rule of natural lords may be compelled through war. As natural slaves cannot rightfully own property (including land), they argued, the "rights of discovery" (*iure inventionis*), as derived from Roman law, pertained to America, which was a *terra nullius* (a land without an owner). However, this extreme position was contested by influential members of the mendicant orders, especially among the Dominicans, and was never made official policy by the crown, who implemented a series of laws intended to limit the power of the conquerors and to undercut the legitimacy of their neo-feudal pretensions while integrating the newly conquered territories within the viceregal structure of the Spanish American empire. In the course of the sixteenth century, Spanish theologians and jurists at the University of Salamanca elaborated a compromise position in which the rights of discovery were presumed to obtain to mineral resources such as gold and silver hidden in the earth but not to the land, which was presumed to be rightfully owned by the indigenous population of America. Also, while Native Americans were presumed to be free imperial subjects of the crown who could not be enslaved except in special circumstances (such as rebellions), they were expected to provide tribute and service in exchange for their evangelization. Nevertheless, once translated into other European languages, the indictment of the injustices, abuses, and cruelties of both the initial conquest and of the encomienda system of tribute labor was used to justify, as the so-called Black Legend, the encroachments by other European nations on territory claimed by the Iberian powers. In addition, rival European nations began to question the legitimacy of both the papal donation and the rights of discovery, arguing that "mere discovery" does not legitimate titles of dominion. Engaged in a search for alternative justifications of empire, imperial rivals of Spain, especially among expanding Protestant nations, began to redefine the terms of "true possession" in terms of "occupation," as demonstrable by European-style agricultural development (and increasingly monocultural development). Though not formalized until the nineteenth century in international law, the appropriation of what was then being referred to as the American *vacuum domicilium* became the central ideological feature of the "cant of conquest" in British America.[50]

While the concept of *vacuum domicilium* was the de facto justification offered by Protestant theorists of empire during the seventeenth century, it would not attain actual currency in international law until the nineteenth century, when most former European colonies in America had gained their independence from European empires. In Latin America, the *encomienda* – a system of extracting Native labor that had never entailed ownership of land – was replaced by the *hacienda*, the modern system of large-scale latifundia agriculture on privately owned estates that turned millions of indigenous tributaries of labor into landless peasantry. In the United States, the doctrine of the "Rights of Discovery" was invoked most prominently in the (now infamous) Supreme Court landmark decision *Johnson* v. *M'Intosh*, in which chief justice John Marshall ruled that private citizens could not purchase land from Native American nations because, by right of "preemption," the title to all Indian lands lawfully belonged to the federal government of the United States and that, therefore, the government held the exclusive right of conferring onto private citizens titles to Native American lands. Ironically, he invoked the example of imperial Spain as a precedent for his ruling, arguing that "Spain did not rest her title solely on the grant of the Pope, ... Her discussions respecting boundary, with France, with Great Britain, and with the United States, all show that she placed it on the rights given by discovery."[51] It would appear that Marshall was not aware, or chose to ignore, the fact that Spanish jurists such as Vitoria had long disposed of this argument by pointing out that the doctrine of discovery "provides no support for possession of these lands, any more than it would if they [the Indians] had discovered us."

Notes

1. For a recent overview of these changes, see Bryce Traister, ed., *The Cambridge Companion to Early American Literature* (Cambridge: Cambridge University Press, 2021). On the hemispheric approach, see especially Allison Bigelow's essay in that volume (218–32).
2. William Spengeman, *A New World of Words: Redefining Early American Literature* (New Haven: Yale University Press, 1994).
3. *Cristóbal Colón: Textos y documentos completos*, ed. Consuelo Varela and Juan Gil (1982; Madrid: Alianza Editorial, 2003), 485–503.
4. See James Akerman, "Introduction," in *The Imperial Map: Cartography and the Mastery of Empire*, ed. James Akerman (Chicago: University of Chicago Press, 2009), 1–9. On the geopolitical tradition of the geographic line, see Carl Schmitt, *The "Nomos" of the Earth in the International law of the "Jus Publicum Europaeum,"* trans. and annotated G. L. Ulmen (New York: Telos, 2003).
5. Amerigo Vespucci, *Letters from a New World: Amerigo Vespucci's Discovery of America*, ed. and introd. Luciano Formisano, trans. David Jacobson (New York: Marilio, 1992), 49.
6. "Relación del Tercer Viaje," in *Cristóbal Colón: Textos y documentos completos*, ed. Consuelo Varela and Juan Gil (1982; Madrid: Alianza Editorial, 2003) 268–94.
7. See Ricardo Padron, *The Indies of the Setting Sun: How Early Modern Spain Mapped the Far East as the Trans-Pacific West* (Chicago: University of Chicago Press, 2020); also Surekha Davies, "*America and Amerindians in Sebastian Münster's* Cosmographiae universalies libri VI (1550)," *Renaissance Studies* 25.3 (2011): 351–73.
8. Fray Juan Gonzalez de Mendoza, *Historia de las cosas mas notables, ritos y costumbres del gran Reyno del a China, sabidas assi por los libros delos mesmos*

Chinas, como por relación de Religiosos, y otras personas que han estado en el dicho Reyno (Madrid: en la casa de Querino Corardo Flamenco, 1586).

9. On the colonial origins of (early) modern totalitarianism, see Irene Silverblatt, *Modern Inquisitions: Peru and the Colonial Origins of the Civilized World* (Durham, NC: Duke University Press, 2004).

10. Richard Hakluyt, *Discourse of Western Planting* [1584], ed. David B. Quinn & Allison M. Quinn (London: Hakluyt Society, 1993). See also David Armitage, *The Ideological Origins of the British Empire* (Cambridge: Cambridge University Press, 2003).

11. See James Muldoon, *Empire and Order: The Concept of Empire, 800–1800* (Basingstoke: Macmillan, 1999) also Andrés Prieto, *The Theologian and the Empire. A Biography of José de Acosta, S.I. (1540–1600)* (Leiden: Brill, 2024).

12. See Anthony Pagden, *Lords of All the World: Ideologies of Empire in Spain, Britain and France c. 1500–c. 1800* (New Haven: Yale University Press, 1995), especially 11–28 on the common Roman legacy. For comparative perspectives on ideologies of conquest in the early Americas, see Lauren Benton and Benjamin Straumann, "Acquiring Empire by Law: From Roman Doctrine to Early Modern European Practice," *Law and History Review* 28 (2010): 20–9; and Robert Williams, *The American Indian in Western Legal Thought: The Discourses of Conquest* (New York: Oxford University Press, 1990), 96–7; and Patricia Seed, *Ceremonies of Possession in Europe's Conquest of the New World, 1492–1640* (Cambridge: Cambridge University Press, 1995). For a comparative perspective of European imperialism in the Americas more generally, see Pagden, *Lords of All the World*; and John H. Elliott, *Empires of the Atlantic World: Britain and Spain, 1492–1830* (New Haven: Yale University Press, 2006).

13. See Perry Anderson, *Lineages of the Absolutist State* (London: Humanities Press, 1974); also José Antonio Maravall, *Culture of the Baroque: Analysis of a Historical Structure*, trans. Terry Cochran (Minneapolis: University of Minnesota Press, 1986).

14. Juan Ginés de Sepúlveda, *Democrates alter de justis belli causis apud Indios*, ed. and trans. Angel Losada as *Democrates Segundo, o de las Justas causas de la Guerra contra los indios* (Madrid: Consejo Superior de Investigaciones Científicas Instituto Francisco de Vitoria, 1951).

15. Cristóbal Colón, 492.

16. Vespucci, Letters from a New World, 49.

17. Ralph Bauer, *The Alchemy of Conquest: Science, Religion, and the Secrets of the New World* (Charlottesville: University of Virginia Press, 2019), 401–29.

18. Francisco de Vitoria, "On the American Indians," in *Political Writings*, ed. and trans. Anthony Pagden and Jeremy Lawrance (Cambridge: Cambridge University Press, 1991), 264–5.

19. See Bartolomé de las Casas, *A Short Account of the Destruction of the Indies*, trans. Nigel Griffin (New York: Penguin Random House, 1992); see also Lewis Hanke, *All Mankind Is One: A Study of the Disputation between Bartolomé de Las Casas and Juan Ginés de Sepúlveda in 1550 on the*

Intellectual and Religious Capacity of the American Indians (DeKalb: Northern Illinois University Press, 1974); and Rolena Adorno, *The Polemics of Possession in Spanish American Narrative* (New Haven: Yale University Press, 2007). On the *Tratado*, see Víctor Zorrilla, "Just War in Las Casas's *Tratado de las doce dudas*," in *Bartolomé de las Casas, O.P.: History, Philosophy, and Theology in the Age of European Expansion*, ed. David Thomas Orique O.P. and Rady Roldán-Figueroa (Leiden: Brill, 2019), 243–59.

20. See Orlando Bentancor, *The Matter of Empire: Metaphysics and Mining in Colonial Peru* (Pittsburgh: Pittsburgh University Press, 2017); also Allison Bigelow, *Mining Language: Racial Thinking, Indigenous Knowledge, and Colonial Metallurgy in the Early Modern Iberian World* (Chapel Hill: The University of North Carolina Press for the Omohundro Institute of Early American History and Culture, 2020).

21. Adorno, *Polemics*.

22. See Walter Mignolo, "El Métatexto Historiográfico y la Historiografía Indiana," *MLN* 96.2 (1981): 358–402, 389; see also his "Cartas, crónicas y relaciones del descubrimiento y la conquista," in *Historia de la literatura hispanoamericana; época colonial*, ed. Luis Íñigo Madrigal (Madrid: Ediciones Cátedra, 1982), 57–116. Roberto González Echevarría, "Humanismo, Retórica y las Crónicas de la Conquista," in *Isla a su Vuelo Fugitiva. Ensayos Críticos sobre Literatura Hispanoamericana* (Madrid: José Porrúa Turanzas, 1983), 9–26; also *Myth and Archive: A Theory of Latin American Narrative* (Cambridge: Cambridge University Press, 1990); and *The Narrative of America* (Cambridge: Cambridge University Press, 1990).

23. On the famous case in which a woman gave a *relación* about her role (in a man's disguise) in the Conquest of America, see Catalina de Erauso's memoir, which has been edited and translated into English by Michele Stepto as *Lieutenant Nun: Memoir of a Basque Transvestite in the New World* (Boston: Beacon Press, 1996).

24. For Guaman Poma de Ayala's chronicle, see the online edition of the Royal Library of Denmark at Copenhagen at The Guaman Poma Website. For an English translation of the first part of Guaman Poma's chronicle, see Felipe Guaman Poma de Ayala, *The First New Chronicle and Good Government*, ed. and trans. Roland Hamilton (Austin: University of Texas Press, 2021).

25. David Brading, *The First America: The Spanish Monarchy, Creole Patriots, and the Liberal State, 1492–1867* (Cambridge: Cambridge University Press, 1991), 59–80; Adorno, *Polemics*, 101–23; also Anthony Pagden, *The Fall of Natural Man: The American Indian and the Origins of Comparative Ethnology* (Cambridge: Cambridge University Press, 1982).

26. Bartolomé de Las Casas' *Brevissima relación* was translated into English in 1583 as *The Spanish Colonie* and in 1656 as *The Tears of the Indians* (1656). It was also translated into other European languages, including the Latin edition by Theodor de Bry as *Narratio regionum indicarum per Hispanos quosdam deuas-tatarum verissima* (Frankfurt in 1598). For a modern English edition, see

   A Short Account of the Destruction of the Indies, ed. Anthony Pagden
   (New York: Penguin, 2004).

27. Quoted in Germán Arciniegas, *Caribbean: Sea of the New World*, trans.
    Harriet de Onís (New York: Knopf, 1946), 118.

28. René Goulaine de Laudonnière, *L'histoire Notable De La Floride Sitvee Es
    Indes Occidentales : Contenant Les Trois Voyages Faits En Icelle Par Certains
    Capitaines & Pilotes François* (Paris: Chez Guillaume Auuray, ruë sainct Iean
    de Beauuais, au Bellerophon couronné, 1586). This account was translated
    into English during the sixteenth century by Richard Hakluyt as *A Notable
    Historie Containing Foure Voyages Made by Certayne French Captaynes Vnto
    Florida* (London: Imprinted by Thomas Dawson, 1587). Both Laudonnière's
    account and Le Moyne's watercolors were published in 1591 by Theodor de
    Bry in both Latin and German. See *Der Ander Theyl, Der Newlich Erfundenen
    Landtschafft Americæ* (Frankfurt, 1591).

29. See Jean de Léry, *History of a Voyage to the Land of Brazil* (Berkeley: University
    of California Press, 1993).

30. Samuel Purchas, *Purchase, His Pilgrimes, part 1 In fiue books* (London: Printed
    by William Stansby for Henrie Fetherstone, and Are to Be Sold at His Shop in
    Pauls Church-Yard at the Signe of the Rose, 1625), 23.

31. See Charles Gibson, *The Black Legend: Anti-Spanish Attitudes in the Old
    World and the New* (New York: Random House, 1971).

32. John Dee et al., *John Dee: The Limits of the British Empire* (Westport: Praeger,
    2004), 43–4. See also John Dee, *General and Rare Memorials Pertayning to the
    Perfect Arte of Nauigation: Annexed to the Paradoxal Cumpas, in Playne: Now
    First Published: 24. Yeres, After the First Inuention Thereof* (London: By Iohn
    Daye, 1577), 2. See also Andrew Fitzmaurice, *Sovereignty, Property and Empire,
    1500–2000* (Cambridge: Cambridge University Press, 2014), 85–124.

33. Dee et al., *John Dee*, 93.

34. Dee et al., *John Dee*, 53.

35. Dee et al., *John Dee*, 48.

36. See Lewis Hanke, James H. Sutton Jr., and Sylvia Leal, eds. *The Spanish
    Struggle for Justice in the Conquest of America* (Boston: Little, Brown, 1965).

37. Thomas Harriot, *A briefe and true report of the new found land of Virginia*,
    introd. Pault Hulton (1590; New York: Dover, 1972), 42. Harriot's account
    was first published in English in 1588 and then republished in Latin, German,
    and French, as well as a new English edition in 1590 as the first volume of
    Theodor de Bry's influential *America* series.

38. Walter Raleigh, *The Discoverie of the Large, Rich and Bewtiful Empyre of
    Guiana*, ed. Neil Whitehead (Norman: University of Oklahoma Press,
    1997), 196.

39. Raleigh, *Discoverie*, 199.

40. Daviken Studnicki-Gizbert, *A Nation Upon the Ocean Sea: Portugal's Atlantic
    Diaspora and the Crisis of the Spanish Empire, 1492–1640* (New York: Oxford
    University Press, 2007).

41. *The Voyages of Pedro Alvares Cabral*, trans. William Brooks Greenlee (London: Hakluyt Society, 1938); see also Paulo Roberto Pereira, *Os três únicos testemunhos do descobrimento do Brasil* (Rio de Janeiro: Lacerda Editores, 1999).
42. On the Portuguese Jesuit missionary networks connecting Brazil and India, see Ananya Chakravarti, *The Empire of Apostles: Religion, Accommodatio, and the Imagination of Empire in Early Modern Brazil and India* (New Delhi: Oxford University Press, 2018); also Stuart M. McManus, *Empire of Eloquence: The Classical Rhetorical Tradition in Colonial Latin America and the Iberian World* (Cambridge: Cambridge University Press, 2021).
43. See Lisa Voigt, *Spectacular Wealth: The Festivals of Colonial South American Mining Towns* (Austin: University of Texas Press, 2016).
44. These include *Des Sauvages, ou Voyage de Samuel Champlain, de Brouage, fait en la France nouvelle* (1603), *Les Voyages de Sieur de Champlain Xaintongeois* (1613), and *Les Voyages et Descourvertures du Sieur de Champlain* (1619). For a comparative study of early French and English colonial American literatures, see Gordon Sayre, *Les Sauvages Américains: Representations of Native Americans in French and English Colonial Literature* (Chapel Hill: University of North Carolina Press, 2000).
45. See *The Jesuit Relations and Allied Documents: Travels and Explorations of the Jesuit Missionaries in New France, 1610–1791*, ed. Ruben Gold Thwaites (Cleveland: The Burrows Brothers Publishing Company, 1896–1901), 71 volumes.
46. See Lester Langley, *The Americas in the Age of Revolution, 1750–1850* (New Haven: Yale University Press, 1997).
47. Purchas, Purchase, His Pilgrimes, 2.
48. John Locke, *Two Treatise of Government* (London: Printed for Whitmore and Fenn and C. Brown, 1821), 219.
49. See Jennifer Greeson, "Speculation and Scientific Method: Thomas Harriot's Virginia IPO," in "The Epistemological Turn in Early American Literary Studies," ed. Alexander Mazzaferro and Ralph Bauer, special issue of *American Literature* 97 (2025): 237–70.
50. Francis Jennings, *The Invasion of America: Indians, Colonialism, and the Cant of Conquest* (Chapel Hill: The University of North Caroline Press for the Omohundro Institute of Early American History and Culture, 2010 [1975]).
51. *Johnson* v. *M'Intosh*, 21 U.S. 543, 5 L.Ed. 681, 8 Wheat. 543 (1823), 573–4.

CHAPTER 2

Against Imperial Nature
Hérard-Dumesle and the Making of Haitian Revolutionary Eloquence

Monique Allewaert

Introduction

By the early nineteenth century, the genre of natural history was one of imperialism's best weapons. From Hans Sloane's *A Voyage to the Islands of Madera, Barbados, Nieves, Saint Christopher and Jamaica with the Natural History of the Herbs and Trees, &c* (1707; 1725), to the Comte de Buffon's *Histoire Naturelle* (1749–67) through Thomas Jefferson's *Notes on the State of Virginia* (1785), early modern natural histories provided the backbone of eighteenth and nineteenth-century North Atlantic naturalism, history, politics, and literature.[1] After the Haitian Revolution, when the French colony of Saint Domingue emerged as Haiti (the second modern republic in the Americas [after the US] to claim independence from imperial Europe and the only one to found its new state on the abolition of slavery and the principle of an equal *noir* or Black identity among its citizens), natural history remained the dominant literary frame through which the island was known in Europe and North America, where Philadelphia served as a hub for French Creole naturalists. Influential and still circulating natural histories of Saint Domingue, including Pere Labat's *Nouveau Voyages* (1724), Jean Nicolson's *Essay sur l'histoire naturelle de l'isle de Saint-Domingue* (1776), and Moreau de St. Mery's *Description topographic* (1796–98), documented the island in terms of resources that could serve the agro-industrial plantation project. As such, these natural histories' modes of categorizing and describing plants, people, animals, soil, minerals, and climatic forces were themselves techniques of capture. The nature these natural histories witnessed was a product and tool of empire.

Nineteenth-century Haitian poet, politician, and naturalist Charles Hérard-Dumesle's massive 1824 *Voyage dans le Nord de Haïti* (Le Cayes) embarked on the daunting project of remaking the imperial genre of natural history so that it served Haitian sovereignty. Early Haitian writers, including not only Hérard-Dumesle but also Pierre Faubert, Ignace and Émile Nau, and Pompée Valentin Vastey (among many others) remained subject to the predations of imperial power and thus inherited a Western intellectual tradition that proved incapable of absorbing the meaning of the world-historical revolution.[2] This tradition viewed the entire Caribbean region through the frame of plantation naturalism, a lens that viewed earth, air, water, and the living beings that populated them as instrumentalizable. For an early Haitian author to write at all in this moment was in the broadest of senses anti-imperial. Hérard-Dumesle's anti-imperialist efforts depended on challenging the nature imperialism produced to generate a nature that benefited Haitians. To forge a Haitian nature, Hérard-Dumesle convoked natural history, politics, poetics, and other-than-human forces that, together, generated a singular Haitian eloquence. This expressly political Haitian eloquence spun a nature that aspired to redress tyranny on a planetary register.

To generate a nature fired by Haitian eloquence, Hérard-Dumesle engages Epicurus, Pliny, and Virgil as well as key figures of the Francophone enlightenment from Voltaire to Buffon to Rousseau to Volney to neo-epicureans (likely the Encyclopedists) and Montesquieu. Working with and against this natural historical tradition, the *Voyage* summons a nature that worked through the intellectual legacies of diverse classes of Haitians, including wealthy elites educated in Europe or descended from those so educated, small-holder agricultors with little formal education; Catholics, Vodouyizans, and practitioners of African religions; denizens of the north and the south recently reunited under the presidency of Jean-Paul Boyer; and also women who are pointedly included in the book's audience in Hérard-Dumesle's frequent addresses to his wife Rose-Estelle.

Across the *Voyage*'s seventeen chapters, Hérard-Dumesle dramatically revises the naturalism that subtended imperial enlightenment and romanticism by subordinating it to a natural history driven by the call and response of tropical human and other-than-human forces. Hérard-Dumesle identifies this mode as a communicative theory embraced both by the Taino people, whom he calls the Haitians' "adopted ancestors," and Afro-diasporic farming cults that he recognizes as central to contemporary Haitian life. Both these adopted indigenous ancestors and Afro-diasporic "cultists" emerge as key sources of the natural history that his book advances. These Amerindian and Afro-diasporic naturalisms also inspired politics and poetry in which Haitian eloquence rerouted lingering plantation-colonial forces and infrastructures into powers that inspired agricultural as well as poetic practices of freedom. Ultimately, the project of Haitian natural history and eloquence that Hérard-Dumesle envisioned contested not simply the intellectual legacy of imperial natural history but the materiality of nature itself.

Revising the Imperial Natural Historical Tradition

Again and again in the *Voyage*, Hérard-Dumesle lambastes European sciences and natural history for having "one purpose only; 'to prove the inferiority of a great portion of the human race'".[3] From the *Voyage*'s opening engagement of the Comte de Buffon to its takedown of Montesquieu's climate science to its sparring with French and English materialists, Hérard-Dumesle sharply contests eighteenth- and early nineteenth-century European natural history and the racializations on which it depended in an effort to make that tradition usable to a Haitian state developing its own public educational projects.[4] This challenge to the natural historical tradition depends on a theory of eloquence that recalls Jay Fliegelman's influential account of post-revolutionary US efforts to articulate a "natural spoken language" that was a "corollary to natural laws."[5] Yet Hérard-Dumesle also pointedly departs from the precedent set by North Atlantic revolutionary eloquence by positing such rhetorical forays not simply as counterparts to natural law but as capable of *changing* natural law and, with it, nature itself.

Hérard-Dumesle's pointed engagement with Montesquieu's climatological theory exemplifies the *Voyage*'s challenge to colonial sciences as well as the account of eloquence he developed to posit a relation between human and other-than-human forces that unraveled the imperial geodesy that Montesquieu's work helped forge.[6] Montesquieu's *Spirit of the Laws* offered a latitudinally based mapping of the globe and its peoples that cast inhabitants of tropical and equatorial regions as so "enervated" by heat as to be lazy, lascivious, less inclined to labor, and prone to despotism as well as slavery. Montesquieu's climatology was one of the less essentializing eighteenth-century theorizations of the concept, origins, and effects of epidermal race, which was increasingly organizing Euro-Atlantic scientific, political, and literary fields. Even so, Hérard-Dumesle understood Montesquieu's climatology underwrote North Atlantic states' presumption that tropical and equatorial places and peoples were inherently incapable of political or civilizational achievement. These states rolled out this climatic theory to justify extractivist and civilizational projects that

produced the affects, despotism, slavery that imperial sciences disingenu-
ously claimed were endemic to tropical or equatorial peoples and places.

In the *Voyage*, Hérard-Dumesle reports that he travels around the island
with the famous French insect scientist Rene de Réaumur's thermometer.
As he trekked from coasts to mountains to mornes (small mountains), to
riverine valleys, he recorded temperatures and collected other data that
contested Montesquivian climatology. He concluded that his climate data
showed significant swings in temperature, humidity, and weather phenomena, including in locations quite proximate to one another.[7] Drawing on
these records, he determined that no generalizations could be made about
the Haitian climate, as its strongest overriding feature was the intense
variability that Montesquieu granted only midlatitudinal regions of the
globe.

If Hérard-Dumesle's Haitian meteorology repudiated the climatic
determinism Montesquieu apportioned to the tropics and poles, instead
of offering a countervailing culturalism as its alternative, he argued for
more and subtler analyses of the imbrications of climatic and social forces.
As he put it:

> It's not true, as many celebrated authors have supposed, that peoples from
> hot climates are fated to despotism, or that they are more easily made to
> submit to it; those [peoples that become despotic] are almost always driven
> by circumstances agitated by a multitude of secondary causes more or less
> influenced by the climate, and that make the sources of eloquence dry up for
> [that people], giving way to dispositions inclined to arts that polish the
> manners and enervate the character, making social commerce agreeable, and
> spreading across an empire an artificial brilliance that makes up for the loss
> of reality, up to the point that despotism, operating to dissolve the morality
> of the state, destroys the effects of climate itself.[8]

Hérard-Dumesle proposes that all climates act on the bodies, nerves, and
affects of the human and other beings living in them. Yet instead of
concluding that climate produces civilizational effects on midlatitudinal
people and retrogressive effects on tropical and polar places and people, he
argues that the influence of climate on people should in all cases be
salutary, not enervating. He elaborates that in Haiti the heat of the climate
fires the ardency of imagination and proliferates metaphors, both of which
incite republican eloquence in Haiti. The real source of a people's and
place's enervation and despotism is not hot climates, as Montesquieu and
other Europeans in his wake supposed, but the artificial polish that fed
social commerce, which ended up becoming a second nature that cut
a people off from the animating force they gained from tuning into their

climates. Despotism so conceived was equally a problem of Bourbon-Restoration France as it had been of Haiti under the reign of Christophe. For Hérard-Dumesle, despotism's root was not anything intrinsic to the earth, the firmament, temperature, humidity, or the tilt of the earth on its axis. Rather despotism emerged from a kind of ecological myopia, from a rigid culturalism that closed itself off from the complex yet ultimately beneficial effects of climates – the effects, that is, that climates had on the life forms that had produced them as such in collusion with historical, celestial, and inorganic forces.

Haitian republican eloquence required finer-tuned attention to climate and closer attention to the imbrications of people and the confluence of forces that together comprised place. To this end, Hérard-Dumesle advises attending to forces Montesquieu did not fully recognize or understand were essential to analyzing nature and its effects on human beings. For one, he argued that it wasn't simply geological features like mountains or rivers that shaped climate but the complex interactions between such geological features. Homing in on the particularities of celestial and atmospheric forces, Hérard-Dumesle proposed that the movements of the moon subtly raised and lowered the sap in plants as well as the circulation of blood in animals and for this was a biological as well as a celestial force.[9] In a selective turn to Greek and Roman precedents that he linked to Africa in a variation of the Black Athena hypothesis, he gave attention to Epicurean theories that foregrounded wind as a key vector of meteorological and poetic processes. As he puts it in one of the book's many poems:

> But Epicurus, a wise one,
> Docile to nature's wishes,
> Came to offer us her delicate flower
> That a light breath sometimes opened,
> That he vivifies, and often colors,
> But which fades in the poisoned breath,
> Fruit of the excesses carried in its wake.[10]

The twice repeated term breath (*souffle*) denotes both breezes and prosodic breathings: the subtle form-giving effects of opening, vivifying, coloring, and fading are, in these lines, equally those of atmospheric forces and of philosopher poets with their oral and mnemonic traditions. That the *souffles* of the poem's fourth and sixth lines might be those of philosopher poets, breezes, or both underscores that the words of philosophers and poets modify the expression of earthly phenomena. That these *souffles* are also winds underscores that other-than-human movements are equally as bound up in this shaping and, moreover, cannot be definitively separated from human voices.

Even if in this verse, and across the *Voyage*, Hérard-Dumesle riffs on Greco-Roman precedents (here the Epicurean-Lucretian tradition),[11] he also urges Haitians to distinguish themselves from these precedents, particularly the excesses he diagnosed in the Epicurean philosophy as well as eighteenth-century neo-epicureans' prioritization of contingency. He supposed the focus on chance cleaved apart natural and moral realms in ways that cast the former as governed by hazard and the latter by human customs and histories. Arguing against the separation of physical and moral causes that increasingly structured the sciences of other modern nation states, Hérard-Dumesle insisted that the yellow fever and other maladies that struck down Europeans during the Haitian Revolution should be understood as a warning – an admonition borne of swarming ecological congeries composed of other-than-human forces alongside human ones – that Haiti's climates were not on the side of the colonists.[12] His vision forces a reckoning with what the historian Dispesh Chakrabarty has called the "climate of history" now perceptible in the so-called Anthropocene: an incongruous cross-hatching of human history with a fundamentally unthinkable and inhuman planetary one. Hérard-Dumesle's meditation suggests that the climate of *Haitian* history follows on the accumulation of exchanges between enslaved and free Black people, colonizers, breezes, and other atmospheric forces, and (as we shall see in the next section) *long durée* geo-historical forces. Exchanges between these social, energetic, and economic forces manifested an epidemic that cut down the colonizers that atmospheric and earth forces wanted banished from the island as much as did enslaved and free Black people.

Call and Response

Instead of simply critiquing North Atlantic sciences, Hérard-Dumesle proposes Haitians should develop their own natural history by drawing scientific and literary inspiration from the rituals of Indigenous Taino peoples as well as those of African nature cults. While walking along the Artibonite River, the voyager announces he is

> delighted … to see these sites testifying to the veneration of the former inhabitants of this island. I remembered an ancient tradition that revealed the respect that those simple people had for the particular god who … presided over the floodings of the river and retained its waves in their beds, and who conserved the memory of the offerings addressed to him in solemn

festivals to make him favorably disposed; however superstitious the cult of our adopted ancestors seemed to me, I found it of a common origin with all of the mythologies of the universe.[13]

Hérard-Dumesle quickly puts to rest his own and European-educated Haitian elites' association of American indigenous practices with superstition by placing the Taino people's celebration of a local river god on par with the celebrations informing "all the mythologies of the universe," which he later qualifies in terms of Babylonian, Greek, and Roman precedents. This sanctioned address to a local river god also recalls Kongo Haitians' veneration of specific water spirits of various sorts called *simbi* that were becoming part of the Haitian vodun pantheon in the early nineteenth century.[14] For Hérard-Dumesle, the religious practices of peoples who consulted natural divinities should not be given the pejorative appellation *superstition*. Well aware of the racialization at play in contemporary European thinkers' charges of superstition, he used the term to critique practices that in one way or another produced artificial second natures, from the incense-steeped Catholicism of *both* Frenchmen and elite Haitians to King Henri Christophe's reliance on the allure of false natures for statecraft, mockingly noting that the king hoarded a huge population of cats that he says Christophe treated as familiars and spies.[15]

Unlike these artificial rituals, the Taino people's river ceremony offered an example of a call and response binding together human with other-than-human forces, and this made these Taino "adopted ancestors" avatars of the climatological eloquence he advocated. He frames the Taino people's presentation of offerings to the Artibonite River as an "address" made with the expectation of a reply in the form of propitious conditions as the river swells and recedes during wet and dry seasons. Whether or not the Taino's regular addresses to the Artibonite River gained the responses for which they hoped, what is certain is that the river produced responses of sorts since the river's conservation of still visible fragments of Taino offerings comprises a concreted riverine memory that Hérard-Dumesle interprets to spin his account of the region's indigenous history and link it to Haitian eloquence.

Marlene Daut suggests moments like these indicate Hérard-Dumesle's effort to pose the land itself as an archival resource that expands the range of records informing historical analysis.[16] Conventional historical archives like the French *Archives Nationales* (themselves a product of the French revolution) and the *Bibliothèque Nationale* (that was itself renamed during the revolution and in the twentieth century became the *Bibliothèque*

Nationale de France [BNF]) were inaccessible to most Haitians and prejudicial to Haiti. While fully in agreement with Daut's thesis, excavating the Haitian eloquence at stake in the *Voyage* indicates that Hérard-Dumesle supposes other-than-human actors and forces *do* respond to his calls. In this sense, Hérard-Dumesle's appeals to the testimony of other-than-human forces is not only a tactic for redressing the racism that structured historical archives but also an analytical mode that developed from human beings' intimacies with earth forces. That Haitian historiography emerges from an eloquence borne of relays between human and other-than-human forces suggests not only an expanded archive that poses the earth, oral stories, and the dead as key sources for a Haitian historiography that developed at the same moment as the famed imperial historiographies of nineteenth-century Europe (Carlyle, Taine, to a lesser extent Michelet). It also demands an interpretive method tuned into the actions and voices of the pulsing other-than-human forces that also compose this archive.

Sometimes the other-than-human forces to whom Hérard-Dumesle calls tell him what he wants to know, as when the Artibonite River discloses fragments of Taino rituals that he draws upon to develop the indigenous history necessary if Haitians were to produce themselves as "adopted" ancestors of the Taino people. In other moments, other-than-human forces read him and reroute his questions and meditations. For instance, after spending a day interpreting the "nearly erased vestiges" and circumstances of the colonial period from the land – all of which recall the horrors of French plantation colonialism and the hollowness of their claims to enlightenment – Hérard-Dumesle begins to further elaborate this history of violence. At precisely this moment, the fog from the morne across from where he stands obscures the landscape he interprets "as if [the morne] wanted to steal from my memories this set of events."[17] The rocks, flowers, rivers, and other "vestiges" and "traces" to which the traveler calls respond "mutely" yet they nonetheless truly record the island's history and serve as an archive, as Daut argues. Moreover, for all of their muteness, these rocks, flowers, rivers, mornes, and mists are not simply channeled into Hérard-Dumesle's narrative voice. Mornes, as well as winds and other meteorological forces also interpret the human beings who call out to them, as happens here when the morne and the winds and fogs it draws to itself together draw a veil over the horrors of the past. This response stops the natural historian from becoming fully enmired in the horrors written across every inch of the Haitian landscape – horrors that other-than-human forces, working through that colonial past in collusion with the chronicler, help to recede but do not disappear.

Hérard-Dumesle's claim that the morne acts "as if" it aims to allay his memory of too-present horrors does not announce a comparison between the categorically distinct phenomena of mountain meteorology and human history. Rather, here, simile announces a connection that moves across, yet does not efface, the differences between the entities whose relation it emphasizes. Hérard-Dumesle's repeated claims of correspondences and "compensations" weaving together seemingly unrelated aspects of the Haitian landscape and people suggests that the *Voyage*'s similes and other figures contribute to a Haitian eloquence that weaves together people and place through an ongoing ecosystemic call and response. In this instance, the call and response borne of this eloquence changes the relation of the present to the past by loosening the grip of a history of colonial violence on the postcolonial present.[18]

This call and response within what Hérard-Dumesle calls an "animated nature" (likely referencing Oliver Goldsmith) changes the materiality of political sentiments and the shapes and powers of nature in ways that underwrite his engagement with the agricultural "cults" he meets during his travels across the island. Observing the festival of a "cult" in the southwest of the island, he supposes these rituals that linked agricultural labor to the celebration of earth forces testified to "our origins."[19] In fact African-derived agricultural celebrations were performed by peoples across the eighteenth and nineteenth century Caribbean diaspora, ranging from harvest festivals to masquerades. In the Haitian case, historian John Thornton documents that African-born persons in late eighteenth and early nineteenth-century Haiti "often looked to organizations formed by their 'nation' – a loose grouping of people from the same part of Africa or the same ethnolinguistic group – to provide leadership and perform mutual aid functions."[20]

These agricultural "cults" and the remembered and imagined African ecologies they venerated proved formidable challenges to Louverture's and then Christophe's efforts to produce centralized governments based on the plantation model.[21] Hérard-Dumesle also notes the tension between such "cultic" practices and statist interests. He explains that while these celebrations testified to the ongoing alliance of human beings with the earth central to agriculture, the pleasure peasants gained from such celebrations proved so great that these cults rapidly multiplied and those who participated in them refused to perform the sort of labor valued by Haitian elites who aimed to scale-up from small-holding agriculture to integrate the island into the global network of trade for plantation goods. I read Hérard-Dumesle as advocating – as his hero Alexandre Pétion, the first president of the Haitian republic, had done – a subsistence-agricultural economic model that he imagines scaling up to a republican governance distinct from plantation-style marketing.[22] For this reason, when he goes on to advocate that the Haitian state should adopt African "cults'" agricultural practices as official state holidays, he is not simply attempting to paper over the real difference between the labor modes of small-holding and large-scale, neo-plantation agricultural production. He is also (however interestedly) also fretting about the different commitments of small-holders and state actors and hoping that state adoption of African agricultural festivals and values might knit together the country and the city, peasants and European-educated elites, the people and the government.

The Revolutionary Eloquence of Haitian Natural History

Hérard-Dumesle's discussion of African agricultural cults might suggest a purely transactional interest in African precedents and the other-than-human phenomena bound up in these precedents. Turning to the *Voyage*'s poetic account of the August 1791 Bois Caïman ceremony, itself one of the earliest written accounts of that Vodou ritual, makes clear the significant role he gave to the intersection of other-than-human phenomena and "cultic" practices.[23] The poem's opening lines drive from the charged intersection of meteorological forces, plantation-colonial infrastructures, and the laments of the enslaved. The poem opens:

> Across the sillions by lightning traced,
> Where shines the glow of a hundred eclipsed [extinguished] fires,
> Groups of the oppressed assemble in silence;[24]

The inaugural "Across" (*à travers*) poses a transversal geometry initiated by the lightning that blazes furrows across a terrain already scored with the sillions of plantation agriculture. This opening overlays the agricultural lines the slave-powered plantation project used to organize and direct planetary forces with Afro-diasporic accounts of meteorological and celestial forces including the Yoruba storm god-cum-Vodou divinity Ogou-Shango and the cross of the Kongo *dikenga*, which referenced the movements of the sun and was itself then being integrated into Vodou vèvès (chalk drawings traced on the earth and that were grounded on the cruciform shape associated with the *dikenga* as well as the Christian cross).[25] As Hérard-Dumesle probably knew well given his sustained engagement with classical and neoclassical precedents, his opening figuration of sillions in alexandrines also evoked the longstanding association of the lines of the plow with the lines of the poet from Virgil's *Georgics* forward.[26]

This storm-driven opening crossing recalls this classical and neoclassical agricultural and poetic tradition only to suspend it. As the speaker explains, the whistlings of enslaved human beings designated as the "sons of the wind," and gusts buffeting the plains from several directions meld into a literally wind-blown song, echoing the previously discussed poem's overlaying of meteorological and poetic movements. On hearing this song, the speaker recounts "Nature is moved ... she suspends those laws that make movement generate harmony,/ And that made famous the sage of Ausonie [Virgil]."[27] Putting into abeyance Virgilian nature and the laws and harmonies it upheld, the speaker poses a nature whose components (men, winds) address it, and on making this address produce an affective and material transformation of nature. In short, here nature is intrinsically plural and the exchanges within this plurality don't only counter any idea of nature as univocity since they also diversify what nature is by making clear it is not one but several.

An orator-priest steps into the void that comes from nature's suspension of the laws that had driven classical agricultural and poetic precedent. This orator-priest sacrifices a bull. On interpreting the sacrifice, he speaks of the relation of meteorological and human forces in a passage of the poem whose importance is signaled by the fact that it is rendered not only in French but also in the Haitian Kreyol in which the Vodou priest spoke:

> This God who lit the torch of the sun,
> Who lifts up the seas and makes the storm roar,
> This God, do not doubt, hidden in a cloud,
> Contemplates this land, sees the badness of the Whites,
> Their cult commits crimes, and ours beneficence,
> But the supreme goodness ordains vengeance
> And will guide your arms; strong with his assistance,
> Let us trample underfoot the greedy idol of our sorrows,
> Powerful Liberty! Come ... speak to all our hearts ...[28]

As Doris Kadish and Deborah Jenson point out, the French and especially the slightly different Kreyol version of this prophecy use demonstrative pronouns that particularize the god who acts (*Ce Dieu* and *Bon dié la – this God/that* good god *there*).[29] These indices specify a polytheistic frame instead of the monotheistic one in which God takes no demonstratives, and in so doing they subtly reinforce the Afro-diasporic cosmologies pulsing through the poem. The Kreyol version of the poem emphasizes that this is not simply a particular god but also a *personal* god, announcing *Bon die la, zot tandé*, or "that good god there, do you hear." The orator's announcement that a god watches the assembled from a cloud coupled with his injunction "do you hear," signals emphasis, to be sure. Yet it also instructs the assembled to listen to the clouds driving the storm buffeting them as the officiant delivers this speech. This synesthetic turn in which a cloud god *looks* upon the assembled who *listen* to that god demands not simply an exchange of perspectives (between looking clouds and listening people): it also emphasizes the *difference* between human and cloud apperception (the regard of the cloud is met by the ear of human auditors) instead of suggesting any easy or spontaneous mutual comprehension.

Already, we see that Hérard-Dumesle's revolutionary meteorology rises from the intersection of celestial, divine, human, wind, vegetable, and animal attentions each to the other. This cross-kind exchange and its effects becomes the poem's explicit subject immediately after the officiant's prophecy when:

> ... The devouring flame
> Rushes swirling turbulently to the brilliant vault
> From which a thousand diamonds whose starry fires,
> Dart onto these deserts veiled in shadows,
> the flickering light of their pale rays[.][30]

Here, on consuming the cultists' sacrificial offering, the bonfire roils its heat and light into a midnight sky illuminated by "starry fires." This sacrificial fire swirling into star-fire forges a celestial illumination that bends back to the earth manifesting as the "flickering light" ("*tremblante lumière*") that illuminates what had previously been obscured, shadowed, and desiccated under the planation-colonial organization of the land.

The revelations and powers the speaker ascribes to this celestial light are delicate and transient. In this sense they are distinct from the hard power, instrumental logic, and direct light that in the poem (and in the *Voyage* more broadly) Hérard-Dumesle associates with what he calls the French "cult" of light and reason. The trembling luminescence that follows on this celestial light brings into relief what was previously present yet not apprehended. Ultimately, Hérard-Dumesle's poem is not simply *about* the Bois Caïman ceremony since it casts itself as a *long-durée* effect of that event's convergence of celestial and meteorological forces, the practices of African "cults," and (neo)classical precedents that together worked to liberate human and other-than-human natures from the capture of colonial naturalism.

This soft reillumination of the terrain is followed by a final celestial response when, just as the assembled strike out, the starry heavens drop down an owl. The orator-priest purifies and interprets this celestial omen, scrying it as a token that the violent uprising against colonists must begin. The officiant distributes a feather to each of those assembled to bind them into a pact with each other and with the storm and astral forces with whom they conspired in remaking nature in the wake of the suspension of classical and neoclassical precedent. Hérard-Dumesle's own plume-drawn production is itself at play in the talismanic oath that concludes the poem, extending the revolutionary meteorology it recounts to the acts of writing and reading by which he and his readers partake in this refiring of nature.

Black Star

In the wake of this pact between people and meteorological, celestial, animal, and vegetable forces fired by the Bois Caïman ceremony, the *Voyage* returns to narrative history. A woman priestess performs a second ceremony after which the assembled stream to the plantations and begin the work of revolution. For three days the sun doesn't appear, and so the uprising unfolds in the soft half human, half astral light that that irradiates the island following the ceremony. After three days, dawn breaks once the revolution is fully underway. Hérard-Dumesle's evocation of astral intensities in the poem from the eclipse that punctuates the poem's opening crossing to the new light that follows on the ceremony recurs in his account of the Haitians' vanquishing of the French in 1804. He proposes that January 1, 1804, the day on which Jean-Jacques Dessalines declared Haitian Independence, opened a new epoch in the universe.[31] He explains that ever since this moment, the annual passage of the sun consecrated a sacrament that bound together the Haitian people, earth forces, and celestial powers:

> And nature sanctified this solemn ceremony [the Declaration of Independence]. Since that day, each year the sun, in beginning once more its course, illuminates that august ceremony in so doing renewing the oath [of independence]; this oath sounds out to posterity to serve as an example to the people and a lesson to tyrants.[32]

The solar movement that Hérard-Dumesle claims is central to this revolutionary oath is not some deistic claptrap cribbed from North Atlantic precedents that mined enlightenment solar symbolics from ancient cultures.[33] Rather, it is the culmination of his concerted engagement with

meteorological, astral, and solar forces he saw as central to Haitian eloquence. This engagement structured his 1819 periodical *L'Obervateur*
whose motto, *au temps et a la verite* – a punning conjunction of time and
weather with truth – was illustrated by a sun bearing a human face. Hérard-
Dumesle's astral logics course through his and other early Haitian poets'
indictments of plantation-colonial ambitions to colonize not only people,
plants, and places but to capture the sun itself in the service of extractivist
ends.[34]

At this seminal moment in the *Voyage,* a liberated sun fires a planetary
chronometry sparked by Haitian Independence. That this chronometry
originates January 1, 1804 stitches into it the European calendrics of the
northern midlatitudes that have been imposed on the colonies, as well as
metropoles, since the adoption of the Gregorian calendar.[35] In Hérard-
Dumesle's reformation, this European calendar and the space-time it imposes
are subordinated to a Haitian space-time that develops through an ecosystemic antiphony – a call and response of voices and regards – by which nature,
acting on itself, becomes other than itself. Across Hérard-Dumesle's oeuvre,
the chronometries, rhythms, and sciences of Europe are sounded as real
space–time making formations that continue into his present. Yet, the
Voyage and the Haitian eloquence it advocates put these European chronometries, rhythms, and sciences in dialogue with Haitian ones. In so doing,
nature is not one but at least two. And by this pluralization, nature is
transformed when the sun – like meteorology, plants, and people – is not
captured in the service of the temporal, energetic, and agricultural economies
of empire but instead constitutes and guarantees Haitian liberation. That the
epoch of Haitian eloquence the *Voyage* announces has not yet been fully
entered in Haiti and certainly not in North Atlantic states speaks not to the
weakness of Hérard-Dumesle's ambition but to the fact that in and outside of
the so-called global south, politicians, historians, poets, and geopolitical
imaginaries have not fully reckoned with the ways that nature has long
been, and remains, imperialism's best weapon. For this, any critique of
imperialism requires engaging and contesting its production of nature as
Hérard-Dumesle did so powerfully.

Notes

1. Chris Iannini, *Fatal Revolutions: Natural History, West Indian Slavery, and the Routes of American Literature* (Chapel Hill: UNC Press, 2012).
2. Marlene Daut, *Tropics of Haiti: Race and the Literary History of the Haitian Revolution* (Liverpool: Liverpool University Press, 2015); Daut, "Nothing in

Nature is Mute," *New Literary History* 49.4 (2018): 493–520; Daut, *Awakening the Ashes* (Chapel Hill: University of North Carolina Press, 2023); Chris Bongie, "The Cry of History: Juste Chanlatte and the Unsettling (Presence) of Race in Early Haitian Literature," *MLN* 130.4 (2015): 807–35.

3. Daut citing Hérard-Dumesle, *Ashes* 116.

4. On early Haitian educational projects see Chelsea Stieber's *Haiti's Paper War* (New York: New York University Press, 2020).

5. Jay Fliegelman, *Declaring Independence* (Palo Alto: Stanford University Press, 1993), 2.

6. The French mapping of the modern-day equator (part of a larger project of determining the shape of the earth) arced from Martinique and St. Domingue to the South American main.

7. He recounts using Réaumur's thermometer to record the temperatures of Haitian cities, mountains, valleys, and coastlines, emphasizing differences in temperature across small distances. Thus, the thermometer "reads from 10 to 10.5 degrees in the heights of Calvaire when it is at 13 or 14d at the bottom of the valley, and at 18d along the nearby coast . . .. This variation is more or less notable at different parts of the island" (386).

8. Charles Hérard-Dumesle, *Voyage dans le nord d'Hayti, ou, Révélations des lieux et des monuments* (Les Cayes: Impr. du Gouvernement, 1824), 269 (my trans.).

9. The phases of the moon, he elaborates subtly move the sap in plants as well as the movement of blood in animals. This intricate dance between geographical, atmospheric, and astral forces explains the waxing and waning of vital and mortuary forces (389, note t).

10. Hérard-Dumesle, *Voyage dans le nord d'Hayti*, 288–9 (my translation).

11. On the link to Lucretius, it seems like that the close of this verse references the plague in the final book of *De Rerum Natura* as well as the excesses and malaise he thinks resulted from Christophe's statescraft.

12. Hérard-Dumesle, *Voyage dans le nord d'Hayti*, 307.

13. Hérard-Dumesle, *Voyage dans le nord d'Hayti*, 296 (my trans.).

14. Wyatt MacGaffey "Twins, simbi spirits and lwas in Kongo and Haiti" in *Central Africans and Cultural Transformations in the American Diaspora* (Cambridge: Cambridge University Press, 2002).

15. Hérard-Dumesle, *Voyage dans le nord d'Hayti*, 182–4; 237.

16. Daut, "Nothing."

17. Hérard-Dumesle, *Voyage dans le nord d'Hayti*, 323.

18. For these correspondences and compensations, see Hérard-Dumesle's discussion of astrology and other natural signs on 307–8 as well as his engagement with, and rewriting of, Rousseau's *Second Discourse* (on the origins of inequality) from *Voyage dans le nord d'Hayti*, 304–6.

19. Hérard-Dumesle, *Voyage dans le nord d'Hayti*, 318.

20. John Thornton, "I am the Subject of the King of Kongo," *Journal of World History* 4.2 (1993): 200.

21. This was in part because peoples from these "nations" were not so fully interpolated into the colonial vision of the world system and the industrial

agricultural practices on which it depended and in part because, profiting little from the plantation system, they refused to work on it for the benefit of the revolutionary or postcolonial state.

22. On subsistence agriculture during Pétion's leadership see Robert Heinl and Nancy Heinl, *Written in Blood* (Lanham: University Press of America, 1996) and Alex Dupuy, *Haiti and the World Economy* (Boulder: Westview Press, 1989).

23. On earlier accounts of Bois Caïman see Daut's *Awakening the Ashes*, 112–13.

24. Hérard-Dumesle, *Voyage dans le nord d'Hayti*, 86 (my trans.).

25. For the relevance of Yoruba gods to the poem, see Doris Kadish and Deborah Jenson, *Poetry of Haitian Independence* (New Haven: Yale University Press, 2015), 272 note 12. On the Yoruba Shango, see Harry Garuba 's "Explorations in Animist Materialism," *Public Culture* 15.2 (2003). On the Kongo dikenga, see Robert F. Thompson's *Four Moments of the Sun* (National Gallery of Art 1981); on the dikenga in early Haiti, see Chris Fennell, *Crossings and Cosmologies* (Gainesville: University Press of Florida, 2010). On the synthesis of the Christian cross and the dikenga, see Cécile Fromont, *Art of Conversion* (Chapel Hill: University of North Carolina Press, 2014).

26. On the *Georgics'* and neogeorgics' association of the plow and the line of poetry, see Kevis Goodman, *Georgic Modernity* (Cambridge: Cambridge University Press, 2008).

27. Hérard-Dumesle, *Voyage dans le nord d'Hayti*, 86 (my trans.).

28. Norman Shapiro has also translated the poem into English for Doris Kadish and Deborah Jenson's *Poetry of Haitian Independence*. He elected to turn the verse into iambic pentameter to signal to English readers the formal properties of Hérard-Dumesle's verse. This is certainly valuable; however, doing so also required slightly changing the sense of the lines to make the meter work. I offer here a more literal but also less formally apposite translation. Although I do not discuss the poem's form at length here, I would note that even if this and other poems seem to fit entirely within the French neoclassical mode, the decision to put Kreyol as well as French into alexandrines, his improvement on alexandrines in the Kreyol version, and his play on the tension between rhythm and meter importantly revises that formal tradition.

29. Kadish and Jenson provide an English translation of the Kreyol text in Appendix A, 225–6.

30. Hérard-Dumesle, *Voyage dans le nord d'Hayti*, 87.

31. Hérard-Dumesle, *Voyage dans le nord d'Hayti*, 219.

32. Hérard-Dumesle, *Voyage dans le nord d'Hayti*, 219 (my trans.).

33. On this point consider Thomas Jefferson's famous letter to Joseph Priestly, which proclaimed that the existence of the United States proved that there was in fact something new under the sun (March 21, 1801).

34. I discuss the plantation-colonial ambition to colonize the sun and anti-colonial refusal of that ambition in forthcoming work.

35. For eighteenth- and nineteenth-century hemispheric American actors, the movement of the new year to January 1 across most of Europe was itself relatively recent memory and loosely timed on the winter solstice.

CHAPTER 3

Apocalypse and Native American Literature
From Samson Occom to the Contemporary Moment

Stephanie Fitzgerald and Hilary Wyss

Empire and Apocalypse

The beginning of empire in the Americas is the beginning of apocalypse. If empire demands uniformity and univocality, it is predicated at its core on the oppression of alterity and the destruction of difference, and so the impulse to diminish or deny Indigenous perspectives within American empire recurs throughout its history. And though the US as an imperial state has often been conceived of as a largely nineteenth-century and later phenomenon, before that empire emerged out of independence from its British forebear, all of the Americas were subject rather than central to prior European empires. This is a useful memory: even the idea of empire is temporally circular, and there is a perennial quality to the complicated settler-colonial narrative of US national identity that is in nearly cataclysmic tension with Indigenous ways of being in this space. In our chapter we will attempt to illuminate and learn from this circularity, focusing on the repetitions and echoes through time as we emerge from our own cataclysmic experience with the COVID pandemic.

If, as Meg Wesling has argued, US literature has in key historical moments functioned as "empire's proxy," then much of recent Indigenous literature works to undo this imperial work.[1] But this contemporary iteration is part of a much larger cycle: identifying an alternative to empire has been the work of Native literature, alphabetic or otherwise, since the first invasion of Europeans. Contemporary literature thus makes visible for our generation what has been visible at every point: that North American Indigenous relationships to empire have been fractured since their inception. From the earliest encounters, Indigenous intellectuals characterize the American empire as apocalyptic rather than triumphant, emphasizing protest over celebration. They have in the process also embedded alternative possibilities to the monoculture of empire. Such alternative knowledge production is ongoing, and the reoccurrence of certain tropes, rather than simply repetition, means and makes something different with each iteration as generations past, present, and future work to dismantle empire and repair its violence.

We contend that the ongoing American empire is built on what can be understood as repeated waves of apocalypse for Indigenous communities. There is not one single ending of a singular world, but endings multiple times over, in waves across the continent, carried by the vehicles of European imperialism and US settler colonialism. Triumphant narratives of empire and conquest have perpetually existed alongside and in conflict with alternative Indigenous narratives that warn of an environmental and cultural apocalypse. From the earliest days, urgent Indigenous voices of protest registered community crisis and balanced between the need for continuity and the necessity of restructuring. In this essay, we explore such alternative anti-imperial visions of possibility and promise, from eighteenth-century counter-colonial narratives to contemporary works of fiction throughout the Indigenous literatures of the space currently known as America.

Scholars have increasingly become aware of the connections between empire's attempt to eliminate Indigeneity, for example, and contemporary environmental devastation. The voracious settler-colonial practice of land accumulation was specifically for the purpose of altering such spaces, and today's American landscape shows the effects of deforestation, overfishing, and overbuilding. The cumulative ecological effects of such practices are compounded for Indigenous communities devastated by their own displacement and alienation in various ways from their own land. And yet the political meaning of Indigenous nationhood and the modern US capitalist state are overlapping and interconnected frameworks that must be understood in relation to each other. From issues as mundane as garbage collection to those as essential as negotiated water rights, Indigenous communities are intimately connected to empire even as they are not fully subject to it.[2] This is a point that contemporary writers are very clear about, and one that Indigenous people have tried to make from early on.

The various literary forms of Indigenous expression, from the earliest days of imperial invasion to settler colonialism today, have a communal component: a potential to speak and to bring concerns to a diverse audience, both Indigenous and non-Indigenous, with varying levels of engagement. Never the only medium of dissent, the earliest written forms put to use by Indigenous writers – such as the petition, sermon, and letter – are a powerful corrective to the growing narrative of empire in the eighteenth century. Later in the nineteenth century, a further engagement with poetic and novelistic forms as well as autobiography continues that anti-imperial corrective.[3] Today Indigenous texts directed to a broadly public audience include novels, poetry, television, and film. All these forms of literary and cultural production are catalysts for transformation, public facing modes of expression in conversation with formal structures of political change, governmental, legal, treaty-bearing, or otherwise. The long history of these various genres – from petitions and letters to contemporary novels and television shows – offers the possibility of renewed public engagement, of a difficult but potentially productive conversation about the relationship between empire and apocalypse. If the varied forms of Native literature and other modes of imaginative expression have long registered the apocalypse of empire, they also express – and constitute enduring and extraordinary evidence of – the ongoing survival and survivance of Native people.[4]

The Practice of Native Literature and Indigenous Theory: Identifying the Apocalypse

A curious problem has defined the United States as a nation: we exist in a world shaped by an apocalypse (past, present, and future) that is willfully made invisible in the everyday lives of most Americans. The historical realities of land appropriation and abusive government policies toward Indigenous people are largely left out of the national narratives, while current practices of land (ab)use and excess consumption threaten the ongoing existence of life as we know it. The double-think that both recognizes impending apocalypse but also pushes it out of mind is visible today in the ways the natural world is buckling under the stress of modernity and its excesses. While the form and structure of apocalypse has changed over time, the fact is that the United States originates in an apocalypse: the attempted eradication of the original occupants of this land by European invaders and the fundamental alteration (indeed desecration) of their homelands. By evading and erasing that origin story, the policies and practices of American nationalism have perpetuated and expanded the forms of apocalypse that are so present in the lives and histories of Native people.

As we enter what some scholars term the Anthropocene, a new geological epoch impacted by human activity, the land itself records the centuries-long multiple events of resource extraction – deforestation, open pit mining, and the discharge of industrial waste into waterways. Through what Rob Nixon terms "slow violence," American empire and its systems of internal colonialism have continuously appropriated and wrought devastation and destruction on the land.[5] The many repeated acts of dispossession of Indigenous land have been part of a continuous attempt to erase Indigenous lifeways and culture, making this *more* than genocide. In relation to Native communities, American empire connects the destruction and appropriation of land to the attempted erasure of Indigenous lifeways and cultures in an apocalyptic cycle. Kathryn Yusoff explains further:

> The Anthropocene might seem to offer a dystopic future that laments the end of the world, but imperialism and ongoing (settler) colonialisms have been ending worlds for as long as they have been in existence. The Anthropocene as a politically infused geology and scientific/popular discourse is just now noticing the extinction it has chosen to continually overlook in the making of its modernity and freedom.[6]

These acts of slow violence have worked to erase histories of imperial and colonial violence.

Indigenous authors as varied as Cherie Dimaline, Louise Erdrich, and Leslie Marmon Silko (to name just a few) have repeatedly identified and decried the relationship between empire and apocalypse.

Today's US global empire is rooted in an origin story of land loss, profound alteration, and desecration of the natural world and massive cultural upheaval for Indigenous communities. The cataclysmically combined loss of family, culture, and land is an apocalypse. It is the nearly unimaginable (and therefore endlessly imagined in popular culture) worst nightmare of any person or community living today. For Native communities this is not an abstraction, a distant fear: it is a reality, a lived experience. One Anishinaabe scholar has characterized this existential challenge for Indigenous people as "Post Apocalypse Stress Syndrome."[7] Daniel Heath Justice, in *Why Indigenous Literatures Matter*, characterizes our own moment as a "Time of trauma."[8]

Indeed, as Indigenous peoples make clear over and over, this is not a thing that happened in the past, it is an ongoing experience – one whose invisibility to mainstream Americans is its most insidious feature. In her book *Firsting and Lasting*, Jean O'Brien identifies the particular patterns of how this Anglo-American narrative of Indigenous erasure came into being. She notes an insistence in nineteenth-century local histories written by white men that "non-Indians held exclusive sway over modernity, denied modernity to Indians, and in the process created a narrative of Indian extinction that has stubbornly remained in the consciousness of Americans."[9] Through what O'Brien terms "firsting" (the absurd idea that "non-Indians were the first people to erect the proper institutions of a social order worthy of notice" [xii]) and "lasting" (the equally preposterous idea that the last Native person had regrettably died and so there were no more Native people in the region – this despite ample evidence that Indigenous communities were and still are ongoing), Indigenous people were pushed out of any community narrative of belonging and endurance.[10]

O'Brien's text has been invaluable in undercutting insidious false notions of history and identity that for many constitute the extent of their engagement with Indigenous New England in particular. She identifies a rhetorical erasure that amounts to a certain kind of apocalypse, and the refusal of certain Indigenous nineteenth-century writers like William Apess to accept those terms. Hartley White makes a similar point in his oral history of the Leech Lake Ojibwe:

> Today I think about how they [the people who sat around and talked {with my} grandfather] preached there, talking this way as they began to address the issue of apocalypse ... these people wanted to talk about that almost constantly ... That's what they talked about – how the white people were taking everything from this earth here – copper bouillon, lead, uranium, anything and everything. They never put anything [back in] here.[11]

White's participation in the long history of oral tradition is a bridge crossing seemingly discrete periods of history as well as discrete divisions between history and literature; at the same time, his work reinforces the presence of ongoing Indigenous literary and historical practices, serving as a counterstrategy and counternarrative to the apocalypses of empire and a rejection of the kind of rhetorical erasure so prevalent in the dominant culture's historical narratives.

Scholar Lawrence Gross notes that "[a]long with many other Native American peoples, the Anishinaabe have seen the end of our world, which has created tremendous social stresses."[12] Gross's discussion of the 1919 consumption epidemic on the White Earth Reservation harkens to a similar apocalyptic moment in Louise Erdrich's historical novel *Tracks* (1988). The novel opens in the winter of 1912 in the aftermath of a tuberculosis epidemic that has struck down entire families across the unnamed reservation. The elder Nanapush and the tribal policeman make the rounds of the reservation dwellings searching for survivors. When they find Fleur, the only survivor in her family's cabin by the lake, Nanapush takes her into his home. The two sit with their grief, staring at the ashes of a cold fire for days on end. It is only when the reservation priest knocks on the door, bringing news of another survivor, that they are roused from their stupor, "numb, stupid as bears in a winter den . . . our lips were parched, stuck together. We could hardly utter a greeting."[13]

Like Gross's discussion of the White Earth Ojibwe, Erdrich's characters must similarly rebuild their worlds in the face of not only the epidemic, but future continuing waves of apocalypse. While Fleur forms a family with Eli and their daughter Lulu, she loses a premature son, and then the deforestation and loss of her allotment land to unpaid taxes and timber speculators. She is unable to recover from this last loss, and retreats from the world into the woods. Nanapush, on the other hand, claims his kinship ties to her daughter Lulu and, through story, rebuilds for the girl her own origin story.

Other Indigenous fiction similarly recounts these cycles of apocalypses and rebuilding. Leslie Marmon Silko's 1977 novel *Ceremony* centers on the experiences of Tayo, a recently returned young Laguna Pueblo veteran who has survived the Bataan death march during World War II. Upon returning home, he finds his community is experiencing the effects of a drought that is both linked to the war and to atomic bomb testing on Pueblo lands. Like the land itself, Tayo is considered irreparably "broken" due to post-traumatic stress disorder (PTSD), but also forges a new path forward, very much in accord with the characterizations of Gross and White.

These examples from Erdrich and Silko vehemently push back against a version of identity that is only erasure and suffering: the settler narrative of melancholy regret and the pathologizing of contemporary Indigenous people. Even as characters like Fleur and Tayo are drawn in relation to very real moments of cultural despair, they refuse their own destruction. Daniel Heath Justice, in *Why Indigenous Literatures Matter*, puts it differently:

> If the 'real' is *only* about language loss, we miss the extraordinary language recovery efforts of many Indigenous communities. If the 'real' is *only* about dysfunctional and abusive families, we don't see the many Indigenous families where substance abuse is not a shattering problem or is only part of a much more expansive and complicated set of experiences, where there is strong and loving support across the generations, where education is valued as an expression of tradition, not in opposition to it. If the 'real' is *only* about dispossession, then we lose stories about communities fighting and succeeding to regain lands and inherent territorial rights and relational obligations to the other-than-human world.[14]

The work of Indigenous literature is navigating the balance between acknowledging empire's apocalyptic effects and ongoing problems and imagining the world differently to give shape to a different world.

**Early Native Literature: Samson Occom and the Genre
of the Petition as a Record of Apocalypse**

Modern writers, culture bearers, and intellectuals have their own ways of
framing the experiences of apocalypse and post-apocalypse, but we see it in
the records from very early on. In New England, one of the earliest
battlegrounds for the settler colonial iteration of empire, we find various
political documents expressing an Indigenous apocalypse. The Pequot War
(now more accurately considered a massacre committed by the English)
concluded with the Treaty of Hartford, signed September 21, 1638, which
outlawed the use of the Pequot language and even the name "Pequot," and
made it a crime for Pequot people to return to their homelands. For one
Indigenous nation among many in New England, this was the political
equivalent of an apocalyptic event – attempted, although never fully
achieved, as the ongoing existence of the Mashantucket Pequot and the
Eastern Pequot Tribal Nation attests.

Less than forty years later, the war known today as King Philip's War
of 1676 engulfed nearly all of southern New England: one historian has
said that proportionally 5 percent of the English and a staggering 40 percent of the Indigenous population of southern New England died. The
war further resulted in the mass deportation of Indigenous New
Englanders into enslavement in the West Indies.[15] Such outright military
engagements overlapped and intersected with other apocalyptic events
including disease and other forms of alienation for those left in their
wake.[16]

For communities throughout southern New England, then, by the
eighteenth century there had already been repeated apocalyptic events.
We see this in the political language of several petitions authored on behalf
of various Indigenous communities by Mohegan Samson Occom, who
uses traditional Indigenous rhetorical structures to make political arguments for the ongoing relevance of Indigeneity in modern life. In one
extended example Occom characterizes a time before the settler colonial
encroachments of the English:

> The Most Great, The Good and The Supream Spirit above . . . saw fit in his
> good pleasure, to Divide this World by the Great Waters, and he fenced this
> great Continent by the Mighty Waters, all around, and it pleased him, to
> Plant our fore Fathers here first, and he gave them this Boundless
> Continent, and it was well furnished and Stored with all Necessaries of
> Life for them, and here they have livd and Spread over the Face of this
> Wilderness World, no man knows how or how long.

After establishing the authority of the human inhabitants, he continues:

> This world was full of all manner of four footed Wild Creatures great &
> small both on the Land and in the Waters and our Lakes, Ponds, Rivers,
> Brooks, and the Seas, were all alive, and [form'd] with Fish of every Sort and
> Bigness, even our Sand and Mud were well stord with Shell Fish, besids with
> Variety of Creeping Shell Fish great and Small, – and our Lands and Woods
> were Loaded with Fuit in a boundence, there were ground Nuts and beans
> in the Earth and Nuts on the Trees plenty, – Thus our Forefathers lived
> upon the Spontaneous Product of this Country.[17]

In another petition Occom uses similar (albeit significantly abbreviated)
language:

> The Great and good Spirit above, Saw fit in his good pleasure, to plant our
> ForeFathers in this great Wilderness ... and he ... Saw it good to give us
> this great Continent & he fill'd this Indian World, with veriety, and
> a Prodigious Number of four footed Beasts, Fowl without number and
> Fish of all kinds great and Small, fill'd our Seas, Rivers, Brooks, and Ponds
> every where.[18]

The space of New England is very explicitly Indigenous: given by "the Great
and Good Spirit" to its Native inhabitants, the "great Wilderness" was
shielded from encroachers by oceans as barriers. Merging traditional world
views with the kind of language settler colonial people could immediately
understand, Occom frames the continent as "fenced" in, and the world order
constituted by a single deity. The abundance of this "boundless continent"
mirrors an Edenic garden, with Native people as its true inheritors.

This abundance and harmony is juxtaposed to a very different present
moment, one shaped by the depredations of the English. In the first
petition, written on behalf of the Brothertown tribe, Occom goes on to
say "all our Hunting, Fishing and Fowling is now gone" and "we are So
poor, we are much dishartend" and even "it is a pinching Necessity that
Constrains us to make our Cried for help."[19] Similarly in the second
petition, written for the Montaukett community, Occom writes: "We
fare now harder than our Fore Fathers –For all our Hunting, Fowling,
Fishing is now almost gone and our Wild Fruit is gone, What little there is
left the English would Ingross or take all to themselves."[20] The cause of the
poverty in both cases is quite explicitly English exploitation, which is
strategically couched by Occom in more generous terms within the petition: he repeatedly uses language to the effect of "our forefather didn't
understand the value of the land and mistakenly signed unfavorable deals
with the English so now it's gone."

For Occom the moment is not called apocalypse, but is clearly framed as one: what was once "an Indian World" is being destroyed – he uses the recurring phrase "is now gone" throughout. The natural world has been enclosed not by the capacious boundaries of the oceans but reshaped and fundamentally altered by the English, and the place of Indigeneity is on the margins of what was once an entire continent for their own use. Through the strategic use of the petition structure, with its balance of humility and critique, Occom both voices his objections and offers an alternative. For Occom the solution is adaptation, and through his rhetoric the shared vocabulary of Indigenous experience and Judeo-Christianity is made new for all: the pre-English world has Edenic qualities, and is framed within a Judeo-Christian worldview but also voices much more than this: disorienting terms upend English assumptions of their own superiority. Occom's embedded critiques of English avarice are framed in categories in opposition to each other such as big and small, (Indigenous) forefathers and English, foolish and cheated. The "we" of the Indigenous speaker calls out for empathy and respect in the spirit not only of Christian teachings brought to the continent by the English usurpers but also in accord with Indigenous worldviews. Through these oppositions the Christian framework is made Indigenous, and an Indigenous worldview is made visible and politically relevant.

From the Seventeenth Century to the Twentieth: The Boarding School as Apocalypse

A skilled orator and political figure even as a young man, Samson Occom had his own run-in with an institution that a hundred years later would become more widespread: the Indian boarding school. The more widely implemented nineteenth- and twentieth-century model celebrated genocide (the phrase "Kill the Indian to save the man" notoriously captured the philosophy of Captain Richard Henry Pratt, the founder of the Carlisle Indian School in the late nineteenth century), but even its earlier incarnation was problematic. The boarding school model was based on a recurring set of practices: separating Indigenous students from their communities, indoctrinating them (often in brutal conditions) in Anglocentric educational and cultural models, and then sending them back out to recruit more Indigenous students. The earliest version, the one that Occom participated in, had a complicated story, with Occom at first willingly inviting his very broad network to participate and engage in white minister Eleazar Wheelock's school, known as Moor's Charity School. For Occom, such a school represented the possibility of Indigenous authority and engagement; with the school situated adjacent to his own home in Mohegan, Occom was a central figure in inviting community members from throughout southern New England and even Iroquoian groups to participate. Occom used his personal and cultural credibility to advocate for the possibilities that he envisioned for Indigenous peoples. Over time, however, that school came to represent a personal and cultural betrayal: after Occom spent over two years in Great Britain raising money for this school, it shifted its emphasis from Indigenous education to an almost exclusively white student body, moving from southern New England to New Hampshire, and incorporating as Dartmouth College. In a biting letter to Wheelock, Occom wrote that rather than becoming an "alma mater" ("nourishing mother"), the school had become an "alba mater" ("White mother") too ashamed to acknowledge her Native students.[21] Occom's hopes for a space of cultural and intellectual exchange vanished into an elite white space that barely acknowledged its Indigenous roots for nearly two centuries.

That cycle of possibility and betrayal took shape in the nineteenth century through the Carlisle Indian school and its various regional iterations. Such schools compounded the community problems produced by Indian Removal (the legal policy from the early nineteenth century that forced the relocation of Tribes east of the Mississippi to lands in the West). Charles Alexander Eastman and Luther Standing Bear write of their experiences with that nineteenth- century version of the boarding school experience, which focused on controlling Indigenous communities caught in the land grab of post–Civil War settler migrations through a military model of dominance and submission. Demanding that the children it took in abandon their Indigenous traditions, these spaces became notorious for abusive conditions and culturally devastating assumptions: children were stripped of their traditional clothing which was replaced by a uniform, had their hair cut into unfamiliar and alienating styles, were forbidden from speaking their own languages, and were taught to pity and condemn their families of origin. Continuing well into the twentieth century, such schools left lasting repercussions on Indigenous communities throughout North America, among them the Wabanaki communities of Maine, as the 2018 documentary film *Dawnland* explores. Focusing on a truth and reconciliation commission, the film documents the community devastation of such boarding schools, as well as other government programs that separated Indigenous children from their families and forced them into foster situations. The film movingly makes the point that we cannot jump to reconciliation without contending with the truth first, and in a powerfully redemptive moment marks the tender ceremonial burning of the tear-stained tissues of the Indigenous people speaking their truth (often weeping) about the suffering such policies have caused.

Modern Indigenous authors have grappled with this history in a number of recent novels. In Louise Erdrich's 1984 novel *Love Medicine*, Margaret keeps one son at home and allows the other to go to Indian boarding school to have one descendant "on either side of the line."[22] More recently, Cherie Dimaline takes on the prehistory and post-history of boarding schools in her novel *The Marrow Thieves* (2017): leaching the dreams of Indigenous people is literalized in her post- apocalyptic narrative. In Dimaline's novel the future apocalypse emerges from the past as well as from modern America. Boarding schools, with their history of cultural violence, are central to this nightmare vision.

For Cherie Dimaline, the apocalypse comes in waves: in *The Marrow Thieves*, it moves from empire and colonization to new imperial formations, from residential schools to the imagined future situation in which colonizers lose the ability to dream. Such schools are embedded in an environmental nightmare and cannot be separated from it. The successive waves of colonization (culminating in the future capture of Native individuals and the harvesting their marrow) follow upon, and in fact are inextricably linked to, the destruction and misuse of land. Empire becomes an apocalypse, albeit an unevenly experienced one, for all, including the dreamless colonizers.

Surviving the Apocalypse of Twentieth-Century Relocation: Urban Experience and the Rebuilding of Worlds

The destruction of Indigenous lands hit Native communities in various forms throughout the centuries: deforestation, drought, flood, and fire are all experienced differently across different regions. And worse: resource extraction; dumping of mining waste and tailings; illness (especially tuberculosis); legal apocalypse; religious and cultural devastation; parceled-out land ownership; language loss as well as the cataclysmic ending of life as it had been lived – all these catastrophes have threatened and continue to threaten Indigenous lifeways.

These waves of apocalypse took shape legally in the twentieth century under a different kind of government policy. Following World War II, Dillon S. Myer was appointed Commissioner of the Bureau of Indian Affairs in 1950. From 1942 to 1946, Myer had been the head of the War

Relocation Authority, the entity responsible for the Japanese internment during World War II, and itself part of US empire building in the twentieth century. This devastating and racially motivated policy presumed that Japanese Americans could not be trusted in wartime and forced their internment in camps suspiciously like some of the harshest Indian reservation settings of the late nineteenth century, enforcing punitive models of citizenship as an entitlement not available to non-white peoples.

When Myer was appointed Commissioner of the Bureau of Indian Affairs, a position he held until the end of the Eisenhower administration in 1953, he was the architect of the twin policies of American Indian relocation and termination (House Concurrent Resolution No. 108, 83rd Congress, August 1, 1953; Indian Relocation Act of 1952 and 1956). While removing federal trust restrictions from tribal lands, the relocation program moved an estimated 100,000 Indians from reservations to target cities such as Chicago, Cleveland, Dallas, Denver, Oakland, San Jose, Tulsa, and Oklahoma City.[23] Between 1953 and 1964, 109 tribes were terminated from their trust relationship with the federal government. The twin policies of relocation and termination are yet two more apocalyptic events for Indigenous communities of the twentieth century and beyond: apocalypses whose effects are still being felt today. Even within a pattern of deeply destructive government policies between Native Nations and the United States, this was a devastating moment.

Contemporary literature maps out the multi-generational effects of twentieth-century American imperialism within its own borders in a variety of ways. As gestured by Lawrence Gross and Hartley White, these include the ongoing devastating impact of the dissolution of family and social structures by disease and by legal mechanisms. Yet even in face of these crushing colonial tools of relocation and termination, modern Indigenous writers describe the experience of rebuilding kinship relations and engaging in what Gross terms "rebuilding worlds."

In one of the earliest fictional depictions of the Indian relocation program, Abel, the protagonist of N. Scott Momaday's Pulitzer Prize-winning novel *House Made of Dawn* (1968) is sent to Los Angeles, one of the program's designated urban centers upon his release from prison in the early 1950s. Both *House Made of Dawn* and Silko's *Ceremony* depict relocation as part of a cycle of departure and return from the reservation that aids in the healing process necessitated by the disruptions of colonialism.

The Jailing of Cecelia Capture (1985) by Janet Campbell Hale is another early urban Indian novel set in the Bay Area during the late 1960s and 1970s. Hale's novel departs from earlier Native novels focused on the experiences of young men by featuring a young female protagonist who is also a mother of young children. Taking place during the span of one night, the novel unfolds with Cecelia Capture reflecting back on her life while jailed on an old welfare fraud charge. While not an actual participant in Relocation, she joined many others who moved to cities from reservation communities for employment and education. She finds work, gives birth to a son whose father has been killed in the Vietnam conflict, and studies at community college while also briefly being caught up in the Indian activism of the time. The novel highlights a protagonist who is able to successfully forge her own destiny in the city even as the state encroaches with its punitive unjust "justice" system.

The most recent novel to explore the history of relocation is Tommy Orange's *There, There (2018)*. The novel showcases twelve alternating characters who are several generations post-relocation, making them the inheritors of protagonists of the earlier relocation novels. *There, There* begins and ends with apocalypse, with the aptly named "Massacre as Prologue" section opening with a sonic and somatic depiction of the Sand Creek Massacre in 1864 and similarly ending with a hail of bullets during a robbery of the Oakland Indian Center powwow. Like the earlier novel by Hale, *There, There* does not directly address Relocation even as it is suffused with its history. Each character faces their own cultural apocalypse. In general, the novel moves from environmental and climate collapse to apocalypse on a more personal level: the threatened destruction of social bonds and kinship relations. The kinship relations between characters enable the practice and process of rebuilding worlds. Colonialism is America's internal version of empire, and the novel makes clear that it continues to devastate Native communities. *There, There* does not offer or celebrate a version of perfect survival: its characters work to maintain cultural connection despite the bullets that keep on arriving.

Contemporary "Wonderworks": Speculative Fictions of the Apocalypse

If much contemporary Indigenous fiction models the remaking of kinship relations in the wake of relocation and termination, Daniel Heath Justice identifies a different generic mode of "rebuilding worlds" within a genre that he terms "wonderworks": a version of fantasy or science fiction that offers us "hopeful alternatives to the oppressive structures and conditions we're continually told are inevitable, material 'reality.'"[24] He explains: "it's a term that gestures, imperfectly, toward other ways of being in the world, and it reminds us that the way things are is not how they have always been, nor is it how they must be."[25] Such works draw on the historical past to imagine an apocalyptic future that nonetheless offers space for rebuilding.

Indeed, Indigenous writers have found the contemporary speculative genres of science fiction and fantasy particularly apt for elaborating the relationship between past and future and for thereby illuminating the apocalypse of empire. Daniel Heath Justice explains:

> when "realistic" fiction demands consistency with corrosive lies and half-truths, imagining otherwise is more than an act of useful resistance – it's a moral imperative . . . It's time for a reappraisal of the relationship between realism and the fantastic, especially when considering the work that marginalized writers are doing to challenge oppressive lived realities through the intentional employment of the fantastic to imagine otherwise.[26]

In a recent foray into speculative fiction, Louise Erdrich's 2017 novel *Future Home of the Living God* opens into a world of ecological and environmental collapse. Like *The Marrow Thieves*, this novel is set in a near-apocalypse time frame, and in it Erdrich returns to familiar themes from her other work, exploring a different iteration of maternal exploitation and family separation. The novel traverses different landscapes from urban to suburban to reservation; pathogens emerging from permafrost may or may not be responsible for what is described as devolving evolution that has also interfered with reproduction and gestation. Legacies of colonialism across generations have decimated entire populations while legislation that worked to undo kinship and social and political structures of Indigenous societies (the Indian Child Welfare Act, the Dawes Act, Termination and Relocation, and so on) all interact in this futuristic world in the story of the protagonist Cedar, her adoptive white family, and her Indigenous maternal relatives.

As the world around them falls apart, the reservation becomes the only safe space, and the community establishes a bitterly ironic reversal of centuries of American empire. As one character, Eddy, explains: "we're just taking back the land within the boundaries of our original treaty. We *were* all set to conduct a compassionate removal of non-tribal people living on our land at present, but I am relieved to tell you that we haven't needed to put removal into action. They've all removed themselves."[27] Land claims are devolving much as the evolutionary processes are; the story is moving backward. Looking at this new map, "we wouldn't see the narrative we think we know."[28] In a countermove, those who have relocated voluntarily or otherwise, are returning (urbans returning to res, non-tribals returning to cities) in a reverse process of relocation. In this way, the policies of removal, relocation, and termination become #LandBack, a dismantling of empire and settler colonialism. At the same time, Eddy's map is a glimpse of a decolonial future, a path forward outside the confines of empire.

Indigeneity in the Contemporary Political and Cultural Moment: New Possibilities, Old Problems, and the Feat of Survivance

We are currently in a moment of growing public interest in the work of Indigenous writers and intellectuals: in addition to the novels in our chapter, recent film and television successes include the three-season television series *Reservation Dogs* (2021–23) as well as the film *Prey* (2022). Indigenous creators are centering Indigenous stories in all their complexity and are being well received by the wider public. Other ongoing investments in centering Indigenous experience and its modernity are all around us: Joy Harjo, Muscogee Creek, was the twenty-third United States Poet Laureate, the first Native American to hold that position; Deb Haaland, a member of the Pueblo of Laguna, is the Secretary of the Interior in the Biden administration; Charles Sams, an enrolled member of the Confederated Tribes of the Umatilla Indian Reservation, is the Director of the National Park Service under Biden, while Lynn Malerba, Mohegan, is the Treasurer of the United States.

And in the circularity of experience, we are in a moment of particular relevance to the "Boundless world" of Samson Occom and the eighteenth-century petitions he helped author: in 2023 the Occom papers were returned to the Mohegan tribe by Dartmouth College, and the papers of Fidelia Fielding, a matriarch of the tribe in the early twentieth century and one of the language-keepers of the community, were returned from Cornell University. Such moments are about reclaiming culture and language; they reject the notion that empire protects and embraces Indigenous culture through its institutions. Anishinaabe efforts to survive PASS or Post-Apocalyptic Stress Syndrome, maintain cultural sovereignty, and rebuild their world are ongoing. Modern Indigenous communities must constantly remake their worlds in the face of seemingly never-ending waves of apocalypse, and that work is apparent all around us, from language reclamation efforts to other forms of community building. These real-world moments reflect what novelists write, over and over. In *The Marrow Thieves* the stories told by the elders Miigwans and Minerva to the younger members of the group are an effort to rebuild world through story and maintain and transmit cultural sovereignty. Minerva's cache of tin tops speaks to her hope for a future of dance and celebration in which jingle dresses, impossible in her world of running and hiding, will once again be worn with pride. In Louise Erdrich's *Future Home of the Living God*, Eddy's conversation captures a similar resistance and persistence:

"Indians have been adapting since before 1492 so I guess we'll keep adapting."
"But the world is going to pieces."
"It is always going to pieces."
"This is different."
"It is always different. We'll adapt."[29]

Academic groups like AISA (founded 1999) and NAISA (founded in 2007) serve as the defining voices of Indigenous studies at the university level; these organizations have used their influence to demand that academic institutions clearly engage with Indigenous communities in ethical and comprehensive ways rather than as imperial extractors. Such efforts, whether they are based within Indigenous communities or in more out-ward facing efforts to challenge the monolithic US empire, speak to ongoing commitments to continuity.

With more awareness comes the recognition of the complexity of the question: whose stories are these to tell, and who are they being shared with? If the Mashantucket Pequot tribal museum and other community-based institutions celebrate their own understanding of contemporary Indigenous life, other kinds of museums and the lack of repatriation remind us that museums are imperial formations. Similarly, Indigenous filmmakers and television exist side-by-side with ongoing representations that range from merely problematic to outright offensive. Empire is insidious: there is a perennial problem of Indigenous traditions peddled to the mainstream in cheap knock-off versions or appropriated and exploited. The hoarding of Indigenous cultural objects by museums and individual collectors is ongoing, as Angeline Boulley's recent novel so chillingly explores: neither explicitly sci fi nor apocalyptic, Boulley's young adult novel *Warrior Girl Unearthed* (2023) nonetheless grapples with the costs and consequences of attempted cultural genocide in a modern world that feels alarmingly tipped toward the apocalyptical, with academics and predatory collectors as the villains and modern missing women looped together with grave robbing and stolen bodies. Sharing stories, then, comes with risks.

To understand the place of apocalypse in Indigenous experience is to upend any comforting version of American identity that has tucked away such horrors into its darkest corners. To see the ongoing waves of apocalypse not only throughout history but also in literature and so many forms of Indigenous expression is to acknowledge what has been visible all along for those willing to listen and see: US empire is built on the alienation of Indigenous lifeways.

While it is tempting to see ourselves in a new and entirely different moment, what the cyclical nature of Indigenous opposition to apocalypse makes clear is that the iterative process of empire means that Indigenous communities are in a longer cycle of survival, and a longer arc of survivance. The apocalypse isn't ending. There is no rolling back; there is not a single turn or event that will change all of it. There is, however, surviving and everything that implies. In the face of apocalypse that is a grand and extraordinary feat.

Notes

1. Meg Wesling, *Empire's Proxy: American Literature and US Imperialism in the Phillipines*. New York: New York University Press, 2011.
2. This is usefully made evident, for example, at the Mashantucket Pequot Museum and Research Center, where a recent tour opened with an emphasis on sovereignty: the tour guide reminds the Center's college student visitors that they have left the state of Connecticut and are on sovereign ground, the invited guests of a community with specific governing structures and cultural practices.
3. The nineteenth century saw significant shifts in forms of writing and publishing among Native people. From autobiographical texts early in the century by William Apess and Black Hawk, to novels, poetry, and other kinds of writing by Eli Parker, Sarah Winnemucca, and John Rollin Ridge among many others, Indigenous writers used a variety of forms to push against American empire.
4. The term "Survivance" was coined by Gerald Vizenor as a combination of "survival" and "resistance." In his 1999 book, *Manifest Manners*, Vizenor forcefully argues that one is not possible without the other, or perhaps even that the terms are interchangeable since the fact of survival is a rebuke to the dominant narrative of extinction. Gerald Vizenor, *Manifest Manners: Narratives on Postindian Survivance* (Lincoln: Univ. of Nebraska Press, 2010).
5. Rob Nixon, *Slow Violence and the Environmentalism of the Poor* (Cambridge: Harvard University Press, 2011), 2.
6. Kathryn Yusoff, *A Billion Black Anthropocenes or None* (Minneapolis: University of Minnesota Press, 2018), xiii.
7. Lawrence W. Gross, "The Comic Vision of Anishinaabe Culture and Religion," *American Indian Quarterly* 26.3 (2002): 436–59, 437.
8. Daniel Heath Justice, *Why Indigenous Literatures Matter* (Waterloo: Wilfrid Laurier University Press, 2018), 155.
9. Jean M. O'Brien, *Firsting and Lasting: Writing Indians Out of Existence in New England.* (Minneapolis: University of Minnesota Press, 2010), xiii.

10. O'Brien, *Firsting and Lasting*, xii.
11. Hartley White, "Ishkwaakiiwan The Apocalypse," in *Living Our Language: Ojibwe Tales and Oral Histories*, ed. Anton Treuer (St. Paul: Minnesota Historical Society Press, 2000), 222.
12. Gross, "The Comic Vision," 437.
13. Louise Erdrich, *Tracks* (New York: Henry Holt & Co., 1988), 7.
14. Justice, *Why Indigenous Literatures Matter*, 147–8 (emphasis original)
15. See Neal Salisbury's introduction to his edition of Mary Rowlandson's Captivity Narrative for these statistics. Another recent narrative of King Philip's War is Lisa Brooks, *Our Beloved Kin: A New History of King Philip's War* (New Haven: Yale University Press, 2018), winner of the Bancroft Prize in History in 2019.
16. For example, Osage/Cherokee scholar George Tinker has suggested the ways Christianity has been used as a vehicle for cultural genocide; the first chapter of his book, *Missionary Conquest: The Gospel and Native American Cultural Genocide* (Minneapolis: Fortress Press, 1993) focuses on John Eliot and the New England missionary impulse of the seventeenth century.
17. Samson Occom, "Brothertown Tribe to US Congress," in *The Collected Writings of Samson Occom, Mohegan: Leadership and Literature in Eighteenth-Century Native America*, ed. Joanna Brooks (New York: Oxford University Press, 2006), 149.
18. Samson Occom, "Montaukett Tribe to the State of New York," in *Collected Writings*, 151.
19. Occom, "Montaukett Tribe," 150.
20. Occom, "Montaukett Tribe, 151.
21. See *The Occom Circle Project*, a digital repository, for this letter and others related to the Indigenous origins of Dartmouth College.
22. Louise Erdrich, *Love Medicine* (New York: Holt, Rhinehart, and Winston, 1984), 17.
23. Donald L. Fixico, *The Urban Indian Experience in America* (Albuquerque: University of New Mexico Press, 2000), 4.
24. Justice, *Why Indigenous Literatures Matter*, 155.
25. Justice, *Why Indigenous Literatures Matter*, 152.
26. Justice, *Why Indigenous Literatures Matter*, 142–3.
27. Louise Erdrich, *Future Home of the Living God* (New York: HarperCollins, 2017), 214 (emphasis original).
28. Erdrich, *Future Home of the Living God*, 55.
29. Erdrich, *Future Home of the Living God*, 28.

PART II

Imperial Nation

Conquest and Compost
James Fenimore Cooper and the Literature of Ecological Empire

Gesa Mackenthun

> I think hard times are coming when we will be wanting the voices of
> writers who can see alternatives to how we live now and can see
> through our fear-stricken society and its obsessive technologies to
> other ways of being, and even imagine some real grounds for hope . . .
> We live in capitalism. Its power seems inescapable. So did the divine
> right of kings. Any human power can be resisted and changed by
> human beings. Resistance and change often begin in art, and very
> often in our art – the art of words.
>
> Ursula Le Guin[1]

Thirty years ago, Amy Kaplan declared the necessity of studying American
literature, from its beginnings, under the rubric of empire.[2] Much important critical work has since been undertaken to delineate the complex
relations between American literature and imperialism, including the
emergence of the critical field of settler colonial studies, with its emphasis
on the territorial and epistemological dispossession of Indigenous populations. This chapter addresses a particular mode of empire I refer to as
ecological-agrarian imperialism,[3] and examines utopian responses to it as
they play out in James Fenimore Cooper's Littlepage trilogy and his late
novel *The Crater*. As the early nineteenth-century's foremost American
novelist, Cooper registers what I argue is a deep critical awareness of the
historical origins of a specific sociocultural conjunction – and one that is
presently assuming a global, life-threatening dimension: the intersections
between soil depletion, food scarcity, biodiversity reduction, and colonial
capitalism. Cooper's works cannot offer a solution to this problem, neither
in his own time nor now. But it can help us think through these pressing
issues.

It is therefore worthwhile taking a fresh look, from a postcolonial-
ecocritical perspective, at the conjunction of colonial dispossession,

intracolonial land conflict, and ecological degradation as they were perceived through the work of one of America's important political thinkers
and writers. Cooper the citizen was notoriously conservative and an
adherent of the semi-feudal property system. Yet Cooper the author offers
significant insights into the cultural response to such pressing issues as
social equality, an equitable distribution of soil, the ecocidal dangers of
agrarian overextraction, and the unfolding of a settler colonial logic of
justified territorial dispossession under the influence of Indian Removal
and the Anti-Rent troubles in upstate New York in the 1830s and 1840s.
While Cooper, as Dana Nelson showed, has important things to say about
constitutional rights and democratic citizenship in the Littlepage trilogy,[4]
these novels also crucially illustrate the micropolitics of territorial acquisition – the transformation of land from Indigenous tenure into the exclusive
property of the manorial elite. At the same time, they articulate twin
concerns about the profitable increase of colonial property and the darker,
ecocidal aspects of such a surplus-oriented economy. In doing so, Cooper's
novels introduce a utopian ecological strain that reappears across nineteenth-
century American literature and lives on today.

Ecological Imperialism: From *The Pioneers* to *The Crater*

The extension of imperial rule to America, which Cooper's novels negotiate in various ways, was not limited to the human sphere. While the study
of ecological imperialism has produced an impressive corpus of critical
work focused on the exchange of plants and animals within the larger
colonial and enlightenment framework, as well as the impact of the
colonial encounter on the emergence of environmental knowledge in the
metropolitan centers of Europe,[5] the effects of the colonial encounter on
the land and soil and the agrarian economies of the newly settled countries
have received less attention. As the critical term "settler colonialism" both
articulates and disguises, European imperial ambition was first and foremost directed at the land and its natural products, with original human
inhabitants posing as a legal and strategic problem, as troublesome con-
tenders for those natural treasures.

One way of approaching James Fenimore Cooper's work is to read his
novels as tireless attempts to rationalize and romanticize the moral
dilemma of white settlers' dispossession of Indigenous inhabitants. Eric
Cheyfitz has shown how *The Pioneers* (1823) works "in concert" with the
coterminous Supreme Court ruling *Johnson* v. *M'Intosh* in producing
historical narratives that legitimize dispossession. By offering Indian land

claims – spelled out as an inferior right of "occupation" in the court ruling – as merely the claims of a white man in disguise, *Pioneers* "romances" the colonial landgrab, thus making it digestible for readers unwilling to engage critically with the complexities of law.[6] The anthropological classification of Native Americans as hunters with no agrarian affinity to the land, formulated in the midst of legal controversies about the forced removal of fully agrarian (the so-called "civilized") tribes, is part of the pervasive fiction of colonial property transactions to which Cooper contributed.[7]

In the later part of his writing career, Cooper fully developed the colonial ideal of taking possession of a fertile but uninhabited country in his island fantasy *The Crater* (1847). Writing ten years after Indian Removal, Cooper dramatizes a process of taking territorial possession by right of "discovery." The mariners Mark Woolston and Bob Betts are shipwrecked on a lonely volcanic island in the middle of the Pacific Ocean in 1796. Benefiting from the ship owner's extensive collection of seeds and farming implements originally destined to be used in "civilizing" Polynesians, and using Bob's boyhood knowledge of farming, the uses of guano, and compost-making, they are able to start a respectable plantation by mixing the barren soil with manure of all kinds, and after a short while melons, cucumbers, squashes, and pumpkins "flourished surprisingly."[8] Soon, "as a result of his own industry and forethought ... Mark found squashes, cucumbers, onions, sweet-potatoes, tomatoes, string-beans, and two or three other vegetables" fit for usage.[9] While Bob Betts is blown away in a storm, the island rises further, proving most fertile. Mark, who reads this as a providential sign – submitted to him alone, we might say, by "Nature's God" (Declaration of Independence) – regards himself as the sole owner of the island. When Betts, whose contribution to the gardening success is effectively suppressed by the narrative voice, returns with a first installment of American settlers, Mark establishes himself as the sole "governor" of the realm, feeling assured that "[it] was scarcely possible for man to possess any portion of this earth by a title better than that with which Mark Woolston was invested with his domains," a remark that prompts the narrator to anachronistically defend the United States' contemporary war against Mexico.[10] While more settlers are transported to Crater Island the land is divided up between Mark, who retains a tract of "quite a thousand acres on the Peak" as his private property while the rest is converted into equal privately owned allotments distributed among the settlers by lottery.[11] Under Mark's benign autocratic rulership, the colony thrives for a while. Soon, dissensions arise due to the toxic impact of demagogic preachers and printers and Mark's helpless imposition of public censorship, and after Mark and his family temporarily leave the island another eruption takes place which submerges the embattled colony.

Cooper's novel imaginatively performs a quick run through American history. Its philosophy of history is inspired by Cooper's acquaintance Thomas Cole's painting cycle *The Course of Empire* (1834–6). While illustrating the mythical construct of America as "Nature's Nation" whose cultural work consists of solving the irreconcilable opposition between Nature and civilization (according to Perry Miller, Henry Nash Smith, and Leo Marx),[12] *The Crater* also plots and predicts social disaster: its ending resembles Cole's last painting, "Desolation," showing a world in ruins and seemingly devoid of life, but a close-up of its lonely pillar shows a sole bird hatching its nest on its top, presumably signaling nature's survival and recuperation after the extinction of man. In its first half, *The Crater* dramatizes the legal fiction of *vacuum domicilium* to Americans seeking to adjust the dismal reality of Indian Removal to their high moral standards. Mark and Bob are engaged in establishing a garden colony by fertilizing, planting, and harvesting from scratch, thus performing the labor that North America's Indigenous inhabitants had performed for between 2,000 and 5,000 years prior to European "discovery." They did so in ways remotely familiar to the colonizers, using mixed planting, crop rotation, and slash burning.[13] Europeans had survived the initial period thanks to Indigenous agriculture; the destruction of native fields became a regular tactic of colonial warfare.

During Bob's absence, Mark lays claim to the island by the divine right of kings, obtrusively buttressed by his many spiritual conversations with God. But in true jeremiad fashion, Cooper then turns the imperial fiction of exclusive ownership into the nightmare of social and geological disaster. The novel is a good illustration of the dialectics of the natural sublime – an aesthetic language, mastered by Cole, that invents a seemingly pristine world ready for rightful possession, while conversely conveying a sensibility for the need to preserve such beauty by taking sustainable conservation measures. As Paul Warde documents, recognition of the need for a sustainable environment was well developed by Cooper's time. A gardener himself, Cooper was familiar with the danger of soil exhaustion, already showing on a large scale in the Eastern states after 200 years of settlement and intensive farming.[14] Thomas Jefferson, for example, knew perfectly well about the soil depletion caused by tobacco farming, "a culture productive of infinite wretchedness" for both the soil and the human workers, that is, slaves. His recognition of a mismatch between the labor necessary for soil conservation and the market price of agricultural products makes him recommend to shift this extractive plant culture to Georgia where it would be grown at much more profitable rates than in the exhausted soil of Virginia and Maryland.[15] By Cooper's time Georgia had become most affected by conflicts about Indian Removal, culminating in the Cherokee Trail of Tears in 1838. Its fertile soils had been conserved by Native Americans.

Cooper solves the problem of social catastrophe and impending ecocide by sinking his island below the sea, uncannily evoking the specter of rising sea levels in present-day climate fiction (as well as contemporary reality). *Crater* inverts the history of Indigenous dispossession in turning the neighboring Pacific islanders into external aggressors who unsuccessfully try to invade the crater colony. The local power dynamic is in turn disturbed by interventionist and profit-seeking Americans. "Friendly" natives are hired as a cheap labor force cutting sandalwood to be traded to China – the colony's only possibility to "coin money."[16] As expected, the sandalwood forests are soon clearcut and the trade discontinues.[17] Had the extractive community not been sunk by geological agency, like ancient Atlantis, we may presume that before long it would have been otherwise subdued by its own agency. Cooper's vision of ecological imperialism proves both historically insightful and uncannily prescient in its focus on the destruction of the commons and the destructive profitability of mono-cultural societies.

Indeed, the narrator of *Crater* obsessively comments on the making of fertile soil out of sand, loam, seaweed, mud, and other manure on the volcanic island. The settlers are continuously engaged in "making soil."[18] Like Jefferson, who repeatedly remarked that a quick profit is to be prioritized over soil protection,[19] Cooper's novel conveys the impression that the physical degradation of the land was a calculated collateral damage of an expanding empire that could always find new soils in foreign parts of the world. It is this logic of expansive destruction, conducted in the expectation of endless natural abundance – the unlimited availability of more fertile soil further west – which eventually led to the Dust Bowl in the 1930s and similar catastrophes. A critical reading of Cooper's novel reveals the aesthetic of abundance pervading settler colonial discourse as the mythical semantic managing global ecocide.

Then again, Cooper's insistence on vegetable diversity implicitly resists the ideology of monoculture ruling over both ecological and human relationships under the conditions of agricultural imperialism. Here again Cooper's work is prescient: had agriculture generally tended as carefully to making compost and raising a great variety of crops, the present global food crisis would be less severe. As Elizabeth Povinelli and Elizabeth DeLoughrey remind us, ecological degradation is not the responsibility of humans as such but rather of a very particular socioeconomic formation practiced by very particular groups of humans.[20] The history of American settlement is a history of settlers abandoning their eastern habitations for better soils, in constant search of the Edenic promise. By the time of the Dust Bowl, the "American phenomenon of destroying the Garden in the search for the Garden" faced the truth that, as Louis Owens writes, there "is no Promised Land and nowhere else to go . . . The American myth of the Eden ever to the west is shattered, the dangers of the myth exposed." Instead of constant deferral of divine fulfillment the commitment should be to "making *this* place, *this America*, the garden it might be."[21] Cooper's Littlepage trilogy indicates some reasons for the failure of yeoman republicanism. It illustrates that the key questions were who does the labor and who owns the land.

The Littlepage Trilogy: Cooper's Cartographies of Lawful Settlement

The novels *Satanstoe* (1845), *The Chainbearer* (1845), and *The Redskins* (1846) directly preceded *The Crater* and can be regarded as thinking through the historical predicament that prevented America from becoming the garden paradise that Cooper evokes in his utopian-dystopian Pacific novel. Like *Crater*, they are mostly set in a nostalgic past but ideologically framed by the immediate context of the Monroe Doctrine and the Mexican War.[22] Next to condemning, and showing the reasons for, Jacksonian "mobocracy," they are seeking to "romance," with waning success, the colonial story of a legal implantation of settler society on American soil. These imaginative accounts of the history of agricultural settlement of the originally Dutch-dominated Hudson River Valley – beginning at the time of the French and Indian War, continuing with the period right after the War of Independence, and ending with the Anti-Rent troubles of Cooper's present – are rendered autodiegetically by three different younger heirs of the landed gentry. They trace the translation of European feudalist structures of landed property and labor to form what Nicole Maskiell refers to as the Anglo-Dutch "northern gentry." The novels confirm Maskiell's insight that the decisive socially binding force in the early colonial Northeast were family networks and "[n]otions of mastery rooted in this shared Anglo-Dutch heritage [that] formed the basis of an . . . elite identity."²³ As novels, however, they also contain the germ of a critique of that perspective.

All three novels begin with a young Littlepage heir visiting the upstate New York family estates Mooseridge and Ravensnest, the latter having entered the family holdings by way of a marriage between Dutch and English gentry at the end of the first novel. *Satanstoe* tells the story of Corny Littlepage who, at age twenty-one, is sent in search of a land claim of 40,000 acres near the Hampshire Grants that his father and a friend had bought from the Mohawk.²⁴ Before going "in search of the land,"²⁵ Corny is overwhelmed by the promise of his future property at the sight of a "large, coarse, parchment map" of the terrain which "excited certain feelings of avarice within my mind. There were streams meandering among hills and valleys, little lakes . . . dotted the surface, and there were all the artistical proofs of a valuable estate, that a good map-maker could devise, to render the whole pleasing and promising."²⁶ In addition to being the only heir to his father's present estate Satanstoe, Corny is looking forward to becoming the proprietor "of all these ample plans, rich bottoms, flowing streams and picturesque lakes."²⁷ Like the surrounding Dutch landowners such as Corny's future father-in-law Herman Mordaunt, the Littlefields are absentee owners of their wilderness estate – which is why they have to go in search of it and actually only find it with the help of the diasporic Onondaga warrior Susquesus.²⁸ The novel illustrates the micropolitics of taking possession, relating the absentee landlords' difficulty in making his settlers continue with their agricultural labor in spite of the nearby battle-line of the French and Indian War. When his settlers consider removing to safer parts, Mordaunt "saw no necessity for this abandonment of advantages over the wilderness that had been obtained at so much cost and trouble . . . he naturally wished to keep the people he had got to his estate with so much difficulty, and at so much cost."²⁹ More concerned about losing his settlers' labor power than the settlers themselves, Mordaunt seems to see only his own monetary and administrative investment in getting his estate running, not the daily "trouble" of "his people" whom he wants to continue farming in frontier precarity. On their way to his estate, "he related to me the cost and trouble" of hiring and keeping the "ten or fifteen families who were on his property."³⁰ His settlement scheme, representing that of historical Dutch- and English-stock manor lords, consists of granting leases for "three lives" plus twenty-one years, that is the lifetimes of three successive family members, at a very low "nominal" fee. In addition, Mordaunt has to pay for an agent and a basic trade and transportation infrastructure. All of these investments will only pay off "a century hence," making "provision for [his] posterity" but not for himself.[31] Cooper here documents the socioeconomic system of dependencies inherent in the futurist temporality of empire. The open-ended temporal frame enables Cooper's complex take on the micropolitics of possession in their seeming repetition, with minor differences, across time and space.

As subsequent events unfold, the novel further reveals the affective social dimension of this feudalist logic. After the ensuing attack by French Indians is fended off, Corny ends up becoming Mordaunt's heir by marrying his daughter. The two sequels sketch the success of Herman Mordaunt's financial scheme. Mordaunt Littlepage, Corny's grandson and narrator of *Chainbearer*, is confronted by his grandfather's agent Jason Newcome whose three lives lease expired sooner than expected because his three children, on whose lives he had bet, had all died prematurely.[32] Instead of commiserating with his tenant for the loss of his children, Littlefield coolly imposes a rent raise on Newcome. He downplays Newcome's labor investment while Newcome questions the legality of the Littlepage land claim: "granted to us by the crown" according to Mordaunt while Newcome refers to the leveling effect of the Revolutionary War.[33] Mordaunt vehemently refuses further discussion pointing out, in the haughty language of feudalism, that his tenants have no rights but merely enjoy the "liberality" of their employers.[34]

If Cooper's authorial sympathies seem to rest generally with his narrator, the latter's pitiless behavior at this juncture forces readers to reckon with the foundations of that sympathy. The Littlepage men act extractively toward both the tenants and the land which they only regard as sources of profit and wealth: "It was a season's work for a skillful axe man to chop, log, burn, clear and sow ten acres of forest land. The ashes he manufactured."[35] Written during the Anti-Rent troubles in the Hudson River valley,[36] Cooper's novels voice the position of the landed gentry but they cannot but note the plausible arguments of their tenants' opposition to a scheme in which absentee landlords should carry away most of the profit while the hardworking farmers are left in poverty and economic insecurity.

Like *The Crater*, then, the trilogy tells a story about original plantation, presumably from tabula rasa. While Cooper's Pacific adventure is set in utopian space (yet marked by contemporary American Pacific colonization), the trilogy is generically tied to keeping a certain faithfulness to the historical record. The Littlepages therefore, unlike Mark Woolston, do not invest the land with their own physical labor but provide the original funding while immigrant settlers are employed in hard and ecologically unsustainable toil: the clearcutting for settlements, fields, and profit by lumber ignores the needs of other life forms. Cooper's plots thus confirm Karl Marx's insight, stated twenty years later with particular reference to the United States, that "[a]ll progress in capitalist agriculture is a progress in the art, not only of robbing the worker, but of robbing the soil; all progress in increasing the fertility of the soil for a given time is progress towards ruining the more long-lasting sources of that fertility."[37] Land and profitable labor are indeed key concerns regulating the relationship between the Littlepage absentee owners and their tenants, as well as that between European and Indigenous American representatives in the novels and society at large.

The novels' cartographies of lawful settlement rest upon the ideology of "improvement," which Cooper explores through the land conflict among his characters. In *Chainbearer*, this conflict escalates between Mordaunt Littlepage and the squatter Aaron "Thousandacres" Timberman who occupies the neglected land claim and who runs a patriarchal family clan to clearcut the forest, floating the wood down to Albany. Thousandacres aggressively rejects the relevance of Mordaunt's title ("He's got a paper title, they tell me, and I've got possession")[38] and justifies his transgression with reference to the Lockean concept of improvement ("What a man sweats for, he has a right to"; "here are my betterments – sixty three as large acres chopped over and hauled to mill").[39] Mordaunt correctly questions Thousandacre's vulgar Lockeanism: "a man might sweat in bearing away his neighbour's goods."[40]

As the dialogue shows, "improvement" in practice does not primarily refer to the sustainable stewardship of land and life but, given the etymology of the term, to the profitable, surplus-oriented use of land.[41] John Locke famously wrote in the section on property in his *Second Treatise of Government* (1690) that although "in the beginning all the world was America" and land was held "in common," Indigenous Americans failed in "improving [the land] by labour."[42] Locke regarded "land that is left wholly to nature, that hath no improvement of pasturage, tillage, or planting," as "waste."[43] It is "labour" which "puts the greatest part of value upon land,"[44] but while labor is necessary for raising the value of the land and also gives a certain "right of property,"[45] it is really the "improvement" effected by mixing one's labor with the soil which gives full title. Locke repeatedly argues that land lying "waste," even if it was enclosed and only temporarily left barren, might become "the possession of someone else."[46] The seemingly "vacant places of America" could therefore lawfully be planted by European settlers.[47] Thousandacres settles in the ambivalences of Locke's theory. Like Locke, he has no sense for the ecological necessity of reforestation or leaving agricultural land to lie fallow. His non-sustainable activity rests on the grounds of biblical and patriarchal discourses of extraction. Socially and economically, he is the egotistical mirror of Andries Coejemans, called the Chainbearer, who voluntarily submits to the Littlepages' social authority and thereby acts as an agent of ecological imperialism in its settler colonial manifestation on the early American frontier.

In sketching the contours of its various land conflicts, the Littlepage trilogy mostly ignores the concerns of regular settlers, whose culmination in the Anti-Rent troubles caused Cooper, writing in an atmosphere of political unrest on the eve of the European 1848 revolutions, to draft these three novels in the first place. Instead, Cooper presents three political camps embedded in particular generic requirements: landed absentee gentry owning the territory, hired settlers denied property title and risking the loss of their homes and the result of their labor if they cannot pay the raised rent, and the libertarian Thousandacres who settles on voluntaristic principles while armed with vulgar doctrines pulled from Lockean labor theory and the logic of colonial discovery.

Chainbearer's property plotline is entangled with its romance plot: Mordaunt becomes enarmored with Ursula Malbone, called Dus, the Chainbearer's niece, who is poor but religious, courageous, and educated, and ultimately becomes Mordaunt's wife. We again encounter her as the elder matron of the family estate in *Redskins*, set in the 1840s, which emplots a direct encounter of the landed gentry and the Anti-Rent pro-testers. Morally, the Littlepages have somewhat degenerated: the narrator, Hugh Littlepage, and his Uncle Ro, recently returned from a pleasure trip in tumultuous Europe, assume the disguise of traveling salesmen in order to avoid direct confrontation with the rebels. Hugh's dismissive attitude toward their claims was probably not shared by all contemporary readers, many of whom were in sympathy with the concerns of the Anti-Renters, if not their means – haunting the Hudson Valley dressed up as "Injins" in calico shirts. A public speaker questions the justification of property based on "antiquity" (the crown grant) and proposes to install "political leap-years ... into the political calendar ... to restore the equilibrium" and "divide up the land."[48] Though the narrator ridicules this idea and has another character speak up against it, it resembles contemporary sugges-tions, by Orestes Bronson and others, for preventing an increase of social and economic inequality.[49]

As in *The Pioneers* and Nathaniel Hawthorne's *House of the Seven Gables*, original Indigenous claims have become invisible through the property transactions between different colonial parties. The *real* legally justified contender for land ownership based on "*antiquity*" are the Mohawk tribe from whom the territory was originally acquired by "pen and ink witchcraft."[50] The Indigenous position is represented in all three novels by the Onondaga Susquesus, who at the end of the saga has reached a biblical age himself. In the final scene of *Redskins* the Anti-Rent protests intersect with a delegation of Indigenous representatives returning from a visit to Washington DC. They make a detour to the Littlepage estate to convince Susquesus, who lives with the Littlepages, to join them and return to his tribe. *Real* "Indians," who at Cooper's time were subject to forced removal, anachronistically interfere with the demands of white tenants *dressed up* as Indians. Knowing that "the land is changed" and in spite of his knowledge that "the pale-face drove off the red-man" with "no treaty between them,"[51] Susquesus sides with the landlords who have given him a home and is resigned to his people's dispossession. His speech, with which the trilogy ends, performs the final translation of ownership, concurring with the determinist message of the Marshall trilogy sealing the fate of Indigenous communities.

Yet the novels betray an interesting slippage within their narrative voice. I concur with Dana Nelson that Cooper's distribution of voice involuntarily sketches the moral demise of the landed gentry.[52] The three narrators become successively less sympathetic. As Nelson shows, Cooper's Littlepage novels are obsessed with the economization of social relations, of love and intimacy getting in the way of economic success and class stability due to various characters marrying "down" the social ladder – a process whose historical equivalent was the growing economic strains of the aristocratic land system increasingly suffering from soil depletion, population pressure, and external market insecurity.[53] Most importantly, perhaps, the trilogy's portrayal of land conflict (manorial vs. yeoman system) occludes both the fact that these conflicts were part of the continuation of the European enclosure policy *and* the recent existence of "a third form of ownership" that was destroyed in full public view: that of the Indigenous commons.[54] That these concerns are voiced at all – by discredited tenants, squatters, and Anti-Rent speakers, by romanticized Indigenous centenarians – is not that surprising in Cooper. The trilogy resembles *The Pioneers* (1827) in constructing, and confirming, a collusion between blood kinship and the increase of property by inheritance, just as the landed blood property system perpetuates a sociology of family

romance. This powerful discursive conjunction of blood and property
forecloses any alternative forms of kinship and land ownership. The novels'
"anarchy" consists in allowing us to see this deeply rooted social matrix,
and, in their messy and unregulated ways, of hinting at epistemic
alternatives.[55]

"Dat Queer!" Topographies of Anarchic Knowledge

The novels' "anarchy" shows in an episode in *Chainbearer* which contains
moments of discursive slippage and semi-digested "messiness" that speak of
missed chances and roads not taken in the process of colonial and transcultural encounter. When Mordaunt Littlepage is searching for the path to his
property in the "virgin" forest, he overhears a beautiful female voice in
a thicket singing a strange song made up of Indian words and a Scots-
Celtic melody. When about to advance he hears the singer's melodious
laugh, but out of the thicket comes Susquesus, who had already helped
Mordaunt's grandfather find the area to be surveyed in *Satanstoe*.[56] When
Mordaunt asks Susquesus about the singing person in the forest, the latter
replies that "'Plenty people dere'," including a "gal" that loves to sing "like
wren."[57] While guiding Mordaunt to his settlement, the Onondaga involves
him in a discussion about the incommensurability of claiming property
without even knowing where that property is located in real space.
Mordaunt reveals to him that he never saw his "patent" before, which
makes the warrior exclaim, "'Dat queer! How you own land, when nebber
see him?'" followed by a discussion about the relevance of written contracts.[58]
Mordaunt arrogantly pontificates about the necessity of farming – an activity
he is never involved in himself – while Susquesus keeps wondering about the
"'queer 'nough'" fact that the white man "'Own land, but don't know
him'."[59] The dialogue reveals that, unbeknownst to his culturally blind
companion, what counts for the Onondaga is not the perpetuation of
property but a wise practice of place-making.

The originator of the culturally hybrid song is revealed three chapters
later. The singer was Ursula Malbone, the Chainbearer's niece and
Mordaunt's future wife. The uncle informs the narrator that he and
Ursula had spent some time among the tribes where she learned the
Onondaga language.[60] Ursula's song is part of the novel's counterhege-
monic epistemology which favors orally transmitted knowledge, transcultural conviviality, and a land-based ethic of truth-telling over against
written titles and false disguises. Both in this and the follow-up novel,
Susquesus and Ursula entertain a special relationship. Ursula's "original

education had been in the forest," her future husband muses, aware that she had ignored gender decorum by assisting her uncle in carrying surveyor chains herself. "It was possible this strange girl might have portrayed to her imagination, in the vista of the future, more of happiness and wild enjoyment, among the woods and ravines of stolen clearings, than by dwelling amid the haunts of men."[61] Once again, Cooper's disjointed, possibilist temporality enables a critique of the argument made through his romancing.

Place-knowledge and "queer" kinship relations converge in *Redskins* when ancient Susquesus still calls Ursula endearingly "wren" during the final scene, a word with which he also refers to the lost love of his youth.[62] Speaking of his and Ursula's impending death, he tells the tribal delegation, "'you hear my voice for the last time. Even the wren cannot sing forever. The very eagle's wing gets tired in time'."[63] The allusion to the Aesopian fable of the eagle and the intelligent and courageous wren hiding in his feather coat speaks of a particular intimacy between these two characters. This conclusion is reinforced by considering Cooper's choice of Edward Coote Pinkney's poem "The Indian's Bride" as motto for the chapter in which both characters are introduced.[64] It is a romantic poem about a transcultural love partnership between an Indigenous warrior and a "graceful female" who left her "pallid countrymen" in order to roam the woods with the "red hunter of the deer," who "humanizes him" while he "educates her to liberty."[65] The strange ending of *Redskins* marks, as Dana Nelson writes, "vanishing intra- and inter-cultural possibilities even as it sketches the hardening racial lines of the nineteenth century."[66] The undeveloped, unnarrated friendship, perhaps even kinship, between Ursula Malbone and Susquesus/the Onondaga tribe forms an "anarchic," but also *anarchistic*-utopian,[67] counterpoint to the three novels' authoritarian emplotment of colonial dispossession. We are left to wonder what kind of story about making kin across cultures Cooper may have handed down to posterity had he had the nerve to focus on these two sympathetic characters!68

This messy and undeveloped textual material, which tells of the deep intercultural friendship between Susquesus and Ursula, is entangled with the novels' dominant discourse of property and landrights. The trilogy opens itself up to a nineteenth-century literary history of alternative imaginings of transcultural interactions and figures. Cooper's intercultural friendship is reminiscent of Mary Jemison's narrative of her life among the Seneca (1824) and the conflicts about property imposed on her by white fortune hunters masquerading as relatives. It could also enter into conversation with Catharine Maria Sedgwick's novel *Hope Leslie* (1827) whose formidable Indigenous character Magawisca is invested with similarly truth-seeking moral positions as Ursula. Cooper's failure of nerve echoes that of youthful Lydia Maria Child who, in her novel *Hobomok* (1824), imagines a cross-cultural family but then has the wife's fiancé reappear and her Native American protagonist vanish in the wilderness.

Through the haze of Cooper's ethnic monoculturalism we gain a glimpse of an alternative "queer" practice of making kin in colonial America – elective kinship by adoption which Cooper tests out, all-male as in the cases of Edward Effingham and Natty Bumppo. Eric Cheyfitz reads *The Pioneers* as translating Indigenous elective affinities and kinship relations into colonial property relations. Indian kinship serves the purpose of telling a story about the translation of property between white men.[69] Mark Rifkin has pointed out the significance of queer kinship and adoption for ideologically regulating property transactions in *The Last of the Mohicans*.[70] These discussions show classic American literature's inability to talk straightforwardly about "queerer" forms of land ownership besides private property, manorial and otherwise. Yet common forms of land use and non-blood-based forms of conviviality existed at Cooper's time, and would continue to exist in the minds of writers later in the century.

Indeed, Cooper's shy utopianism, exemplified in the cross-cultural friendship between Susquesus and Ursula, points to realizations of land management and kin-making beyond established kinship economies undertaken in his own moment and later in the century. These contemporary and future utopian communities, experimenting with different forms of kin-making and compost-making based on the teachings of socialist radicals like Charles Fourier and Robert Owens, were largely forged by and for white communities of settler-citizens.[71] Indigenous forms of livelihood, struggling for survival under the brutal conditions of Allotment privatization, had vanished from the view of the urban intelligentia.[72]

In spite of their racialist tendencies and short duration, these utopian communities were important vectors of social reform. Real and literary non-extractive and communitarian forms of existence formed a counterpoint to postbellum and fin-de-siècle predator capitalism. Repelled by acts of wanton deforestation and the poverty of eastern farmers, Mr. Homos in William Dean Howells' *A Traveler from Altruria* tells of his homeland in which monopoly capitalism and social inequality have been overcome and all citizens cultivate the earth in common.[73] Charlotte Perkins Gilman's geologically removed garden community

Herland overturned patriarchal social relations and installed a science-based form of female government.[74] And American literary resistance to ecological imperialism did not end with the nineteenth century. More recently, Ursula Le Guin, Ernest Callenbach, Octavia Butler, and Kim Stanley Robinson have all used the utopian mode in imagining ecologically sound societies making crops and compost without conquest. At the same time, "Land Back!" is the response of a motley alliance resisting the continuation of extractive enclosure policies causing misery and evictions.

Reading Cooper's literary meditations on the early history of the socioeconomic formation of agrarian imperialism, and attending to the anarchy of ecological empire in his novels, is instructive in analyzing the present conjunction. Then as now, alternatives to extractive and ecocidal practices seem impossible; but the divine right of kings invoked by Cooper's proprietors will hopefully remain defunct. Then as now, to cite Fredric Jameson's famous bonmot, "it seems to be easier for us . . . to imagine the thoroughgoing deterioration of the earth and of nature than the breakdown of late capitalism."[75] This is because the logic of "improvement" has a strong grip on our imaginations, successfully channeling our utopian impulses into blockbusting dystopian disaster narratives. But as Ursula Le Guin reminds us at the end of her acceptance speech, the name of the value of literature is not profit – but freedom.

Notes

1. Ursula Le Guin, National Book Award acceptance speech, 2014. https://vimeo.com/112654091.
2. Amy Kaplan, "'Left Alone With America': The Absence of Empire in the Study of American Culture," *Cultures of United States Imperialism*, ed. Amy Kaplan and Donald Pease (Durham: Duke University Press, 1993), 3–21.
3. The concept focuses on the agricultural and soil-related aspects of settler colonial practices. It is inspired by Hannah Holleman, *Dust Bowls of Empire: Imperialism, Environmental Politics, and the Injustice of "Green" Capitalism* (New Haven: Yale University Press, 2018), as well as the work of John Bellamy Foster and David Worster.
4. Dana D. Nelson, *Commons Democracy: Reading the Politics of Participation in the Early United States* (New York: Fordham University Press, 2016), 105–32.
5. Most of these works focus on the development of the modern natural sciences within the European, especially British, colonial framework of the classical episteme, as well as plant transports and botanical gardens. See Richard Grove, *Green Imperialism: Colonial Expansion, Tropical Island Edens and the Origins of Environmentalism, 1600–1860* (Cambridge University Press, 1995) and Richard Drayton, *Nature's Government: Science, Imperial Britain, and the*

"Improvement" of the World (New Delhi: Orient Longman, 2000). A more transcultural approach is Londa Schiebinger, *Plants for Empire: Colonial Bioprospecting in the Atlantic World* (Cambridge: Harvard University Press, 2004).

6. Eric Cheyfitz, "Savage Law: The Plot Against American Indians in *Johnson and Graham's Lessee v. M'Intosh* and *The Pioneers*," in *Cultures of United States Imperialism*, ed. Amy Kaplan and Donald Pease (Durham: Duke University Press, 1993), 109–28.

7. Cheyfitz, "Savage Law," 117.

8. James Fenimore Cooper, *The Crater; or Vulcan's Peak* (1847; reprint, ed. Thomas Philbrick (Cambridge, MA: Harvard University Press, 1962), 74–4; 107.

9. Cooper, *The Crater*, 114.

10. Ibid., 296.

11. Ibid., 329–32.

12. Miller's reading still signifies in the context of contemporary science fiction film like Nolan's *Interstellar*: see Alexandra Ganser, "Astrofuturism," in *Critical Terms in Future Studies*, ed. Heike Paul (London: Palgrave Macmillan, 2019), 35–43.

13. On the familiarity of mixed planting methods see Edmund Morgan, *American Slavery American Freedom* (New York: Norton, 1975), 53–4.

14. Paul Warde, *The Invention of Sustainability: Nature and Destiny, c. 1500–1870* (Cambridge: Cambridge University Press, 2018).

15. Thomas Jefferson, *Notes on the State of Virginia* (1787; reprint, ed. William Peden , Chapel Hill: University of North Carolina Press, 1982), 166.

16. Cooper, *The Crater*, 296, 352.

17. Ibid., 352, 358.

18. Ibid., 341, 343, 346.

19. In his classic *Soil Conservation* (New York: McGraw-Hill, 1939), Hugh Hammond Bennett gives a depressing account of the ignorance of early American settlers concerning soil and manure (869). Cooper's knowledge was much advanced by comparison, possibly due to the influence of the recent publication of Justus Liebig's *Chemistry in its Application to Agriculture and Physiology* (Cambridge: J. Munro and Co., 1842) and of his acquaintance, the American economist Henry C. Carey. See Thomas Philbrick, "Introduction," in *The Crater*, xviii; and Warde, *Invention of Sustainability*, 300–6.

20. Elizabeth Povinelli, *Geontologies: A Requiem to Late Liberalism* (Durham: Duke University Press, 2016), 12; Elizabeth deLoughrey, *Allegories of the Anthropocene* (Durham: Duke University Press, 2019), 15.

21. Louis Owens, *The Grapes of Wrath: Trouble in the Promised Land* (New York: Twayne/Simon&Schuster, 1996), 53, 55.

22. April Gentry, "Created Space: *The Crater* and the Pacific Frontier" (James Fenimore Cooper Society, 2002). https://jfcoopersociety.org/content/04-crit/articles/other/2002other-gentry.htm?Highlight=April%20Gentry.

23. Nicole Saffold Maskiell, *Bound by Bondage: Slavery and the Creation of a Northern Gentry* (Ithaca: Cornell University Press, 2022), 2. Maskiell's main interest is in the aspect of slave counterculture which is underrepresented by Cooper. The incredible life span of his main slave character, Jaap, connects the stories of all three novels, as does that of the main Indigenous character, Susquesus.

24. James Fenimore Cooper, *Satanstoe; or, the Littlepage Manuscripts* (1845; reprint Albany: State University Press of New York, 1990), 52.

25. Cooper, *Satanstoe*, 124.

26. Cooper, *Satanstoe*, 137.

27. Cooper, *Satanstoe*, 137.

28. Cooper, *Satanstoe*, 299–302.

29. Cooper, *Satanstoe*, 273.

30. Cooper, *Satanstoe*, 294.

31. Cooper, *Satanstoe*, 295.

32. James Fenimore Cooper, *The Chainbearer* (1845; reprint Albany: SUNY Press, 2020), 160.

33. Cooper, *The Chainbearer*, 158, 160.

34. Cooper, *The Chainbearer*, 161.

35. Cooper, *The Chainbearer*, 154, 163.

36. The historical model of Cooper's landowners is the van Rennselaer dynasty.

37. Karl Marx, *Capital: A Critique of Political Economy* (1867/ engl. 1887, vol.1; reprint: London: Penguin, 1976), 637–8 (chapter 15, section 10 of the English translation; chapter 13, section 10 of the German original). For an extended analysis of Marx's ecological thought, see John Bellamy Foster, *Marx's Ecology: Materialism and Nature* (New York: Monthly Review Press, 2000).

38. Cooper, *The Chainbearer*, 211.

39. Cooper, *The Chainbearer*, 207, 211.

40. Cooper, *The Chainbearer*, 207.

41. "Improve" is derived from the Old French "emprouwer," "to turn to profit." Ellen Meiksins Wood, *The Origin of Capitalism* (orig. 1999, London: Verso, 2017), 105–15; and Drayton, *Nature's Government*, 51.

42. John Locke, "An Essay Concerning the True Original, Extent and End of Civil Government" (1690). *Two Treatises of Government* (reprint, ed. W. S. Carpenter, London: Everyman, 1990), 140, 146.

43. Locke, "An Essay," 137.

44. Locke, "An Essay," 137.

45. Locke, "An Essay," 138.

46. Locke, "An Essay," 135.

47. Locke, "An Essay," 134. What Locke regards as "wasteful" – letting fields lie fallow for a few seasons to allow the soil to regenerate, or less fertile areas used for foraging in common – was a widespread practice before the beginning of extractive monoculture since the early modern period (Morgan, *American Slavery*, 53–5), and it is presently practiced by organic agriculture. Locke apparently knew little about soil.

48. James Fenimore Cooper, *The Redskins, or Indian and Injin* (New York: Burgess & Stringer, 1846), vol. 1, 244.

49. Nelson, *Commons Democracy*, 168. Thomas Paine suggests a land inheritance tax and limitation of inheritance in *Agrarian Justice* (1796). The speaker's "leap-year" theory is the ancient Hebrew concept of Jubilee, promoting the cyclical liberation of slaves and redistribution of property (Book of Leviticus 25: 8–13; Ezekiel 46:17).

50. Colin G. Calloway, *Pen and Ink Witchcraft: Treaties and Treaty Making in American Indian History* (Oxford University Press, 2013).

51. Cooper, *Redskins*, vol. 2, 208.

52. Nelson, *Commons Democracy*, 138.

53. Nelson, *Commons Democracy*, 157–8.

54. Nelson, *Commons Democracy*, 177.

55. Amy Kaplan describes the "anarchy of empire" integral to much nineteenth-century American literature as "the breakdown or defiance of the monolithic system of order that empire aspires to impose on the world," an order built on dualisms such as domestic v. foreign. Empire, she argues, tries in vain to domesticate this anarchy, e.g. by articulating it in the language of haunting, but it is potentially "a figure of empire's undoing" (*Anarchy*, 13). The imaginative breakdown of hegemonic social constructs is of course a general potential of literature as described by various critics, among them M. M. Bakhtin and Pierre Macherey.

56. Cooper, *Chainbearer*, 86.

57. Cooper, *Chainbearer*, 90.

58. Cooper, *Chainbearer*, 94.

59. Cooper, *Chainbearer*, 97.

60. Cooper, *Chainbearer*, 127.

61. Cooper, *Chainbearer*, 255.

62. Cooper, *Redskins*, 176, 218, 213.

63. Cooper, *Redskins*, 218.

64. Cooper, *Chainbearer*, 77.

65. Edward Coote Pinkney, "The Indian's Bride," in *The Miscellaneous Poems of Edward Coate Pinkney* (New York: Morris, Willis & Co., 1844), 3–4.

66. Nelson, *Commons Democracy*, 166.

67. The liaison, like the one in Pinkney's poem, has an anarchistic ring by its embracement of voluntary kinship and its defiance of existing hierarchies.

68. Cooper toys with transcultural love relations in *The Last of the Mohicans* (1826) and *The Wept of Wish-ton-Wish* (1829), but makes both end tragically.

69. Cheyfitz, "Savage Law," 117–18, 124–5.

70. Mark Rifkin, *When Did Indians Become Straight? Kinship, the History of Sexuality, and Sovereignty* (Oxford University Press, 2011), 45–98.

71. Abby L. Goode explores the "whiteness" and eugenics discourse of nineteenth-century agrarian utopian communities in *Agrotopias: An American Literary History of Sustainability* (Chapel Hill: University of North Carolina Press, 2022).

72. Jean M. O'Brien, *Firsting and Lasting: Writing Indians out of Existence in New England* (Minneapolis: University of Minnesota Press, 2010).

73. William Dean Howells, *A Traveler from Altruria* (1894; reprint Boston: Bedford St. Martin's Press, 1996).

74. Charlotte Perkins Gilman, *Herland* (1915; reprint London: Vintage, 2015).

75. Fredric Jameson, *The Seeds of Time* (New York: Columbia University Press, 1994), xii.

CHAPTER 5

Manifestly Queer Domesticity
Empire and Nineteenth-Century Queer Fiction
Rafael Walker

The meteoric, if overdue, rise of empire studies in the last decades has taught scholars across disciplines to detect imperial thinking beyond the obvious places. Empire is no longer just a facet of political discourse; we've learned to see it, too, as an all-pervading force infiltrating even the crevices of intimate life. This broadened perspective is in no small measure thanks to Amy Kaplan's pioneering scholarship on empire. One of its chief contributions was to demonstrate that prevailing conceptions of nineteenth-century American domesticity, seemingly the most private of institutions, operated in the service of the nation's acquisitive enterprise to expand its territory and influence.

As Kaplan demonstrates, domesticity, coded in the nineteenth century as the separate sphere of women, abetted empire by providing it a moral foundation. "Domestic discourse," she suggests, "both redressed and reenacted the anarchic qualities of empire through its own double move-ment: to expand female influence beyond the home and the nation, and simultaneously to contract woman's sphere to that of policing domestic boundaries against the threat of foreignness."[1] Central to the first of domesticity's double movements in this context is the way it worked to "efface all traces of violent conflict" in the making of empire by bringing the aggressive, acquisitive energies associated with striving white male colonizers under the tempering influence of white women in the home – a harmonious conjunction of public with private. This dynamic, Kaplan shows, played out in domestic fiction of the mid-nineteenth century in novel after novel, most notably Susan Warner's *The Wide, Wide World* (1850) and Maria Susanna Cummins's *The Lamplighter* (1854).[2]

While Kaplan is everywhere alert to the gendered and racial dimensions of domesticity's relation to empire, she takes for granted that this relation is structurally heterosexual. This feature of Kaplan's study is attributable, no doubt, to the paucity of queer fiction readily available at the time of her study. With the benefit of recent literary discoveries from the nineteenth century, we are now equipped to broaden our understanding of the impact of imperial thinking on literature.[3] Many writers, as this chapter shows, used the affordances of this apparently heterosexual imperial paradigm to carve out space for lives and desires otherwise considered deviant or unspeakable. In so doing, these authors exceed the ideological standpoints that most cultural historians of empire recognize. For example, in a study of empire that self-consciously consigns queer people more or less to the footnotes, John Carlos Rowe identifies three such standpoints: (1) supportive of empire, (2) opposed to it, and (3) "divided between obligations to a certain national consensus and ... outrage at specific failures of U.S. democracy."[4] But there are writers who do not fall into (or refuse to stay in) these neatly divided categories. Moreover, these particular nineteenth-century authors, when writing about marginalized people, traffic less in the pernicious kinds of "internal colonialism" discussed by many scholars. If, for more orthodox writers of the era, domestic-imperial discourse helped to exclude groups understood as foreign from the national home, as Kaplan and others have argued, that same discourse helped writers depicting queer lives to weave their sexually nonconforming subjects into the national fabric.

I begin this investigation with a central and familiar figure in the queer history of nineteenth-century American letters, Walt Whitman. Of Whitman's much-celebrated poetics of same-sex desire, we know a great deal. However, given fiction's ostensibly greater compatibility with the discourse of "manifest domesticity," it is not surprising that Whitman's narrative work, though far less esteemed, would prove a site more suitable for examining his queer improvisation with imperial-domestic discourse.[5] Whitman's little-known short story of 1841, "The Child's Champion," is exemplary in this respect. A story initially so scandalous that Whitman would later feel compelled to revise it – motivated, perhaps, by personal trauma[6] – "The Child's Champion" focuses on Charles, a young boy living with his widowed mother but spending most of his waking hours apprenticed to an abusive master, Mr. Ellis, described as "a soulless gold-worshipper."[7] While midcentury domestic ideology imagined children under the authority of strong mothers in loving homes, the story calculatedly alienates Charles from both his mother and his home. The problem is not that his mother does not love him; it's that she, widowed and indigent, lacks the means to provide for him and direct his life. As he returns home for lunch at the story's beginning, for example,

> Tears started in the widow's eyes. She dared not trust herself with a reply, though her heart was bursting with the thought that she could not better his condition. There was no earthly means of support on which she had dependence enough to encourage her child in the wish she knew was coming; the wish – not uttered for the first time – to be freed from his bondage.[8]

In emphasizing the brokenness of Charles's home and impotence of his mother, the story at once casts the child adrift and exposes him to a world of alternative forms of kinship. In contrast to past readers – who, with scarce exception, concentrate overmuch on its eroticism – I view the rethinking of prevailing modes of affiliation as the story's primary concern. And this concern, I maintain, is inextricable from concerns about empire.

The convergence of empire with the story's exploration of alternative kinship comes into view immediately after the above-quoted dilemma besetting Charles's mother. In begging not to be sent back to Mr. Ellis, the child warns, "if I have to work there much longer, I know I shall run away, and go to sea, or somewhere else."[9] Charles is, of course, coaxed into making his way back to Mr. Ellis's, but the story interrupts this itinerary to sketch the implications of his threat to go to sea, as Whitman's own brother, Jesse, had done earlier.[10] En route to Mr. Ellis's, he stops at a public house, drawn in not to drink – having promised his mother always to abstain – but by childish curiosity about the merriment inside. The place brims with sailors, the very roughnecks whose numbers he had just warned of joining if forced to remain in Mr. Ellis's service. But these nautical roughnecks, contemptible though they appear, were essential to nineteenth-century America's effort to situate itself in an imperial relation to the world. Endlessly roving in search of new lands and riches while defending their nations' borders, sailors are the nineteenth-century's prime embodiments of the aggressive, masculine energies of empire.[11] The rollicking mirth of one particular sailor in the bunch, a one-eyed and very loud man, morphs into just such aggression when Charles declines a drink proffered. However, as Michael Moon has shown most amply, the one-eyed sailor's confrontation is not simply abrasive but distinctly erotic, delivered "in terms that sound as much like an order to fellate him as an offer to drink."[12] The bar scene is awash in erotic references to liquids and injunctions to sup: "curse me if you shant have a suck at my expense," "a goodly amount of fluid was spilled upon the floor," "blast my eyes if he shant go down on his marrow bones and gobble up the rum we've spilt," and so forth.[13]

It would be ridiculous to try to portray the flamboyant Walt Whitman as some prig sheepish about frank expressions of sexuality. After all, he would stage a scene not dissimilar to the one above in section 11 of his masterpiece poem *Song of Myself* (1855), in which twenty-eight male bathers frolic in orgiastic abandon and "think not whom they souse with spray."[14] In the case of "The Child's Champion," though, Whitman, exploiting the prudish domestic discourse of his day, associates the sailor's excessive eroticism with a kind of affiliation no healthier than an inert home or a punishing apprenticeship. A mother's love without money or power, a master's discipline without love, a sailor's pleasure seeking without moral anchor – each of these options is ruled out in its turn.

Whither, then, the child? Enter his champion, John Lankton, the enigmatic stranger in the corner of the public house who forcibly rescues Charles from the clutches of the one-eyed sailor. Although Lankton and Charles are strangers, the story characterizes the former's compulsion to intervene as deriving from an instinct toward eros: "he felt that he should love him."[15] Notably, just after revealing Lankton's personal feelings, the narrator shifts abruptly to an appeal to the reader, a paean to universal love too mawkish to quote at length here. This is a move straight out of the playbook of the woman-dominated genre of sentimental fiction inundating the literary market of Whitman's day, which strove, in large part, to improve readers through eliciting their sympathy. Yet, curiously, Whitman disavows this connection, grumbling, "No scrap is this of sentimental fiction; ask your own heart, reader, and your own memory, for endorsement to its truth."[16]

The key to that paradox is this: Whitman wanted to have his cake and eat it, too – to have same-sex desire both recognized *and* sanctioned. On the one hand, the sentimental mode and the domestic discourse from which it arose provided a morally safe cover for Whitman to enact this illicit melodrama of intergenerational, same-sex love. On the other, by explicitly distancing his story from a literary tradition routinely panned for its excesses, its distortions of the emotions, he implores readers to take this transgressive union seriously. In other words, Whitman cannily exploits the "cult of domesticity" to transmute sex – the sordid behavior we observe in the appetitive sailors – into its sanitized, socially permissible analogue: intimacy. This hybrid strategy is most succinctly displayed when, as the pair lies together in Lankton's bed, an angel – a male angel, significantly – enters the room and blesses the union by kissing each of them on the lips. The highly conventional *angelus ex machina* papers over the highly unconventional detail that they "slumbered there in each other's arms."[17] At work here is the logic of Kaplan's "manifest domesticity": just as an idealized woman's sphere sublimates unruly masculine energies, the feminized conventions of sentimental fiction sanctify this otherwise obscene episode.

We find the logic of empire operating elsewhere in a fashion more recognizably consonant with the era's domestic discourse: in the transformation of Charles and Lankton. Hitherto Lankton, though a man of means, had been "a dissipated young man – a brawler – one whose too frequent companions were rowdies, black-legs, and swindlers."[18] In keeping with nineteenth-century domestic ideology, his waywardness is imputed to his corrupted home life: he is "parentless," and "he had no one to attract him to his home."[19] In Whitman's queer adaptation of this ideology, after the annexation of Charles to his life, "he enjoyed his home, and loved to be there," exchanging his dissipated lifestyle for something more wholesome.[20] That this something more wholesome is an intimate life with another male is Whitman's Trojan horse, his smuggling in of a celebration of same-sex love under the cover of nineteenth-century sentimental conventions. Further in line with the logic of empire, the transformation of Lankton is not so much predicated upon eradicating all aggressive urges in him; no, as his violent defense of Charles from the sailors suggests, it's about rerouting those urges to more productive channels – the protection of the domestic sphere.

It might be tempting to construe this relationship as exploitive, as one critic has, by focusing on the power imbalance seemingly inevitable in an intergenerational relationship of this kind.[21] But such a cynical interpretation necessarily overlooks the fact that Charles is no less the beneficiary of this union – not only in that his material conditions are improved through Lankton's largesse but also in that he, too, is redeemed from vice. (Recall Charles's earlier threat to go to sea – the result, we have seen, of his dysfunctional home life.)

The nitty-gritty details of this male pair's future together are strategically suppressed, the narrator declaring, "It needs not to particularize the subsequent events of Lankton's and the boy's history," yet he alludes to these auspicious developments:

> How the reformation of the profligate might be dated to begin from that time; how he gradually severed the guilty ties that had so long galled him – how he enjoyed his own home, and loved to be there, and why he loved to be there; how the close knit love of the boy and him grew not slack with time; and how, when at length he became ahead of a family of his own, he would shudder when he thought of his early danger and escape.[22]

Whitman's focus on the propitious effects of their union, without disclosure of the presumably indelicate means through which those effects are brought about, coalesces provocatively with the final lines' cryptically enjoining readers to draw out the moral of the story for themselves. To accept that they are both reformed is to accept that their love reformed each other. And to concede that fact is to concede the legitimacy of same-sex desire – and in the very terms structured by a heterosexual discourse derived from the needs of empire building.

Indeed, Whitman treats the relationship between Charlie and Lankton as a healthy training ground for heterosexual marriage, gesturing toward a happy domestic life for Lankton as a "head of family" following his time with his young ward and possibly (though not certainly) for the young ward as well. This too conforms to and yet queers the logic of manifest domesticity, which separates its own imperial training grounds from the domestic hearth that renders them innocent.[23] We might regard the dalliance enjoyed by Charlie and Lankton as the male correlate of the common phenomenon among women at the time famously characterized by Carole Smith-Rosenberg as "the female world of love and ritual" – an emotionally, sometimes sexually, charged homosocial environment in which adolescents of the same sex prepared for heterosexual life in a society intensely segregated by gender.[24]

About forty years later, Bret Harte would write a story about same-sex desire similar to Whitman's. Though published in 1895, Harte's "In the Tules" is set, like "The Child's Champion," in the antebellum US – only in Gold Rush–era California rather than Long Island. In light of this retrograde historical setting and Harte's choice of a nomadic frontiersman for his protagonist, it seems likely that the author was seeking to place his story about same-sex love within the seemingly safer, more innocent context of westward expansion – that dreamy period in American history that Americans already had begun nostalgically romanticizing by Harte's time. In so doing, Harte was able to draw more fully on that epoch's domestic discourse, which, as we have seen, served Whitman similarly as he attempted to render in more socially acceptable terms what otherwise would have been condemnable material.

The story's main character is Martin Morse, an archetype of the hundreds of lone frontiersmen peopling California during the Gold Rush. The language of empire suffuses Harte's description: his arrival at a bay of the Sacramento River is "the *ultima thule* of his journeyings"; "the land would be his by discovery and occupation"; he is said to possess "the roving instincts of the frontier-man."[25] For all his roving instincts, however,

Morse is also conspicuously domestic, as we learn very early in the story, when the narrator explains that Morse "convert[s] his halted wagon into a temporary cabin," where "he resolved to rest and . . . 'settle.'"[26] It would appear, from Harte's scare quotes, that he is punning on the word *settle*, employing a double entendre combining the domesticity-inflected meaning of the word (as in "to settle down") with its empire-inflected one (as in "to settle new territory").

It's not long before we discover that Morse also is in the market for someone to settle down with. With only his oxen for company, he is lonely, his sole communion with the human world the affluent revelers aboard the steamship that passes his settlement in the distance. Despite his concern that his rustic lack of sophistication would unfit him for socializing with that crowd, Morse nonetheless watches for the steamship with an obsessive longing. "He watched it the next night and the next," we're told; "Hereafter he never missed it, coming or going – whatever the hard and weary preoccupations of his new and lonely life."[27] Suddenly, one night, the world of the steamship crashes into his, in the form of a murdered sheriff washed ashore along with, as we later learn, the sheriff's murderer. The latter, who introduces himself pseudonymously as Captain Jack, inspires immediately in Morse "complete fascination."[28] Harte is strikingly unsubtle in characterizing this fascination as erotic, continuing his description of the encounter with the following passage:

> [Morse] found himself shyly pleased with even the slight interest he had displayed in his affairs, and his hand felt yet warm and tingling from his sudden soft, but expressive grasp, as if it had been a woman's. There is a simple intuition of friendship in some lonely, self-abstracted natures that is nearly akin to love at first sight. Even the audacities and insolence of this stranger affected Morse as he might have been touched and captivated by the coquetries or imperiousness of some bucolic virgin.[29]

It is worth noting the way that Harte tempers this provocative description. The narrator briefly exchanges his more risqué register for universalizing generality in order to normalize what risked appearing aberrant: two men in "love at first sight." This sentence would have been easily at home in Whitman's "The Child's Champion," and the consonance between the tactics of these two writers, separated by two generations, is important. Remember how Whitman calls in the angel in order to give divine sanction to Charlie and Lankton's union and divine distraction from the fact that these two men are sharing a bed, likely engaged in much more than friendly chitchat. Similarly, Harte cuts the eyebrow-raising pair of similes for Morse and Captain Jack's first encounter – in which the latter is likened first to a woman and finally to a "bucolic virgin" – with a hyper-generalizing and sanitizing sentence about friendship. Later, Harte's narrator goes on to conflate all the terms: "Friendship and love – and, for the matter of that, religion – are eminently one-ideaed," each, for Harte, one side of the same coin.[30]

There are also significant differences between Whitman's story and Harte's. The most salient is the latter's tragic ending, which is partly linked to the fact that Harte does not portray the relationship between his two male characters as preliminary to a normative heterosexual one. While, as in Whitman's story, the same-sex relationship proves ennobling for both characters – we're told, for example, that Morse is inspired to work harder "that it might make him more worthy of his friend" – the improvement that each strives after is wholly for the other man, not for some unspecified future wife and family.[31] In fact, such is their devotion that they die for each other. Happening upon the crowd poised to lynch Captain Jack for murdering the sheriff earlier in the story, Morse hurls himself at them and is quickly dispatched, shot in the heart, literally and figuratively, "his arms outstretched and his head at the doomed man's feet."[32] Although observing Morse's sacrifice moves the mob to the point where it seems they're disposed to show Captain Jack clemency, Captain Jack spurns them, flinging out "a curse so awful and sweeping" as to nullify any pity he might have earned. He is killed, and, in recognition of their mutual devotion, the mob of men bury Morse and Captain Jack together in a single grave.[33]

One might be moved to interpret Harte's decision to give this love story a tragic ending as his ultimately retreating from the more scandalous or more radical implications that he has raised. But, if he backpedaled, we can hardly blame him. Unlike Whitman, Harte was writing at a time that, thanks to psychoanalysis, was learning to understand same-sex intercourse as comprising an identity rather than a behavior – as part of who someone was rather than as something a person did. Once named, homosexuality became more visible and therefore more prone to being stigmatized. An ending in which these two men lived happily ever after in gay bliss probably wouldn't have been published and, if published, might have landed Harte into serious trouble. More importantly, though, such an ending would have been terribly implausible. And one of the most valuable contributions of "In the Tules," I think, is the fact that it presses readers to ask why. Why couldn't two perfectly sane men who are devoted to and improve each other enjoy a fulfilling amorous relationship? As we ponder this question, it becomes increasingly clear that what makes their relationship inconceivable has little to do with them and virtually everything to do with the arbitrary heteronormative conventions on which both conceptions of the home and of the state are based. Harte at once persuades us to condemn these norms and to imagine that the world could be otherwise.

The intense gender-bending and male-male eroticism central to Harte's story is well-documented in the history of the American Western frontier. Although his characters' behaviors may not have obvious links to empire – occurring as they do entirely within the nation – the historical inflection points on which they rely make the connection between empire and the representation of queerness clearer. Literary critic Peter Stoneley, for example, notes, "Close and loving male-male relationships were not invented with the gold rush, but they became newly conspicuous against the otherwise grim background of a struggle for wealth."[34] As Kaplan's work has already established, the home functioned earlier in the nation's history as a check against the more antisocial urges associated with empire building. Harte applies that logic to home-building on the frontier and substitutes homosexual coupling for heterosexual coupling (much more difficult in a setting so overwhelmingly dominated by men). In so doing, not only does Harte elevate domesticity while tempering the acquisitiveness and violence associated with westward expansion (indeed, Morse is there to discover gold and had participated in "the Indian massacres"); he also uses the unusual social conditions of Gold Rush–era California to characterize homosexual love as having the same ameliorative potential that was widely attributed to heterosexual love – no matter that circumstances compelled Harte to treat such relationships as nonviable.

Harte was not the only writer at the end of the nineteenth century to extend domestic discourse to the Gold Rush, and neither was homosexuality the only queer practice that the opposition between frontiersman aggression and domesticity was used to vindicate. Harte's contemporary, Mary E. Wilkins Freeman, relied on this contrast to justify celibacy, which Benjamin Kahan's groundbreaking scholarship has taught us to view as "a coherent sexual identity."[35] Louisa Ellis, the titular character of one of Freeman's most famous short stories, "A New England Nun" (1891), offers a case in point. At the outset of this Gold Rush-related story, Louisa has spent the last fifteen years betrothed to a man who, a year after their engagement, left to pursue his fortunes in the mines of Australia. Joe Dagget has made good on his promise to "secure a competency" and now means to make good on his promise to Louisa.[36] But, of course, people change in fifteen years, and the protagonist has changed so drastically as to become wholly unfit for wedlock: "Louisa's feet had turned into a path, smooth maybe under a calm, serene sky, but so straight and unswerving that it could not meet a check at her grave, and so narrow that there was no room for any one at her side."[37]

Freeman foreshadows this fact earlier in the story, by the way she identifies Louisa so closely with her domestic environs. It's not simply that she is a fastidious housekeeper; she "could not remember that ever in her life she had mislaid one of these little feminine appurtenances, which had become, from long use and constant association, a very part of her personality."[38] In figuring the relationship between Louisa and her belongings in this intensely intimate fashion, Freeman exemplifies cultural theorist Bill Brown's thesis about subject–object relations in the period, according to which American authors of this time discovered more personal alternatives for conceiving of relations between people and things than the uninspiring terms afforded by capitalism.[39]

Such a charged conception of objects serves at least two narrative functions in "The New England Nun." First, it helps Freeman emphasize how utterly out of place Joe Dagget is in the life that Louisa has cultivated over the course of his long absence. Even before his character is sketched for us, we are presented with a punchy, three-sentence paragraph emphasizing his unsuitability for Louisa's home: "He filled up the whole room. A little canary that had been asleep in his green cage at the south window woke up and fluttered wildly, beating his little yellow wings against the wires. He always did so when Joe Dagget came into the room."[40] On his departure, she "swept Joe Dagget's track carefully," literally removing all traces of him from her sacrosanct haven.[41] Joe, for his part, feels no more welcome there than Louisa feels him invasive. Imagining himself "surrounded by a hedge of lace," Joe "was afraid to stir lest he should put a clumsy foot or hand through the fairy web."[42] Freeman's intimate construction of Louisa's home, in short, serves to mark it as a space where the aggressive, masculine forces that the gold-seeking Joe Dagget embodies have no place.

But this construction is also at least as much about what Louisa's life includes as it is about what it excludes. Bodied forth by Louisa's dog that, for fourteen years, has been kept tied to a chain for biting a stranger when a puppy, the story's moral is that one need not hold oneself in sober maturity to decisions made in the blush of youth. (Freeman, we must remember, would go on to separate legally from her own husband.) Besides this moral, Freeman's story, through its union of its protagonist with her domestic surroundings, suggests that celibacy can have a positive, even relational content. As Kahan has argued, it is not necessarily synonymous with asexuality or "a nonexperience or nonknowledge of sexuality."[43] It can be, as it is in this story, an informed decision, a preference for one sexual domain over another. Freeman makes it clear that this is her view of the matter with respect to Louisa. Joe Dagget is left free to pursue the "fairer and firmer" young woman possessing "just the qualities to arouse the admiration."[44] And Louisa is left with the "serenity and placid narrowness [that] had become to her as birthright itself."[45] Everybody wins.

Or do they? While Freeman has left little room to doubt whether Louisa Ellis will be content in her celibacy – figured as a deliberate choice that she has spent years practicing and settling into – it is not so clear whether Joe Dagget and his young bride will be able to establish a happy home. After all, Freeman suggests in her depiction of Joe that his masculine aggressiveness, while vital in the gold mines, is inimical to domesticity – that it tears the home apart like a bull in a china cabinet. Such a suggestion might register a shift in the culture's attitude toward manifest domesticity. For, if, earlier in the nineteenth century, men's and women's spheres were viewed as harmonious and complementary, they now are presented as mutually antagonistic.

A reorientation of this kind would comport with the increasingly popular opposition to imperial expansion that Amy Kaplan and many other scholars have identified in this generation of writers, which would come to a head as the nation approached the Spanish-American War of 1898. Even such literary luminaries as Mark Twain and William Dean Howells publicly opposed it. Howells deserves special mention here, for, in his short story "Editha" (1905), he crafts a plot in which the very gender dynamics celebrated in the nineteenth century result in domestic disaster.[46] In brief, the protagonist's warped understanding of war as heroic and patriotic leads her to persuade her main suitor to join the budding war effort; in fact, she makes it a condition of her hand. He enlists and is slain ingloriously in the first skirmish. To make matters worse, in the end, we learn that Editha's mind has been so deformed by the culture's inveterate idealization of violence – evident in the discourse of manifest domesticity and its sublimation of harm – that not even his needless death alters her views.

It is difficult not to wonder whether this repudiation of masculine aggression explains why one of Freeman's happiest fictional households is shared by two women, the protagonists of her 1887 story "Two Friends."[47] Or why, in Sarah Orne Jewett's 1886 short story "A White Heron," her main character, Sylvia, would ultimately reject the attentions and the financial bribe of the handsome hunter who seeks her beloved bird – beginning the opposition between feminine nurture and masculine avarice that she would elaborate in her novel *A Country of Pointed Firs* (1896).[48]

As I have tried to sketch here, the history of the American queer short story reveals a dynamic relationship between queer domesticity and empire: if, earlier in the century, imperial thinking provided an opening for writers to insert queer lives into the national imaginary, by the turn of the century, queer forms of affiliation seem to provide the antidote to much of the viciousness of empire.

Even in its queerest form, however, nineteenth-century representations of domesticity do scarcely better at concealing the racism propelling empire and underpinning the construction of American identity. After all, is it not "Black Dave" whose racialized siren's song lures the child of Whitman's story into the licentious pub when he should instead be on his way back to work?[49] According to Amy Kaplan, the nation's ruling class in the nineteenth century feared that the "incorporation of alien races would introduce a kind of anarchy into the unity of the nation."[50] In light of Kaplan's observations about race and empire, what at first seems little more than a casual instance of nineteenth-century racism becomes something more deeply structural. Black Dave is depicted as a Svengali who beguiles white men from labor and into wanton unproductivity. Though his presence in the story is dim and short-lived, the threat that he represents is made representative and – since Dave belongs to a whole "race whose fondness for melody is so well known" – anything but isolated.[51] If it seems that I am making too much of this peripheral figure, consider how easy it would have been for Whitman to make Dave white (perhaps one of the sailors) in a story where everyone else is white.

As Dave demonstrates, caricatures of black people and other nonwhite groups helped to establish the need for the conjunction of empire with domesticity, the implication in Whitman's story being that good homes will keep white men on the straight-and-narrow – on, that is, their way to work. Moreover, the "Indian massacres" in which Harte's protagonist had been engaged before meeting Captain Jack—atrocities receiving only passing mention in the story—are shadowy reminders of the violence inhering in any act of settling, including settling down. Are these nineteenth-century writers revolutionary for depicting queer lives in a world where heterosexuality was so entrenched that it didn't even require a name? Certainly. But they also demonstrate how efforts at inclusion can end up replicating some of the most heinous exclusions of the very paradigms that those well-intentioned efforts were meant to combat.

Notes

1. Amy Kaplan, *The Anarchy of Empire in the Making of US Culture* (Cambridge: Harvard University Press, 2005), 28.
2. Susan Warner, *The Wide, Wide World* (New York: The Feminist Press, 1989); Maria Susanna Cummins, *The Lamplighter* (New Brunswick: Rutgers University Press, 1988).
3. Christopher Looby's 2017 collection of queer short stories from the American nineteenth century, for example, brings to light a stunning array of hitherto forgotten fictional accounts of queer life from the era. To that volume, cited repeatedly, this chapter is deeply indebted.
4. John Carlos Rowe, *Literary Culture and US Imperialism: From the Revolution to World War II* (New York: Oxford University Press, 2000), x.
5. Although scholars of domestic ideology are rarely explicit about the generic constraints of their work, of why they focus on fiction rather than, say, poetry, one can infer that they are drawn to the distinct capacity for fiction to create certain cause-and-effect relations through its storytelling, such relations being requisite to the formation of ideology. John Carlos Rowe's note about the generic parameters of his study helps to illustrate this point: "in the history of modern US culture, a wide variety of prose genres are used both to justify and challenge the dominant hierarchies of the national mythology" (14).
6. Whitman biographer David S. Reynolds unearthed an alleged scandal of the same year that "The Child's Champion" involving Whitman and one or more boys while he was teaching in the small Long Island town of Southold. Rumor has it that Whitman had inappropriate relations with the children – which might have included sharing a bed, a fact directly relevant to this short story – and was consequently run out of town tarred and feathered. See David S. Reynolds, "Dark Passages: Teaching and Early Authorship", in Reynolds's *Walt Whitman's America: A Cultural Biography* (New York: Knopf, 1995), 52–80.
7. Walt Whitman, "The Child's Champion," in *"The Man Who Thought Himself a Woman" and Other Queer Nineteenth-Century Short Stories*, ed. Christopher Looby (Philadelphia: University of Pennsylvania Press, 2017), 5.
8. Whitman, "The Child's Champion," 4.
9. Whitman, "The Child's Champion," 4.
10. As Whitman scholars have noted, Jesse Whitman's departure from the family for seafaring deeply affected Whitman. The experience ruined Jesse, so much so that "Whitman subsequently committed [him] to an insane asylum, without any obvious remorse." See Vivian Pollak, *The Erotic Whitman* (Berkeley: University of California Press, 2000), 95.
11. Ishmael, the first-person narrator of Herman Melville's *Moby-Dick* (1851), alludes to the way the closing of the frontier led the enterprising men once involved in westward expansion to seafaring when he refers to "Vermonters and New Hampshire men, all athirst for gain and glory in the fishery . . . who have felled forests, and now seek to drop the axe and snatch the whale-lance."

See Herman Melville, *Moby-Dick*. 3rd ed., ed. Herschel Parker (New York: Norton & Co., 2018), 38.

12. Michael Moon, *Disseminating Whitman: Revision and Corporeality in* Leaves of Grass (Cambridge: Harvard University Press, 1993), 27–8.

13. Whitman, "Child's Champion," 6–7.

14. Walt Whitman, "Song of Myself," in Leaves of Grass *and Other Writings*, ed. Michael Moon (New York: W.W. Norton & Co.), 34.

15. Whitman, "Child's Champion," 8.

16. Whitman, "Child's Champion," 8.

17. Whitman, "Child's Champion," 11.

18. Whitman, "Child's Champion," 10.

19. Whitman, "Child's Champion," 10–11.

20. Whitman, "Child's Champion," 12.

21. Attempting to place the many varieties of nineteenth-century American temperance fiction – including Whitman's – on an oscillating continuum between empowerment and patriarchal exploitation, Karen Sánchez-Eppler argues, "In these stories, children may prove effective disciplinary agents, but, in reforming their fathers, they do not empower themselves." Yet, as I try to make clear above, I do not think it possible to read Charles as anything but empowered in the reciprocal loving relationship he enters with Lankton. To read the story as Sánchez-Eppler does requires overlooking both Charles's maleness and, concomitantly, the danger of degeneration he faced in the absence of a nurturing home. See Karen Sánchez-Eppler, "Temperance in the Bed of a Child: Incest and Social Order in Nineteenth-Century America," *American Quarterly* 47.1 (1995): 25.

22. Whitman, "Child's Champion," 12.

23. The 1861 novel *Cecil Dreeme* – whose modern publishers tout as "one of the queerest American novels of the nineteenth century" – similarly characterizes gay sex as a preliminary to maturity. According to Travis M. Foster, "While at the beginning of the novel Robert Byng begs off "Young Americanism," asking for opportunity to mature "before you expect a man's work of me," we're meant, by the novel's end, to see his near liberation from desire for either Densdeth or Emma Denman as evidence of having accomplished just that (ch. 1). This novel is, in no small sense, the coming of age of the white queer as Young American." See Travis M. Foster, "The Queer Young American Comes of Age." *Commonplace: The Journal of Early American Life*. http://commonplace.online/article/the-queer-young-american-comes-of-age/.

24. Carroll Smith-Rosenberg, "The Female World of Love and Ritual: Relations between Women in Nineteenth-Century America," *Signs* 1.1 (1975).

25. Bret Harte, "In the Tules," in *"The Man Who Thought Himself a Woman" and Other Queer Nineteenth-Century Short Stories*, 185–6.

26. Harte, "In the Tules," 185.

27. Harte, "In the Tules," 187.

28. Harte, "In the Tules," 191.

29. Harte, "In the Tules," 191.
30. Harte, "In the Tules," 199.
31. Harte, "In the Tules," 194.
32. Harte, "In the Tules," 202.
33. Harte, "In the Tules," 202.
34. Peter Stoneley, "Rewriting the Gold Rush: Twain, Harte and Homosociality," *Journal of American Studies* 30.2 (1996): 192.
35. Ranging from the nineteenth century to the twentieth, Kahan's *Celibacies: American Modernism and Sexual Life* works to distinguish celibacy as a coherent sexual identity in a field of other kinds of sexual identities, with which celibacy is often confused, sometimes treated as a cover for those other identities. Although Kahan does not discuss Freeman's story, I understand it as fully exemplifying his argument. See Benjamin Kahan, *Celibacies: American Modernism and Sexual Life* (Durham: Duke University Press, 2013), 2.
36. Mary E. Wilkins Freeman, "The New England Nun," in *The Norton Anthology of American Literature*. Shorter 9th ed., eds. Robert Levine et al. (New York: Norton & Co., 2017), 463.
37. Freeman, "The New England Nun," 463.
38. Freeman, "The New England Nun," 460–1.
39. See Bill Brown, *A Sense of Things: The Object Matter of American Literature* (Chicago: University of Chicago Press, 2003). Decades earlier, Herman Melville published a story in which normal subject-object relations had shifted too far in the other direction. Rather than subjects dominating objects, "I and My Chimney" (1856) features a first-person narrator who has become enthralled to an object to the point of pathology. Despite the syntax of the title, the narrator insists that "my chimney tak[es] precedence of me" (225). Such moments as the following reveal that things have gotten out of hand: "In vain my wife – with what probable ulterior intent will, ere long, appear – solemnly warned me, that unless something were done speedily, we should be burnt to the ground, owing to the holes crumbling through the aforesaid blotchy parts, where the chimney joined the roof. 'Wife,' said I, 'far better that my house should burn down, than that my chimney should be pulled down, though but a few feet'" (230). This unusual relationship between a man and his belongings, while surely queer, is presented in a light less favorable than the more mutualistic, less obsessive relationship existing between Louisa Ellis and her domestic world. See Herman Melville, "I and My Chimney," in *"The Man Who Thought Himself a Woman" and Other Queer Nineteenth-Century Short Stories*, 225 and 230, respectively.
40. Freeman, "New England Nun," 461.
41. Freeman, "New England Nun," 463.
42. Freeman, "New England Nun," 463.
43. Kahan, *Celibacies*, 13.
44. Freeman, "New England Nun," 467.
45. Freeman, "New England Nun," 468.

46. William Dean Howells, "Editha," in *The Norton Anthology of American Literature.*

47. Mary E. Wilkins Freeman, "Two Friends," in *"The Man Who Thought Himself a Woman" and Other Queer Nineteenth-Century Short Stories.*

48. Sarah Orne Jewett, "A White Heron," in *The Norton Anthology of American Literature*; Sarah Orne Jewett, The Country of Pointed Firs *and Other Stories* (New York: Signet Classics, 2009).

49. Whitman, "Child's Champion," 5.

50. Kaplan, *Anarchy*, 7.

51. Whitman, "Child's Champion," 5–6.

CHAPTER 6

Herman, or the Ambiguities
Melville, US Imperialism, and the Participant Critic

Emilio Irigoyen

Both Melville's writings and their rich critical afterlife hold a central place in discussions of US literature and empire. His works project and question deep imperial assumptions about the role of his country in the world. Across his oeuvre, a full range of attitudes, actions, and events, tied to US expansionism, neocolonialism, and imperial interventionism, appear to be the object of withering analysis as well as a motif for exultant celebration – a varied, ambiguous and, at times, seemingly contradictory approach that has led to a wide range of interpretations. The history of this criticism, in turn, has uniquely reflected the changing racial and colonial imagination of both US scholarly discourse and society at large. After briefly reviewing this critical history, this chapter approaches Melville's complicated engagement with US imperialism from several angles, first by exploring how the opacity of otherness undermines the imperial self and then by examining the rhetorical and ideological ambiguities of some of his most prominent comments on US empire. To address these ambiguities, and sometimes outright contradictions, we must also examine Melville's own direct involvement in US interventionism. This chapter argues that doing so may not only illuminate the role of Melville criticism in the long history of empire, but also situate the contemporary critical moment within that history and recognize that the critic can also be a participant in this narrative.

Imperial and Anti-imperial Melville: A Critical History

The history of Melville's reception is famous for its variability. Critical readings of US imperialism in his works have been similarly fluctuant. Early commentators tended to accept Melville's narrators at face value when they celebrate the exceptionalism of the US, its Manifest Destiny of expansion, and the virtues of its interventions abroad – be they orchestrated by private enterprises or military interventions.[1] Melville's work was often perceived, either explicitly or indirectly, as a literary manifest-ation of US moral, political, or cultural superiority and a celebration of the nation's commanding role in the world. One reader who viewed it this way was Rudyard Kipling. His poem "The White Man's Burden," one of the most famous literary glorifications of imperialism in the nineteenth-century, appears to have been inspired by a passage from *White-Jacket* (1850).

While addressing one of the novel's main issues, flogging in the US Navy, Melville's narrator contends that this practice is contrary to the nation's very identity: "we Americans are the peculiar, chosen people – the Israel of our time; we bear the ark of the liberties of the world." At this point in Melville's text, the argument against flogging sailors on US ships transforms into one for world domination, with the narrator claiming that the USA, like Israel, "was given an express dispensation":

> God has given to us, for a future inheritance, the broad domains of the political pagans, that shall yet come and lie down under the shade of our ark, without bloody hands being lifted. . . . The rest of the nations must soon be in our rear. We are the pioneers of the world; the advance-guard, sent on through the wilderness of untried things, to break a new path in the New World that is ours.[2]

The USA has the duty to forge paths in that world because of the nation's unique, exceptional condition. It must do it, the narrator contends, because no one else can. This is at the core of Kipling's text: it is the "burden" to which it refers. We know that *White-Jacket* was on Kipling's mind – and most likely on his desk – in the two periods when he composed the poem. "The White Man's Burden" originated as a piece for Queen Victoria's 1897 Jubilee, but Kipling soon abandoned it. In the latter half of 1898, shortly after the conclusion of the US-Spanish War, he returned to it and reframed it as an argument in favor of the US annexation of the Philippines; the final version includes this subtitle: "The United States and the Philippine Islands."[3] During this period, Kipling made two trips with the Channel Squadron of the Royal Navy and chronicled them in *A Fleet in Being*, a first-hand account of navy life that quotes *White-Jacket* as its closest literary source.[4] In September of 1898, while he was working on *A Fleet*, Kipling wrote to the future President Theodore Roosevelt, urging him to "put all the weight of your influence into hanging on permanently to the whole Philippines."[5] In November, (the same month *A Fleet* was serialized), he followed up by sending Roosevelt "The White Man's Burden."[6] The poem's organizing motif, in its final version, is the notion of colonial expansion as a mandate imposed on the USA, much the same as in the passage from *White-Jacket*. While Melville's narrator presents this in religious terms (God's design, in the form of a "future inheritance"), Kipling's turn-of-the-century text grounds it in the positivist notion of bringing progress and civilization to the backward peoples of the world, but he keeps Melville's biblical reference: the story of Israel escaping from Egypt,[7] which is used in both texts to depict imperialism as a source of freedom.

After the "Melville Revival" of the 1920s, scholarly production in the US departed from the kind of nineteenth-century imperialist readings exemplified by Kipling's use of the passage quoted above. By the mid-twentieth century, amid rising authoritarianism and World War II, Melville began to embody the literary expression of US democratic endeavors and their beneficent effects on the world. However, this new image still retained an aura of exceptionalism and superiority, which would be employed in various ways from the post–World War II era until the end of the Cold War.[8] F. O. Matthiessen's 1941 *American Renaissance*, which was written in part as a US response to European totalitarianism and was key in the development of the field of US (or "American") literary studies, was instrumental in establishing this new reading, in part by contrasting a totalitarian Ahab with a democratic Ishmael in *Moby-Dick*. Like most critics would do until the 1980s, Matthiessen focused on Melville's liberal and progressive passages while ignoring others, such as the one that caught Kipling's attention. At one point, for example, Matthiessen quotes Ishmael's claim that the "peaceful influence" of whaling "eventuated the liberation of Peru, Chili, and Bolivia from the yoke of Old Spain, and the establishment of the eternal democracy in those parts."[9] Yet he does not mention Ishmael's remark, made a few chapters earlier, that the USA would follow the War against Mexico by conquering other neighboring lands and, potentially, annexing the whole continent.[10]

Many scholars have examined the ways in which the institution of Melville as an epitome of the national genius was coextensive with the consolidation and legitimization of the national scholarly field of US literary studies at the outset of what would become known as "Americanism," the ideological and discursive fabric that, in both conscious and unconscious ways, would hold together a number of notions about the country's identity and its outsized role in the world. William V. Spanos goes so far as to claim that

> nothing in the history of [US] American cultural production and consumption can teach us more about the ideological operations of canon formation

in general and the formation of the American canon in particular than the apparently erratic history of the reception of the texts of a writer whose *raison d'être* ... was to interrogate the relationship between cultural monuments and sociopolitical power.[11]

Spanos argues that the rehabilitation of Melville and especially *Moby-Dick* by the pre–Cold War critics "was a symptomatic manifestation of the achievement of the hegemony of the [US] American *anthropologos:* the Emersonian principle of 'self-reliance' or, more precisely, 'central man,' which, in the name of 'American' freedom, was ultimately intended to domesticate the threat of resistance by a multiplicity of 'alien' subject positions against the dominant sociopolitical order."[12] Throughout the age running from the 1920s revival to mid-century "Americanism," critics usually took Melville to be the exemplar of a US democratic spirit that was necessarily interventionist yet never imperial in nature.

During the countercultural decade of the 1960s, however, some critics began to recognize a more skeptical, less nationalist Melville in the references to racism and colonialism appearing in many of his works. This initiated what Andrew Lawson has described as "the critical effort to rehabilitate Melville as an anti-imperialist."[13] A major antecedent to this is C. L. R. James' 1953 *Mariners, Renegades, and Castaways: The Story of Herman Melville and the World We Live In* (a book the Caribbean critic wrote while awaiting deportation), although James's focus is on race and class rather than empire.[14] The recognition of Melville's critique of racism and imperialism would solidify in the 1980s, bolstered in part by studies of "Benito Cereno";[15] in that decade, it became common, for the first time, to perceive in the novella "a critique of racism that now seems quite evident"[16] and that has dominated scholarship on "Benito Cereno" ever since. By the late 1990s, a critical consensus had firmly established Melville as one of the most formidable critics of both racism and imperialism in the antebellum canon.[17] This remains the standard critical view.[18] And while this chapter largely aligns with this perspective, it focuses on the ambiguities and contradictions of Melville's scriptural engagement with imperialism. As many critics have argued, the ostensible celebrations of US superiority and "destined" expansionism that abound in Melville's works must be read as ironic; but so are many of his denunciations of US imperial actions and attitudes laden with double-voiced irony. Both Melville's celebrations and his denunciations of US empire are at once powerful and equivocal. Moreover, as the next section suggests, these ambiguities deliberately involve Melville's readers, inviting them to consider their own contradictions, especially those regarding the racial and colonial otherness produced by empire.

Opacity, Ambiguity, and Power in "Benito Cereno"

As one of the most widely traveled writers of the nineteenth-century US canon, Melville set foot on all six inhabited continents, engaging in both commercial and military enterprises and interacting – often in close quarters, and from various positions of power – with a diverse array of people in different contexts. To name a few, he was a low-ranking worker in one of the most brutal and hierarchical jobs of the time (whaling), a guest/captive among Polynesians suspected to be cannibals, an ordinary seaman in the US Navy, a tourist in Europe, and a pilgrim in Palestine. Thus, it seems only natural that one of the most frequent motifs throughout his writings is the encounter of a first-person narrator with geopolitical, ethnic, and cultural others. Melville's experiences, as well as the works that emerged from them, starkly contrast with what Brickhouse and Gillman describe in the introduction as "the imperial selves dreamed into being by American writers" such as Emerson and Whitman. Beginning with his first novel, *Typee* (1846), many of his narratives undermine "the prototypes of colonial mastership" by opposing the (always precarious) physical control over others with the impossibility of discerning "their interiors," a "failure to master" that has a destabilizing effect over the imperial self.[19]

The unsettling opacity of the racial-colonial other is a recurrent subject in Melville. The most repeated motif in his writings is perhaps that of a character, animal, object, or event that is in front of us, but remains elusive, resisting either complete visibility, identification, comprehension, or translation. Some specific images of this opacity reappear uncannily throughout Melville's writings. The most recurring one is probably the figure of a woman covered by a *saya y manto*, a Peruvian outfit that concealed the whole female body except for one eye, allowing women to avoid recognition, which is recalled in at least six texts. Time and again, US characters are disturbed by the covered woman's eye leering at them, a reversal of the conventional scene where a naked nonwhite female is exposed to the gaze of the white male.[20] There are two texts where this disturbing unreadability of the other is the foundational and propelling force of the whole narrative: "Benito Cereno" (1854) and Melville's last full-length novel, *The Confidence-Man* (1857). Opacity also plays a prominent role in *Typee*, where the protagonist, haunted by the terror of being cannibalized, agonizes over whether the natives he encounters on a Polynesian island are friendly hosts or savages with cannibalistic intentions, or perhaps both. This duality presented in Melville's first novel reflects the two fundamental ways characters engage with otherness in his works: either by attempted understanding and solidarity, or by brutal and blind domination. The most famous example of the former is the relationship between Ishmael and Queequeg in *Moby-Dick*. Ishmael begins with the same question that torments *Typee*'s hero: is the Polynesian with whom he shares quarters a cannibal? But contrary to Tommo, he soon disregards that possibility and decides to treat Queequeg as "my fellow man," an expression he uses three times in quick succession.[21] Within *Moby-Dick*, other examples include Ishmael's rapports with his "friends" King Tranquo and the young Peruvians in Lima. What all these instances have in common is that no side claims or seeks a position of dominance over the other.

The binary opposition between fellowship or friendship on one side, and domination on the other, is most bluntly addressed in "Benito Cereno." US Captain Amasa Delano, a character invested in, among other denials, ignoring the unescapably brutal reality of slavery, at one point praises an enslaver's relation with his enslaved in these terms: "I envy you such a friend; slave I cannot call him."[22] If "*Typee* is one of the first US literary texts to establish a connection between the institutions of slavery in the United States and Euro-American colonialism in Polynesia,"[23] "Benito Cereno" revisits the symbiosis of slavery and colonialism, exploring how it has historically affected Euro-American consideration of the intraspecific limits of what means to be human (most notably, through the constructs of the cannibal and the slave), and how it shapes contemporary antebellum US society. Above all, the novella focuses on Melville's insight that the oppressed racial and colonial other remains inherently opaque. When Delano boards a South American ship in distress near the coast of colonial Chile, he encounters a starving and convalescing crew, a weak "Spanish" captain who is unable to command, and a group of slaves being carried from one port to another, who due to the lack of provisions and manpower are left to roam unsupervised.[24] At the core of the plot is a secret hidden from both Delano and the readers: the Blacks have revolted and taken control of the ship. To mislead Delano and evade capture, they feign subservience, pretending to be still enslaved while coercing the white sailors to assume the roles of masters. Eventually, the ruse is revealed and Delano sends his crew to suppress the revolt and restore the previous order.

The masquerade performed by the rebels capitalizes on racial and cultural stereotypes, deceiving Delano by conforming to his preconceived notions about the behavior of "Blacks" and "Spaniards." The text sets a similar trap for the readers. Initially, we are introduced to the events through Delano's perceptions, with whom most nineteenth-century US readers may be expected to identify. Melville combines a strong focalization on Delano with a third-person narrator who distances himself from the character. While we read what appears to be a neutral account, we experience events through Delano's eyes, receiving the same information that he does. The problem is that Delano's perception is affected by his racist, ethnocentric, and jingoistic worldview. In the second part of the text, after the hoax is revealed, the story is retold through the testimony of other (non-US) characters, which affords readers an opportunity to assess, in retrospect, how much they were deceived and therefore to evaluate their own capacity to see beyond the stereotypes that have been acted out in front of them, as well as their willingness to accept Delano's perceptions at face value. The novella elaborately critiques racial and geopolitical bias, then, by not only exposing the prejudices of the character (a self-righteous captain from Massachusetts), but also, potentially, those of the readers. As Sophia Mihic has put it, in Melville's texts "states of artifice meet states of artifice. They frame us as much as we frame them."[25]

As Loren Goldner and others have pointed out, critics tend to subsume Melville's references to Latin America into other, US-specific agendas.[26] Although "Benito Cereno" tells the intervention of a US Captain and his crew in a slave revolt in South America, US scholarship, with few exceptions, has read the story from a national perspective, generally as a tale about US slavery. The critical tendency to deem the setting irrelevant, or of minor significance may be supported by the fact that Melville is rewriting a previous text on a historic event, but critical readings of Melville's other narrative that reformulates a previous non-fictional text, *Israel Potter*, regularly assume that the US and European settings of the novel are of the highest significance. In the case of "Benito Cereno," the few studies that pay attention to the story's non-US setting usually consider it in the context of the Black Atlantic, although the action happens entirely in the Pacific; one recent study that does consider the story in a Pacific context refers mostly to the Asian Pacific.[27]

While issues of race in antebellum US have dominated the vast body of scholarship on the novella, a number of studies have also connected the text to US imperial actions and attitudes. Since Melville's time, some readers have noticed that the comments on the "sullen inefficiency"[28] of Spanish colonial rule and the allusions to the shortcomings of postcolonial Spanish America matched some of the arguments made in favor of US military intervention and imperial expansion, spanning from 1840s Texas to 1890s Cuba. The narrative also echoes, even more vividly, images and stories that circulated in the US about postcolonial Haiti – the only country in the Americas where Black people ruled, as a direct result of a successful revolution of the enslaved.[29] The text has also been considered in the context of what was then the most influential formulation of US policy toward the rest of the Americas, which became known as the Monroe Doctrine. Outlined in President James Monroe's 1823 address to Congress, it portrayed the independent republics in the rest of the continent as both "our Southern brethren" and the natural and legitimate sphere of influence of the United States – and therefore, a potential object of its imperial expansion.[30] If Delano says that a man's slave can be his friend, Monroe's speech suggests that a country's satellites can be its "brethren." The ambiguous relationship between Delano and his Chilean counterpart Benito Cereno may evoke parallels with Monroe's speech: legally and formally they are equals (captains of two different ships), and the local authority is the Chilean Cereno, (as they are on his ship), but the visiting US character immediately assumes control. Like the "white man" of Kipling's poem and the USA in the passage of *White-Jacket* that inspires it, Delano *must* take charge of things, since the locals are unable to do so.

But while Delano possesses power and agency, he lacks Cereno's awareness. At the end of the text, Melville opposes the profound effect the events have had on the South American with Delano's inability or unwillingness to learn anything from them (as he famously asks, "why moralize upon it?"). In their last conversation, the US hero appears disappointed and even angry that the Chilean cannot just happily turn the page: "'You are saved,' cried Captain Delano, more and more astonished and pained; 'you are saved.'" After this exchange, Delano, the visiting liberator, safely returns to the US, while Cereno, the helpless local victim to whom he has "saved," stays in Lima and dies soon after.[31] If Cereno's paralysis and languishing death may symbolize the decline of the Spanish empire, post-1980s scholars have read in Delano's forward-looking complacency an expression of racial and colonial bad faith, suggesting that both "monarchic" and "democratic" empires are condemned.

Melville's sustained attention to both imperialism and race would significantly diminish in his postwar works, which is why this chapter focuses on his antebellum works. After publishing ten books in eleven years, nine years would pass between *The Confidence-Man* (1857) and *Battle-Pieces and Aspects of the War* (1866). In the meantime, Melville had abandoned prose and turned to poetry. The volume of verses on the Civil

War displays an attitude that is more "patriotic,"[32] or at least more unequivocally and uniformly so. This is particularly emphatic in the book's "Supplement," which insists on images of national unity but also, incidentally, of a racial (white) unity, a combination that would be frequent in both discourses and policies during Reconstruction.[33]

Collaboration and Ambiguity: Herman's Actions and Melville's Rhetorical Devices

Critics today consider Melville to have been an astute observer of the nineteenth-century workings of empire. He is seen, for example, as "the first canonical US author ... to have perceived the effects of gunboat diplomacy ... from the standpoint of its indigenous victims."[34] This perception can be linked to his exceptionally insightful view of power relations, the fact that he personally witnessed Euro-American imperialism in various places and circumstances, and the profound empathy he shows with a vast range of suffering and oppressed people. But it can also be related to his direct involvement in gunboat interventionism. For fourteen months he served as an ordinary seaman on the USS *United States*, a frigate assigned (to use the US official parlance) to "protect American interests"[35] in Polynesia and the Spanish American Pacific – the settings, respectively, of *Typee*, *Omoo*, and *Mardi* and of "Benito Cereno" and "The Encantadas." The text most closely related to Melville's time on the flagship of the Pacific Squadron is *White-Jacket* (1850), which largely takes place in South American waters. A short "Note" prefacing the narrative states that the story incorporates the author's "experiences and observations" on "a United States frigate," a generic form of referring to what was, in fact, *the United States* frigate.[36] The note both establishes the autobiographical basis of the novel and avoids its specifics. A distinctive characteristic of *White-Jacket* within Melville's body of work is that it bypasses almost entirely both the context and the purpose of the enterprise in which the narrator is involved. While Melville's next novel, for instance, will explain in painstaking detail the whole enterprise of whaling and how the *Pequod*'s path relates to (mainly by deviating from) that enterprise, here we are not even told why the US vessel is in the South Pacific. The narrative's exceptional decontextualization may help to explain why critics have seldom considered it in the context of US interventionism: in a sense, they are following the narrator's lead. The text offers a vivid depiction of life on a US military ship, per the subtitle, *The World in a Man-of-War*, while saying surprisingly little about the man-of-war in the world.

The incident recounted in Chapter V is the only one that somewhat relates to the actual duties for which US military vessels were stationed in the South American Pacific. While anchored on the coast of Peru, a contingent of soldiers, "every man armed to the teeth," boards a Peruvian warship to seize a Briton who had deserted from the frigate and is now serving in the South American navy. The Captain of the Peruvian ship is called "Don Sereno," connecting this military intervention to the civilian and humanitarian one of "Benito Cereno." As in the novella, US sailors board a South American ship and take control over a weaker local authority.[37] In the narrator's telling, even the US crew is shocked: "What? when a piping-hot peace was between the United States and Peru, to send an armed body on board a Peruvian sloop of war, and seize one of its officers, in broad daylight? – Monstrous infraction of the Law of Nations!"[38] While this incident is based on a historic event, the sailor's return was voluntary, and a friendly Peruvian admiral interceded for him. Melville's fictional version presents instead a forced imposition of US interests over the local authorities, reminiscent of events Melville must have heard on board and/or read about, such as the capture of Monterrey by the *United States*, which took place less than a year before he enlisted in the frigate. Commodore T. A. C. Jones decided to seize the city believing that the United States might have declared war on Mexico (although it had not, and Jones had to return control of the city to the Mexican authorities).

While Melville's fiction reshapes the historical incident into a recognizable portrait of the kind of actions and attitudes that characterized US interventionism in the region, the events are presented in an ostensibly mocking tone. The narrator's bombastic and short-lived indignation both underscores the intrinsically imperialist character of the incident and invites readers to dismiss it with laughter. Melville employs a similar formula in *Moby-Dick* to make a more explicit reference to US imperial policies regarding the Americas. Chanting the exploits of Nantucket whalemen, Ishmael compares them to the imperial conquests of the US and the British Empire: "Let America add Mexico to Texas, and pile Cuba upon Canada;[[39]] let the English overswarm all India, and hang out their blazing banner from the sun; two thirds of this terraqueous globe are the Nantucketer's. For the sea is his; he owns it, as Emperors own Empires."[40] Here again, the narrator's exuberance, now in the form of foolish exaggeration rather than grandiloquent outrage, seems to undermine or distract from what he is very pointedly stating: in one case, that the US warship, much like the nation itself, is not a friendly peer, but a bully to the Spanish American republics; and in the other, that the continent's geopolitical future is not one of brotherly freedom but an "American" empire.

One possible function of these rhetorical deviations is to deflect the kind of censorship and condemnation that Melville experienced with the publication of *Typee*.[41] Like many US writers of his time, Melville directed most of his explicit critique of imperialism toward European countries. In *Typee*, the claim that Western missionaries and military forces were bringing salvation and progress to the Polynesians is belied by the actual devastation caused by those colonial enterprises, but the focus of this denunciation is on European endeavors. And yet, Nukuheva (Nuku Hiva), where both Melville and the narrator stayed, is the main island of a group that, as John Carlos Rowe noted, "might be termed [the US's] first imperial venture outside North America."[42] As Rowe argues, in *Typee* "Melville anticipates . . . the extent to which US imperialism would be predicated on commercial, rather than territorial, control of other cultures and peoples."[43] Ishmael's casual remark, instead, foresees the country simply piling one conquest upon the other.

Melville's first novel was published the same year the US went to war with Mexico, a conflict he, like others at the time, viewed as a tipping point in the shift from republic to empire, as Ishmael plainly states in the passage just quoted. In the quasi-allegorical novel *Mardi* (1849), an anonymous text found in a scroll accuses President Polk, in the figure of the "great chieftain" of Vivenza (the USA), of having done a "still more imperial thing" than the king of England: he has "gone to war without declaring intentions" (a reference to Polk's decision to enter into hostilities with Mexico, bypassing congress). The anonymous author then turns the criticism to the people: "You yourselves were precipitated upon a neighboring nation, ere you knew your spears were in your hands."[44] But he soon shifts his emphasis, however, and proposes not to abandon the expansionist "ambition" but to slow it down, stating that "it is best served, by waiting events. Time, but Time only, may enable you to cross the equator; and give you the Arctic Circles for your boundaries."[45] Having first denounced that "he who hated oppressors, is become an oppressor himself,"[46] the tract concludes by recommending more efficient ways of conquest. Thus, it is challenging to attribute any single, clear position on the subject to the text in the scroll; it appears as if, at different moments, it considers the issue in a different light.

This is something that Melville does quite frequently. As mentioned above, at different times, and for different purposes, Ishmael may present whaling as either imperial or liberatory. Both of these images are, of course, employed to celebrate whaling, a point Ishmael emphasizes in chapter 24, "The Advocate." After attributing to whaling, the first US private industry to reach planetary impact, "the establishment of the eternal democracy" along the Western coast of South America, he goes on to mention other parts of the world that also have been, or would be, integrated into the capitalist-colonialist system due to whaling's beneficial influence: Australia ("The whale-ship is the true mother of that now mighty colony"); Japan, which only the whaleship may make "to become hospitable" (to Western visitors and commerce); and Polynesia, whose islands "do commercial homage to the whale-ship, that cleared the way for the missionary and the merchant, and in many cases carried the primitive missionaries to their first destinations."[47] This panegyric to whaling is, quite transparently, a celebration of democratic capitalism. It is also, if less directly, a show of national pride. The USA excels at this great extractivist industry, as we are repeatedly reminded in the novel, while "the rest of the nations" (to quote the jingoistic passage from *White-Jacket* discussed earlier) are now "in our rear." If in *White-Jacket* the narrator foresees a future of US global dominance, Ishmael presents it as having already been achieved, at least with regards to whaling. *Moby-Dick* recapitulates that process in detail: the linguistic progression of terms about whales, the evolution of the techniques, the expansion of both the species that are killed and the parts of the world where they are hunted, and so on; in most of this, the USA whaling industry is placed, either explicitly or implicitly, at the end of the evolution: "the advance-guard" that has "break[ed] a new path," as predicted in *White-Jacket*.

However, we cannot take Ishmael's glorification of whaling at face value. His exalted tone, like the grandiloquent one in which expansionism and interventionism are denounced elsewhere, makes clear that all this is an exaggeration, at best. Throughout Melville's oeuvre, both critique and celebration are often ironic. The linking of whaling with "missionary and merchant" activities in Polynesia, for instance, must have reminded some 1851 readers of *Moby-Dick* of the scathing – and much criticized – comments made in *Typee*, Melville's most famous novel at the time, on the devastating effects of Western commerce and religion on the people of the islands. How might those readers – and how may today's scholars – be expected to read the passage? Ishmael's praise of whaling is punctuated by references (such as "the now mighty colony"), which depending on our perception of this Gestalt image of sorts can be interpreted either as the global benefits or the horrific downsides of whaling. Whatever we make of this, it appears that we need to consider all aspects simultaneously: the nationalistic, "democratic," capitalist, imperial celebration; the ironic and/or contradictory frame in which it is constructed; the pointed critique of all that seems to be celebrated; and the ambiguous status of this critique. As Samuel Otter argued in 1999, while Melville explores and denounces "the rhetorical structures and ideological functions of antebellum discourse," he also realizes "that he cannot sustain an outsider's privilege" and, "instead of dismissing contemporary beliefs about race, nation, and self, . . . acknowledges their appeal and probes their sources and sway." Melville's "verbal doubleness," as Otter terms it, is neither "the deus ex machina of irony often used to redeem him from the taint of his culture or . . . the too-easy ambivalence used to describe an author said to see 'both sides.'"[48] We can know Herman's actions to the extent made possible by his biographers. But the rhetorical ambiguities of his writings on empire leave Melville the author in an always uncertain light in which, as argued in the conclusion to this chapter, we too may find ourselves implicated.

Conclusion: "The Encantadas" and the Participant Critic

Recent studies on Melville and imperialism have paid an increasing attention to "The Encantadas, or Enchanted Isles" (1854), recognizing its setting, much like the isles themselves, at the intersection of multiple forms, histories, and narratives of imperialism, particularly "trans-American authoritarian violence."[49] Many elements in this text, beginning with its bilingual title and its archipelagic structure – ten sketches that have no clear chronological, narrative, or thematic order – underscore the impossibility of integrating the islands into any single image, conceptualization, perspective, or language. Their original name, chosen by the narrator over the already established "Galapagos," was coined, he says, precisely because of this "apparent fleetingness," the impossibility of pinning them down.[50] The second sketch, "Two Sides to a Tortoise," is devoted to one of Melville's recurring figures of opacity, the archipelago's eponymous creatures; or more exactly, as per the title, to the irreducible ambivalence they embody. After recounting that three Galapagos tortoises have been brought on board, the narrator expends much of the sketch trying to convey how these "mystic creatures" affected him, "in a manner not easy to unfold," both by their "worshipful venerableness of aspect" and their amazing characteristics as actual living beings: "What other bodily being possesses such a citadel wherein to resist the assaults of Time?"[51] This citadel is the animal's shell, and the "two sides" to which the title refers are, in the simplest formulation, those of this shield, which, like the doubloon nailed to the mast in *Moby-Dick*, has only one face visible and therefore readable.

Fascinated, the narrator embarks on a series of musings that occupies most of the sketch, touching upon history, philosophy, religion, and so on. Then, the long reverie suddenly stops, and the whole experience is quickly summarized as a "wild nightmare begot by ... the tortoise,"[52] with this sentence concluding the sketch: "But next evening, strange to say, I sat down with my shipmates, and made a merry repast from tortoise steaks and tortoise stews; and supper over, out knife, and helped convert the three mighty concave shells into three fanciful soup-tureens, and polished the three flat yellowish calapees into three gorgeous salvers."[53] What, up to this point, may seem a mindful, sensitive ecological discourse ends with the rapid reification of the animal as raw material for human consumption and consumerism. As if it were a parody of *Moby-Dick* in a nutshell, the profound text examining profound questions concludes by casually asserting that at the end of the day it is really all about extractivism – and perhaps, having a good time with the mates. The narrator's nonchalant action suggests, as he himself acknowledges, a "strange" disconnect with everything we have known thus far about his perceptions, sensibility, and discourse, marking a shift in his reclusive and reflective character to that of cheerful participation in mindless communal utilitarianism.

Here, I believe, some of the main questions and concepts touched upon in this chapter converge: ambiguity and uncertainty, inescapable contradictions, the binarism of the relationships with otherness, the acceptance that one may participate in what criticizes (and the equivocal ways in which we sometimes process that reality), the toll of being a social critic and the necessity or desire of also being a participant in one's own society.[54] These questions are not solely relevant to the issue of imperialism, of course; and neither is Melville's sketch, which like the rest of "The Encantadas" many scholars have linked to imperial matters, but not, (that I know of), on account of its last sentence. This sole phrase, however, in the tension (or resolution?) that it manifests, may illuminate Melville's relationship with US imperialism more succinctly than the many explicit references to the subject. It may also illuminate the multidimensional ambiguities and contradictions – primarily between thoughts and actions – that many of us may recognize in ourselves, regarding multiple issues, from empire to race to animal welfare to the future of the planet.

As the editors suggest in the introduction, literature is ideally situated to become the medium of both imperial denial and acknowledgment, as well as an imaginative resource for contestation. This chapter has attempted to demonstrate that in Melville's works, acknowledgment, denial, contestation, as well as participation, may be all involved, sometimes concurrently. This may help to explain why his writings have triggered such a wide range of interpretations. It is also one of the aspects that have made and continue to make these writings and their profound and at times unsettling insights so present to readers across so many eras, places, and positions.

American Postscript

As I write this chapter from Montevideo, Uruguay, I am newly struck by the necessity – given the purposes of this volume – of placing Melville's writings within a continental American critical tradition. Melville's vivid and complex engagement with empire belongs to a rich history of hemispheric writings about transamerican imperialism, one that includes many non-US American writers. While space limitations prevent an accounting of this tradition, I will turn briefly here to one exemplary text: José Martí's "Nuestra América" ("Our America"), first published in 1891 during the author's exile in New York, in the same year that Melville died in that city.[55] In "Nuestra América," the most famous Spanish American essay on imperialism written in the nineteenth-century, Martí presents the geopolitical region in which "Benito Cereno" is set in a manner reminiscent of the novella itself: as transitioning between a fading Spanish empire still ruling Cuba and Puerto Rico and an emerging US power poised to supplant it. Martí's text also argues that, as Melville's story implies, the new nations are condemned if they fail to embrace their multiracial condition. In "our mestizo America" ("nuestra América mestiza"), Martí insists, the body is "a motley of Indian and criollo" ("el cuerpo pinto de indio y criollo").[56] As suggested earlier, the refusal of that American body is one of the reasons all the characters in "Benito Cereno" are doomed, in one way or another: there is no genuine exchange, let alone mixing – in any area or sense – between the *white, Black*, and *brown* people on the *San Dominick*. Even the briefest consideration of Melville's and Martí's texts together brings into relation the national and regional traditions within which they are usually – and separately – read. To study "empire and American literature," as this collection aims to, requires a truly *American*, transnational approach that is unfortunately still too rare.

Notes

1. Exceptionalism (the belief that the United States was unique and exemplary compared to other countries), and Manifest Destiny (the view that white Anglophone settlers were destined to expand across North America and

potentially beyond) were two of the most common justifications for the country's expansion of its borders and areas of influence.

2. Taken at face value, this passage supports Dimock's well-known argument in *Empire for Liberty*, which sees in Melville's "individualism" a "conjunction of freedom and dominion" that corresponds to Jefferson's expression, "empire for liberty," where "the former stands to safeguard the latter and the latter, in turn, serves to justify the former." Dimock does, indeed, take the passage at face value, since she does not see *White-Jacket*'s "rhetorical apparatus" as undermining the narrator's voice, but rather projecting an "image not only of trusted readers, but also of a narrator presumably as trusted by them as they are by him." Herman Melville. *White-Jacket; or, The World in a Man-of-War*, ed. Harrison Hayford, Hershel Parker, and G. Thomas Tanselle (Evanston: Northwestern University Press, 1970), 151. Wai-chee Dimock, *Empire for Liberty: Melville and the Poetics of Individualism* (Princeton: Princeton University Press, 1989), 9, 14, 93.

3. Rudyard Kipling, *The Cambridge Edition of the Poems of Rudyard Kipling*, ed. Thomas Pinney (Cambridge: Cambridge University Press, 2013), 528.

4. Kevin J. Hayes, "Kipling and the Rise of *White-Jacket*." *Notes and Queries* 64.1 (2017): 147.

5. He also advised him against entering politics and suggested a career as "colonial administrator" instead, since "the country will need 'em pretty bad in a few years." Rudyard Kipling, *The Letters of Rudyard Kipling*, ed. Thomas Pinney (London: Palgrave Macmillan, 1990), vol. 2, 350.

6. Patrick Brantlinger, *Taming Cannibals: Race and the Victorians* (Ithaca: Cornell University Press, 2011), 204.

7. Kipling, *Poems*, 112.

8. In occupied Japan, for instance, Melville held a prominent place in the efforts to promote "Western" political and cultural values, and the image of the USA as their champion. This appears to have had long-term effects, at least in academia: still today, Japan produces a larger body of Melville scholarship than probably any country in the world, except the USA.

9. Herman Melville, *Moby-Dick, or, The Whale*, ed. Harrison Hayford, Hershel Parker, and G. Thomas Tanselle (Evanston: Northwestern University Press and The Newberry Library, 1988), 110. F. O. Matthiessen, *American Renaissance: Art and Expression in the Age of Emerson and Whitman* (London: Oxford University Press, 1946), 417.

10. Melville, *Moby-Dick*, 64.

11. William V. Spanos, *The Errant Art of Moby-Dick: The Canon, the Cold War, and the Struggle for American Studies* (Durham: Duke University Press, 1995), 4.

12. Spanos, *The Errant Art of Moby-Dick*, 17.

13. Andrew Lawson, "Moby-Dick and the American Empire." *Comparative American Studies An International Journal*, 10.1 (2012): 45–62.

14. C. L. R. James, *Mariners, Renegades, and Castaways: The Story of Herman Melville and the World We Live In* (Hanover: University Press of New England, 2001).

15. Allan Moore Emery, "'Benito Cereno' and Manifest Destiny." *Nineteenth-Century Fiction*, 39.1 (1984): 48–68.

16. Brian Yothers, "Introduction," in Herman Melville, *The Piazza Tales*, ed. Brian Yothers (Peterborough: Broadview, 2018), 23–4.

17. The relatively sudden nature of this shift may explain why Melville is not considered in the 1993 *Cultures of United States Imperialism*, a groundbreaking collection that epitomized the broader turn taking place in US Studies at the time. Amy Kaplan and Donald E. Pease, eds. *Cultures of United States Imperialism* (Durham: Duke University Press, 1993).

18. This is not a uniform consensus, of course. Kennan Ferguson, for example, argues that in *Typee* and *Omoo* Melville, all while denouncing European imperialism in the Pacific, "created a new template of imperialism for the American imaginary, one that holds itself as protecting cultures from foreign influence while manipulating them to its own ends" (23); see Kennan Ferguson, "Who Eats Whom? Melville's Anthropolitics at the Dawn of Pacific Imperialism," in *A Political Companion to Herman Melville*, ed. Jason Frank (Lexington: University Press of Kentucky, 2013), 21–41.

19. Christopher Freeburg, *Melville and the Idea of Blackness: Race and Imperialism in Nineteenth-Century America* (New York: Cambridge University Press, 2012), 14.

20. Herman Melville, *Typee, a Peep at Polynesian Life*, ed. Harrison Hayford, Hershel Parker, and G. Thomas Tanselle (Evanston: Northwestern University Press, 1968), 86; *Mardi: And A Voyage Thither*, ed. Harrison Hayford, Hershel Parker, and G. Thomas Tanselle (Evanston: Northwestern University Press, 1970), 186; *Pierre; or, The Ambiguities*, ed. Harrison Hayford, Hershel Parker, and G. Thomas Tanselle (Evanston: Northwestern University Press, 1971), 149; *The Piazza Tales, and Other Prose Pieces, 1838–1860*, ed. Harrison Hayford, Alma A. MacDougall, and G. Thomas Tanselle (Evanston: Northwestern University Press, 1987), 47; *Clarel: A Poem and Pilgrimage in the Holy Land*, ed. Harrison Hayford, Alma A. MacDougall, Hershel Parker, and G. Thomas Tanselle (Evanston: Northwestern University Press, 1991), 4.26.100, 494; *Published Poems: Battle-Pieces; John Marr; Timoleon*, ed. Robert Charles Ryan and Hershel Parker (Evanston: Northwestern University Press, 2009), 239.

21. Melville, *Moby-Dick*, 52.

22. Melville, *The Piazza*, 57.

23. John Carlos Rowe, *Literary Culture and US Imperialism: From the Revolution to World War II* (Oxford: Oxford University Press, 2000), 77.

24. Melville's story follows, for the most part, Delano's 1817 chronicle of the historic events. Amasa Delano, *Narrative of Voyages and Travels in the Northern and Southern Hemispheres: Comprising Three Voyages Round the World; Together with a Voyage of Survey and Discovery, in the Pacific Ocean and Oriental Islands* (Boston: E. G. House, 1817), 318–53.

25. Sophia Mihic, "'The End Was in the Beginning': Melville, Ellison, and the Democratic Death of Progress in Typee and Omoo," in *A Political*

Companion to Herman Melville, ed. Jason Frank (Lexington: University Press of Kentucky, 2013), 53.

26. Loren Goldner, *Herman Melville: Between Charlemagne and the Antemosaic Cosmic Man: Race, Class and the Crisis of Bourgeois Ideology in an American Renaissance Writer* (New York: Queequeg Publications, 2006), 201.

27. Colleen Tripp, "Beyond the Black Atlantic: Pacific Rebellions and the Gothic in Herman Melville's 'Benito Cereno'," *Journal of Transnational American Studies* 8.1 (2017). For an example of more reasonable spatial and geopolitical contextualizations of the novella, see Alexandra Ganser, "From the Black Atlantic to the Bleak Pacific: Re-Reading 'Benito Cereno'," *Atlantic Studies* 15.2 (2018): 218–37. For a detailed and wide-reaching contextualization of the historical episode in English, see Greg Grandin, *The Empire of Necessity: Slavery, Freedom, and Deception in the New World* (New York: Picador, 2015).

28. Melville, *The Piazza*, 52.

29. One of Melville's most prominent changes to Delano's account is that of the ship's name to *San Dominick*, which recalls Haiti's colonial name, *Saint-Domingue*. The gruesome details about the rebels' treatment of their white captives, including references to torture and allusions to cannibalism, are also Melville's, and they would likely make many US readers of the time recall the events in Haiti.

30. [USA] National Archives. "Monroe Doctrine (1823)." www.archives.gov/mile stone-documents/monroe-doctrine. June 25, 2021.

31. Melville, *The Piazza*, 116–17.

32. Herman Melville, *Published Poems: Battle-Pieces; John Marr; Timoleon*, ed. Robert Charles Ryan and Hershel Parker (Evanston: Northwestern University Press, 2009), 184.

33. Melville, *Published Poems*, 184–5. On Melville's variable portrait of and relationship with the national self, see Robert S. Levine, "Melville and Americanness: A Problem," *Leviathan* 16.3 (2014): 5–20; for the significance of the "Supplement" to this, p. 17.

34. Lawrence Buell, "Melville and the Question of American Decolonization," *American Literature* 64.2 (1992): 239.

35. Barbara Salazar Torreon and Sofia Plagakis, *Instances of Use of United States Armed Forces Abroad, 1798–2023* (Washington: Congressional Research Service, 2023), 3–4.

36. Melville, *White-Jacket*, ix. This curious formula is absent from the much longer preface to the London edition, published the same year, where Melville explains: "As the object of this work is not to portray the particular man-of-war in which the author sailed" but "general life in the Navy, the true name of the frigate is not given." Herman Melville, *White-Jacket; or, The World in a Man-of-War* (London: Richard Bentley, 1850), iii.

37. Melville, *White-Jacket*, 18–19.

38. Melville, *White-Jacket*, 19.

39. Ishmael's vision of US "adding" and "piling" recalls what Hannah Arendt and others have considered a defining characteristic of imperialism: its never-

ending, all-consuming progression, or to use Arendt's words, "its idea of unlimited expansion." Hannah Arendt, *Imperialism,* in *The Origins of Totalitarianism* (San Diego: Harvest, 1968), 150.

40. Melville, *Moby-Dick*, 64.
41. On editorial changes and moral condemnation of the novel, see Melville, *Typee*, 279–90, 294. Melville would write in 1849 to an editor and friend: "What a madness & anguish it is, that an author can never – under no conceivable circumstances – be at all frank with his readers." Herman Melville, *Correspondence*, ed. Lynn Horth (Evanston: Northwestern University Press, 1993), 149.
42. Rowe, *Literary Culture*, 82.
43. Rowe, *Literary Culture*, 85.
44. Melville, *Mardi*, 528.
45. Melville, *Mardi*, 529–30.
46. Melville, *Mardi*, 526.
47. Melville, *Moby-Dick*, 110.
48. Samuel Otter, *Melville's Anatomies* (Berkeley: University of California Press, 1999), 4.
49. Nicholas Spengler, "Tracking Melville's 'Dog-King': Creole Sympathies and Canine Warfare in the Americas," *Leviathan* 21.3 (2019) 71.
50. Melville, *The Piazza*, 128.
51. Melville, *The Piazza*, 131.
52. Melville, *The Piazza*, 132.
53. Melville, *The Piazza*, 132–3.
54. To mention one example, Melville's service in the Navy had little to do with nationalism or supporting interventionism: it was a means of returning to the US.
55. For a rare study pairing Melville and Martí, see Anamaría Flores, "Toward a Revolution in American Studies: The Counter-Narratives of José Martí and Herman Melville," *Socialism and Democracy* 21.1 (2007): 55–74.
56. José Martí, *Nuestra América* (Caracas: Biblioteca Ayacucho, 1985), 35, 34.

CHAPTER 7

Cultures of US Torture
Entertainment and Clandestine Spectacle

Rodrigo Lazo

In the years following September 11, 2001, films and television shows featured torture scenes with disturbing regularity. As the excesses of the so-called War on Terror made their way into mainstream media – most shockingly in the photos at the infamous Abu Ghraib prison in Iraq – torture moved from the clandestine sites of dark ops to the spectacle of representation in a variety of written and visual texts. Television shows such as *Homeland* (2011–20) and movies such as *Rescue Dawn* (2006), the latter set in Vietnam, came to feature torture scenes, which became routine in the representation of violence. The most infamous examples emerged on the television show *24* (2001–10), which featured a federal agent who used torture to extract information from terrorists, sometimes to avert the detonation of ticking dirty bombs.[1] Literary productions were not exempt: Viet Thanh Nguyen's *The Sympathizer* (2015) featured a torture scene toward the end of the narrative after having raised questions about how filmmakers depict violence against Vietnamese people for entertainment. Meanwhile, film studies scholars debated the relationship of the War on Terror to the emergence of the horror subgenre called, perhaps erroneously, "torture porn."[2] Touching many genres, torture depictions reached their apogee in the somewhat comical movie *Deadpool*, in which the physical mutation that gave the eponymous super-hero his strength was the result of prolonged torture.

The cultural productions of the 2000s grappled with a post-9/11 US national fixation on the role of torture as part of anti-terrorism operations and as a form of power display on the international stage. Various forms of entertainment contributed to a discursive proliferation that included debates in the journalistic sphere about whether it was defensible (or justifiable) to operate a US-run torture program and commentary from political figures about US operations in response to the threats from the likes of Al-Qaeda. The many voices in the media justifying such actions treated torture as an acceptable practice, and the result, to use Rebecca Gordon's phrase, was "mainstreaming torture."³ Given the political will in the Bush Administration to use torture and make legal arguments to support its position, the torturing of people framed as "enemy combatants" became another instance of the spectacle of US power that was on full display in the invasions of and bombing campaigns in Afghanistan and Iraq, which is to say, entertainment followed the violence of the war.

Torture as practice and representation – the former through dark ops, the latter public – offers a recent window into how the US empire engages in clandestine spectacle, simultaneously showing and veiling its power through contradictory positions in relation to international legal and ethical norms. US culture participates in the display of torture as power and thus it offers a window into the way literature and film normalize the operations of empire. From the nineteenth to the twenty-first centuries, the US empire has simultaneously flaunted and disavowed its use and abuse of violence. The cultural work of literature and film, in both the past and the present, buttresses the US ability's to maintain contradictory and complicated positions in relation to the nation's relationship to violence. To shed light on how easily torture can be deployed as entertainment in imperial conflicts, this chapter seeks historical insight from a little-known novelette published in 1851 about a young couple from New York who elope and end up imprisoned in Cuba, only to be tortured by sadistic colonial Spanish authorities. This work of fiction provides a surprising look backward and forward to the conflicting ways that the cultures of US torture represent US actions in visual ways. As Amy Kaplan wrote in *Cultures of United States Imperialism*, imperial politics deploy denial, displacement, and projection abroad. "If the vehemence and persistence with which something is denied mark its importance and even formative power, the characterization of a nation's ideological opponents reveals as much about that nation's self-conception as it does about its enemies."⁴ Torture as both representation and practice in recent decades shows how denial and projection can also facilitate displays of power.

The obscene power wielded by the US empire was evident in the torture program's critical rejoinder, *The Senate Intelligence Committee Report on Torture* (2014), a black-covered tome replete with charts and names of people detained and abused under the CIA's not-so-covert program. The *Report* was not part of a critique of the type associated with truth and reconciliation commissions, which were established in many countries from South Africa to Argentina following historical periods of extreme human rights violations. No one was held responsible for the US torture program. Instead, the Senate Intelligence report was a salvo from one branch of the US government taking issue with decisions of the executive branch. Taken together, the US covert-ops program and the Senate report showed that the US empire not only tortured people but simultaneously produced a discursive imperial practice, a monumental record that raised questions about the nation-state's own methods. Put another way, while the Bush Administration showed its willingness to flout the Geneva Conventions' prohibition against torturing of prisoners of war, the US Congress flaunted its investigative powers in a 6,700-page classified document from which the *Senate Intelligence Report* was produced. By the time discussions of the torture program waned in the late 2010s, it was clear that cultures of US torture included not only military practices and governmental oversight but also an entertainment industry that was more than willing to portray the empire's "enhanced interrogation methods," as they were euphemistically called.

Popular culture helps circulate that complicated display of clandestine spectacle. The contradiction generated by dark ops in the public eye has been building for decades. Michael Rogin, writing in the wake of the Iran/Contra scandal of the 1980s, noted that covert operations in the Reagan era were public shows not only for audiences in the United States but also for allies and enemies abroad "Political spectacle in the postmodern empire, in other words, is itself a form of power and not simply window dressing that diverts attention from the secret substance of American foreign policy," Rogin wrote.[5] But if the outing of Ollie North and Iran/Contra's diverting of dubious funds to unlawful attacks on Nicaragua still had the taint of international embarrassment (scandal), Bush II's torture program was accompanied by a White House legal team (and political supporters) justifying it in public. Those talking points filtered down into culture.

The recognition, acceptance, and even defense of the torture program created a discourse that inspired popular culture's showing of torture scenes, representing agents and victims of torture that allowed viewers to gawk if not cringe. This point can be taken up more specifically with an analysis of arguably the most important filmic representation of the War on Terror's depravity: the blockbuster *Zero Dark Thirty* (2012). Based on events related to the search for Osama bin Laden and bringing torture scenes to the big screen, *Zero Dark Thirty* circulated images of people being tortured, framing political-ethical debates in a form of entertainment. That conjunction is not new. As our nineteenth-century example of popular fiction will show, the cultural appeal of torture has a long history. These two texts, more than 150 years apart, are marked by differences in medium, the historical conditions of production, and the international contexts depicted, and yet they are both exemplary of culture's turn to torture for and as entertainment – or what we might call "torturetainment." While the word *entertain* derives from the Old French *entretenir*, meaning to hold together or to hold up (*tenir*), "torturetainment" is meant to imply the holding of a viewer or reader in thrall to a torture scene. As we will see, torturetainment is the vehicle by which the hidden spectacle of dark ops advertises the US empire's power even while intertwining elements of disavowal.

Darkness Visible: *Zero Dark Thirty*

The title, as the filmmakers made clear, referred to military time, thirty minutes after midnight (when the Navy Seals sent to kill Osama bin Laden were en route) with "dark" emphasizing the clandestine, secretive elements of the operation.[6] A tension between what parts of the dark ops were visible and which were hidden was central to the content of the film and also made its way into the hype surrounding the release of *Zero Dark Thirty*. On the one hand, the film made torture visible, opening with a prolonged scene that included "water boarding" and gave viewers a representation of what the public had heard for years about the War on Terror. Less clear was exactly where the scene was taking place. The location of the scene was identified as "Black Site. Undisclosed Location," which suggested an operation outside of national US territory (perhaps one of the notorious sites such as Abu Ghraib or Guantánamo). Running dark ops in extra-national locations was essential to the US torture program, to avoid juridical consequences for torturers. And yet places like Guantánamo emphasized the paradox of clandestine spectacle, the notion of an out-of-sight setting about which the public well knew. On another level, the term "water boarding" served as a euphemistic cover, a language distraction that sounds almost like an activity at a water park or boogie-boarding, for what is effectively the pouring of water down someone's throat until they start to drown.

By the time *Zero Dark Thirty* played in theaters, it was not a secret that US operatives were carrying out the types of actions portrayed. Any shock from the film resulted from the sensational depiction of violence rather than a documentary-like revelation of activities carried out with the Bush Administration's sanction. *Zero Dark Thirty* made visible the actual torture practice and therefore inserted entertainment into debates over torture with a major publicity campaign that featured Hollywood superstars. The film based its characters on intelligence operatives, military activity, and even governmental actions. Opening with an announcement to the audience that "The following motion picture is based on first-hand accounts of actual events," *Zero Dark Thirty* paraded as film à clef. The main character, Maya, is based on a CIA agent who worked on the bin Laden case, albeit with a different nom de guerre. Not long after the film's release, *Slate* magazine published an article – "Who Are the People in *Zero Dark Thirty*?" – which lined up characters with CIA operatives, a member of the Bush II presidential cabinet, and suspected terrorists. "One of the more obvious correlations between character and real-life inspiration is the key suspect in Maya's hunt, Bin Laden's courier, Abu Ahmed al-Kuwaiti," the *Slate* article noted, reminding us that in addition to the heroine of the movie, actual people suffered under the torture program.[7]

When the film was released, it became apparent that the CIA had been in touch with the filmmakers, and in response, the US Congress balked. The release was accompanied by the surfacing of a memo that screenwriter Mark Boal and director Kathryn Bigelow communicated with CIA personnel on the story of "Maya" and her dogged search for the supposed 9/11 mastermind. In turn, a trio of senators with access to classified intelligence – Dianne Feinstein, Carl Levin, and John McCain – sent a letter to the Sony Pictures chief, "We write to express our deep disappointment with the movie 'Zero Dark Thirty.' We believe the film is grossly inaccurate and misleading in its suggestion that torture resulted in information that led to the location of Usama bin Laden."[8] While critics have debated whether the film actually presents such a causal relationship – the filmmakers argue that it presents various information-gathering methods as leading to bin Laden's location – the narrative arc of the film is such that torture scenes early in the film lead to additional intelligence operations that ultimately help to locate bin Laden.

The dust-up with the senators revived an ongoing national debate on whether torture was an efficacious intelligence-gathering practice. Released the same year as *Zero Dark Thirty*, *The Senate Intelligence Committee Report on Torture* addressed the issue in its first finding: "The CIA's use of its enhanced interrogation techniques was not an effective means of acquiring intelligence or gaining cooperation from detainees." This was followed by a second major conclusion: "The CIA's justification for the use of its enhanced interrogation techniques rested on inaccurate claims of their effectiveness."[9] No wonder some of the senators involved in bringing forward this report found the need to respond to a popular film. And yet just as important was a troubling result: the report's primary finding effectively ceded the terms of debate – the ethical ground – by accepting the question of torture's efficacy as a primary consideration.

Zero Dark Thirty was the most visible of representations of torture circulating in the fifteen years after the 9/11 attacks. The mid-2010s brought a proliferation of torture-laced entertainment forms, including the video game Grand Theft Auto (GTA) 5, released in 2014, in which a player was presented with a scenario involving implements of torture (a hammer, plyers, electric shock) to be used for extracting information from a potential informant. If GTA made torture a game, the many movies and shows that featured torture scenes turned the practice into spectacle as a highly visible form of participation that brings to the forefront something that was previously kept in clandestine settings. Part of the participation involved repetition. Many different kinds of shows during this decade seemed to feature a requisite torture scene. The constant repetition from one entertainment form to another also created what Jacques Derrida's wordplay on torture would call torsion (a turning, a returning). Derrida writes,

> As you know, torture (*torqueo, tortum, torquere*), sometimes in the form of an inquisition or inquisitional questioning, never far from some Torquemada, some grand inquisitor, is always a matter of turning, of torsion, indeed of the re-turn of some re-torsion. There is always a wheel [*roue*] in torture. Torture always puts to work an encircling violence and an insistent repetition, a relentlessness, the turn and return of a circle.[10]

That repetition can refer to a practice that emerges at various points in history – what comes to be known as "water boarding" was a modification of the Medieval "water cure." Water boarding also was part of US military action in the Philippines in the early twentieth century. But the repetition also emerges in the copy-cat energy of popular culture, the willful embrace of torture that results from its own repetitive momentum.[11]

Torturetainment as an element of the War on Terror both depicts the violence and flaunts the empire's power through the challenge to ethical conventions, the human rights discourse that emerged after World War II. Torturetainment is an advertisement for power. *Zero Dark Thirty* makes visible the role of empire (as nation-state) in the carrying out of a practice that becomes mediated by film and other forms of entertainment. This should prompt us to pause, if not reconsider, whether a historical shift in the visibility of torture took place in the early twenty-first century. To develop this question, it is useful to return to the critic Michel Foucault's arguments about changes at the end of the eighteenth century. An early section in *Discipline and Punish*, titled "Torture," notes how, at that historical point, the infliction of pain by the state goes private, away from public hangings and toward penal violence behind bars. Foucault calls it "a new age for penal justice" connected to the rise of the modern prison system, which led to "the disappearance of torture as a public spectacle."[12] Did we in the first two decades of the twenty-first century reverse that shift and return to torture as spectacle? This time the mediation of entertainment replaced the in-person experience of witnessing public executions. In the spirit of public display, Russian authorities paraded before the media suspects who had been tortured following a terrorist attack on a music venue in Moscow in 2024. Showing signs of having endured electric shocks and mutilation, the accused men became an exhibit in the willingness of the Russian empire to break with international norms. "There was no attempt to hide the evidence of torture," *The Guardian* reported.[13] For anyone keeping track of the extent to which torture scenes had appeared in entertainment, the public display by Moscow continued the spectacle, this time no longer pretending to be clandestine.

And yet, counterintuitive as it seems, the very visibility of the entertainment and media process inserts the possibility of disavowal. If the characters in a video game or the people portrayed on television are not real and the people tortured are separated from viewers by entertainment forms, an empire can both practice torture and flaunt it while neutralizing ethical objection. The publicizing of torture, whether in the years following 9/11 or in more recent examples, creates a structure in which pain and power become intertwined. In *The Body in Pain*, Elaine Scarry discusses torture in a way that clarifies the role of entertainment in a long historical process of disavowal: "The denial ... occurs in the translation of all the objectified elements of pain into the insignia of power, the conversion of the enlarged map of human suffering into an emblem of the regime's strength."[14] This is what a film like *Zero Dark Thirty* displays and the Russian show of tortured prisoners makes all too clear: the empire's admission of torturing people turns someone else's pain into what Scarry calls "insignia of power." When the US dispatches the practice to a semi-official setting, the dark ops site, the disavowal persists as an element in the process.

Disavowal is part of cultures of US torture in that elements of secrecy are themselves part of the spectacle. That is why the modifier *clandestine* is so important in the naming of the torture spectacle. With different arms of the US government working separately, one or another governmental US agency can always deny that it sanctioned such actions or had anything to do with them, relegating torture to the work of supposed rogue operatives in "undisclosed locations." That, after all, was the result of the infamous

Abu Ghraib photos. While the US and particularly the military were responsible for military operations and the structural conditions – meaning the role given soldiers in these wars – for committing acts of violence against prisoners, disavowal was possible through a recourse to individual actors, and here a gendered dynamic emerged. It was Lynndie England and her codefendants who took the fall for Abu Ghraib. The infamous photos of England pointing at bound prisoners, even pretending to walk one on a leash, became the face of dark ops. England was convicted of mistreating prisoners while the unnamed water boarders never were even taken to trial; the empire could claim rogue agents while bypassing the charge of rogue state.

Zero Dark Thirty gave us its own form of disavowal as it distanced itself from the torture debates. As the controversy over methods heated up, the studio and director Bigelow quickly embraced marketing a storyline and interpretation that placed gender at the center of the story. "'Zero Dark Thirty' Goes Feminist'" was the headline in a *Salon* magazine interview with writer Boal. "[I]t's a historical fact that a lot of the people instrumentally involved in the hunt for bin Laden were women, and that there was a small group of women in particular who persisted on the courier lead – and [that's] what the Maya character is all about," Boal told Salon. "In a sense that's emblematic of a larger shift within the culture of women taking on jobs that were previously reserved for men, in the intelligence community, but also, as we see, in the military."[15] Jessica Chastain, who played Maya, was also involved in the media blitz to shift the discussion toward the heroine, touting Maya's independence and work ethic. "She doesn't have a love interest in this movie, and in real life she didn't; she was focused" Chastain said in an interview. "She becomes a servant in her work. She loses some friends on the almost decade-long journey to find Osama bin Laden. And it just keeps the fire going within her until she finds the compound and she finds the man himself."[16] All of which is to say that a movie trafficking in torturetainment billed itself as a story about the glass ceiling.

The point becomes clear if we consider the film's storyline and Maya's ascent within the gendered power dynamics of the CIA. While depictions of torture take up most of the film's opening half hour, the story shifts toward Maya's struggles as a woman working against being dismissed in the workplace. She has to challenge her superiors as part of the effort to continue the hunt for bin Laden. The drama becomes woman-centered when Maya and Jessica, a fellow CIA operative and sometimes roommate, are sharing dinner and discussing their personal lives (Maya declares she does not have romantic entanglements) and a bomb goes off and sends them fleeing while holding hands. The full dimensions of the gender plot come forward later when Jessica is killed by a suicide bomber. Maya is then left to fend for herself as she battles against not only the male-dominated terrorist networks but also by the male-dominated CIA, which provides only lukewarm support for her crusade. "It's her against the world," one CIA operative says. In the process, Maya becomes a role model for other women trying to rise through the ranks at the CIA. "You inspired me to come to Pakistan," one young woman operative tells her.

Maya as corporate climber appears at the start of the film. In the opening torture seen, she wears a business suit. Her participation is derided by the men. In numerous scenes Maya is alone facing a group of men who do not believe in or do not care about the search for bin Laden, and she must stand against male-imposed limitations on her actions and the operation. One scene cuts between Navy Seals dressed in combat gear and Maya herself dressed in a business suit. "You're going to kill him for me," she tells the Seals, a line that captures the disjunction between the male-run operations of the empire and her own struggle to get the job done. That is to say, by the terms established in the film, the Seals are doing this for Maya, not country or even justice. The hunt for bin Laden is no longer about national security interest but about Maya's individual trajectory of professional progress at the CIA. Will Maya be able to break the glass ceiling?

That shift in the dominant plot line from public to private contributes to the film's ultimate disavowal of trafficking in torture. The heroine plot line moves past the detailed physical torture of a 9/11 terrorist, presented as a brown man, in the opening sequence. In the film's final scene, Maya is being escorted out of the Middle East on a military plane. She is the only person on the manifest, and she sits inside the plane all alone. The pilot asks her, "Where would you like to go?" She does not respond, and instead drops a couple of tears. By then, viewers are focused on her as character, not on the practice of torture that opens the film. *Zero Dark Thirty* effectively disavows the torture elements leading to Maya's success and thus connects to a much broader history of culture and imperialism which covers structures of power and violence through discourses of equality and freedom.

Door-to-Door Spectacle

More than 150 years before viewers flocked to theaters to view torture scenes in *Zero Dark Thirty*, a curious fictional work featured a nineteenth-century version of torturetainment. In order to consider the long history of clandestine spectacle, we can turn to a relatively unknown entry in this textual record: the sensationally titled *A Thrilling and Exciting Account of the Sufferings and Horrible Tortures Inflicted on Mortimer Bowers and Miss Sophia Delaplain by the Spanish Authorities, for a Supposed Participation With General Lopez in the Invasion of Cuba* (1851).[17] This story received some critical attention in 2007, when it was included in the collection *Empire and the Literature of Sensation*, which sought to emphasize how popular forms registered "the excitement and anxiety of this era of empire-building."[18] This was a historical moment when the US was spreading its settler colonial towns across North America and engaged in a war of conquest with Mexico.

The Sophia Delaplain story was among hundreds of short fictional titles that saturated the antebellum market with accounts of corruption, intrigue, kidnapping, and a variety of salacious topics. "Supply as well as demand drove the popularity of such short forms of fiction, since they were cheaper to produce than longer hard-bound volumes, and could be plausibly disguised as periodicals, thus qualifying for much lower postal rates than those that applied to books," writes the literary critic Paul Erickson.[19] "Delaplain" was part of the catalog of E. E. Barclay, a door-to-door purveyor of lurid tales that have been compared to contemporary true crime.[20] These stories were set in the context of actual events and sometimes supposedly written by the participants, which would explain the pseudonymous Delaplain as the author of the account. Imagine sitting at home and receiving from Barclay's team of door-to-door salespeople a flyer promising a story of "suffering and horrible torture," and if that wasn't enough to attract you, the title also referred to one of the most celebrated US news events of the day, the Narciso López filibustering expeditions to Cuba that failed in their attempts to take over the island from Spain. Thomas M. McDade describes how "Barclay decked his books in bright-colored pictorial drawings to enliven, as if that were necessary, the already lurid text."[21] If GTA 5 brought torture to the technology of color associated with video games in our period, Barclay connected torture to color, using print media.

The Delaplain account is graphic, visually and linguistically, in its depiction. It follows the structure of torture as defined much later by the Geneva Convention, in which a state official attempts to extract information from the victim through physical torment. After Delaplain is asked for information about the filibustering expedition (information she does not have), the following scene ensues:

A small rope, drawn over a pully, was suspended from the ceiling, in the end of which rope was fastened a small hook, somewhat resembling a fish-hook, except that the beard was wanting.

We were now partially strangled, in order that the organ linguae might protrude from the mouth. The tongue was then perforated with an awl, and the hooks attached to the rope were inserted therein. The ropes were then drawn over the pullies until they became so tight that we were under the necessity of standing on tip-toe to prevent our weight from being wholly borne by the tongue.[22]

For those readers who wanted a visual of this scene, the pamphlet featured a drawing of Delaplain suspended by the tongue.

How does Delaplain end up in that situation? The story involves a young woman from a prominent family in New York who elopes with a suitor against her family's wishes. To do so, she cross-dresses as a man. After boarding a packet for California, they find themselves on a ship that is commandeered for a Narcisco López-like filibustering expedition in Cuba. Among the adventurous elements are filibusters engaged in a battle on the ship, the capture of the ship's passengers by Cuban officials, and the appearance of a tribunal run by sadists representing the Inquisition. Delaplain is tortured before escaping and returning home. Her beloved Bowers is killed.

The Delaplain story shifts the usual torture frame so that the otherness of the victim (viewed by the torturer as having an ideological, national, ethnic, and/or religious difference so profound as to uphold the inhuman treatment) is transferred to the torturers, Inquisitorial Spaniards, whose connection to the Catholic Church invokes the Black Legend. Delaplain tells us, "The prison in which we were confined was in the basement of St. Andrew's church . . . it answered the purpose well, and is well supplied with the instruments of torture."[23] In the illustration a group of monks stands in the background as the torture is taking place. And to emphasize the full participation of the Catholic Church, the execution of Bowers is carried out with "a Catholic priest being in attendance."

[Bowers] was then ordered to stand on a small platform, immediately in front of what appeared to be the image of a beautiful virgin. . . . I was horror-struck at beholding the image raise its arms for the purpose of returning the embrace, and in the place of what should have been its arms, two sharp instruments, in the shape of sickles presented themselves, and clasped the body of Mortimer in their embrace. Bowers writhed in agony, but all to no purpose. I was struck dumb. The image continued to tighten its embrace, until the body of Mortimer fell, in four separate pieces, upon the floor.[24]

A torture device connected to a figure of the Virgin Mary is not unheard of in the history of torture, and in the mid-nineteenth century, US periodicals circulated accounts of the Iron Maiden (a cabinet with a Virgin image in the front that can hold a person and pierces the occupant as it closes). As early as 1833, the New England weekly *The Religious Intelligencer* had published an article titled "Popery Illustrated," describing a torture contraption as a "wooden statue, made by the hands of Monks, representing the Virgin Mary." The front of this statue was covered with nails and small daggers and "As this statue extended its arms and gradually drew them back, as if she would affectionally embrace, and press some one to her heart," the daggers pierced the person two or three inches deep. "This statue is a fair representation of Romanism," *The Religious Intelligencer* concludes.[25]

In literary historical terms, the story owes much to Gothic conventions, especially the narrative of Ambrosio and Matilda in Matthew Lewis's 1796 *The Monk*, which also features a cross-dressing female lover and torture by the Inquisition. But in the Delaplain story, the actions of Catholics are connected to a racialized Cuban subject. "In order that my reader may know, or form an idea, of the nature of the Cuban Spaniard, I shall describe each torture separately," Delaplain says.[26] By invoking "nature" in relation to colonial/national identity, Delaplain hints at US racial perspectives that view Cubans as "Creole" or "swarthy." The racialized association of Cubans and Spaniards could be read in opposition to the description of Mortimer Bowers: "His hair was of the pure auburn, and fell in natural glossy ringlets upon a neck whose lily hue told that the sons of Africa, the Spanish Moor, the Eastern Celestial, or the Aboriginal American, could claim no affinity. Nothing but the pure Circassian blood flowed there."[27] The passage simultaneously situates Bowers among the whitest of the white – a population of the Northern Caucasus – while associating his killers with Africa (Spanish Moor) and presumably "aboriginal Americans." The references to various sites of descent, including Eastern Celestial, in opposition to "Circassian blood" emphasize the importance of racialized appearance to this torture scene. The effect is that racialized bodies inhabit different sides of a dyad in which torture becomes a way to emphasize the structural and social separation of racial otherness.

My discussion so far has emphasized how *A Thrilling and Exciting Account* offered its own brand of nineteenth-century spectacle, but part of torturetainment is the simultaneous disavowal of the structure of torture. That part becomes clearer when we turn to the way the story handles gender difference. It is possible that nineteenth-century readers were thrilled and excited not by the torture but rather the series of gender transgressions that precede those scenes. Delaplain ends up in Cuba because she challenges patriarchal conventions. Her father tells her she is to engage only with those in their "elite society." She is not allowed to socialize with, much less marry, Mortimer Bowers because he is from lower-class circles. Although Delaplain protests that Mortimer's character is what should be considered, her father responds that he is a "young man without fortune, without friends, and whose parents are in so straitened circumstances, that they with difficulty sustain themselves."[28] In the ultimate rebuke, Delaplain's father turns the eagle into a metaphor for class distinctions: "Eagles must sleep in an eagle's nest."[29] As such, Delaplain transgresses not only gendered limitations but also her family's Manhattan conventions on status.

Delaplain responds by cross-dressing and boarding the ship *Henry Clay*; s/he appears "on ship-board in the habiliments of the masculine gender" and flaunts it as a way "to add to the interest of the adventure."[30] Becoming "Harry Blain," a name that rhymes with Delaplain, she forgets about "the propriety of having the marriage ceremony performed before we left the shores of our native country."[31] When filibusters try to take over the ship and a battle breaks out, the masculine Blain is in the middle of it, fighting against the freebooters. But that is no protection when the couple goes on shore for water and Spaniards suspect them of being filibusters – a term which implies piracy, deception, and opportunism and connects the story to the highly publicized expeditions to Cuba. Authorities in Cuba interpret the cross-dressing as evidence of deception, and the punishment of torture is a response not only for the supposed military action but also the social transgressions against gender norms.

The question of gender roles and the place of women in society is the ultimate payoff to this story. The action is motivated by a question of whether Delaplain would be able to escape the confines of her patriarchal home. By leaving New York for the newly acquired territory of California and ultimately ending up in the Caribbean, Delaplain seems to say that for a young woman to exert independence in choosing a husband she would have to leave her home country. *A Thrilling and Exciting Account* concludes with a reactionary position on Delaplain's independence. Having witnessed her paramour's execution, Delaplain escapes from Cuba and makes her way to Baltimore, where she writes her account. The moral? More "discretion" was necessary from her parents and herself. Dejected and planning to withdraw from the world, Delaplain concludes her tale by saying, "I would remind both the old and the young, that it is as necessary now as formerly, to observe the old adage – 'LOOK BEFORE YOU LEAP'."³² Like the pedagogical imperatives of so many eighteenth and nineteenth century fictions, the story warns women of the dangers posed by thrilling and exciting adventures which it peddles. The tale ultimately uses torture to work through the social position of a woman trying to gain independence, and in that sense it shares a plot direction with *Zero Dark Thirty*.

Taken together, these two texts depict the long history of representing torture in American culture. The contexts are vastly different and so are the forms of culture being circulated; nevertheless, among the effects of torturetainment is the turning of violence into entertainment. Like cultures of US imperialism, cultures of US torture enable a disavowal of the effects of violence under the guise of benevolence or entertainment. Torture emerges in the texts for its narrative value, but it is not presented as an integral part of the US nation-state. In the early nineteenth-century, as US expansionism under the guise of a white supremacist ideology of "Manifest Destiny" decimated indigenous groups and justified the invasion of Mexico, torture was often associated with another, competing empire – Spain. In the case of the 1851 text, the torture is carried out by evil Spaniards in Cuba, enacting a type of projection to another imperial power. In the 9/11 film, US agents torture prisoners at some off-shore location, keeping the US empire at a distance from its own operations. Despite settings and plots that are at the center of US imperial objectives, these texts ultimately divert attention from the military operations that are the engine driving expansionist territorial acquisition and imperialist control. In other words, the requisite torture scene in popular culture, and torturetainment more generally, are simultaneously a display of US power and a cover for the machinations of empire.

Notes

1. For a discussion of *24* as portraying what she calls a biopower "torture fantasy" that circulates a notion of the body as holding information that can be extracted, see Hillary Neroni, *The Subject of Torture: Psychoanalysis and Biopolitics in Television and Film* (New York: Columbia University Press, 2015), 95–114.
2. Steve Jones argues that the horror subgenre "torture porn" precedes and postdates the War on Terror, even though some films that came out after the revelation of the Bush administration's torture program gesture toward allegorical elements associated with Abu Ghraib and Guantánamo, including the

use of orange jumpsuits and black hoods. *Torture Porn: Popular Horror After Saw* (New York: Palgrave Macmillan, 2013), 63–70.

3. Gordon argues that the US relationship to torture changed after 9/11. While the criticisms of Vietnam-era excesses, and particularly torture as part of that war's Phoenix Program, marked a national turning away from torture as acceptable practice, the post-9/11 period saw torture normalized in the social and political realms. Rebecca Gordon, *Mainstreaming Torture: Ethical Approaches in the Post-9/11 United States* (New York: Oxford University Press, 2014).

4. Amy Kaplan, "Left Alone with America," in *Cultures of United States Imperialism*, ed. Amy Kaplan and Donald Pease (Durham: Duke University Press, 1994), 13.

5. Michael Rogin, "'Make My Day!': Spectacle as Amnesia in Imperial Politics," *Representations* 29 (Winter 1990): 100.

6. Advertisements for the film explained the title as a "metaphor for the search." *Universal UK*, "The Meaning of Zero Dark Thirty," January 4, 2013, 1:17 www.youtube.com/watch?v=dOz7DXYeFWU.

7. David Haglund, Aisha Harris, and Forrest Wickman, "Who Are the People in *Zero Dark Thirty?*" *Slate*, January 4, 2013. www.slate.com/blogs/browbeat/2013/01/14/zero_dark_thirty_fact_vs_fiction_who_are_the_real_life_inspirations_for.html.

8. Steven Zeitchik, "Senate Leaders Feinstein and McCain Condemn 'Zero Dark Thirty,'" *Los Angeles Times*, December 19, 2012. www.latimes.com/entertainment/movies/la-xpm-2012-dec-19-la-et-mn-feinstein-mccain-condemn-zero-dark-thirty-20121219-story.html.

9. *The Senate Intelligence Committee Report on Torture* (Brooklyn: Melville House, 2014), 3–4.

10. Jacques Derrida, *Rogues: Two Essays on Reason*, trans. Pascale-Anne Brault and Michael Naas (Palo Alto: Stanford University Press, 2005), 7–8.

11. Derrida's project in *Rogues* is thinking through a democracy to come with an awareness of the violence inherent in present-day democratic efforts.

12. Michel Foucault, *Discipline and Punish: The Birth of the Prison*, trans. Alan Sheridan (New York: Vintage, 1995), 7.

13. Andrew Roth and Pjotr Sauer, "Russia Officials Lauding Torture was Unthinkable: Now It is Proud to Do So," *The Guardian*, March 25, 2024. www.theguardian.com/world/2024/mar/25/russian-officials-lauding-torture-was-unthinkable-now-it-is-proud-to-do-so.

14. Elaine Scarry, *The Body in Pain* (New York: Oxford University Press, 1985), 56.

15. Irin Carmon, "'Zero Dark Thirty' Goes Feminist," *Salon*, February 1, 2013. www.salon.com/2013/02/01/zero_dark_thirty_goes_feminist/.

16. Artisan News Service, "Zero Dark Thirty Tops Box Office," January 13, 2013, 1:47, www.youtube.com/watch?v=ifKvswiZJ3w.

17. Miss Delaplain [pseud.], *A Thrilling and Exciting Account of the Sufferings and Horrible Tortures Inflicted on Mortimer Bowers and Miss Sophia Delaplain by*

the Spanish Authorities, for a Supposed Participation With General Lopez in the Invasion of Cuba (Charleston: E. E. Barclay, M. B. Crosson & Co., 1851).

18. Jesse Alemán and Shelley Streeby, eds., *Empire and the Literature of Sensation* (New Brunswick: Rutgers University Press, 2007), xxvii. Alemán and Streeby's collection tracked how the operations of empire appeared in texts and fomented ideological positions vis a vis US expansionism in the mid-century.

19. Paul Erickson shows that while the antebellum period is usually associated with major writers such as Nathaniel Hawthorne, the marketplace of fiction opened the way for writers to publish a variety of "cheap, ephemeral urban sensation and adventure fiction." "New Books, New Men: City-Mysteries Fiction, Authorship, and the Literary Marketplace," *Early American Studies* 1:1 (Spring 2003): 273–312.

20. Barclay was a publisher and entrepreneur did a brisk business between 1841 and 1888 in sensationally titled tales such as *A Confession of the Awful and Bloody Transactions in the Life of Charles Wallace, the Fiend-Like Murderer of Miss Mary Rogers* (1851). More than 160 Barclay publications appeared before the end of the century, most out of his publishing houses in Cincinnati and Philadelphia. Many of the tales involved a young heroine who runs away from home and comes into contact with pirates, murderers, or soldiers. Thomas M. McDade, "Lurid Literature of the Last Century: The Publications of E.E. Barclay," *The Pennsylvania Magazine of History and Biography* 80.4 (Oct. 1956): 453.

21. McDade, "Lurid," 454.

22. Miss Delaplain, *A Thrilling and Exciting Account*, 28–9.

23. Miss Delaplain, *A Thrilling and Exciting Account*, 27.

24. Miss Delaplain, *A Thrilling and Exciting Account*, 29–30.

25. "Popery Illustrated," *The Religious Intelligencer*, December 14, 1833, 461.

26. Miss Delaplain, *A Thrilling and Exciting Account*, 29.

27. Miss Delaplain, *A Thrilling and Exciting Account*, 6.

28. Miss Delaplain, *A Thrilling and Exciting Account*, 12.

29. Miss Delaplain, *A Thrilling and Exciting Account*, 11.

30. Miss Delaplain, *A Thrilling and Exciting Account*, 16.

31. Miss Delaplain, *A Thrilling and Exciting Account*, 17.

32. Miss Delaplain, *A Thrilling and Exciting Account*, 31.

PART III

Ongoing Empire and Speculative Worlds

The Du Bois Genealogy
Three Worlds and Three Writers on Black Anti-Imperialism
Alex Lubin

In his 1903 book, *The Souls of Black Folk*, the African American sociologist W. E. B. Du Bois predicted, "the problem of the twentieth century is the problem of the color line."[1] This famous line, predicting an era of counter-revolutionary energies following Reconstruction and ascendant Jim Crow racial terror, has helped scholars comprehend the making of racial segregation and inequality in the twentieth-century United States. Yet, Du Bois's famous line originally appeared three years prior to the publication of *Souls* in a different context. Delivered to the Pan-African Congress that had been convened in Paris, Du Bois delivered an address in which he followed his line about the color line's prominence in the twentieth century with the following: "the basis of denying to over half the world the right of sharing to their utmost ability the opportunities and privileges of modern civilization."[2] Cast in this way, Du Bois's prophetic statement about the enduring power of racism to determine the fate of the twentieth century was a global, and not just national, statement. As Brent Edwards has pointed out, this most famous statement of Du Bois's was as much an internationalist prophecy as well as a national one.

Du Bois's oeuvre casts a long shadow over studies of empire because of the ways it recognized racism as constitutive of a state-centric world system. *Souls* was written in the context of US overseas imperial expansion, as the United States acquired Guam, the Philippines, and Puerto Rico and annexed the independent state of Hawaii in the Spanish American War (1898). In 1915 the United States invaded the independent nation of Haiti and began a decades-long intervention in Cuba. In 1919 the worldwide convulsions of inter-imperial rivalries led to World War I, followed by the emergence of an international order governed by nation-states instead of empires. In this new international context, the fate of what Du Bois called, "the darker nations" of Afro-Asia were determined by Anglo-Atlantic nations.[3] The color line, then, was a synecdoche for understanding race and racism in the context of a worldwide international order.

Du Bois published *The Souls of Black Folk* not only in the context of a global reordering of imperial power, but also in the context of a decades-long backlash, or counterrevolution, against the possibilities of Black freedom, or what he termed "abolition democracy," within the US.[4] The counterrevolution took the form of Jim Crow segregation, vigilante white terror, and legal sanctioning of second-class Black citizenship. Du Bois saw the US domestic counterrevolution as connected to US imperial expansion. Black soldiers recruited to fight in World War I demanded equal citizenship after the war as the wages of participation. Concurrently, people living in the Afro-Asian world who were colonized by US and European imperial expansion faced new forms of racist control. Du Bois understood the dialectic between US overseas expansion and domestic racism as the "anarchy of empire."[5] Understanding how Black Americans were paradoxically situated as both citizens of the US *and* as members of a diaspora that connected them to the geographies targeted by European and US imperial projects helped him to identify the creative and imaginative ways that Black Americans have seen themselves as part of Pan-African "commonwealth"[6] engaged in global Black anti-imperialist movements.

Pan-Africanism is the historical banner under which several modes of Black anti-imperialist agendas have existed, including back-to-Africa emigration plans and more conceptual and cultural notions that articulate global Blackness as a political project. Pan-Africanism has been a strategy to imagine Black freedom within and beyond Western modernity.[7] While there are many varieties of Pan-Africanism, Du Bois was most interested in Pan-African political projects focused on anti-imperialism across the Africa continent. He was foremost among Black Americans in developing an anti-imperialist Pan-Africanism through the formation of the Pan-African Congress. The Pan-African Congress convened annual meetings that attracted African and African American intellectual leaders to discuss shared struggles and to plot a political way forward against European and American imperialism.

Pan-African projects, whether based in emigration plots or in political organizing, had to confront "the anarchy of empire," to reconcile how African Americans could be part of a Black world even while located in the imperial West. Moreover, Pan-African projects had to theorize bonds of Blackness – that is, to create an imagined community – despite linguistic and geopolitical differences within the Black world.[8] Pan-African literature was one of the most important ways to build Pan-Africanism, to experiment with representing Blackness in order to overcome the linguistic and geopolitical differences that threatened to make diasporic or international connection impossible. Pan-African literature offered a means to forge community out of difference, to define alternative global definitions of Blackness, and to test modes of political struggle as the waging of anti-imperialist and anti-racist struggle, attuned to varied and uneven geopolitical and historical conjunctures.

W. E. B. Du Bois was the most famous writer contributing to the project of creating a Black anti-imperialist literature in this era. But he was not the only one – nor even the only one to write under the name Du Bois. Indeed, for most of the twentieth century, we can find a writer with the surname Du Bois taking up the Black anti-imperial literary tradition: W. E. B. Du Bois, his wife Shirley Graham Du Bois, and his stepson David Graham Du Bois. Together these three writers and their key texts frame a miniature world history of literary anti-imperial politics in the US and beyond. First, W. E. B. Du Bois's 1928 novel, *Dark Princess*, theorizes Black anti-imperialism in the interwar years, at the dawn of the international geopolitical order based in the nation-state. Second, Shirley Graham Du Bois penned journalistic essays and biographies at the height of the Cold War, when Black anti-imperialists aligned with the Third World movement. Third, David Graham Du Bois wrote journalistic essays and a novel, *And Bid Him Sing*, after experiencing the Afro-Asian movement in Cairo, Egypt and as an editor for the Black Panther Party newspaper in the US The Du Bois genealogy requires centering the planetary in Black literary and political anti-imperialism. In referring to the planetary, I mean to invoke Wai Chee Dimock's call for analyses of "denationalized" texts that transgress nationalist literary borders and circulate or flow globally. Unlike Benedict Anderson, who postulates the rise of the novel as a phase in the making of nationalism's imagined community, Dimock argues that literature "holds out to its readers dimensions of space and time so far-flung and so deeply recessional that they can never be made to coincide with the synchronic plane of the geopolitical map."[9] In what follows I read the Du Bois genealogy and its engagement with the Pan-African literature of anti-imperialism against the grain of nationalist histories to identify its planetary formations and imaginaries.

A prolific writer of manifestos, monographs, poetry, fiction, journalism, autobiography, and more, W. E. B. Du Bois employed varied modes of literary address to imagine the possibilities for political projects, to experiment with alternative worlds, and to test theories and methods. His 1928 novel, *Dark Princess* (one of the five novels he published) is a potent example of how he employed fiction to imagine the possibilities for Pan-Africanism. *Dark Princess* was among the first works of fiction to narrate the possibilities of Black internationalism at a time of massive international geopolitical transformation. Published after World War I and on the cusp of World War II, Du Bois's novel speculates on the possibilities of Black American anti-imperialism in a world increasingly divided along the color line. Following the Treaty of Versailles, the European powers met to divide the globe into gradations of freedom and unfreedom. Enshrined in the formation of the League of Nations were assumptions about which polities were fit for self-rule, which were required to undergo varieties of trustee-ships and mandates, and which were to assume mentorship from European powers. In this new global arrangement, nation/states would be ranked, often along racialized lines, as self-ruling or under trusteeship.

From his vantage point at the London-based 1912 Universal Races Congress, and as a witness to the 1921 "Red Summer" in the US when African American soldiers returning from World War I were brutally attacked as they demanded equality, Du Bois believed that African Americans had a stake in joining with the so-called "darker nations" in the post–World War I world order, to establish the horizons of Black freedom in a global terrain and not merely within the United States. *Dark Princess* is an attempt to theorize the relationship of Black Americans to the "darker nations;" it joined his political work in forming the Pan-African Congress and in writing manifestos in the National Association for the Advancement of Colored People (NAACP)'s *Crisis Magazine* advocating for a planetary approach to confronting the color line.

Dark Princess was published during an era that literary critics call the Harlem Renaissance or the New Negro Movement. While Du Bois is usually considered an elder at the edge of these movements, the most prominent concerns in *Dark Princess* echo work by other Renaissance-era writers, including George Schuyler (*Black Empire*), Claude McKay (*Banjo* and *Amiable With Big Teeth*), among others.[10] *Dark Princess's* protagonist is Mathew Townes, an African American with roots in the US South who struggles to find a political strategy to overcome racist violence. Each of the four sections of *Dark Princess* offers an experiment in global Blackness and in Black political activism. Ultimately, Townes realizes that anti-imperialism is the only viable path to freedom. In the first section readers meet Townes as an "exile" in Berlin studying to become a medical doctor. Despite his excellence as a student, Townes's advancement is stunted by the color line; he is overlooked for jobs and promotions and therefore decides to abandon a medical career. Even beyond the United States, in

Berlin, Townes realizes the color line prevents his advancement through the normative routes of education and achievement.

In the second section of the novel Townes joins the sleeping-car porter's union, where he learns of a plot to derail a train carrying members of the Ku Klux Klan, a plot that if successful would lead to several deaths, including his own. Although reluctant to engage in violent sabotage as a mode of Black resistance, he ultimate embraces this path when he experiences the lynching of a fellow porter. In this section, Townes experiments with Black trade unionism and armed resistance as routes to liberation. Yet, he abandons this route when he learns that the train derailment will also kill his love interest, the Indian Princess Kaultilya, leader of a cadre of Third World activists, who happens to be on the train.

In the third section of *Dark Princess* Townes experiments with political power within the United States as a route to freedom. Readers follow Townes's work with a Black congressman in Chicago and his ultimate advancement through the political process by taking advantage of compromises with people in power. Townes's political advancement includes concessions made to capitalists and to white supremacists in the service of his own career and at the expense of the Black masses. Again, he abandons this route to Black freedom, realizing that the true revolutionary potential to overcome the global color line lies in the metaphorical (and in his personal case, literal) marriage of Black Americans to the darker nations beyond the United States.

The final section of *Dark Princess* sees Townes abandon his dreams of economic and political power within the United States and his decision to join with Princess Kaultilya both in marriage and a global struggle against racism and colonialism. Where Townes had struggled with the question of how African Americans could fit within the darker nations, by the end of the novel he recognizes not only that Black Americans are part of the world's darker nations, but also that the Black working class, especially in the Southern US, can be a vanguard in a global movement to overcome racial and imperial violence. The role of Black Americans in the Third World movement is articulated most clearly by Princess Kaultilya, who convinces him that the US Black belt is part of the darker nations.

> here in Virginia you are at the edge of a black world. The black belt of the Congo, the Nile, and the Ganges reaches by way of Guiana, Haiti, and Jamaica, like a red arrow, up into the heart of white America. Thus I see a mighty synthesis: you can work in Africa and Asia right here in America if you work in the Black Belt ... You may stand here, Mathew – here, halfway between Maine and Florida, between the Atlantic and the Pacific, with

Europe in your face and China at your back, with industry in your right
hand and commerce in your left and the farm beneath your steady feet; and
yet be in the Land of the Blacks.[11]

Princess Kaultilya's "synthesis" links nation-states to political imaginaries
like the "black belt of the Congo" or to rivers like the Nile and Ganges, and
it transposes "I" to "you." In doing so, Kaultilya outlines a planetary
imaginary that transcends and transgresses a world system made problematic by the color line. In this way, *Dark Princess* foreshadows an argument
Du Bois develops in *Black Reconstruction in America* (1935) that southern
Black Americans, during reconstruction, represent a vanguard of future
planetary abolitionist democracy.

During the two decades following the publication of *Dark Princess* the
world was radically altered again. World War II transformed the US Black
freedom movement as it began to wage legal battles for civil and political
rights within the United States. Across Africa and Asia, decolonization
movements began to see victories in the formation of newly independent
states. In 1955 Bandung, Indonesia hosted the inaugural Afro-Asian conference, an event that marked the beginning of the nonaligned movement.
Bandung (as it became known) attracted the heads of newly decolonized
states who articulated some of the demands of nonalignment, including
political and economic independence from the global superpowers and
nuclear disarmament.[12] Globally, the military and economic rivalry
between the Soviet Union and the United States crystalized into the
Cold War, where winning over the countries of the global south to US
or Soviet orbits was foremost. Within these transformed contexts, Black
American relationships to empire shifted from their pre-war orientations
toward decolonization movements across Africa and Asia, including
Bandung, to new locations. A growing number of decolonized spaces
across the global south – from Havana, to Accra, to Beijing, to Cairo –
served as liberated spaces for African Americans who sought to experience
freedom beyond the color line.[13]

Egypt became a hub for anti-colonial movements across the African
continent due its successful 1952 war for independence followed by the 1956
nationalization of the Suez Canal and its defense from British, French, and
Israeli militaries during the so-called, "Suez crisis." Gamal Abdel Nasser
became one of the preeminent African anti-colonial leaders, successfully
defending Egyptian independence. Nasser's vision for Egyptian independence, as articulated in his book *Egypt's Liberation: The Philosophy of the
Revolution*, sought to unite three prominent and sometimes competing

political trends in the Afro-Asian world: Pan-Africanism, Pan-Islamism, and Pan-Arabism.[14]

Nasser's vision proved attractive to several African Americans, who began to travel to Egypt along with places like Ghana, and African anti-imperialists used Cairo as a base for plotting their liberation movements. In 1954 the African Association, convened by African university students across Egypt and supervised by members of the Egyptian Free Officers who had participated in the 1952 Egyptian revolution, was formed in Cairo to unite "a general congress of peoples from colonized African territories." Through the African Association, Cairo hosted African intellectuals and artists who represented newly independent states as well as those exiled from their still-colonized countries. For example, the African Association hosted Vusumze Make, the South African freedom fighter who lived in Cairo with his spouse, the African American poet, Maya Angelou. During her time in Cairo, Angelou contributed to the nonaligned movement's Cairo-based magazine, *The Arab Observer*, and facilitated the travel and settlement of several African American artists in Cairo.

One of the African Association's most important functions was thus to curate art and new aesthetic forms of literature and writing to forge Pan-African and anti-imperialist connections. Pan-African art, including literature, helped bridge political and linguistic differences across African anti-imperialist movements. The Association published a literary and political magazine called, "Africa Rising" that was coedited by the Egyptian poet, Abdu Badawi, and was published in Arabic, English, and French. Further, drawing on the support of Nasser's government, the African Association built support and capacity via Cairo Radio, which offered the association a radio program in Swahili, Amharic, and other African languages and was broadcast across the continent.

Due to the success of the African Association, as well as the growing stature of Nasser within the Afro-Asian movement, the nonaligned movement chose Cairo to be the home of the inaugural 1957 Afro-Asian People's Solidarity Organization (AAPSO) meeting. AAPSO was committed to adopting political resolutions on the possibilities for the nonaligned movement, including the need for political independence and decolonization, the demilitarization of Afro-Asian countries, and nuclear nonproliferation. Like the African Association, AAPSO acknowledged the need for a cultural front of artists from within the Third World to publish and share their work; it established a writer's bureau that hosted conferences in Tashkent, Uzbekistan, Conkary, Guinea, Cairo, Egypt, and Beirut, Lebanon. The first writer's conference was inaugurated by Egyptian leftists and artists including novelists like Taha Hussein and Naguib Mahfouz, and the journalist and novelists, Ihsan Abd Al-Qudus. AAPSO's writer's bureau was intended to help inspire and support poetry and fiction anthologies produced within the Afro-Asian world, including the publication of the trilingual *Lotus Magazine*.[15]

The cultural front was at the center of AAPSO's anti-imperialist politics because it desired not only to place Afro-Asian anti-colonial politics at the center of political culture, but also to be a space to promote a different sort of modernity than the one promoted by the global superpowers. As AAPSO delegates argued at the first writer's conference, the fight against imperialism went beyond a rhetorical debate between competing sides to an epistemological struggle centered on self-representation and decolonization from Western cultural imperialism.

> Our politics is cultural because it does not mean to us a simple conflict between opponents anxious to conquer and dominate; but we struggle to create a new order the setting up of which is inspired by the suffering of all those who have known slavery, racial discrimination, colonialism, and imperialism. Our cultural aspirations are far more fundamental for our political actions than the power of the west, which has depersonalized us and so altered our institutions.[16]

The writer's bureau was a space to theorize the anti-imperialist cultural front as well as to promote Afro-Asian writers, anthologies, and short fiction.

If the cultural front helped translate geopolitical and linguistic differences across a vast territory, AAPSO's feminist politics helped to locate women's politics across Afro-Asian countries at the center of its vision of anti-imperialism. To that end, it organized a women's bureau and eventually organized the 1961 Afro-Asian Women's Conference, held in Cairo. The conference, chaired by the Egyptian feminist Bahia Karam hosted 240 delegates, from thirty-five countries who presented anti-imperialist politics as feminist politics. As Karam told delegates at the opening session of the conference,

> Our Conference is meeting at a crucial time, not only for our two continents but for the whole world. It is meeting at a time when the forces of imperialism and colonialism are fighting its last-ditch battle, and when the struggle for liberation and independence is at its height. And we, the women of Africa and Asia are playing our part in this great struggle, which I have no doubt, will meet with victory and success.[17]

The agenda for the conference focused on the "economic status of women, social status and rights of women, the cultural rights of women, political and legal rights of women, and the role of women in the struggle for national liberation."

AAPSO's writers and women's bureaus forged bonds of anti-imperialism across linguistic and geopolitical terrain. Moreover, the cultural and feminist leanings of AAPSO worked to translate the nonalignment movement to Black anti-imperialist politics, especially its feminist varieties. Although African Americans were not the primary audience for AAPSO's politics, increasingly Afro-America became a place of concern for the nonaligned movement. Recognizing the importance of the US Black belt as a front in the nonaligned movement's anti-imperialist politics, the *Arab Observer*, the Egyptian-based, multilingual magazine of the nonaligned movement, began to publish dispatches from "Afro-America" in the early 1960s. The contributions of African American writers, including Maya Angelou, Shirley Graham Du Bois, and David Graham Du Bois, were a major avenue to nonaligned publications, such as the *Arab Observer*.

The transformed post-war context for Black freedom movements in the US and beyond gives us a special historical perspective on the life and work of Shirley Graham DuBois. Shirley Graham had built a radical political life prior to meeting and marrying W. E. B. Du Bois. Born in 1896 in Indianapolis, Indiana, Lola Shirley Graham was the daughter of an AME (African Methodist Episcopal) minister, who spent her childhood moving across the country while her father established new churches. After a relatively short first marriage that produced two sons, Graham left her children with her mother while she attended Oberlin College. At Oberlin, she earned her BA and MA degrees in music history, and she completed an opera, *Tom-Toms: An Epic of Music and The Negro*, performed at Cleveland Stadium in 1932 to a crowd of 10,000. In producing *Tom-Toms* Graham became the first African American woman to write and produce an opera with an all-Black cast. She went on to become a field organizer with the NAACP, a novelist of several short children's books on Black history, and a founding member of the Progressive Party. At age forty-four, Graham married the eighty-four-year-old W. E. B. Du Bois and joined him in Ghana at the apex of Nkrumah's independence movement.

Shirley Graham Du Bois was an observer at AAPSO events and reported on AAPSO in *Freedomways*, a US-based magazine she founded with Paul Robeson and others, and in the *Egyptian Gazette* as well as several Soviet-based journals. Her reporting encouraged readers to view Nasser as a model for Black anti-imperialism, and she repeatedly argued to Black American readers that Egypt and Arab nationalist politics should be considered at the center of Black radical politics. She argued that Egypt was at the center of the Black diaspora and its anti-imperialist politics fostered a cultural and feminist agenda to which Black Americans should aspire.[18] Typical of Graham DuBois's admiration for the internationalism of Afro-Asian politics was her description of the final day of the 1961 AAPSO women's conference, when, on a "warm and sunny afternoon," the delegates assembled outside the National Assembly Building and marched through the streets of Cairo, each woman carrying her national flag. As the marchers moved through Cairo's streets, onlookers cheered and threw flowers, chanting, "Honor these women of Africa and Asia! They are our women – the mothers of our sons. Long live Afro-Asian solidarity!"

The AAPSO provided Shirley Graham Du Bois as a writer with a space where Black internationalist feminist politics translated to Third World internationalism. The multiple places she lists in her description of AAPSO's Afro-Asian Women's Conference signal that Black internationalism.

> We marched together: the delicate women of China with their flower-like little faces – thin refugees from Palestine and from South Africa – women of Guinea – Iran – Indonesia – Kenya – Nigeria – Tunisia – North Korea – Jordan – Cambodia – Libya – Morocco – thirty five flags fluttered in the breeze and the women of thirty-five countries marches through the streets of Cairo for three hours and then came to the home of President Nasser.[19]

The cultural and feminist front against imperialism echoes the romance of Black anti-imperialism in *Dark Princess*; yet, Graham Du Bois's vision differs from the novel in that she sees women are independent political theorists, and the Arab world has a prominent political voice in the Third World movement.[20]

Like all internationalist movements, the political terrain on which delegates assembled was always uneven – there were serious political disagreements, differences in economic status among delegates, differences in national rights among delegates, differences in language, race, socioeconomic status. Moreover, global debates splitting the world into the Eastern and Western blocs exerted tremendous pressure on all nonaligned organizations. These pressures came to a head for Cairo's African American community in June 1967 when the so-called six-day war with Israel (with considerable US sponsorship) led the Egyptian government to expel all US citizens from the country. As they evacuated Egypt, African Americans encountered the conundrums of being US citizens in the nonaligned movement: despite a preference to engage in a different sort of modernity, their passports connected them to a US project they ultimately could not escape.

Shirley Graham Du Bois helped introduce Anglophone readers to the anti-imperialism of the nonaligned movement through her journalism and her biography of Gamal Abdel Nasser. Her son, David Graham Du Bois, the stepson of W. E. B. Du Bois, carried the torch by translating Cairo's nonaligned movement to US contexts throughout the 1970s. David Graham Du Bois straddled Egypt and the United States during his literary career and in doing so was able to influence the Black Panther Party's internationalist vision for Black anti-imperialism. In his capacities as a journalist and editor in Cairo, David Graham Du Bois befriended dozens of Black American Muslims who came to Cairo to study Islam at Al-Azhar University, artists in residency at the American Research Center or at the American University in Cairo, and political activists, like Malcolm X, who addressed the Organization of African University (OAU) in 1964. In his capacity as a tour guide and insider to Cairo's political and culture scene, Du Bois was uniquely situated to analyze the complex relationships African Americans formed to the Afro-Asian movement, and how these relationships contributed to Black anti-imperialism.

David Graham Du Bois moved to Cairo with his mother in 1962 and became a journalist working for *The Arab Observer* and the *Egyptian Gazette*. He published dispatches on Afro-America in the nonaligned movement's press. This genre presented news coverage of civil rights struggles and racial abuse in the United States intended to show that the West had not overcome its history of anti-Black racism and that Egypt was more progressive. However, in making this case, Graham Du Bois had to confront racial tensions between African American expats and tourists and Egyptians, misunderstandings and occasional discrimination that was directed in both directions. Even as he recognized the tensions between the African American community in Cairo and Egyptians across the country, Du Bois also knew that cultural exchanges had successfully bridged these divides. For David Graham Du Bois the importance of the cultural front of the Afro-Asian movement was its dynamic enabling African Americans to translate their experiences of racism to the global anti-imperialist movement.[21]

More than most American journalists, this Du Bois helped make American readers aware of the African American expatriate and tourist community in Cairo during the era of the Third World Movement. As an editor for the English-language *Egyptian Gazette,* Du Bois covered Malcom

X's 1964 visit to Cairo. After touring North Africa and the Middle East
that year (for the second time), Malcolm arrived in Cairo to address the
recently formed OAU. Afterwards, he sought to build a US-based organization based on the OAU called the Organization of African American
Unity, and he tasked Maya Angelou to help lead this organization in the
US David Graham Du Bois also reported on a cadre of Black Muslims,
most of whom were members of the Nation of Islam, who had received
scholarships to study orthodox Sunni Islam at Al-Azhar University. Several
of these religious students were also musicians and writers, who shared
their cultural productions with Egyptian colleagues. Other African
Americans were drawn to Cairo due to the flowering of Egyptian modernist art and culture that bloomed in age of the Third World movement.[22]

In many ways, David Graham Du Bois's writing and experiences in
Cairo represent the fulfillment of his parents, W. E. B. and Shirley Graham
Du Bois's vision of Black anti-imperialism. While this Du Bois genealogy
is markedly more intellectual than biological, David Graham Du Bois
continued to engage the stepfather whose name he took, W. E. B. Du
Bois's experiments in Blackness and questioning of the roles of the US
Black freedom movement in a global struggle against the color line.
Moreover, David Graham Du Bois fulfilled his mother's insistence that
the Middle East was an epicenter of Cold War era racial and imperial
warfare. The Du Bois genealogy comes to fruition in David Graham Du
Bois's novel And *Bid Him Sing*.[23]

And Bid Him Sing is a genre of historical realism based on fictionalized
accounts of actual events and figures. The novel was published in 1972,
after David Graham Du Bois had returned from Cairo and became the
editor of the Black Panther's newspaper. Du Bois's novel is a retrospective
on the African American expat community in Cairo in the era of the Afro-
Asian movement; yet its publication occurs following Nasser's 1970 death
and therefore serves as a usable history of Black anti-imperialism as it was
developing in the Black Panther Party. The novel is set in 1964, as the
narrator, Bob Jones (based on Graham Du Bois himself) serves as the hub
for the African American expat community in Cairo at the of peak of
Gamal Abdel Nasser's pan-Arab and Pan-African organizing. The expat
community at the center of the novel are comprised of former and current
Nation of Islam members, as well as intellectuals like Graham Du Bois,
who were attracted to Cairo as the crossroads of the Pan-African world.
And Bid Him Sing's protagonist is Suliman Ibn Rashid, a Black American
Muslim poet who travels to Cairo to escape racism in the US, to study
orthodox Islam at Al-Azhar University, and to engage in the transnational

anti-imperialist political currents that ebbed and flowed across the Nile delta. Readers follow Rashid's experiences reading poetry in jazz clubs across Cairo and meeting other African American expats and fellow travelers, including Malcolm X, who appears in the novel as he prepares to address the 1964 OAU conference. The novel's climax is when the African American expat community meets with Malcolm X prior to his OAU speech. At one of these meetings, Malcolm articulates the need for an Organization of African American Unity (OAAU) that can be modeled on the OAU. When pressed to explain to his listeners why he believes there is a need for an OAAU, Malcolm frames the need in terms of the racial violence experienced in the US South. Yet, to an audience of Black Americans living in Cairo, Malcolm's framing seems narrowly focused on the United States. Bob Jones asks Malcolm, "Could we establish an OAAU group here in Cairo?" To this question, Malcolm begins to expand his understanding of the OAAU to a global movement of Black anti-imperialism. As he explains to his audience,

> Cairo is a good place to have one of the first groups. Anywhere brothers and sisters are outside the States OAAU units can be formed. They will be established throughout Latin and South America and the Caribbean. We will pattern ourselves after the Organization of African Unity and create and maintain close ties with the OAU.[24]

David Graham Du Bois's restaging of Malcolm's commitment to linking OAAU to global anti-imperialist movements fills important gaps that were left silent following Malcolm's assassination shortly after his visit to Cairo. Moreover, reminding US readers in 1975 of the unfulfilled anti-imperialist politics of the OAAU offered a usable past for Black anti-imperialist in the Black Panther Party and beyond struggling to link the Black freedom movement to global movements against imperialism and racism.[25]

Throughout *And Bid Him Sing*, readers encounter Egypt as a cosmopolitan third-world capitol, where African American Muslims like Rashid, read anti-racist poetry to Cairo café audiences comprised of, "young black students from West and East Africa, young African diplomats and freedom fighters from southern Africa, some Pakistanis and Indian students from South Africa. They included some Palestinians and some Egyptians."[26] Graham Du Bois understood that the cultural politics of the Third World movement allowed particularistic histories of racial violence and colonialism to be translated across linguistic and geopolitical divides. Hence the protagonist of the novel is not Bob Jones (the editor), nor Malcolm X (the leader), but the relatively unknown cadre of African American expats who happen to make art while in Cairo.

Although David Graham Du Bois was one of the few Americans allowed to stay in Cairo following the June 1967 six-day war due to his status as a journalist for the *Egyptian Gazette*, most of the African American expat community had to evacuate. Graham Du Bois eventually moved back to the United States where he became the editor of the Black Panther Party's newspaper. As an editor of the *Black Panther Intercommunal Newspaper*, Du Bois curated what Black Panther Party members learned about Third World and anti-imperialist politics. In his capacity as an editor, Graham Du Bois infused the newspaper with information about decolonization and anti-imperialist struggle in the Middle East and North Africa. The Black Panther newspaper became one of the most consistent venues in the US to report on the Palestinian refugees' struggle to return to their homelands; indeed, leaders of the Palestinian Front for the Liberation of Palestine (PFLP) had a regular column in the newspaper under Graham Du Bois's editorship. Moreover, Graham Du Bois helped encourage and perhaps facilitate Black Panther Party members' tours of Palestinian refugee camps.

At the core of the Panther's politics and their newspaper was the theory of intercommunalism, a version of Black anti-imperialism that sought to forge global solidarity with peoples fighting imperialism and racism, without abandoning the history and experiences of African Americans. As Huey Newton wrote in the Panther's newspaper, "We see very little difference in what happens to a community here in North America and what happens to a community in Vietnam . . . We see very little difference in what happens to a Black community Harlem and a Black community in South Africa, a Black community in Angola and Mozambique."[27] Graham Du Bois's experience as an editor and author of *And Bid Him Sing* helped the Black Panthers forge a politics of intercommunalism. At the center of Cairo's Third World era, he knew that international solidarity was fraught with all sorts of obstacles. Yet, he also understood that cultural politics – literature, in particular – could help liberate the minds of readers in ways that would encourage them to confront the obstacles to revolutionary change. Hence, *And Bid Him Sing*'s importance is not only in retelling the history of the African American expat community in Cairo, but also in modeling how the Black Panther's politics of intercommunalism could operate within a global Third World left.

The Du Bois genealogy as sketched out in this essay makes visible less a singular thread of Black anti-imperialist writing than a series of different historical conjunctures when Black anti-imperialism flourished. While each Du Bois confronted the particularities of their geopolitical context, they share an interest in theorizing how Black American experiences of racial terror translate to global anti-imperialist struggles, especially in the long era of the nonaligned, Third World movement. For all three Du Boises the complexities of Black American anti-imperialism were best recognized and navigated through writing, the various literary and political genres that imagine ways to link Black America to global currents. The bonds of this linkage, like the Du Bois genealogy itself, were rooted in shared understandings of Black anti-imperialism and not in essentialist categories of racial fraternity or belonging. In this, each Du Bois modeled ways for Black American anti-imperialism to harmonize, sometimes with discordant notes, with global anti-imperialist currents.

Notes

1. W. E. B. Du Bois, *The Souls of Black Folk* (Oxford: Oxford University Press, 2008), 32.
2. Quoted in Brent Hayes Edwards, *The Practice of Diaspora: Literature, Translation, and the Rise of Black Internationalism* (Cambridge: Harvard University Press, 2003), 1.
3. W. E. B Du Bois, *Darkwater: Voices from within the Veil* (New York: Harcourt, Brace, and Howe, 1920), 10.
4. W. E. B. Du Bois, *Black Reconstruction in America* (New York: Atheneum, 1992).
5. Du Bois, *Darkwater*, 276. Amy Kaplan *The Anarchy of Empire in the Making of US Culture* (Cambridge: Harvard University Press, 2005) offers an especially brilliant analysis of this dialectic.
6. In his essay, "In Search of a Pan-African Commonwealth" Cedric Robinson criticizes Pan-African formations rooted in the nation-state and thereby repro-duce forms of bourgeois leadership that undermine Black mass movements. Instead, he identifies revolutionary Pan-Africanism as a form of imagined community that works against the nation/state, that resists identitarian categories as its rationale, and that provide belonging to the many. Cedric J. Robinson, "In Search of a Pan-African Commonwealth," in H. L. T. Quan (ed.), *Cedric J. Robinson: On Racial Capitalism, Black Internationalism, and Cultures of Resistance* (London: Pluto Press, 2019), 45–53.
7. The long history of enslavement and the failures of emancipation to guarantee Black freedom in the United States encouraged Black leaders from Henry McNeil Turner to Marcus Garvey to plan back-to-Africa emigration projects, sometimes with the aid of white segregationists who believed that Black people could never assimilate to the United States. Henry McNeil Turner, for example, planed three African emigration projects to Liberia and Sierra

Leon. In the second decade of the twentieth century, Chief Sam organized emigration routes for black Americans to various African continental destinations. Perhaps the most significant black-to-Africa movement was led by Marcus Garvey, whose United Negro Improvement Association purchased ships with plans to transport Black Americans to Liberia. See, for example, Hakim Adi, *Pan-Africanism: A History* (London: Bloomsbury Academic, 2018).

8. Benedict Anderson, *Imagined Communities: Reflections on the Origins and Spread of Naitonalisms* (London: Verso Books, 1983).

9. Wai Chee Dimmock, "Literature for the Planet," *PMLA*, 116.1, Special Topic: Globalizing Literary Studies (January 2001): 175.

10. Robert A. Hill, ed. *George Samuel Schuyler, Black Empire* (Boston: Northeastern University Press, 1993); Claude McKay, *Banjo: A Story Without a Plot* (New York: Harcourt, Brace, Jovanovich, 1929); and Brent Hayes Edwards and Jean-Christophe Cloutier, eds., *Claude McKay, Amiable With Big Teeth* (New York: Penguin Publishing Group, 2018).

11. W. E. B. Du Bois, *Dark Princess: A Romance* (Oxford: Oxford University Press, 2007), 205.

12. For example, the African American writer Richard Wright covered the Bandung conference and published a report called, *The Color Curtain*. Recognizing the potential of the Bandung moment to radicalize African Americans in the United States, the State Department prevented Paul Robeson and W. E. B. Du Bois from traveling to Bandung, although both would later participate in writer's and film conferences sponsored by Third World organizations.

13. Du Bois spent the final years of his life in the newly decolonized nation/state of Ghana, where, in 1957, Kwame Nkrumah led a successful decolonization movement that attracted several Black Americans in solidarity. See, for example, Kevin Gaines, *American Africans in Ghana: Black Expatriates and the Civil Rights Era* (Chapel Hill: University of North Carolina Press, 2012).

14. Gamal Abdel Nasser, *Egypt's Liberation: The Philosophy of the Revolution* (Ann Arbor: Public Affairs Press, 2008).

15. W. E. B. Du Bois was an official observer of the 1958 Tashkent conference, as was Franz Fanon, who served as a member of the Algerian delegation at the 1958 and 1960s conferences.

16. Duncan McEachern Yoon, "The Global South and the Cultural Struggles: On the Afro-Asian People's Solidarity Organization," *The Global South Project*. www.globalsouthproject.cornell.edu/the-global-south-and-cultural-struggles.html. At the 1962 Cairo writer's conference, Egyptian actress, Faten Hamama called for AAPSO to curate a film library to share cinema produced in AAPSO delegate countries across the nonaligned world. The Egyptian novelist, Naguib Mahfouz called for a transnational exchange of literature across AAPSO delegate countries. Hamama's and Mahfouz's recommendations were part of the "Cultural Resolutions and Recommendations" at the center of the conference.

17. Quoted in Shirley Graham Du Bois, "The First Conference on African and Asian Women," *Political Affairs* (March 1961), 61.

18. See, for example, Keith Feldman, "Towards an Afro-Arab Diasporic Culture: The Translational Practices of David Graham Du Bois," *Alif: Journal of Comparative Politics* 31 (2011): 152–72.

19. Shirley Graham Du Bois, "The First Conference of African and Asian Women," 63.

20. On Black internationalist feminism, see Cheryl Higashida, *Black Internationalist Feminism: Women Writers of the Black Left, 1945–1995* (Champaign: University of Illinois Press, 2013).

21. On translational politics, see Keith Feldman, "Towards an Afro-Arab Diasporic Culture."

22. The African American artist Robert Colescott accepted a professorship at the American University in Cairo (AUC) in 1965, was enamored with Egyptian modernist painters. Colescott created AUC's first art gallery and his own art was transformed following his time in Cairo.

23. David Graham Du Bois, *And Bid Him Sing* (Palo Alto: Ramparts Press, 1975).

24. Du Bois, *And Bid Him Sing*, 137.

25. David Graham Du Bois likely based the character Suliman Ibn Rashid on Ibrahim Ibn Ismail, who published to chapbooks of poetry while living in Cairo and studying at Al-Azhar.

26. Du Bois, *And Bid Him Sing*, 103.

27. Huey Newton, "Let Us Hold High the Banner of Intercommunalism and the Invincible Thoughts of Huey P. Newton, Minister of Defense and Supreme Commander of the Black Panther Party," *Black Panther* 5.30 (January 23, 1971).

CHAPTER 9

Harry Foster Dean and the Project of Black Maritime Empire

Nadia Nurhussein

Six years before he died, the singular but understudied figure Captain Harry Foster Dean wrote a memoir about an extraordinary period in his life and named it for his ship: *The Pedro Gorino*. In it, he recounts his thwarted attempts to establish a powerful Black empire in Africa in the early twentieth century. From his Cape Colony headquarters, Dean attempted to raise funds for his project but failed to elicit interest from any of the major leaders of African descent in the United States. His adventure concluded with his ejection from Africa by European imperialists, one of whom allegedly called him "the most dangerous 'Negro' in the world."[1] Today Dean has been largely forgotten, but he belongs to a lineage of Black Americans active in African repatriation movements from at least the early nineteenth century onward. (In fact, Dean claimed to be the grandson of early American emigrationist Paul Cuffe, but that claim has been challenged by several scholars.) His entire life was driven by the spirit of what we may call maritime Pan-Africanism – a variant of Pan-Africanism built upon aspirations of maritime capability. According to Dean, a transnational Black empire, such as the one he dreamt of, could not succeed without proving itself as a maritime power. Just as he and many other advocates of African repatriation of the nineteenth and twentieth centuries emphasized that the racial environment in the United States was unhealthy for people of African descent, Dean believed, in addition, that "only the ozone of the multitudinous oceans will cleanse our race from the degrading arena" and that a truly successful Pan-African empire needed to be tied to the world ocean.[2]

Among major figures of maritime Pan-Africanism, perhaps the best known is Marcus Garvey, an internationally recognized race leader popularly called the "Black Moses," once destined to usher an exodus of his people across the Atlantic. With his Back-to-Africa efforts, Garvey was enormously successful for a time. He believed not only in the concept of

Black nationality but in the concept of Black imperialism, through which Africans and the diaspora would join forces, culminating in the establishment of a powerful territorial empire in Africa. In his essay "Africa for the Africans," he writes that those of African descent around the world are "in sympathetic accord with the aspirations of native Africans" and "desire to help them build up Africa as a Negro Empire."[3] At that time, in the early twentieth century, Liberia and Ethiopia were the only nominally independent nations in Africa. Liberia was ostensibly a democracy, but this status was belied by the dominance of Americo-Liberians, who formed an elite stratum in Liberian society. In addition, Liberia's nineteenth-century history as a project of the American Colonization Society appeared to link the nation's founding to European imperialism, which reached its pinnacle with the so-called Scramble for Africa and partition of the continent at the 1884 Berlin Conference. In contrast to Liberia's modern republicanism, Ethiopia had preserved an imperial line that claimed to reach back to the union of King Solomon and the Queen of Sheba. As an ancient African nation, it loomed as a symbol for Garvey, who, in the aforementioned essay, asks, "was not the Negro a power, was he not great once?," citing a historical past that included "Egypt, Ethiopia and Timbuctoo tower[ing] in their civilizations" above the rest of the world.[4]

Though the model of imperial Ethiopia may have resonated more closely with Garvey's nostalgic vision of Black empire, Liberia was the most practical choice geopolitically to serve as center of his project; he aimed, to quote historian Tamba E. M'bayo, "to use Liberia as a bridgehead for the eventual liberation of the rest of Africa from European colonialism."[5] As a result, Garvey attempted to establish a formal relationship with the Liberian government. By 1924, that relationship had soured.[6] As M'bayo points out, "It is unclear how, as part of his plan to liberate Africa, Garvey planned to implement his multifaceted project in Liberia without simultaneously undermining the Americo-Liberian government."[7]

Equally ill-fated was the most grandiose, spectacular, and romantic element of Garvey's plan: the shipping line that would have carried members of his Universal Negro Improvement Association (UNIA) over the Atlantic to settle in Liberia. A shipping corporation established by Garvey in 1919, the Black Star Line was in operation until 1922, when Garvey was found guilty of mail fraud, and was, as W. E. B. Du Bois put it, "the foundation stone of Garvey's rise to popularity among Negroes."[8] According to a statement in the *Negro World*, the UNIA newspaper, the company's aim was "to put our ships on the seas, to link up our people throughout the world, to convey to them their commerce and their trade, to make them a greater people industrially and commercially, to lay through such a source the foundation of empire."[9] The shipping line then served a practical purpose as well – although it was handled impractically and, in fact, disastrously – in part by transporting New World Africans back to their native land, where the work of building a Black empire could begin. In other words, Garvey's navigation of the ocean was largely a means to an end.

With this chapter, I hope to reveal what Garvey's more familiar program can tell us about Dean's significance to both Black Oceanic studies and the study of empire. There has been scholarly interest in the relationship of the Black world to the ocean since, at least, the publication of Paul Gilroy's *The Black Atlantic: Modernity and Double Consciousness* more than thirty years ago, and this interest has reached an even higher pitch more recently with major publications such as Christina Sharpe's *In the Wake: On Blackness and Being* and Tiffany Lethabo King's *The Black Shoals: Offshore Formations of Black and Native Studies*. Also of note is Elizabeth DeLoughrey's career-long work on oceans: her first monograph, *Routes and Roots: Navigating Caribbean and Pacific Island Literatures*, begins with the Barbadian poet Kamau Brathwaite's influential concept of "tidalectics," which she summarizes as "a dynamic and shifting relationship between land and sea."[10] Despite the fact that Dean considers the charting of this movement between land and sea the central figure of his life's work, he and his work have been mainly ignored in this rich body of scholarship. In fact, Gilroy acknowledges in a footnote to his introduction that *The Pedro Gorino* "contains interesting material on the practical politics of Pan-Africanism that go unrecorded elsewhere," and yet Dean is mentioned nowhere else in Gilroy's book.[11]

By the time *The Pedro Gorino* was published in 1929, Garvey was living in Jamaica after his US imprisonment. Dean's efforts would echo those of his much more familiar and successful peer, but also prefigure them, because the events in Dean's book take place years before the birth of Garveyism. As Dean wrote, "There seems to be one fact of agreement between Marcus Garvey and myself and that is our marriage to the Ideal of the Emancipation of our race . . . from the dominance of the white man[,] the restoration of Africa and the culture of the African race."[12] Dean and Garvey, as John S. Burger points out, "had ties that offered avenues of cooperation," such as mutual colleagues who led the Los Angeles branch of the Universal Negro Improvement Association, but "there is presently no information as to why Dean and Garvey did not work together."[13] This is especially surprising considering how few master mariners of African descent existed at the time; Dean would have been a valuable associate for Garvey.

Roughly contemporaneous with the Black Star Line was Dean's own proposed commercial shipping line, running between California and Monrovia, with the possibility of transporting immigrants as well as goods. On its face, Dean's scheme had more potential than Garvey's, as Dean's nautical knowledge and familiarity with ships would have allowed him to avoid the fiascos that befell Garvey. For example, Garvey notoriously overpaid for multiple unseaworthy ships to add to his fleet. As Du Bois noted, Garvey himself "alleges his own lack of experience in the shipping business: 'Marcus Garvey is not a navigator; he is not a marine engineer; he is not even a good sailor.'"[14] In addition to Dean's superior skill and knowledge, he appears to have considered his route carefully. California seems at first glance an inconvenient site from which to sail for the west coast of Africa, but Dean's thoughtful list of "advantages in Liberia via Los Angeles" – including "tolls," "insurance rates," and so forth – aims to silence skeptics.[15] Dean's plans, therefore, would appear to have been much more practicable. Instead, however, Dean encountered even more obstacles than Garvey. He was unable even to purchase a ship: the only tool of Black liberation, in his view. The United States Shipping Board stood in the way of Dean's repeated attempts. As reported in the *San Francisco Chronicle* in 1922, Dean determined that he was being prevented from purchasing a ship due to racial discrimination and even somehow obtained written proof explicitly proving as much. As a result, he drafted a letter to the US Secretary of State, Charles Evans Hughes, to protest his treatment. In addition to racist bureaucratic obstruction, Dean failed also to garner popular support. He managed to connect with numerous influential figures throughout his life, but apparently lacked the charisma and organizational skills necessary to connect with the masses.

However, what the omission of Dean from histories of African American repatriation – as well as his frustration about his status as race leader *manqué*, ignored by potential followers – illuminates most clearly is that the racial project he proposed depended upon a limited epistemology for which he could not successfully make a case. While both Dean and Garvey saw the ship as "a living, micro-cultural, micro-political system in motion," to quote Gilroy, Garvey's ship functioned mainly as a symbolic tether between the old terrestrial world and the new. Dean's understanding of maritime Pan-Africanism, on the other hand, emphatically shifted the focus from land ("fatherland" or "motherland," although he uses the word "motherland" multiple times in his memoir) to sea as a productive site of solidarity. In other words, Dean emphasizes nautical knowledge as the crucial means by which the race could connect, succeed, and even gain imperial strength. This orientation ran counter to other visions of African repatriation, many of which originated in an impulse toward homecoming that necessarily emphasized African land. Despite Dean's compulsory interest in agriculture, logging, animal husbandry, mining, and other activities common to the land-based orientation associated with most emigration projects, his racial project prioritizes industries associated with the ship itself, the coasts, and the global ocean. As he writes in his diary, while "Garvey believes in organization," Dean simply "believe[s] that sea power tools and machinery will set us right."[16]

The ship becomes for Dean a reparative Afrocentric tool, in a literal and practical sense, animating empire as it travels from port to port. Whereas Garvey's plan was "to unite Negrodom by a *line* of steamships" (my emphasis), to quote Du Bois, Dean viewed his ship not as a line but as a point – or, *the* point.[17] In articles (such as the *San Francisco Chronicle* article mentioned above), in his memoir, in his diaries, and elsewhere, Dean conceives of the heart of his maritime empire as a "nucleus." As the coauthor of Dean's memoir, Sterling North, wrote of Dean's perspective of the Pedro Gorino, "It seemed to him that the African fleet had its little nucleus and that it was merely a matter of years before his dream would be a reality."[18] An *Oakland Tribune* article about Dean cited his desire to found "upon the continent of Africa a great maritime nation," this time describing the "little Republic of Liberia" as "its nucleus."[19]

Rather than dismiss this recurring descriptor as an example of eccentric phraseology, I would like to underscore Dean's desire to view the Pedro Gorino, or alternatively the "maritime nation" of Liberia, as the atomic nucleus around which his project revolves, a maritime core around which empire orbits with a powerful force. In this light, it is noteworthy that Dean's diaries demonstrate an interest in and basic knowledge of science, tinged with his own eclectic spirituality. For example, as he treated his diaries frequently as commonplace books, he recorded notes in one of his 1921 diaries on an article published in *Nautilus*, a popular New Thought magazine, including the barely altered transcription, "an electron is a whirling hole of energy in space ... held together by the infinitely extensive attracti[ve] energy called 'God.'"[20] The atomic model of the day – scientists Ernest Rutherford and J. J. Thompson had discovered the atomic nucleus in 1911 and the electron in 1897, respectively – held a special attraction for Dean, who then filtered it through his own peculiar metaphysical perspective.

He believed that nautical science was not simply an isolated vocational field of study; it was physics, philosophy, psychology, and so forth, all wrapped in one. As a result, one of the strategic goals of Dean's maritime Pan-Africanism was the founding of a nautical college in 1925 in Alameda, California, with several other campuses ostensibly founded earlier throughout Africa, in order to train a generation of Black men to become effective race leaders through knowledge of the sea.[21] Dean's "Academy for Vocational Training," as he called it – presumably an early name for Dean's Habashi College – set forth a "syllabus" of thirty-three subjects: various unsurprising topics such as "Maritime History," "Nautical Astronomy," and "Theory of Seamanship" were to be taught alongside a *mélange* that included "Applied Psychology," "Magnetism," "Eugenics," and "Vocal Music."[22] Another of his curricular documents underscores the link between this particular educational approach and the building of Black empire, as he sees it:

> The curriculum will consist of a three years' course of instruction in geography, mathematics, logic, astronomy, business law and maritime subjects designed to prepare an average youth with the knowledge and ideals necessary for a successful nautical career in which he can contribute his full measure to society, and aid in rehabilitating the great continent of Africa and drawing its people from their present submerged state.[23]

Students enrolled in this program of study, according to Dean, should approach each of these disciplines through the lens of "rehabilitation." He offers them knowledge – especially nautical knowledge – in exchange for their service as agents of Black maritime empire. Even Dean's metaphor of "drawing its people from their present submerged state" hints at this philosophy: his particular brand of racial "uplift" imagines a drowning race being thrown a flotation device or boarding a rescue boat. At every turn, he emphasizes that only a profound understanding of the sea can save us.

Dean articulates his goals for his students in terms that evoke both astronomy and quantum physics: he intends to offer them an "environment as extensive as the Expanse between an electron and the Magellan nebula in which their fancies may expand." It is no surprise that the aspiration is expansionist. The Magellanic Clouds to which he refers are even named for the Portuguese explorer Ferdinand Magellan. His students' "fancies" are expected, like Dean's, to be imperialist in nature, encompassing the space between the smallest unit then conceivable and the distant firmament. This is not to say that the sort of imperialism promoted by Dean conforms to models of European imperialism that would have been familiar to him at the turn of the century. He was adamantly anti-imperialist when it came to the white colonial presence in Africa. His was an anti-imperialist imperialism, common among Pan-Africanist leaders and thinkers of the early twentieth century. These visions of Black empire were restorative and reparative, attempting to rebuild what white imperialist progress had destroyed. The objective of his expansionist mindset was to promote a restorative Afrocentric vision of empire built upon nautical knowledge:

> The sea training I give will develop a spirit of fidelity and vigilance. A continuous inspection of the stars develops a cosmic mind. Navigation will develop a broad knowledge of geography. The darkness of the night develops a sixth sense of position. It develops a strong imagination of one's ability to conquer nature's forces and fear of nature's phenomena thus increasing our control of nature and our knowledge of it.
>
> The knowledge of pure science is mastered through it. A maritime people cannot be enslaved. The description of the effect of the sea on man would take a volume.[24]

What Dean calls a "cosmic mind" – influenced here perhaps by his reading of New Thought publications and those of similar spiritual movements of the era – he also describes elsewhere as a "plastic alert flexible mind," which is "developed through the discipline of the sea." The "fancies," as they are encouraged to expand between the microscopic and the telescopic, take on a completely novel imaginative sense, a plasticity that could not be culti-vated outside of the sea. Celestial navigation – for example, knowing what it means to observe the Magellanic Clouds, or some other celestial body, and how to proceed – deepens the mental and physical capacities of anyone willing and able to study it, to the point where they are strong enough to confront any element of the natural world. According to his notes, sailing the sea at night has such an effect upon proprioception ("a sixth sense of position") that it fosters a new kind of thought and a new kind of action, and the thought and action spawned by this proprioceptive awareness foster a productive expansionism.

To illustrate Dean's insistence that the nautical mind was best suited to build a Black empire, I would like to turn to a pivotal moment in *The Pedro Gorino*. At one point in his travels, Dean's mind drifts and he allows his own fancies to expand:

> In three days of dreaming I rebuilt the Ethiopian Empire. In three days of dreaming I recaptured Africa for the Africans. Once more Mashonaland was

Ophir, and gleaming black bodies brought gold from the mines. The ruins of Zimbabwe were no longer ruins, but stately masonry. The sons of the ancient race who raised those piles of stone to forgotten gods once more were proud possessors of all they surveyed. And those dark descendants of the Phœnicians, still workshiping the crane and the ram, reattained the genius of their ancestors, sailing their ships to every country, bearing the wealth of Africa. As in the ancient days, precious stones and metals poured from Sheba northward through all Arabia, and westward down the wide rivers of the jungle. Nowhere were there slaves, or poverty, or ignorance. In three days of dreaming I dammed the rivers to water the karoo until the desert bloomed like the rose. I built cities in trackless thickets and from the forests of Africa constructed such a fleet of graceful ships as the world has never seen.[25]

This vision of Pan-Africa flourishes because of its people's successful navigation of rivers and oceans. Even the agricultural marvels, Dean is quick to note, follow from a manipulation of waterways: the land will not come alive until he waters it with the rivers, demonstrating his "control of nature." Conversely, before taking to the sea, one must control the land, as the ships upon which maritime empire depend are constructed from native lumber found in Africa's forests. The maritime empire then reflects a dynamic, well-balanced cycle between land and water – in line with what Brathwaite would call "tidalectics" – with the ship as its apotheosis.

This land–sea dynamism is intrinsic to Dean's conception of maritime empire. The "psychology of the sea," as he puts it, "is wrapped up in the longing at Sea for the land and once at sea then the longing for it when on land which makes for a healthy ambition[,] industry and thought. It is an education out of which grows civilization and the acquirement of culture."[26] The agitation itself produces, in other words, the necessary conditions for collective Black empire. Alternative visions of Black empire, according to Dean, lack this productive dynamism, because "it is only in Oceanic industries that persons iron out the disharmonies within their souls and character."[27] As a result, these visions of Black empire, plagued by "disharmonies," will never be sound.

Dean believed he had developed the best program for a harmonious and kinetic Black social world. He finds the form of his maritime empire in the solar-system-like relationship between the nucleus and the electron – again, described contemporaneously by Landone, and transcribed by Dean, as "a whirling hole of energy in space." The nucleus of maritime empire, as Dean views it, must be surrounded by the constant mental and physical motility of its people as if energetic electrons in flux; as he puts it, "so long as human beings are disciplined and influenced by [the sea] there is no stagnation."[28] The metaphor is one that depends upon racial collectivity: the literal bonds of subatomic particles writ large. His dream maritime empire is an Ethiopianist vision, one that imagines a cooperative restoration to past glory through activity and industry. What seems lost to history can be reimagined – through the sea – as a vital African future.

Notes

1. Captain Harry Dean, *The Pedro Gorino: The Adventures of a Negro Sea-Captain in Africa and on the Seven Seas in his attempts to Found an Ethiopian Empire. An Autobiographical Narrative* (New York: Houghton Mifflin, 1929), 119.
2. Captain Harry Dean Papers, Box 1, Folder 18, DuSable Museum of African American History, Chicago, Illinois. Spelling errors from the Captain Harry Dean Papers have been silently corrected.
3. Marcus Garvey, "Africa for the Africans," in Amy Jacques Garvey, ed., *Philosophy and Opinions of Marcus Garvey, or, Africa for the Africans* (New York: Universal Pub. House, 1923–25; rpt. Majority Press, 1986), 71.
4. Garvey, "Africa," 77.
5. Tamba E. M'bayo, "W.E.B. Du Bois, Marcus Garvey, and Pan-Africanism in Liberia, 1919–1924," *The Historian* 66.1 (2004): 32.
6. See Frank Chalk, "Du Bois and Garvey Confront Liberia: Two Incidents of the Coolidge Years," *Canadian Journal of African Studies* 1.2 (1967): 139.
7. M'bayo, "Du Bois," 41.
8. Du Bois, "The Black Star Line," *Crisis*, September 1922, 210.
9. Garvey, "Gentlemen, Can You Let the Tiger Loose?," *Negro World*, June 23, 1923, 1.
10. DeLoughrey, *Routes and Roots* (Honolulu: University of Hawai'i Press, 2007), 3.
11. Gilroy, *Black Atlantic* (Cambridge: Harvard University Press, 1993), 227, n. 34.
12. Dean Papers, Box 1, Folder 20.
13. Burger, MA Thesis, Roosevelt University, January 1973, 53. Dean Papers, Box 4, Folder 110.
14. Du Bois, "The Black Star Line," 214.
15. Dean Papers, Box 1, Folder 7.
16. Dean Papers, Box 1, Folder 3.
17. Du Bois, "The Black Star Line," 210.
18. North, Preface to *The Pedro Gorino*, x–xi.
19. Dean Papers, Box 1, Folder 21.
20. Dean Papers, Box 1, Folder 7. This language is taken from "The Idealized Process of Unfailing Methods of Healing" in the July 1921 issue, and rephrased later for Landone's 1922 self-help book, *How to Turn Your Desires*

and Ideals into Realities. New Thought was a spiritual movement, popular in the late nineteenth and early twentieth centuries, that believed in the power of the mind to heal the body or to manifest good things (that is, "the law of attraction").

21. "In his diaries he wrote that he started nautical schools at Mombasa, East Africa in December 1906; in Cape Town, South Africa in January, 1909 and at Sinoa, Liberia in 1910. There is only Dean's word that he started these schools." Burger, 87. Dean Papers, Box 4, Folder 110.
22. Dean Papers, Box 4, Folder 116.
23. Dean Papers, Box 1, Folder 11.
24. Dean Papers, Box 1, Folder 18.
25. Dean, *The Pedro Gorino*, 154–5.
26. Dean Papers, Box 2, Folder 22.
27. Dean Papers, Box 4, Folder 107.
28. Dean Papers, Box 1, Folder 18.

CHAPTER 10

Elusive "Sun-Bright Hardness"
The Caribbean Horizons of Black Renaissance Fiction in an Age of Rising US Empire

Jak Peake

> For this peculiar tint that paints my house
> Peculiar in an alien atmosphere
> Where other houses have the same pale hue . . .
> Claude McKay, "My House"[1]

> All of this has been done in the name of the Government of the United States; however, without any act by Congress and without any knowledge of the American people. . . . Nothing that might reflect upon the Occupation administration in Haiti is allowed to reach the newspapers of the United States.
> James Weldon Johnson, "Self-Determining Haiti"[2]

In the mid-1920s, a Black cultural movement, some called it a Negro Renaissance, took hold in US cities, Harlem, New York City especially, and more broadly Chicago and Washington DC – but also in Caribbean places like Panama's Canal Zone and Port-au-Prince, Haiti – and became part of a global zeitgeist. White US modernists such as Gertrude Stein, T. S. Eliot, and Ezra Pound joined in and ventriloquized Black voices in rebellion against the strictures of Old World English.[3] Put simply, in Langston Hughes's words, the "Negro" was "in vogue."

This vogue for Blackness roughly coincided with the expansion of the United States into the Pacific and the Caribbean – what some started to call, following the Spanish-American War of 1898, the Greater United States (even if little to no official documentation recognized it as such).[4] With the occupations of Cuba (1899–1902; 1906–09), the Dominican Republic (1916–24), Haiti (1915–1934), Nicaragua (1912–33); and the outright acquisition of the Panama Canal Zone (1903–79), Puerto Rico (1899–present), and the US Virgin Islands (1917–present), the Caribbean proved a strategic backyard for US expansion, and was clearly intertwined with

Black culture, given the region's Afro-Caribbean demographic. Afro-Caribbeans and African Americans might well be considered New World siblings, in many respects, but the connections between the two groups, who encountered each other frequently in New York City, were neither clear-cut nor typically well defined. In the intellectual and artistic world, US imperial ambitions in the region – and its racializing and racist dynamic – did not go without critique in left-leaning magazines like *The Nation*, and Black periodicals like *The Crisis*, *The Messenger*, and *The Crusader*. Yet Black fiction that touched on Caribbean matters did not typically invite much in the way of anticolonial – or what we might call postcolonial – commentary.[5]

This critical lapse – the failure of contemporary commentary on 1920s fiction to attend to Caribbean countries – left them too often obscured, their political contours vanishing or barely discerned. This elision was mirrored in popular and academic discourse on US culture and history for over a half-century and more.[6] Building on the work of Amy Kaplan and Mary Renda, this chapter examines how such silencing of the Caribbean was actively produced, manufactured in the coverage of contemporary Black Renaissance fiction in the late 1910s and 1920s, and in striking contrast to equivalent discourse about, and produced by, nonfiction.[7] Examining periodical responses to four key Renaissance texts on the Caribbean – *The Emperor Jones*, *Nigger Heaven*, *Home to Harlem*, and *Tropic Death* – the chapter departs from conventional close reading to examine instead their reading by commentators in contemporaneous magazines. This history of print cultural practices and discourse reveals the extent to which US cultural producers apprehended or engaged with the notion of a US Empire, or imperialism, in regions such as the Caribbean. Reading *con-* and *para*-textually (e.g. examining adverts, images, and other paraphernalia) and dialogically between and among authors, issues, and texts, offers suggestive new routes for engaging with print culture. This approach necessarily upends the dynamic whereby the book – the novel, play, or poetry collection – is seen as the final product in contrast to the testing ground, via the circulation of earlier drafts, of the magazine and its milieu. Thinking *con-* or *para*-textually about that which comes "with" or "alongside" a text, but also about where words, texts, images, and meanings converge, may prove especially productive in print-historical recovery, where – as is the case with magazines or newspapers – there are multiple agents of production (e.g. editors, writers, illustrators), and editorial decision-making is complicated by such collectives. Following this modus operandi, the chapter examines seminal themes which emerged in 1910s–1920s periodicals over Black representation, race, art, and propaganda – the latter a key term given prominence by Du Bois's famous pronouncements on the role of propaganda in Black art.[8] In doing so, it aims to demonstrate how Black fiction produced in New York was often narrowly interpreted in light of the metropole's own cultural-geographic – as well as US national – imaginary, at the exclusion of wider regional and global trends and, crucially, US imperialism.

In 1929, Carl Van Doren – a Columbia professor who had supported Black writers' literary efforts – stated that "the people of the United States should be reminded that they are no longer merely citizens of a republic but also citizens of an empire." While his phrasing elides the sense of a continuum between the US's colonial past and its early twentieth-century makeup, the context in which Van Doren affirms the US imperium is itself telling. His short article, published in *Wings*, a magazine of the Literary Guild (which allowed its members to acquire editions that were cheaper than the trade publisher's) set out for readers why the Guild's editorial board had chosen William Seabrook's notoriously exoticizing and occupation-justifying travel book, *The Magic Island*, for its subscribers. Not only did Seabrook's book serve as a reminder of the fact that the US was an empire, in Van Doren's eyes, it also proved that "ancient human moods and ideas" existed within it, and could not be willed away by "the modern, rational, scientific temper" of the age.[9] Van Doren was quietly affirming not only the choice of Seabrook's volume as a Guild selection, that is, but the necessity of US military empire itself.

Nine years before this, James Weldon Johnson presented a four-part exposé of the US occupation in Haiti ("Self-Determining Haiti") in *The Nation*, outlining imperial praxis in all but name: Haiti was, so Johnson told his readers, controlled by the US military and the National City Bank of New York. While the word "empire" is absent from Johnson's *Nation* articles, he did use the word "imperialism" once in the conclusion of his last piece. Johnson evoked US Empire as a set of practices which had become corrupt or malign in Haiti, and which could be corrected if the US lived up to its ideals of "fair play" and a "sense of justice," ideals which differed from the "ruthless imperialism" used to justify conquest over inferiors.[10]

Whatever their merits or blind spots, Van Doren's and Johnson's accounts, produced almost at opposite ends of the 1920s, are revealing for what they tell us about nonfiction writing on US Empire. Nonfiction like Johnson's or Seabrook's could be read as something like testimony or evidence of US Empire, whether stated explicitly (as is the case with Van Doren in 1929) or evoked (as Johnson did in 1920). And yet, in contrast to nonfiction such as journalism or travel writing, which invited at least acknowledgment, if not anticolonial critique, of US imperialism, New York's literary fiction – especially where Haiti or the Caribbean served as a backdrop – was rarely read in terms of the growth of the US Empire into the Caribbean Basin, "[o]nly six hundred miles from the Florida coast," or of US-Caribbean relations more broadly.[11]

Why, we might ask, considering various authors' investments in Caribbean allusions, representation, and settings, were commentators unable to see this terrain for what it was (sometimes *just* the Caribbean, but quite typically a fully or semi-colonized space of US territory or occupation in the Caribbean)? What made this fiction such "hard reading," to borrow from Du Bois's review of Guyanese-born writer Eric Walrond's *Tropic Death* (as cited in an incisive article by Imani Owens)?[12] The problem arguably related, to mapping, and the tendency, even today, to map the United States imaginatively within the boundaries of the then forty-eight (now fifty) states – what Benedict Anderson and, more recently, Daniel Immerwahr call the "logo map" of the country. By contrast, images of the Greater US, which included alongside the US mainland the territories of the Caribbean (Puerto Rico, US Virgin Islands), Guam, American Samoa, and the Philippines, not to mention the occupation of various Latin American/Caribbean countries in the early twentieth century, were rare.[13] An 1899 map of Greater America (see Figure 10.1), which features in a book about global conflict, would have been unfamiliar to most US citizens.

With the Greater US, as mapped below stretching outwards into the Atlantic and Pacific Oceans, a more complex – not to mention more accurate – territory extends beyond the "logo map" of the US mainland. But it was not a map that most US readers – and especially those readers primarily interested in fiction – had ever seen. Moreover, just as the "logo map" was exerting its ideological mainland force onto readers' conceptual maps, modern fiction was simultaneously turning away from didactic and moralizing narrators prone to guiding readers and imparting their worldviews through extensive commentaries. If readers were not told how to think – for example not told that countries like Haiti, Puerto Rico, and Panama, in and around the Caribbean Basin, were colonies or semi-/para-colonies of the US – they could hardly be expected to join up the dots. Without any access to a map of the Greater US – that is, a map of US Empire – the absence of empire in the literary critical conversation was (and to some extent still is) inevitable.[14]

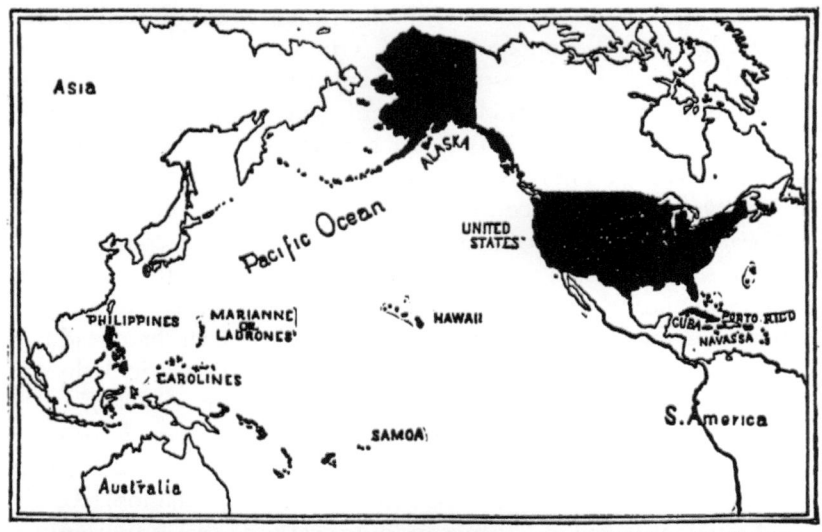

OUTLINE MAP SHOWING THE TERRITORY OF GREATER AMERICA.

Figure 10.1 Greater America (US) map from Marshall Everett and H. I. Cleveland, eds., *Startling Experiences in the Three Wars: War in China, the Philippines, South Africa*. Chicago: Educational Co., 1899–1900, p. 149.

In his 1940 biography *The Big Sea*, Hughes wrote of the Black vogue years at the opening of the chapter, fittingly titled "When the Negro was in Vogue," accordingly:

> The 1920's were the years of Manhattan's black Renaissance. It began with *Shuffle Along*, *Running Wild*, and the Charleston. Perhaps some people would say even with *The Emperor Jones*, Charles Gilpin, and the tom-toms at the Provincetown. But certainly it was the musical revue, *Shuffle Along*, that gave a scintillating send-off to that Negro vogue in Manhattan.[15]

Hughes dated this vogue-cum-Renaissance – a period he associated with Black Manhattan – to the 1920s and the all-Black Broadway musical hit, *Shuffle Along*, which opened to downtown New York audiences in 1921. Composed by Eubie Blake, with lyrics by Noble Sissie and a script by the comedy duo Flournoy Miller and Aubrey Lyles, this hit show represented a super-quartet of Black talent from the vaudeville circuit, launching the careers of future Black stars including Josephine Baker, Paul Robeson, Florence Mills, Fredi Washington, and Adelaide Hall. Hughes's retrospective links *Shuffle Along* with *Runnin' Wild* and the Charleston.

A huge musical hit on Broadway in 1923, *Runnin' Wild* not only reunited Miller and Lyles as performers, but also featured James P. Johnson – a pioneer of the stride piano – performing his composition "The Charleston" which popularized the dance.[16]

Hughes presents us then with a distinctly musical opening to this Black Manhattan vogue: the jazzy, ragtime, bluesy sound that echoed in uptown Harlem cabarets, and gripped midtown Manhattan theaters.[17] Notably, in Hughes's historicizing of this vogue not only is the culture Black, but also its producers: composers, lyricists, musicians, and performers. Yet Hughes's Black musical entrée to this era is not without vacillation. "Perhaps," he ruminates, "some people" – the tone is peculiarly detached, suggesting he does not subscribe to such a view – date its opening to "*The Emperor Jones*, Charles Gilpin, and the toms-toms at Provincetown."[18] With this, Hughes gives us an alternative genesis to Black Manhattan's vogue. One might be forgiven for thinking *The Emperor Jones* is a Black play, performed by Black artists, over a backdrop of African tom-toms, with little to no Caribbean content. Hughes's omission is telling: namely the white playwright's name, Eugene O'Neill, of *The Emperor Jones*, which debuted on Broadway in 1920 with the Provincetown Players, a white bohemian theater company comprising writers, artists, and radicals including Djuna Barnes, Louise Bryant, Max Eastman, John Reed, and Edna St. Vincent Millay – a fact which highlights the interracial collaborations in the arts at the time.[19] Furthermore, a significant proportion of the play takes place on a fictionalized Caribbean island, very reminiscent of Haiti, and the tom-tom rhythms, however much associated with Africa, are in fact Caribbean.

So why might Hughes only partially acknowledge the role of O'Neill's play? White critics were quick to hail *The Emperor Jones* and O'Neill in glowing terms during its first run at the Provincetown Theater in Greenwich Village. On November 4, days after its opening, *New York Tribune* drama critic, Heywood Broun, stated that *The Emperor Jones* was "just about the most interesting play which has yet come from the most promising playwright in America."[20] Toward the end of its first Broadway run at the Princess Theatre, Black intellectuals W. E. B. Du Bois and the radical Virgin Islander Hubert Harrison were in lockstep in their praise of O'Neill's production. On June 4, 1921 in *Negro World*, Harrison defined the play as a "joint product of the genius of Eugene O'Neill and Charles Gilpin." Furthermore, he rejected a racial uplift agenda in art whereby only positive representations of Blackness – for example, "self-help, racial solidarity, temperance, thrift, chastity, social purity" – were reinforced.[21]

In Harrison's view, Black critics who disliked the play because it "does not elevate the Negro" misunderstood it. Such drama had merit as a "mirror" of life.[22] In the same month, Du Bois offered a parallel view to Harrison's on *The Emperor Jones* and the role of art in *The Crisis*:

> We want everything that is said about us to tell of the best and highest and noblest in us. We insist that our Art and Propaganda be one.
> This is wrong and in the end it is harmful ... we face the Truth of Art. We have criminals and prostitutes, ignorant and debased elements just as all folk have. When the artist paints us he has a right to paint us whole and not ignore everything which is not as perfect as we would wish it to be.
> ... Sheldon, Torrence and O'Neill are our great benefactors – forerunners of artists who will yet arise in Ethiopia of the Outstretched Arm.[23]

Philosopher Alain Locke and Montgomery Gregory, director of the Howard Players from 1919 to 1924, agreed with Du Bois, praising O'Neill, Ridgely Torrence, and Paul Green as playwrights who recognized "the potentialities of Negro life and folkways" paving the way "for the theatre of tomorrow."[24] In doing so, Locke and Gregory presented a decidedly white foundation to Black US drama, even as they recognized the talents of Black playwrights and authors Willis Richardson, John Matheus, Georgia Douglas Johnson, Eulalie Spence, and Richard Bruce Nugent.[25]

This view was not uniform, however. In *The New Negro: An Interpretation*, veteran New Negro W. S. Braithwaite argued that O'Neill's "pre-occupation, almost obsession" in plays like *The Emperor Jones* with racial atavism suggested that "the real tragedy of Negro life is a task still left for the Negro writer to perform."[26] A blistering review of the play by William Bridges, *The Challenge* editor, featured in the *Negro World* some three months before Du Bois's and Harrison's positive reviews of O'Neill's work.[27] For Bridges, O'Neill's play rivaled the work of Thomas Dixon, author of *The Clansman*, and surpassed Lothrop Stoddard, the white supremacist author of *The Rising Tide of Color*.[28]

The Emperor Jones, then, divided opinion, even as it opened the door to a white origins story for Harlem's Black theater. It is perhaps no surprise then that Hughes presented a muted case for O'Neill's play as a generative seed for what he calls multifariously the "Negro," "New Negro," "Manhattan's Black," and "Harlem" Renaissance.[29] Further, its Caribbean setting "on an island in the West Indies" resembling Haiti, "yet un-self-determined by white marines" poses complications about such a text, which takes readers off the topic of race relations or the "relations of representation" in the US, and rather broadens the frame, to a wider "politics of representation" concerning the US Empire, Caribbean sovereignty, and US-Caribbean foreign policy/relations.[30] O'Neill's inter-textual reference to James Weldon Johnson's articles for *The Nation* – headlined "Self-Determining Haiti" and critical of US marine rule and the export of racism from the US South to a formerly sovereign Black repub-lic – simultaneously evokes the US occupation of Haiti while pointing to an earlier chronological frame, prior to the imperial intervention from the north.[31] Brutus Jones, who rises to become the Black titular emperor of the island in *The Emperor Jones*, serves several roles, recalling a US-takeover of Haiti (albeit by an African American), but also the nineteenth-century Haitian revolutionary leader and monarch Henry Christophe, Haitian president Jean Vilbrun Guillaume Sam, and the Jamaican political activist Marcus Garvey. From Jones's suicide by silver bullet which is reminiscent of Christophe's suicide, to the mob's pursuit of him, which echoes the fates of Christophe and Guillaume Sam (Sam was killed by a mob in 1915 and his death would precipitate Woodrow Wilson's order of US troops to seize Port-au-Prince), he appears an amalgam of these two Haitian leaders. As such, the character could be said to represent a near zenith and nadir of Haitian sovereignty, as Christophe's reign and building of the Sans Souci citadel might be read as a highpoint of Haitian achievement in contrast to Guillaume Sam's tenure which was succeeded by US occupation. In another reading, Jones's love of pomp, military apparel, and migrant status in Haiti recalls Marcus Garvey (albeit with the migrant status reversed, and an African American residing in the Caribbean) – an allusion touched on by Hubert Harrison, Robert Morss Lovett, and Charles S. Johnson and noted in the press in the run-up to Garvey's 1923 trial.[32]

Hughes's summary suggests that the Caribbean – Haiti especially – and the Black arts in Harlem and its surrounds were bound up with one another, and yet we could only know this through not so much context, but rather as *sub*text, akin to a kind of political unconscious of Hughes's autobiography.[33] The US occupation of Haiti posed questions about race, race relations, and the US Empire, just as Haiti's legacy as the only country to have led a successful Black revolt raised questions about what US domination of this once proud Black republic meant in the twentieth century. If, as Michael Dash has argued, Haiti could be seen a version of Harlem in the Caribbean, then Harlem was also a window on to Haiti, a factor amplified by leading Black periodicals, like *The Crisis*, *The Messenger*, *Opportunity*, *The Crusader*, and *Negro World.*[34]

On August 20, 1926, amid the *Crisis*'s symposium on the artist's respon-sibilities with respect to Black representation ("The Negro in Art: How Shall He Be Portrayed?"), and two months after Du Bois's apparent reversal on art and propaganda ("I do not care a damn for any art that is not used for propaganda"), white writer, photographer, and patron Carl Van Vechten published his now notorious novel *Nigger Heaven*.[35] On the day of its release, Augustus Granville Dill, Du Bois's protégé, wrote to Du Bois to say that he had received a preliminary summary from *Crisis* literary editor, Jessie Fauset, who believed that Du Bois was "the only one who will give it what it deserves" (a "slap" was her apparent suggestion), on account of Van Vechten's pervasive influence among Harlem's Black intellectuals. The novel was, so she putatively said, "an insult to the negro group."[36]

From the outset, *Nigger Heaven*, with its obviously provocative title, courted controversy, inviting responses from distinct and intersecting modernist and New Negro wings in the US and Europe. Writing from Paris, Gertrude Stein found it "awfully good and made up of light and delicate work"; Charles S. Johnson thanked Van Vechten for his "honesty," stating he had let slip what many Black folk regarded as "family secrets"; Nella Larsen felt it to be "too close, too true."[37] Much of the Black press was damning, with few other than the "new school" of New Negroes – Langston Hughes, Zora Neale Hurston, Nella Larsen, and Wallace Thurman – standing firmly behind by their friend, mentor and sometimes patron, "Carlo." Both of the Johnsons (Charles S. and James Weldon) and Walter White were positive about the text among the old school New Negroes.[38] Even Alain Locke praised it privately to Van Vechten, though he held back from publishing a review which he had been considering – perhaps judging that to do so risked his own reputation.[39] However, it was also this senior wing that gave the book its stiffest criticism. In a lacerating review, "Homo Africanus Harlemi," for the *New York Amsterdam News* on September 1, 1926, Harrison concluded that Van Vechten's novel was "cheap shoddy," had "neither atmosphere, depth nor character" and "smelt . . . like a stable."[40] In the December 1926 *Messenger*, Joel Rogers called it "smut with a sympathetic setting."[41] That month, Du Bois would deliver on Fauset's wish, publishing his review of *Nigger Heaven* in *The Crisis*. "[A] blow in the face," according to Du Bois, it was "an affront to the hospitality of black folk and to the intelligence of white." Perhaps anticipating the various ways in which the novel would cause offense, Van Vechten toned down some erotic scenes, as well as sexual innuendos, in the proofing stage.[42] Yet even with this, the text was too prurient and exoticist for the likes of Du Bois, Harrison, and Rogers. "[N]either truthful nor artistic," Du Bois bristled, it was a "caricature" too routed in the cabaret to give a genuine reflection of life for the ordinary Harlemite: "To him the black cabaret is Harlem."[43] Charles S. Johnson's alternative take, in his letter to Van Vechten, was not so much that the cabaret was a metonym for Harlem, but rather a foundational literary moment: "the cabaret scene has been described once and for all."[44]

Whether because of, or despite, the controversies, *Nigger Heaven* sold fantastically well.[45] Almost immediately 100,000 copies were sold, and over two years it had gone through fourteen printings.[46] What united both advocates and skeptics, among them Nella Larsen and Charles S. Johnson on one side, and Rogers and Harrison on the other, was the wish that Black writers would write such work themselves, a point Van Vechten made in his nonfiction and *Nigger Heaven*.[47] In the latter, the editor Russett Durwood explains the risks of overlooking such material to the protagonist Byron Kasson, "Well, if you young Negro intellectuals don't get busy, a new crop of Nordics is going to spring up who will take the trouble to become better informed and will exploit this material before the Negro gets around to it."[48]

Two years later, Claude McKay appeared to accept Durwood's – or Van Vechten's – advice, publishing his debut novel, *Home to Harlem*, which presented a Black writer's take on the underworld of Harlem's dives, cabarets, and nightlife. From the off, the novel was read and reviewed in the shadow of Van Vechten's novel, with a good deal of reviewers noting the parallels between the two. In one review, for example, by Thomas Young, entitled "Harlem's Prodigal Son" – a reference to *Nigger Heaven*, which Van Vechten had defined as a retelling of the Prodigal Son – McKay's novel was compared directly to Van Vechten's precursor, with both failing "to give the real picture."[49] In another by Dewey R. Jones, the comparison was even more explicit, with the review's title, "More 'Nigger Heaven,'" suggestive of McKay's extension and imitation of Van Vechten's novel. For Jones, *Home to Harlem* was "'Nigger Heaven' in a larger and more violent dose."[50] Langston Hughes would joke to Van Vechten about McKay's novel: "If yours was 'Nigger Heaven,' this is 'Nigger Hell.'"[51]

A Harper advertisement for *Home to Harlem* in *The Forum* also played on its association to Van Vechten's novel: "packed in the pantry hole of a Pullman and dancing, drinking, fighting, loving in that world of 'ebonies' and 'high yallers' – the side of Nigger Heaven that the 'ofays' do not see, by the newest recruit to negro literature."[52] *Nigger Heaven*'s smash hit had made it the obvious comparator, and – whatever dissent there was in the Black press – this was unlikely to impact white audiences.

Du Bois's now infamous review of McKay's novel – which apparently made the *Crisis* editor long for a bath "after the dirtier parts of its filth" – is notable for its silence as to any connection to *Nigger Heaven*. Rather Du

Bois claimed that the novel satisfied the "prurient demand on the part of white folk for a portrayal in Negroes of that utter licentiousness which conventional civilization holds white folk back from enjoying."[53] For Du Bois, McKay had gone astray. Guided by the market and white appetite, rather than artistic integrity, his vision of Harlem was simply "untrue." A year and a half before, Du Bois had made the same claim about *Nigger Heaven* ("it is not a true picture of Harlem life").[54] Du Bois saw McKay's text as falling on the wrong side of the propaganda debate, but McKay set his work against dictums on propaganda, stating in his correspondence to Louise Bryant that his novel contained "no propaganda. It is a story first of all."[55] Du Bois evidently read both *Nigger Heaven* and *Home to Harlem*, then, through the prism of a dubious, racist marketplace which encouraged authors like Van Vechten and McKay to warp Harlem's image.[56]

Nowhere in either review does the role of US Empire in the early twentieth century receive any consideration or even mention. Yet in both, Haiti is vaguely indexed and simultaneously sublimated into a broader landscape of Black representation bound up with Harlem and Black America. With respect to McKay's novel, Du Bois saw "glimpses of the Haitian, Ray" that possessed the potential for development, while Van Vechten's novel read as a "notebook [of] every fact he has heard about Negroes and their problems; singularly irrelevant quotations, Haitian history, Chesnutt's novels, race poetry, 'blues' written by white folk."[57] Inadvertently, that is, Du Bois's two reviews of the most well-known cabarets novels of the "Negro" Renaissance, underscore an undercurrent, or "cross currents" – a phrase Du Bois used in his double review of Nella Larsen's *Quicksand* and *Home to Harlem* – of Caribbean geography that somehow related to Harlem.[58] John Lowney notes the irony with which the same issue of the *Crisis* featuring Clement Wood's critique of the US occupation of Haiti is silent on Haitian matters in Du Bois's *Home to Harlem* review.[59]

This absence of commentary on US foreign policy and/in the Caribbean, even the lack of mere observation, is emblematic of literary criticism in this period. The divide between the political and the literary was also a divide between nonfiction and fiction, yielding a discourse discrepancy quite easily exhibited by a single spokesperson – in this case Du Bois – shifting between these modes of expression. In October 1920, for example, Du Bois harangued "the impossible Wilson and his lackeys" for being made "the catspaw of thieves" in Haiti, and yet eight years hence, he had little to say about the role of empire in fiction which touched on Haiti.

Fig 10.2 (left): "Harper Books of the Month," advertisement, *The Forum* LXXIX, no. 4 (April 1928): ix. Fig 10.3 (top right): Mahlon Blaine dust jacket illustration from John Vandercook, *Black Majesty: The Life of Christophe, King of Haiti* (New York and London: Harper & Brothers, 1928). Fig 10.4 (bottom right): Aaron Douglas dust jacket illustration from Claude McKay, *Home to Harlem* (New York; London: Harper and Brothers, 1928).[60]

Similarly, Harper's *The Forum* advertisement of *Home to Harlem* is silent on the novel's Haitian/Caribbean undercurrents, despite the promotional material for John Vandercook's *Black Majesty*, a history of the Haitian King, Henry Christophe, set to its right (see Figure 10.2).[61] Above this is a small black-and white illustration by Mahlon Blaine from *Black Majesty*'s dust jacket of Christophe (top right, Figure 10.3), towering, sword in hand, Samurai-like, his cape billowing out behind. Beneath the copy for both texts, and confusingly situated between the copy for Roark Bradford's *Ol' Man Adams an' His Children* and Josef Bard's *Shipwreck in Europe*, is a jazz-inspired image: a Black man, with arms outstretched, stands between two tall edifices, one a skyscraper, the letters "CABA" arching behind him, the full word, "CABARET" in caps presumably cut off. The picture is a miniature of Aaron Douglas's illustration for *Home to Harlem*'s dust jacket (Figure 10.4), but there is no signpost for readers to know this, as the image is free-floating and untitled, as is the case with Blaine's image (which is positioned directly above *Black Majesty*'s copy). The publishers and readers of both texts may have drawn the connections implicitly, but Harper made no explicit reference to the Haitian connection between Vandercook's and McKay's texts. And if readers compared the dust jackets of both books, they would have noted the contrast between Blaine's rural Haitian setting, as the totemic Black hero stands in tall grass, and Douglas's urban, New York environs with a Black figure surrounded by tall buildings and jazz symbolism. Pace Douglas, Harlem is the book's key geographical site, but Haiti is completely absent from his cover illustration.

This divorcing of related context between *Black Majesty* and *Home to Harlem* – somewhat understandable in light of the constraints of short, marketing copy – becomes even more contorted when reviewers who considered them side by side made no connection between the two. In Robert Cortes Holliday's *New York Evening Post* review of both, McKay's novel – misnamed *Back to Harlem* – is presented as a more authentic portrait of Harlem than *Nigger Heaven*: a "virile, pulsating novel . . . as a Negro sees it," echoing similar sentiment to Gwendolyn Bennett who saw McKay's text as more realistic than *Nigger Heaven*.[62] However, neither Ray nor his Haitian background is mentioned – though just paragraphs before Holliday dedicated significant column inches to a summary of Vandercook's Haitian history. Similarly, T. S. Matthews's *The New Republic* review describes *Home to Harlem* as a book of "documentary interest" about "a jungle nigger in the jungle city" but does not refer to Ray by name, only identifying him as "an educated Negro – morose, ineffectual and priggish" who makes the reviewer "uncomfortable."[63] As George Hutchinson argues, Matthews's review purveys a white liberalist racism, shaped by primitivist and exoticist ideas, in which a pure untainted Black experience is prized over all else. As such, Matthews – who reviews *Home to Harlem* alongside *Quicksand*, Roark Bradford's *Ol' Man Adams an' His Children*, and John Vandercook's *Black Majesty* – singles out Vandercook's history of Christophe as his favorite text.[64] Unsurprisingly, Ray – the problem figure – is given short shrift because he does not fit with the image of Haiti as primitive, primordial, African and "pure Black."

A further irony attending the comparisons drawn between *Nigger Heaven* and *Home to Harlem* in contemporary reviews of the period is that they miss the ways that McKay's text might be plausibly read as a response to a lack of geographical and historical understanding of the Caribbean, which Van Vechten's novel registers metafictionally. In two key scenes in which the protagonist Byron Kasson is presented with alternative directions for his writing, the Caribbean surfaces. First, when agonizing about subjects to write about, Mary – his soon to be girlfriend – suggests the topic of Henry Christophe: "Do you know anything about Christophe? It seems to me that the story of Christophe would make a gorgeous subject for a novel."[65] Second, Russett Durwood, the magazine editor, who rejects Byron's short story, intimates that he is keen "to find a good character study" of Marcus Garvey.[66] Whether about the Caribbean, or about a Caribbean subject in Harlem, the region's significance and potential interest to audiences is registered. Likewise, one could argue that Van Vechten's Caribbean call here echoes O'Neill's Brutus Jones, who functions as something like a Christophe and Garvey figure – both of whom had come to symbolize Caribbean sovereignty and agency, with the latter an advocate of a Black empire.

It is striking, therefore, that so many contemporary reviewers either missed or were silent about McKay's presentation of Caribbean matters in *Home to Harlem*. Ray's education of Jake in Haitian history, and on Black history more broadly, clearly serves a special purpose in the text. Jake learns from Ray about the father figure of the Haitian Revolution, Toussaint L'Ouverture, a historical icon perhaps less fetishized than Christophe (or differently so), if more often mythologized and revered. Ray's lament for the homeland from which he is in effect exiled – his father, we learn, jailed for speaking out against "Uncle Sam," his brother executed by marines – presents a damning critique of US imperial practices whereby dissent is paid for with one's liberty or life.[67]

Ray's dislocation and migration to Harlem is symptomatic of the violence and hegemony now exerted by the US in Haiti. However, there are vague parallels with Jake's transatlantic journey as a soldier amid the First World War, and his returnee status to the US while AWOL. In a world system dominated by old and emerging imperial nations, Black bodies are not only devalued, but are also dictated to by world powers like the United States and Britain, whether from the standpoint of an African American citizen, a Black émigré in London (as Jake is), or a Haitian in US-occupied territory. Woodrow Wilson's notion of self-determining nations does not apply to Ray's Haiti, or Jake's (Black) America (which, having never been officially recognized as a separate nation, is purely an imagined community). Ray recognizes how US occupation serves as a great leveler for Afro-Haitians, making them little different from African

Americans. Furthermore, Jake and Ray's friendship in *Home to Harlem*
provides the potential seeds for an imagined community which extends
beyond national borders and speaks to, in various ways, a Black internationalist and/or Black Atlantic outlook.

Where in fiction the Caribbean took center stage, as is the case in Eric
Walrond's short story collection, *Tropic Death*, critics' parameters were
very much guided by the Black and white debates shaping discourse about
Harlem, the New Negro, and the United States. While the collection
succeeded in bringing the Caribbean to critics' attention, few if any
could see the wider geopolitical horizon, whereby an emerging US
Empire and foreign policy were deeply enmeshed in the region.

Focusing predominantly on the Panama Canal Zone, a pan-Caribbean
"contact zone" under US territorial control, Walrond's collection presents
a heterogenous cast of Caribbean characters from across the region.
Notably, in "Subjection," Ballet is unlawfully shot dead by a US marine
for speaking out against marine brutality and, in the words of his killer,
"sticking [. . . his] mouth where [. . . he] hadn't any goddam business."[68] In
a striking parallel, Walrond's story transplants the horrors of marine
brutality and assassination which James Weldon Johnson reported on in
Haiti in 1920 to the Canal Zone. Where Johnson wrote of marines talking
unguardedly of hunting down "cacos" (Haitians associated with armed
resistance) and letting "them have it," Walrond supplies the volley of "[t]
here sure, dead shots" ("vap, vap, vap") which result in the murder of an
Afro-Caribbean man (Ballet) in cold blood.[69]

While, as James Davis notes, there was a tendency among critics to
homogenize the heterogenous cast of Walrond's stories, with
V. F. Calverton, for example, reading the text in terms of "the Negro,"
many reviews did at least register, as did the reviewer of the *New York
Times*, "the teaming multitudes" contained in *Tropic Death*, from the
"islands of Jamaica and Barbados" to the "jungles of the Guianas of
South America."[70] For the vast bulk of reviewers, Walrond was read
curiously as impersonal and objective.[71] According to Robert Herrick, for
example, Walrond had "no propaganda," did not raise the "race question"
and was not stirred by "a mutinous background of controversy or
resentment."[72] This commentary on his impersonal approach reads as
code – or shorthand where the word "propaganda" is used – for both the
art-propaganda debate opened up by Du Bois, and the long-running
discourse about the role of propaganda and objectivity in race literature
of which Du Bois's debate was itself a part.[73] Indeed, John Dos Passos's
comments about Walrond's book – used in the advertising material sent

out by Harper – may have shaped reviewers' perceptions of Walrond's impartiality, since he emphasized the universal, rather than racially-specific, appeal of *Tropic Death*: "Like any book that deeply expresses the essence of any race, it's much more human than it is racial."[74]

Of reviewers attuned to this propaganda-impartiality debate concerning Walrond's book, Langston Hughes and J. A. Rogers arguably took the most forceful positions. Where Hughes argued that "[w]hether it is good Negro propaganda or not should be of no moment" – a clear riposte to Du Bois – Rogers found *Tropic Death* "TOO darn impersonal – so impersonal that one would fancy it was some Negro-despising Englishman or Southerner ... that was speaking."[75] *Tropic Death* may have opened the door to the Caribbean, but it could not escape a US-centered Harlem discourse.

And from the standpoint of Harlem, *Tropic Death* appears to have made for, in Du Bois words, "hard reading." Not only did he and other reviewers struggle with the dialect, language, and "impressionism," but the text's presentation of exploitation proved difficult for reviewers to interpret or even respond to. Du Bois – ironically one of the few reviewers not to frame it in terms of propaganda – saw it as a truthful, vivid, and tragic account of the "life of black labourers of the West Indies," but said nothing about its presentation of US forces.[76] Du Bois's fellow National Association for the Advancement of Colored People (NAACP) colleague, Mary White Ovington, read the stories as "vivid pictures of the West Indies and Central America" and noted the "stark tragedy" of the narratives.[77] Yet for her, the portraits not only troubled her vision of the Caribbean as a happy-go-lucky US vacation spot, but also seemed too incredible and morbid:

> To those of us who know the West Indies as a pleasant winter resort, ... Eric Walrond's picture is like a stunning blow. One asks oneself, can it be true? Is life so terrible in this exquisitely beautiful and seemingly happy land? We saw laughter, but Walrond sees little but tears.[78]

For Ovington, Walrond's prose was also "at times trying" because of his modernist style and linguistic choices. Given "his milieu" was "unusual," she felt "he must take a little more pains in presenting them."[79] In many respects, Ovington exposes an insularity of the New York-US milieu here, unfamiliar with and uncertain of the Caribbean world depicted by Walrond. Like Du Bois, Ovington read the text in tragic terms, but such tragedy was not linked to US hegemony, foreign policy, or empire. Even the Jamaican journalist, J. A. Rogers, read the work as "overtouched" and

unrepresentative of "the average dweller in the tropics [. . . or] even the life
of the average West Indian peasant." Rogers, though, a mixed-race
Jamaican, had a very different experience of the Caribbean than
Walrond, who had had a truly pan-Caribbean upbringing. Born in
British Guiana, Walrond moved to his mother's home island of
Barbados at eight, and then to Panama at age twelve in 1911, amid the
Panama Canal's construction, when the Canal Zone was itself an especially
pan-Caribbean melting pot.[80]

Beyond *Tropic Death*'s apparent unrepresentativeness, Rogers was critical of its genre, style, and approach. For him, it fit within a category of
literature designed for a white consumer market demanding "the exotic,
the sexy, the cabaret side of Negro life" as presented in books like *Nigger
Heaven* and plays like *The Emperor Jones*.[81] While the notion that *Tropic
Death* contains some exoticist aspects was debated, the linkage to cabaret –
even as an aesthetic – particularly where little dancing and no cabaret
features, suggests that Walrond's work could not be read as distinct from
Harlem. The New York world then was keenly alert to the aesthetic
considerations, the literary modes of expression, the language and diction
of Harlem's fiction. Politically, it was also highly charged with respect to
representations of Blackness and, furthermore, the supposed intentions
and race of such authors. But when this fiction veered into the Caribbean,
outside clearly defined US parameters, the geo-political and anti-imperial
contours of such writing remained obscure – proving "hard reading" in
various senses of the term: sensitive and potentially painful subject matter
as well as difficult to discern.

While New York's nonfiction – especially journalism and essays – may
have proved "easier" (if not easy) political reading, often inviting commentary on US foreign policy and Caribbean sovereignty, the same could not
be said for its Black literary fiction. Such fiction was typically read narrowly
in terms of Harlem's aesthetics or literary geography, sometimes in
national terms, but rarely in relation to broader regional currents – an
approach that kept the Caribbean generally hidden out of sight. Why few
could bridge the hermeneutic gap between these different modes of writing
is indicative perhaps not only of a disconnect between political and literary
analysis at the time, but also of the newness of Black fiction in a literary
world which was only just getting to grips with this so-called vogue, not to
mention with the very concept of anything like a US Empire.

In the *Nation*, Johnson talked of the culture of silence, propaganda,
misinformation and censorship, inculcated by the US, to ensure the
general public remained in the dark about US marine practices which

extended to torture, rape, and murder. In *Tropic Death*, Ballet's cold-blooded murder is justified through misinformation as a brief falsified report praises the unspecified US Department for keeping casualties down to only one following armed resistance. In nonfiction and fiction respectively, Johnson and Walrond set out to expose not only the brutalities of US rule in the Caribbean, but the mechanisms by which Americans were kept in the dark about their nation. When it came to fiction, at least, even when the light was given to "sun-bright hardness" as Hughes said of Walrond's prose, much remained in shadow.[82] One can only imagine that somewhere in the US State Department at the time, such narrow readings would be judged as a major success.

Notes

1. Claude McKay, "My House," *Opportunity* 4.47 (November 1926): 342.
2. James Weldon Johnson, *Self-Determining Haiti* (New York: The Nation, 1920), 8–9. Originally printed as James Weldon Johnson, "Self-Determining Haiti: I. The American Occupation," *The Nation* III.2878 (August 28, 1920): 236–8, at 236–7.
3. Michael North, *Dialect of Modernism: Race, Language, and Twentieth-century Literature* (New York: Oxford University Press, 1994), 8–9.
4. Daniel Immerwahr adopts this term to describe the full territory of the United States; the term itself emerged following the Spanish-American War of 1898, and the US's subsequent acquisition of Puerto Rico, the Philippines, Guam, Hawai'i, American Samoa, as well as the occupation of Cuba. See Daniel Immerwahr, *How to Hide an Empire: A History of the Greater United States* (New York: Farrar, Straus and Giroux, 2019), 9. Daniel Immerwahr, "The Greater United States: Territory and Empire in US History," *Diplomatic History* 40.3 (2016): 373–91, at 381, https://doi.org/10.1093/dh/dhw009.
5. See note 10 on *The Nation*. James Weldon Johnson, "The Truth About Haiti," *The Crisis* 20.5 (September 1920). Cyril Briggs, "Editorials," *The Crusader* III.4 (December 1920): 8–13, at 11. "Editorials," *The Messenger* II.X (November 1920): 127–34.
6. As Amy Kaplan has argued, the US Empire remained also obscured in scholarship because discourse about it was habitually buried or dismissed in US historiography and studies of US culture, or occluded in postcolonial studies, because its imperialism did not fit pre-existing European paradigms. Since Kaplan and Donald Pease's *Cultures of United States Imperialism* was published, various studies – e.g. Mary Renda's *Taking Haiti* or Vicente Rafael's *White Love and other Events in Filipino History* – have addressed this gap, deepening the ways in which postcolonialist, US cultural and historical approaches intersect with one another, and with this, analyses of race, gender, sexuality, and so on. Amy Kaplan, "'Left Alone with America': The Absence of Empire in

the Study of American Culture," in *Cultures of United States Imperialism*, ed. Amy Kaplan and Donald E. Pease (Durham: Duke University Press, 1993), 14, 17. Mary A. Renda, *Taking Haiti: Military Occupation and the Culture of US Imperialism, 1915–1940* (Chapel Hill: University of North Carolina Press, 2001). Vicente L. Rafael, *White Love and Other Events in Filipino History* (Durham: Duke University Press, 2000).

7. I prefer the label of the Black Renaissance, or simply the shorthand of the Renaissance, as I feel it closest to the original terms first used to describe this Black-led artistic movement, typically called the Negro or New Negro Renaissance, prior to its post hoc naming as the Harlem Renaissance. For more on the discussion of the history of this terminology, see: Jak Peake, "'Watching the Waters': Tropic Flows in the Harlem Renaissance, Black Internationalism and Other Currents," *Radical Americas* 3.1 (2018): 1–52, https://doi.org/10.14324/111.444.ra.2018.v3.1.013.

8. I use the term "Black art" here to refer to art which represented Black people, not art which was necessarily produced by Black people.

9. Carl Van Doren, "Why the Editorial Board Selected The Magic Island," *Wings* 3.1 (January 1929): 2–7, at 3.

10. Johnson, *Self-Determining Haiti*. Originally published as four articles in the *Nation* from August 28 until September 25, 1920. See Johnson, "Self-Determining Haiti: I. The American Occupation." James Weldon Johnson, "Self-Determining Haiti: II. What the United States has Accomplished," *The Nation* III, no. 2879 (September 4, 1920): 265–267. James Weldon Johnson, "Self-Determining Haiti: III. Government of, by, and for the National City Bank," *The Nation* III.2880 (September 11, 1920): 295–7. James Weldon Johnson, "Self-Determining Haiti: IV. The Haitian People," *The Nation* III.2882 (September 25, 1920): 345–7, at 347.

11. Van Doren, "Why the Editorial Board Selected the Magic Island."

12. Imani D. Owens, "'Hard Reading': US Empire and Black Modernist Aesthetics in Eric Walrond's *Tropic Death*," *MELUS* 41.4 (2016): 96–115.

13. Immerwahr, *How to Hide an Empire*, 8. Benedict R. Anderson, *Imagined Communities: Reflections on the Origin and Spread of Nationalism*, Revised ed. (London: Verso, 2006), 179.

14. Sean X. Goudie uses the term "paracolonial" to describe the US's global conduct, especially in the Caribbean, which was in his words both "colonialist and not colonialist." Sean X. Goudie, *Creole America: The West Indies and the Formation of Literature and Culture in the New Republic* (Philadelphia: University of Pennsylvania Press, 2006), 12–13.

15. Langston Hughes, *The Big Sea: An Autobiography*, 2nd ed. (New York: Hill and Wang, 1993), 223.

16. See C. W. E. Bigsby, *The Cambridge Companion to Modern American Culture*, (Cambridge: Cambridge University Press, 2006), 358.

17. Langston Hughes, *The Weary Blues* (New York: Knopf, 1926). Langston Hughes, *Fine Clothes to the Jew* (New York: A.A. Knopf, 1927).

18. Hughes, *The Big Sea: An Autobiography*, 223.

19. George Hutchinson, *The Harlem Renaissance in Black and White* (Cambridge: Belknap Press of Harvard University Press, 1995).

20. Heywood Broun, "'The Emperor Jones' by O'Neill Gives Chance for Cheers," review of *The Emperor Jones*, *New York Tribune*, November 4, 1920, 8.

21. For this definition of racial uplift see Kevin Kelly Gaines, *Uplifting the Race: Black Leadership, Politics, and Bulture in the Twentieth Century* (Chapel Hill: The University of North Carolina Press, 1996), 2. Quoted in Shane Vogel, *The Scene of Harlem Cabaret: Race, Sexuality, Performance* (Chicago: University of Chicago Press, 2009), 4.

22. Hubert Harrison, "The Emperor Jones," review of *The Emperor Jones*, *Negro World*, June 4, 1921, 4.

23. W. E. B. Du Bois, "Negro Art," *The Crisis* 22.2 (1921): 55–6.

24. Alain Locke, "Introduction," in *Plays of Negro Life: A Source-book of Native American Drama* (New York: Harper & Brothers, 1927), n.p.

25. In the bibliographical subsection entitled "Negro Drama" at the end of Locke's *The New Negro: An Interpretation*, three of O'Neill's plays are listed, eclipsed only by the entries for Paul Green, Willis ("Willie") Richardson, Ridgely (misnamed Ridgeley) Torrence among twentieth-century playwrights. See Alain LeRoy Locke, ed., *The New Negro: An Interpretation* (New York: A. and C. Boni, 1925), 430–1. I have borrowed the phrases, the "old school" and "new school" of New Negroes from Emily Barnard. See Emily Bernard, ed., *Remember Me to Harlem: The Letters of Langston Hughes and Carl Van Vechten* (New York: Vintage Books, 2002), xxi–xxii.

26. William Stanley Braithwaite, "The Negro in American Literature," in *The New Negro: An Interpretation*, ed. Alain LeRoy Locke (New York: A. and C. Boni, 1925), 35.

27. William Bridges, "'Emperor Jones' A Travesty on the Negro Race," review of *The Emperor Jones*, *Negro World* X.6 (March 26, 1921): 2.

28. See Lothrop Stoddard, *The Rising Tide of Color: Against White World-Supremacy* (New York: Charles Scribner's Sons, 1920). Lothrop Stoddard, *The French Revolution in San Domingo* (Boston: Houghton Mifflin Company, 1914).

29. Hughes, *The Big Sea*, 271, 274, 278 (Negro Renaissance), 271, 275 (New Negro Renaissance), 223 (Manhattan's Black Renaissance) and 334 (Harlem Renaissance).

30. Eugene O'Neill, *The Emperor Jones* (Cincinnati: Stewart Kidd Company, 1921), n.p. I am using Stuart Hall's notion of the "relations of representation" and "politics of representation" as discussed in Stuart Hall, "New Ethnicities," in *Modern Criticism and Theory: A Reader*, ed. David Lodge and Nigel Wood (Harlow: Pearson Longman, 2008), 585.

31. Erez Manela, *The Wilsonian Moment: Self-Determination and the International Origins of Anticolonial Nationalism* (Oxford: Oxford University Press, 2007), 40–1.

32. See Hubert H. Harrison, *A Hubert Harrison Reader*, ed. Jeffrey B. Perry, 1st ed. (Middletown: Wesleyan University Press, 2001), 378–383. See also "The

Garvey Movement is Commanding Attention," *The Richmond Planet*, September 9, 1922, 4.

33. Fredric Jameson, *The Political Unconscious: Narrative as a Socially Symbolic Act* (London: Routledge, 2002).

34. J. Michael Dash, *Haiti and the United States: National Stereotypes and the Literary Imagination*, 2nd ed. (Basingstoke: Palgrave Macmillan, 1998), 34.

35. The first part of the symposium, which ran until November 1926, began in March 1926: W. E. B. Du Bois, "The Negro in Art: How Shall He Be Portrayed; A Symposium," *The Crisis* 31.5 (March 1926): 219–20. The symposium was also preceded by a questionnaire, see W. E. B. Du Bois, "Questionnaire," *The Crisis* 31.4 (February 1926): 165. While "Criteria of Negro Art," was published in *The Crisis* in October 1926, Du Bois had presented it as a Chicago NAACP conference address in June 1926. W. E. B. Du Bois, "Criteria of Negro Art," *The Crisis* 32.6 (October 1926): 290–7, at 296. Carl Van Vechten, Day Books, 1926, Box 208, Folder 5, Carl Van Vechten Papers, MssCol 3142, see entry August 20, Manuscripts and Archives Division, The New York Public Library. Edward White, *The Tastemaker: Carl Van Vechten and the Birth of Modern America*, 1st ed. (New York: Farrar, Straus and Giroux, 2014), 208.

36. Augustus Granville Dill, letter from Augustus G. Dill to W. E. B. Du Bois, August 20, 1926, W. E. B. Du Bois Papers, MS 312, Special Collections and University Archives, University of Massachusetts Amherst Libraries. While Fauset correctly pre-empted Du Bois's dislike of Van Vechten's book, she was wrong about Du Bois being the only Black intellectual brave enough to knock *Nigger Heaven*.

37. Gertrude Stein, letter from Gertrude Stein to Carl Van Vechten, n.d. 1926[?], Box 19, Folder 6, Carl Van Vechten Papers, MssCol 3142, Manuscripts and Archives Division, The New York Public Library. Charles S. Johnson, letter from Charles S. Johnson to Carl Van Vechten, August 10, 1926, Box 19, Folder 9, Carl Van Vechten Papers, MssCol 3142, Manuscripts and Archives Division, The New York Public Library. Nella Imes (Larsen), letter from Nella Imes (Larsen) to Carl Van Vechten, August 11, 1926, Box 19, Folder 7, Carl Van Vechten Papers, MssCol 3142, Manuscripts and Archives Division, The New York Public Library.

38. White was on friendly terms with Van Vechten, and it was White's novel *The Fire in the Flint* which had sparked Van Vechten's interest in Harlem.

39. Robert F. Worth, "Nigger Heaven and the Harlem Renaissance," *African American Review* 29.3 (1995): 463, https://doi.org/10.2307/3042395, http://www.jstor.org/stable/3042395.

40. Hubert Harrison, "Homo Africanus Harlemi," review of *Nigger Heaven*, *New York Amsterdam News*, September 1, 1926, 20. Nine days after the publication of this article, Harrison gave a lecture at the Educational Forum on 200 W. 135th street on the topic. See Hubert Harrison, "A Reply to 'Nigger Heaven': With a Sizzling Summary of Blasé Neurotics and the so-called 'Literary' Set in Harlem," 10 September 1926, Series VIII: Sub-series 8.1: Box 16, Folder 38,

Hubert Harrison Papers, Rare Book & Manuscript Library, Columbia University, https://dlc.library.columbia.edu/catalog/cul:j9kd51c6zf.

41. Joel Rogers, "The Critic: Do They Tell the Truth," review of *Nigger Heaven*, *The Messenger* 8.12 (December 1926): 365.

42. Where in an earlier draft Byron's head "lay cushioned between" Lasca's "nude, golden brown breasts," the published version placed his head "on her shoulder." A few pages later, an "eel-eater" whom Lasca is told is not for "the little lady" is designated "queer" in the published version. Carl Van Vechten, Nigger Heaven, "Galley proof," 1926, Box 93, Folder 1, Carl Van Vechten Papers, MssCol 3142, 240, 244, Manuscripts and Archives Division, The New York Public Library. Carl Van Vechten, *Nigger Heaven* (New York: Alfred A. Knopf, 1926), 240, 244.

43. W. E. B. Du Bois, "Books," review of *Nigger Heaven*, *The Crisis* 33.2 (December 1926): 81.

44. Johnson, letter from Charles S. Johnson to Carl Van Vechten.

45. Joel Rogers make this point in Rogers, "The Critic: Do They Tell the Truth," 365.

46. Cary D. Wintz and Paul Finkelman, eds., *Encyclopedia of the Harlem Renaissance*, vol. 2: K-Y Index (New York: Routledge, 2004), 1203.

47. See Imes (Larsen), letter from Nella Imes (Larsen) to Carl Van Vechten. Johnson, letter from Charles S. Johnson to Carl Van Vechten. Rogers, "The Critic: Do They Tell the Truth," 365, 380. Harrison, "Homo Africanus Harlemi." Carl Van Vechten, "Moanin' Wid a Sword in Ma Han'," *Vanity Fair* 25 (February 1926).

48. Van Vechten, *Nigger Heaven*, 223.

49. Thomas W. Young, "Harlem's Prodigal Son," review of *Home to Harlem*, *Norfolk Journal and Guide* xxviii.16 (April 21, 1928): 16.

50. Dewey R. Jones, "The Bookshelf: More 'Nigger Heaven'," review of *Home to Harlem*, *The Chicago Defender*, March 17, 1928, Sec. 2, 2.1.

51. Bernard, *Remember Me to Harlem*, 61.

52. "Harper Books of the Month," Advertisement, *The Forum* LXXIX, no. 4 (April 1928): ix. The notion that McKay was a new recruit to negro literature, nine years on from the poem, "If We Must Die," and six since the publication of his poetry collection *Harlem Shadows*, stretches credibility, but it suggests that Harper and Brother's marketeers pitched the novel at a white audience, or at least one unfamiliar with his writing.

53. W. E. B. Du Bois, "The Browsing Reader: Two Novels," review of Home to Harlem and Quicksand, *The Crisis* 35.6 (June 1928): 202.

54. Du Bois, "Books," 81.

55. Claude McKay, letter from Claude McKay to Louise Bryant, August 23, 1926, Louise Bryant Papers, MS 1840, Series 1, Box 5, Folder 68: Manuscripts and Archives, Yale University Library.

56. Du Bois reviewed *Home to Harlem* alongside Nella Larsen's *Quicksand*, describing the latter as "the best piece of fiction that Negro America has produced since the heyday of Chesnutt." Yet, curiously Du Bois dedicated fewer words to Larsen's novella, and ended with a fillip against the market: New York

columnists would not find it "near nasty enough," while it was "too sincere for the South and middle West." Du Bois, "The Browsing Reader: Two Novels," 202.

57. Du Bois, "Books," 82. Du Bois, "The Browsing Reader: Two Novels," 202.

58. Du Bois, "The Browsing Reader: Two Novels," 202.

59. John Lowney, "Haiti and Black Transnationalism: Remapping the Migrant Geography of Home to Harlem," *African American Review* 34.3 (2000): 413–29, at 413, https://doi.org/10.2307/2901381, www.jstor.org/stable/2901381.

60. "Harper Books of the Month." Mahlon Blaine dust jacket from John Vandercook, *Black Majesty: The Life of Christophe, King of Haiti* (New York: Harper & Brothers, 1928). Aaron Douglas dust jacket from Claude McKay, *Home to Harlem* (New York; London: Harper and Brothers, 1928): see General Research Division, The New York Public Library, "Home to Harlem," New York Public Library Digital Collections, https://digitalcollections.nypl .org/items/510d47db-d153-a3d9-e040-e00a18064a99.

61. "Harper Books of the Month."

62. Robert Cortes Holliday, "The Negro in King Christophe's Haiti, in Sir M. Garvey's Harlem, In Sunday School and at Large," review of John Vandercook's *Black Majesty*, Howard W. Odum's *Rainbow Round my Shoulder*, Claude McKay's *Home to Harlem* and Roark Bradford's *Ol' Man Adams an' His Children*, *New York Evening Post*, April 21, 1928, Sec. 3, 12. Gwendolyn Bennett, "Blue-Black Symphony," review of *Home to Harlem*, *New York Herald Tribune*, March 11, 1928, Sec. XII, 5–6.

63. T. S. Matthews, "What Gods! What Gongs!," review of Roark Bradford's *Ol' Man Adams an' His Children*, Nella Larsen's *Quicksand*, Claude McKay's *Home to Harlem* and John Vandercook's *Black Majesty*, *The New Republic* LV.704 (May 30, 1928): 50.

64. Hutchinson, *The Harlem Renaissance in Black and White*, 247–8.

65. Van Vechten, *Nigger Heaven*, 122. Van Vechten almost appears to be anticipating John Vandercook's *Black Majesty*, which though technically a history, has a novelistic feel. He dined with Vandercook and his wife on November 28, 1926, just prior to their setting sail to Haiti, and read Vandercook's book *Tom-Tom* a month prior to this. Van Vechten, Day Books: see entries for October 18 and November 28, 1926.

66. As editor of the American Mars, Durwood is most likely modeled on the *American Mercury* editor, H. L. Mencken. Van Vechten, *Nigger Heaven*, 225.

67. McKay, *Home to Harlem*, 152.

68. Eric Walrond, "Subjection," in *Tropic Death* (New York: Boni & Liveright, 1926), 139–60, at 158.

69. Johnson, *Self-Determining Haiti*; 18. Walrond, "Subjection," 158.

70. "Eric Walrond's Tales and Other New Works of Fiction," *New York Times*, October 17, 1926, Sec. BR., 6; V. F. Calverton, "Ground Swells in Fiction," review of *Tropic Death*, *Nigger Heaven*, H. G. Well's *The World of William Clissold*, Jim Tully's *Jarnegan*, Ruth Suckow's *Iowa Interiors*, Dorothy Canfield's *Her Son's Wife*, Rose Macaulay's *Crewe's Train*, Carl Van Doren's

The Ninth Wave, Joseph Hergesheimer's *Tampico*, Fritz Mauthner's *Mrs. Socrates*, Elizabeth Madox Robert's *The Time of Man*, Louis Bromfield's *Early Autumn* and Ellen Glasgow's The Romantic Comedians, *The Survey* 57.3 (November 1, 1928): 159–61, at 160.

71. See, for example, Calverton, "Ground Swells in Fiction." Robert Herrick, "Tropic Death," review of *Tropic Death*, *The New Republic* XLVIII, no. 623 (November 10, 1926): 332. Langston Hughes, "Marl-Dust and West Indian Sun," review of *Tropic Death*, *New York Herald Tribune*, December 5, 1926, Sec. VII, 9. Eric Walrond's Tales and Other New Works of Fiction." J. A. Rogers, "Book Review," review of *Tropic Death*, *The Pittsburgh Courier*, March 5, 1927, Sec. 2, 8. James Davis, *Eric Walrond: A Life in the Harlem Renaissance and the Transatlantic Caribbean* (New York: Columbia University Press, 2015), 184.

72. Herrick, "Tropic Death."

73. "Eric Walrond's Tales and Other New Works of Fiction." Calverton, "Ground Swells in Fiction." For an example of an article discussing race and propaganda prior to Du Bois's "Criteria of Negro Art," see Newman I. White's review, and particularly the comments concerning Benjamin Brawley who is described "as unique among negro writers in not allowing sympathy of race propaganda to warp his critical judgement." Newman I. White, "Review of T.S. Stribling's Birthright, Ernest Howard Culbertson's Goat Alley, Claude McKay's Harlem Shadows, Thomas W. Talley's Negro Folk Rhymes, James Weldon Johnson's The Book of American Negro Poetry and Benjamin Brawley's The Negro in Literature and Art," *The Southern Atlantic Quarterly* 22.1 (January 1923): 93–95, at 95.

74. See, for example, "Tropic Death by Eric Walrond," Harper and Brothers advertisement, *The New York World*, October 26, 1928, 17. "Tropic Death by Eric Walrond," Harper and Brothers advertisement, *The Saturday Review of Literature*, October 30, 1928, 268. For a facsimile of the advert, see Charles Egleston, *The House of Boni & Liveright, 1917–1933: A Documentary Volume*, vol. 288, Dictionary of Literary Biography, (Detroit: Gale, 2003), 406.

75. Hughes, "Marl-Dust and West Indian Sun." Rogers, "Book Review."

76. W. E. B. Du Bois and Alain Locke, "Five Books," review of Eric Walrond's *Tropic Death*, Leo Weiner's *Mayan and Mexican Origins*, Rossa B. Cooley's *Homes of the Freed*, and James Weldon Johnson and J. Rosamond Johnson *The Second Book of American Negro Spirituals* (by Du Bois); John Vandercook's *Tom-Tom* (by Alain Locke), *The Crisis* 33.3 (January 1927): 152.

77. Mary White Ovington, "The Bookshelf: West India Tales," review of *Tropic Death*, *Chicago Defender*, January 1, 1927, Sec. 2, 1.

78. Ovington, "The Bookshelf: West India Tales," 1.

79. Ovington, "The Bookshelf: West India Tales," 1.

80. Davis, *Eric Walrond*, xv. Lara Putnam, *Radical Moves: Caribbean Migrants and the Politics of Race in the Jazz Age* (Chapel Hill: University of North Carolina Press, 2013), 61.

81. Rogers, "Book Review."

82. Hughes, "Marl-Dust and West Indian Sun."

CHAPTER 11

What We Know That We Don't Know
Nella Larsen, James Baldwin, and Ocean Vuong on US Empire and Desire

Meg Wesling

How does a focus on sexuality help us to understand the relationship between US empire and American literature? What kind of work does sexuality do in normalizing or contesting the conditions of empire? And what can literature teach us about sexuality and its relation to empire? To think through these questions, I will begin by establishing some of the key findings of recent scholarship and then turn to three novels that together comprise a particular strand of queer fiction, running from the early twentieth century through the contemporary moment, that helps us to glimpse the interworking of literature, sexuality, and empire's racializing project: Nella Larsen's *Passing*, James Baldwin's *Giovanni's Room*, and Ocean Vuong's *On Earth We're Briefly Gorgeous*.

A first key point emerges from scholarship on race and US empire over the past several decades: that the organization of US empire and the perpetuation of white supremacy have long depended upon the logic of sexual normativity for their natural-seemingness. Projects of US state-building, including settler colonialism, chattel slavery, extraterritorial expansion, and US military aggression have promoted a vision of Americanness as iconographically and ideologically synonymous with the white heteropatriarchal family, and a long history of legal and literary representations of racialized subjects as sexually non-normative, whether perverse, primitive, or promiscuous, continues to serve the project of US empire. From the push toward extraterritorial expansion in the late nineteenth century to the rising nationalist populism of the early twenty-first century, US literature has been at the center of a political debate about the meaning of American identity and the racial and sexual norms constituted within it.

When we look back to consider how the development of an American literary canon was structurally and ideologically tied to the US imperial project in the late nineteenth century, we should therefore not be surprised to see the culture wars of the present play out in terms of debates about what books can be taught, read, and circulated. For example, my book, *Empire's Proxy*, posited that the field of American literary studies found the conditions for its own institutionalization as a tool in the expansion of US empire at the close of the nineteenth century. The project of "Americanizing" the US's new colonial subjects was often described by pro-expansionists through the paradigm of colonial tutelage; through the ideological characterization of US imperialism as a project of education, American literature became a privileged tool for communicating American identity, history, and values. As such, American literary study found the conditions for its emergence as a field of knowledge in the project of empire. In considering how sexuality functioned within the paradigm of colonial tutelage, I am struck by the ways in which late-nineteenth century imperialists like William Howard Taft shared with anti-vice crusaders like Anthony Comstock the belief that literature had a strong moral (or immoral) effect on the reader. Having little appreciation for the nuanced and often contradictory ways that readers make sense of, identify with, and draw lessons from literary texts, these parties placed the literary as a powerful form of moral education or a threatening challenge to the "natural" values of the white heteropatriarchal family. Thus, the very idea of literature as a persuasive tool is one site where the conditions of empire and the regulation of sexuality merge in the literary.

A second key point emerging from American literary studies on empire studies is that US settler colonialism has functioned as an *epistemological* project, one that continues to exert a powerful force on our frameworks for understanding and articulating what sexuality means. For example, J. Kehaulani Kauanui has written compellingly about how the settler colonial system imposed long-lasting transformations in Hawai'i long before the US-backed overthrow in 1893 and unilateral annexation in 1898, including the imposition of heteropatriarchy and heterosexual monogamy as part of an American Christian missionary project that promoted gendered and racialized ideas of "civilization" linked to capit-alism and land ownership.[1] Kauanui has demonstrated how everything regarded as Indigenous was feminized as part of rendering it "savage" in relation to the patriarchal Christian ideal as the model of the modern subject/nation. This scholarship highlights what David Scott describes as the "paradox" of "colonial enlightenment" as knowledge production with the "permanent legacy that has set the conditions in which we make of

ourselves what we make and which therefore demands constant renego-
tiation and readjustment."[2]

Recognizing the legacy of US settler colonialism as an epistemological
project requires that we attend to the ways that it continues to impact the
very frameworks through which we theorize the categories of resistance
and opposition by setting the terms for what is legally legible, practically
viable, and cognitively imaginable. For example, Scott L. Morgensen's
work offers a compelling analysis of the way that "the biopolitics of settler
colonialism was constituted by the imposition of colonial heteropatriarchy and the hegemony of settler sexuality, which sought both the elimination of Indigenous sexuality and its incorporation into settler sexual
modernity."[3] Drawing on work of scholars such as Andrea Smith and
Mark Rifkin, among others, Morgensen demonstrates how the disciplin-
ing of Native American sexuality was a critical part of the formation of
modern normative sexuality as white and heteropatriarchal; the "queering of Native peoples by colonial heteropatriarchy" constituted what he
calls, drawing on Ann Laura Stoler, the "education of desire" as
a principal part of settler colonialism.

The epistemological frameworks that have maintained white supremacy
through its association with sexual normativity shaped the history of
chattel slavery and have been a central part of racialization after the formal
end of enslavement. The popularization of knowledge about the emergent
category of sexual identity known as "the homosexual" in the late nineteenth century was disseminated through the work of sexologists like
Havelock Ellis, who famously used the Black female body as a sign of
sexual Otherness.[4] For his argument, he drew heavily from the traditions of
comparative anatomy and race science in arguing that the body itself was
the locus of sexual identity and he looked to genital size and form to find
"anomalies" that he interpreted as indicators of sexual perversion. Not only
did Ellis draw on the assumptions of race science to purport that visual
corporeal difference indicated invisible differences in sexual desire and
gender presentation, but he also drew on nineteenth-century racial ideologies and fantasies to provide supporting evidence for his claims. The racial
ideologies of the nineteenth century most frequently took the form of
fantasies of African American sexual excess; depictions of African American
men as sexual predators were used to stoke fear of miscegenation and to
justify lynching as a form of racial terror in the name of protecting white
women's sexual purity. Images and tales of African American women's
sexual promiscuity and lasciviousness were used, conversely, to erase the
systemic rape and sexual assault of African American women by white men.

Thus, the nineteenth-century understanding of sexual norms must be understood in the context of the legal, medical, and social apparatuses of racial management. As Evelyn Brooks Higginbotham argued, "The exclusion of black women from the dominant society's definition of 'lady' said as much about sexuality as it did about class. The metalanguage of race signifies, too, the imbrication of race within the representation of sexuality."[5] Ideas about African American women's sexuality as excessive and dangerous constitute an important facet of the ideological system of white supremacy, and figure into the literary, often, as absence; as Evelynn Hammonds has argued, "the sexualities of black women have been shaped by silence, erasure, and invisibility" as a response to the overdetermination of Blackness and sexual excess within white patriarchal discourse.[6]

For scholars of queer studies, this means a fundamental rethinking of the categories of knowledge that subtend the field. Marlon Ross argues that the foundational paradigm of "the closet" only works if the homosexual in question is not already marked by another kind of sexual non-normativity, which is to say, marked by race. Inasmuch as race is, as Higginbotham has argued, a "metalanguage" that constructs gender and sexuality's signifying power at the outset, then the closet as a "raceless paradigm" allows us only to imagine the invention of the Anglo-Saxon homosexual (elite male) homosexual whose sexuality could be presumed normative. Ross argues, "Perverting the procreative purpose of the healthy Anglo-Saxon male, the homosexual necessarily also carried within his body a latent racial perversion, implicitly fostering the threat of racial reversion by failing to do his part to propagate the Anglo Saxon race."[7]

To think through the ways in which Ross's argument raises questions about the "truth" of sexual identity, I turn here to Nella Larsen's 1929 novel *Passing*.[8] If Larsen is subtly depicting sexual desire between Irene and Clare, as critics have argued persuasively, then how does the novel trouble the paradigm of the closet and coming out in ways that might differ significantly from, for example, Eve Sedgwick's field-defining readings of Henry James or Herman Melville? How are the contours of secrecy, knowledge, and disclosure understood differently when we take into account how the historical emergence of "the homosexual" as a type of person, or a "species," to use Michel Foucault's words, appears as the sign of an emergent modern understanding of sexuality only if the homosexual in question is not inhabiting a body already marked as sexually non-normative – that is to say, a racialized body? For African American men and women, racially coded as always already sexually excessive and non-normative, what closeted space is exited in the name of revelation or liberation? Or, as Ross puts it, "what does it mean for African Americans to uncloset their sexuality within the context of a racial status already marked as an abnormal site over and against white bourgeois identity and its various signifiers of racial normativity?"[9]

Nella Larsen's *Passing*, in this light, speaks to the profoundly influential factors in the way that sexuality and empire play out in American literature. First, the novel's central concern with crossing the color line demonstrates all the ways in which the policing of racial identity is inextricably linked to the regulation of sexuality. The novel's hint that Irene Redfield may desire Clare Kendry is inseparable from Clare's status as someone who, by passing as white, has already dared to violate the racial boundaries that Irene takes quite seriously; even as Irene recognizes that the visual signs of racial belonging are laughable and she mocks the repertoire of bodily markers that white people rely on to signify racial difference, for Irene the sense of racial and sexual propriety are inseparable. Irene's terror at glimpsing her desire for Clare – or perhaps, her refusal to really see that desire at all – must be read in the context of enormous pressure she carries as part of her self-understanding as a paragon of African American respectability, with her careful attention to manners and social convention, her participation in the rituals of Black cultural life, and her iron-fisted management of the home as the site where not only hers, but her husband's and her sons' sexuality is carefully managed. Irene's careful crafting of self, with her highly con-strained avenue for the expression of sexuality, and the very coded ways that Larsen suggests Irene's desire for Clare, bring to mind the archive of Black feminist scholarship that has identified how histories of enslavement and systemic sexual violence leave a legacy of silence, secrecy, and opacity in literary representations, making the exploration of such representations an important site for political work.[10]

Such work asks us to read into the gaps and silences around sexual desire for a more complex navigation of the reality of Black women's ontological status as Other to white American normative sexuality. But we must also read Irene's subtle fears about her husband Brian as animated by a powerful understanding that heteronormativity and anti-Blackness work powerfully in tandem. When Irene frets about "That strange, and to her fantastic, notion of Brian's of going off to Brazil which, though unmentioned, yet lived within him; how it frightened her, and – yes, angered her!", Larsen is acknowledging the specifically *US-American* history of sexual regulation that sets the terms of respectability and survival for Irene as an African American woman.[11] Thus, Irene's comment that "Brian doesn't care for ladies" and her dismay that "it's South America that attracts him" must be understood within the context of the extreme threat such desire poses to Irene's security.[12] This reference also contrasts Irene and Brian's bourgeois life in Harlem with the reputation of Brazil as a place of sexual freedom and racial integration; as Zita Nunes has demonstrated, articles in the African American press throughout the 1920s lauded South America in general, and Brazil in particular, as a place of "true democracy" where "racial peace and good will prevail."[13] At the same time, Larsen complicates this image by locating South America as the source of the "untold gold" that makes Clare's husband Jack's vast fortune. Jack's openly racist attitudes undermine the fantasy of South America as a haven of racial integration. Nevertheless, for Brian and for many of Larsen's readers, given the overdetermined relationship between Blackness and sexual pathology in US legal and literary domains, racial and sexual freedom can only be imagined outside a US framework.[14]

A key point that becomes clearer when we look at sexuality through its entanglement with US empire is thus the historically contingent nature of sexual identity. I would argue, then, that the work of American literary studies must be to continue to illuminate the culturally contingent, often collective nature sexual identity. We are living in a moment in which the presumption of the *innate* and immutable nature of sexuality operates as liberal orthodoxy in the public sphere. Major research institutes continue to investigate the possible biological causes of homosexuality, and legal "wins" for gay and lesbian rights are increasingly predicated on the argument that sexuality is an immutable characteristic.[15] Meanwhile, the notion that sexual identities could be contingent and culturally specific in nature is wielded by the extreme Right as a threat to family and nation. Legislation like the "Don't Say Gay" bill in Florida promotes a paranoid fantasy that to *read about* homosexuality is to risk becoming queer. Yet to maintain that sexual identity is an innate and immutable category of being is to erase the ways that sexual norms and identities have been central to the enforcement of racial hierarchies and white supremacy.

What if, instead, we consider how sexuality is, as Indigenous scholar Kim TallBear has argued, not an innate immutable characteristic, but a way of relating to others, a way of being that "mediates social relations across the family, clan, pueblo, tribe, and other forms of relations ... "?[16] To think about sexuality as a way of relating allows us to investigate how the desires that seem natural, spontaneous, and personal to each of us are also deeply imbricated in social relations – and to embrace the possibilities for resistance and change that the sexual might open up. Sharon Holland has asked, "can work on 'desire' be antiracist work? Can antiracist work *think* 'desire'?".[17] In a similar vein, feminist philosopher Amia Srinivasan recently asked, "what would it mean to desire more ethically, more justly?"[18] In posing these questions, Holland and Srinivasan demystify the ways that desire molds itself around historically calcified, politically charged categories of identity and power. To ask if we can desire more ethically, more justly, is to insist that our desires have both a social life and a collective political history. It is to suggest that our desires are not simply internal to us, emerging from the depths of an inscrutable psychic terrain, but produced in relation to the values and logics of the world around us. It is to grapple with the reality that the intimacy of our desires, the sense of their immediacy and interiority, is an after-effect of our lived experiences and the disciplinary forces that shape us.

In the remaining pages, I want to turn to two further examples to explore these ideas, asking in particular how literature can help not only to illuminate the relationship between sexuality and empire but to push back against its deterministic frameworks by imagining new modes of desire. Sexuality, like Americanness itself, has always been, under contestation – and the intriguing fact of literature is that it can be offered as a model but there is no guarantee how it will be read or interpreted. Opportunities for misreading and resistant interpretations abound. My hope in the readings that follow is to explore what Tiffany Lethabo King has named "the potential of the erotic and the sexual under conditions of conquest" – to examine not just how US literature has perpetuated a racialized logic of sexual normativity but also how, at times, it exceeds or upends that logic.[19]

I turn here to James Baldwin's 1956 novel *Giovanni's Room* to explore how this mid-century text illuminates the collective work of managing empire through sexual norms. The growing and important scholarly canon on *Giovanni's Room* has brilliantly explored how race and sexuality shape and define each other in the novel; there remains much to be said, however, about Baldwin's trenchant critique of the imperial state.[20] The opening scene establishes US imperialism as a central concern in the novel; the protagonist, David, addresses the reader directly, asserting that "My face is like a face you have seen many times. My ancestors conquered a continent, pushing across death-laden plains, until they came to an ocean which faced away from Europe with a darker past."[21] David links his white American identity to the legacy of Anglo-European settler colonialism, establishing empire as a central concern of the novel. Moreover, Baldwin links American racial, imperial, and sexual histories through the subtle but persistent racialization of David's queer lovers. While David's "blond hair gleams," his first male lover, Joey, is described as "very quick and dark," whose "curly hair darken[s] the pillow" and David notices after their coupling that "his body was brown."[22] The central love affair in the novel is that between David and Giovanni, an Italian barman who has immigrated to Paris after the birth of his stillborn son. Giovanni, too, is described as "dark and leonine," and his economic and geographical marginalization and his legal precarity as a working-class immigrant stand in contradistinction to the impunity that David's whiteness and his Americanness provide him.[23] For David, white American masculinity is so intimately connected to heteropatriarchal privilege that to express queer desire is to become racialized.[24] That is to say, *Giovanni's Room* offers us a vision of whiteness and heteropatriarchy so interdependent that the protagonist, David, can only imagine his queer desire as a loss not just of his manhood but of his whiteness.

US empire enters in more subtle ways, too. In one early reflection, David makes a passing reference to an affair "while [he] was in the Army which involved a fairy who was later court-martialed out."[25] This is a telling moment, both for its false tone of casual recollection and for the dismissive reference to the "fairy" who, unlike David, paid a more public price for their affair. We also learn that David once caused a "minor sensation by flirting with a soldier" in the Parisian gay bar he occasionally frequents, even as he carefully maintains his position that he is not gay, but only there to cajole a free drink or two from a wealthy friend.[26] Such scenes evoke the paradoxical history of the military in relation to gay and lesbian life; the military has functioned as a site for the international reproduction of an aggressive masculinity and the global imposition of American gender and sexual norms; at the same time, particularly during and after WWII, it provided unprecedented opportunities for homoerotic desire and same-sex intimacy for men and women who left families and hometowns to enter the war effort.[27] The homosocial, extra-familial space of the military as a site endowed with extraordinary opportunity for but also punishment of same-sex desire explains the novel's depiction of the inconsistency of David's desire, his incessant back and forth between desire and repulsion toward Giovanni, and his terror at the desire he feels growing in himself, a desire he says both "shamed and frightened me."[28] This nod to the relationship between sexuality and the military foreshadows the more spectacular way that Giovanni's queer identity will be exploited in the name of the imperial state.

Baldwin sets this tragic love affair in Paris, the center of a French imperial state fighting, at that moment, for control of its colonial projects

in Asia and Africa. The novel's publication coincides with the intensifica-
tion of what Baldwin elsewhere referred to as "the battle going on ... for
the domination of the world," and Baldwin's readers would have received
the book in the context of the escalation of the French war in Indochina
and the fall of Dien Bien Phu, as well as the brutal conflict between France
and the Algerian National Liberation Front that would end in Algeria's
independence.[29] The novel's publication was also timed with the powerful
emergent post-war internationalist anti-colonial, anti-racist organizing
represented, to cite one example, by the First International Congress of
Black Writers and Artists, which was held in Paris the year of the novel's
publication and in which Baldwin participated as a journalist. This context
illuminates how and why *Giovanni's Room* implicitly situates the question
of American racial and sexual norms within the broader militarized context
of anti-imperialist struggles and the global resistance to European and
American domination.

The context of the US Cold War is essential here, too; David's obsession
with the criminality of his desire for Giovanni speaks not just to the
pathologizing of same-sex desire in the US, but the specifically American
paranoia that homosexuality represented a threat to the US nation-state.[30]
David's framework for understanding his desire for Giovanni is firmly
rooted in a set of beliefs and practices that are tied to the particular ways
that white supremacy and homophobia mingle in an anti-communist US
framework. For one thing, David refuses Giovanni's nonchalance regarding the future of their relationship, shouting "it is a crime – in my country"
and he recognizes that fleeing American soil does not mean shaking off the
ideological framework it imposes: "after all, I didn't grow up here, I grew
up there."[31] Similarly, when David tells himself that his desire for another
man "would be something that had happened to me once – it would be
something that had happened to many men once," he rejects the minor-
itizing logic of mid-century gay liberation discourses and instead locates his
affair within the logic of a Cold War paranoia that universalized queer
desire as a threat that might be, could be anywhere.[32] In so doing,
Giovanni's Room explores the pervasive nature of queer desire and the
particular ways that the state, in the form of family, media, and economy,
work in tandem to contain and to criminalize that desire but *not to
eradicate it*. To the contrary, the imperial heteropatriarchal state,
Baldwin demonstrates, depends on the continued, but always marginalized
and inherently racialized queer subject as its radical Other.

We see this most clearly when Giovanni is accused of murdering
Guillaume, the owner of the gay bar where Giovanni once worked and

where David and Giovanni met; Guillaume is described by David as an "old queen," and David speculates that Giovanni was driven by poverty and desperation to submit to Guillaume's sexual advances before finally murdering him in a fit of rage and humiliation. The murder becomes an event of "terrific scandal" in the media—a familiar scenario that allows Baldwin to note that "such a scandal always threatens, before its reverberations cease, to rock the very foundations of the state."[33] Why does this murder in Paris challenge the very foundations of the imperial center? Baldwin offers an analysis with precision:

> when Guillaume's corpse was discovered, it was not only the boys of the street who were frightened; they, in fact, were a good deal less frightened than the men who roamed the streets to buy them, whose careers, positions, aspirations, could never have survived such notoriety. Fathers of families, sons of great houses, and itching adventurers from Belleville were all desperately anxious that the case be closed so that things might, in effect, go back to normal and the dreadful whiplash of public morality not fall on their backs.[34]

Here, then, we have a clue about the peculiar challenge of queerness to empire. It is not queer criminality, putatively located in Giovanni, or even queer desire that challenges the state, but the fact that it cannot be contained within the urban underworld of working class and marginalized subjects. The fact that "sons of great houses"—including the "adventurers" associated with conquest and empire – can be caught up in this scandal, their standing tainted by their connection to this world, demonstrates that the state's main objective is not to extinguish the reality of queer desire but to stamp out the evidence that its existence is diffuse and everywhere, that it is not contained in the pathologized, racialized, foreignized body of the pervert or the criminal. In this context, Giovanni, whose marginal status has already made him part of the low-paid urban underclass, now becomes a useful tool for the media and for the state. Baldwin thus suggests how the association between homosexuality and criminal deviance, a mainstay of popular fiction and journalistic sensation since the late 19th century, also serves the needs of the modern imperial state.[35]

Baldwin also invites us to consider that the "normal" that these "fathers of families, sons of great houses" go back to is not a clear distinction between gay male subcultures and heteropatriarchal domesticity. Rather, queer desire is a part of everyday life, a quotidian reality whose geographic and ideological marginalization serves both the fantasy of the heteropatriarchal family as the norm, and the maintenance of a queer subculture where young men like Giovanni are easily financially and sexually exploited, having no recourse to the law or the state in their defense. Giovanni's status as Other to the French imperial state is crucial to the way that the state manages the scandal of queer desire:

> It was fortunate, therefore, that Giovanni was a foreigner. As though by some magnificently tacit agreement, with every day that he was at large, the press became more vituperative against him and more gentle towards Guillaume. It was remembered that there perished with Guillaume one of the oldest names in France .... Guillaume's name became fantastically entangled with French history, French honor, and French glory, and very nearly became, indeed, a symbol of French manhood.[36]

For Guillaume's name to be "fantastically entangled with French history, French honor, and French glory" means, of course, that it is also entangled with French empire, which is the generative force of the ideological and economic infrastructure of that history and that glory. The symbolic and representational force of the association of poverty with deviance on the one hand, and wealth with power and prestige on the other, allows Giovanni's death to recuperate Guillaume into the heteropatriarchal order. But it symbolically cleanses David as well; as in the earlier example of the "fairy" who was court-marshaled out of the Army, here too the evidence of David's queer past is safely contained when the apparatus of the state steps in to protect the figure of white heteropatriarchal authority. The story told in newsprint across the nation depicts Giovanni as a "criminal ... of the dullest kind, a bungler" whose status as a foreigner and as someone suspected of "having what the French ... call *les goûts particuliers*" makes him a convenient suspect.[37] Conversely, Guillaume is elevated to stand for both the glory and the precarity of the white patriarch as the symbol of the state. Inasmuch as Giovanni's impending death propels Guillaume's reputation very nearly to the status of a symbol of "French manhood," it also allows David to recuperate his own fantasy of returning to the privilege of white American manhood, returning to his fiancée Hella's suffocating embrace, where she pleads with him, "Just let me be a woman, take me. It's what I want. It's *all* I want."[38]

While *Giovanni's Room* illuminates an American narrator's participation in the collective cultural work of managing race and sexuality from the center of French empire, I now turn to a more recent novel to think more about the epistemological legacies of US empire on our ways of knowing and expressing desire. Ocean Vuong's poetic novel, *On Earth We're Briefly Gorgeous*, offers an opportunity to examine the connections among sexuality, empire, and literary imagination through the lens of language. The structure of the novel places the limits of language at the center of the book's project; written as an epistolary novel to his mother, Rose, Little Dog acknowledges that she will never be able to read what he writes. Though each chapter is addressed to her, it is not clear if his writing brings him closer to her or pushes him further apart: "Dear Ma, I am writing to reach you – even if each word I put down is one word further from where you are."[39] Little Dog's literacy and his mastery of English distinguish him from his mother and his grandmother, a distinction that Vuong closely connects to the enduring trauma of the Vietnam War and the subsequent experience of US racism. It is his mother's language that marks her as Other to American identity; because of Rose's fair skin she can pass for white until she begins to speak, when "[her] tongue out[s] her." As Vuong puts it, "One does not 'pass' in America, it seems, without English."[40] Similarly, the bullying Little Dog experiences at school, he notes, is meted out by boys who have already "mastered the dialect of damaged American fathers," thus indicating how violence, too, is a language that we teach and learn from one generation to the next.[41]

Language also constructs the meaning of Little Dog's particular experience of being queer, of being one further step from the normative framework of white American masculinity, highlighting how American nationalism and imperial violence shape the contours of his sexual identity and desires. Little Dog and his mother are in a Dunkin' Donuts when he announces to her, "I don't like girls." His declarative statement fills a particular linguistic void between them; he explains that he is stuck with the vocabulary of a colonial history that names and defines terms for sexuality:

> I didn't want to use the Vietnamese word for it – pê-dê – from the French word pédé, short from pédéraste. Before the French occupation, our Vietnamese did not have a name for queer bodies – because they were seen, like all bodies, fleshed and of one source – and I didn't want to introduce this part of me using the epithet for criminals.[42]

Little Dog must translate from a French colonial context to an American neocolonial one, finding, finally, that the reality of his sexual identity exceeds the linguistic and, perhaps, the epistemological registers available to them.

Little Dog's queer identity is molded by his linguistic legacies of Vietnamese and his proficiency in English, particularly in his role as the translator for the family. Through English, he learns how gender and sexuality work in a US frame, and he helps his mother produce her gender for this unfamiliar public. His fluency in English makes Little Dog the translator for the family, and it is not insignificant that the memory that stays with him is the role he played in calling Victoria's Secret to order his mother's bras and underwear, the telephone operators mistaking him for a young woman. He accompanies his mother shopping and reads for her the tags on a dress she considers buying, a dress that he would wear a few days later, in secret, only to be witnessed by a neighborhood boy and be taunted with "freak, fairy, fag."[43] Little Dog's mastery of English thus establishes an intimacy with his mother that upends the hierarchy between parent and child and traverses the boundary between feminine and masculine. In one sense, this linguistic interdependence and intimacy "queers" Little Dog from the start. It also renders his mother's American femininity a strategic construction that requires collective labor within the family.

These scenes illuminate the ways that American empire is embedded in the linguistic possibilities and the definitional categories of sexuality that are available at any particular historical moment, which is to say they are not static, but dynamic in relation to our personal experiences of violence, trauma, and love, among other things. *On Earth We're Briefly Gorgeous* asks how this distinction is already playing itself out, mostly without our awareness, in the contours of our fantasies and desires themselves. This is not to say that US empire determines those desires, but it does challenge the idea that our desires and our sexual identities emerge solely from within us, indifferent to our experiences and the knowledge that we carry in our very bodies. Instead, they represent an internal working-out of complex historical, collective memories. The intimacy of sex and empire are repeated in Little Dog's relationship with Trevor, the white boy who becomes his lover. As he and Trevor have sex, Little Dog makes explicit the connection between violence and intimacy: "'Keep going,' I begged. 'Fuck me up, fuck me up.' By then, violence was already mundane to me, was what I knew, ultimately, of love. Fuck. Me. Up. It felt good to name what was already happening to me all my life. I was being fucked up, at last, by choice."[44]

This is not just a personal history, however, but an intimacy with US empire as well. After Trevor dies of a heroin overdose, Little Dog recalls their first summer together:

> He grabbed the WWII army helmet off the floor and put it back on, the one he was wearing the day I met him. I keep seeing that helmet – but this can't be right. This boy, impossibly American and alive in the image of a dead

soldier. It's too neat, so clean a symbol I just have made it up. And even now, in all the pictures I looked through, I can't find him wearing it. Yet here it is, tilted to hide Trevor's eyes, making him seem anonymous and easy to look at.[45]

That the helmet renders Trevor "anonymous and easy to look at" indicates how the symbolic figure of the soldier renders Little Dog's fantasies a space where love and violence are inseparable. Vuong insists that the legacy of US imperialism seeps into even our most intimate desires. In reality, Trevor is not a soldier, but the grandson of a Korean War veteran and nephew of a Vietnam vet, making the Army helmet a fitting symbolic representation of the militarized roots of his own identity. Trevor's dad boasts admiringly of the wartime violence that Trevor's uncle James inflicted during his military deployment in Vietnam: "He whooped them in that jungle. He did good for us. He burned them up. You know that Trev? . . . He told you yet? How he burned up four of them in a ditch with gasoline? He told me that on his wedding night, can you believe it?"[46] Trevor's father interpellates his son as the inheritor of white American masculinity predicated on military force, casually mentioning a grotesque scene of carnage as evidence of "good." Vuong links this to sexual normativity through the setting of a wedding night confession, begging the question of how this violence is not contained to the theater of war, but becomes part of our most intimate selves.

In such scenes, Vuong pushes back against the fantasy of a separation between public and private, between past and present. The histories of US imperialism and racism inform every aspect of the novel's intimate relationship. Little Dog has to recall, time and again, that the intertwined US histories of race and sexuality situate him and Trevor differently in relation to their desire.

> He was white, I never forgot this. He was always white. And I knew this was why there was a space for us: a farm, a field, a barn, a house, an hour, two. A space I never found in the city, where the tenement apartments we lived in were so cramped one could tell when a neighbor had a stomach flu in the middle of the night. To hide here, in a room in a broken-down mobile home, was, somehow, a privilege, a chance. He was white. I was yellow. In the dark, our facts lit up and our acts pinned us down.[47]

Little Dog understands, finally, that this is the way that the distribution of power in the world is not something that sex liberates you from, but something that defines the contours of sexuality itself: "I had thought sex was to breach new ground, despite terror, that as long as the world did not see us, its rules did not apply. But I was wrong. The rules, they were already inside us."[48]

To say that the "rules" are already "inside" us is to say that our desires are already linked to the political and social world. The history of American literature and empire demonstrates for us that sexuality is inherently political; that its characterization as something internal and natural is itself a political position, one that carries with it its own history and its specific ideological stakes and compromises. Desire is itself part of the political world; its conditions for emerging, its contours and colors are filtered through the relations of race and power that operate in the public sphere. As much as we would like to think that there is something radical about queer desire, Vuong demonstrates that queer desire doesn't necessarily upend these relations; one of the important messages of the text is to meditate on how closely queer desires can, and often do, absorb and replicate the violence of the world around us.

I opened this chapter recalling how American literature was consolidated as a knowledge project to be used as a tool in US empire in the Pacific. But one thing we know we don't know is that there is way to ensure how books will be read, or what will become of that epistemological field once it gets to the reader. In one early letter Little Dog recounts for his mother that he "fled my shitty high school to spend my days in New York lost in library stacks, reading obscure texts by dead people, most of whom never dreamed a face like mine floating over their sentences – and least of all that those sentences would save me."[49] American literature's imperial history is inextricably linked, also, to this other, unpredictable outcome: to be changed, or as Vuong puts it, "saved" by the literature that was intended to subordinate you. Those dead people who "never dreamed" of a reader like Little Dog remind us that the relationship between American literature and American empire is not a static one; even old texts change as they are read by new eyes.

My title references Carolyn Porter's 1994 essay, in which she traces the difficulties of "remapping American literary studies" in ways that neither cling to the traditional field-defining coordinates nor attempt to add new voices and perspectives without dramatically deconstructing the norms, assumptions, and methods of the field.[50] While my project here is much less expansive, my nod to Porter's work is meant to underscore the unknowability of sexuality as central to its relation to American literary studies. Despite decades of research, debate, and scholarship on its origins, we still don't know what causes one set of desires and not another. Valerie Rohy has argued the terms we use to name and understand our sexualities are insufficient because sexuality itself is "too heterogeneous to totalize."[51] Judith Butler argues that "If a sexuality is to be disclosed, what will be taken as the true determinant of its meaning: the phantasy structure, the act, the orifice, the gender, the anatomy? And if the practice engages a complex interplay of all of those, which one of this (sic) erotic dimensions will come to stand for the sexuality that requires them all?"[52] What I am proposing, then, is that there is a lot we don't know about sexuality: it is too amorphous a collection – desires, acts, ideas, feelings, fantasies, and more – to claim dominion over. What we know, however, is that US empire's remapping of power relations, norms, identities, and territory operates with and through the desires we hold to be most intimate, and that American literary study is key to better understanding the sexual scope of empire's reach.

Notes

1. J. Kehaulani Kauanui. *Paradoxes of Hawaiian Sovereignty: Land, Sex, and the Colonial Politics of State Nationalism* (Durham: Duke University Press, 2018).
2. Kauanui, *Paradoxes of Hawaiian Sovereignty*, 20.
3. Scott L. Morgensen, *Spaces Between Us: Queer Settler Colonialism and Indigenous Decolonization* (Minneapolis: University of Minnesota Press, 2011), 34.
4. Siobhan Somerville has explored how sexologists drew from comparative anatomy and racial ideologies of the nineteenth century to scan the body for visible signs of sexual anomaly and invest those anomalies with the significance of sexual perversion; whether the ostensible signs of sexual perversion were in the "unusually large clitoris" or in another part of the genital structure, these studies mobilized racialized ideas about sexual normativity and sexual perversion to make meanings for the emergent categories of sexual identity they studied. Ellis, in particular, focused much more on "abnormal passion" between women, and posited that both lesbians and African American women had "irregular" genital structures that made them less sexually differentiated than white women, whose bodies were taken as the standard of sexual normativity. This is to say, then, that the meaning of sexual inversion and "abnormal passion" were already mapped onto a racial hierarchy of sexual difference, and thus that the emergence of sexual deviance is inseparable from the context of white supremacy, chattel slavery, and colonialism. Havelock Ellis, *Studies in the Psychology of Sex*. Vol. I, *Sexual Inversion*. 1897 (London: University Press, 1900). Quoted in Siobhan B. Somerville, *Queering the Color Line: Race and the Invention of Homosexuality in American Culture* (Durham: Duke University Press, 2000), 28.
5. Evelyn Brooks Higginbotham, "African-American Women's History and the Metalanguage of Race," *Signs* 17.2 (1992): 263.

6. Evelynn Hammonds, "Black (W)holes and the Geometry of Black Female Sexuality," *differences: A Journal of Feminist Cultural Studies*. 6.2–3 (1994): 141.

7. Marlon Ross, "Beyond the Closet as a Raceless Paradigm" *Black Queer Studies*, ed. E. Patrick Johnson and Mae Henderson (Durham: Duke University Press, 2005), 168.

8. Nella Larsen, *Passing* (New York: Alfred A. Knopf, 1929; Rpt. Dover Publications, 2004).

9. Ross, "Beyond the Closet as a Raceless Paradigm," 183.

10. In addition to Hammonds and Higginbotham, see also Cynthia Blair, "African American Women's Sexuality" *Frontiers: A Journal of Women's Studies* 35.1: 4–10; Sara Clarke Kaplan, *The Black Reproductive: Unfree Labor and Insurgent Motherhood* (Minneapolis: University of Minnesota Press, 2021); and Deborah E. McDowell and Arnold Rampersad, *Slavery and the Literary Imagination* (Baltimore: Johns Hopkins University Press, 1989).

11. Larsen, *Passing*, 43.

12. Larsen, *Passing*, 31.

13. Zita Nunes, *Cannibal Democracy: Race and Representation in the Literature of the Americas* (Minneapolis: University of Minnesota Press, 2008), 118.

14. An anonymous article from the *Chicago Defender* from October 1925 argues that "there is no stigma attached to Negro blood, such as obtains here. Mixed Negroes [sic] feel no discrimination – they mingle with people on similar social levels, and there is no race problem in Brazil." My thanks to Jessica Graham for the background information on the ways that Brazil often functioned in the African American imaginary as a place less controlled by anti-Black racism and by homophobia. See also David L. Blackmore, ""That Unreasonable Restless Feeling": The Homosexual Subtexts of Nella Larsen's *Passing" African American Review* 26.3 (1992): 475–84.

15. *Obergefell* v. *Hodges*: Same-Sex Marriage Legalized (R44143). n.d. See also *Brief Amicus Curiae of American Psychological Association, Obergefell* v. *Hodges*, March 6, 2015, nos. 14–556, 14–562, 14–571, and 14–574, 7, 9, www.apa.org/about/offices/ogc/amicus/obergefell-supreme-court.pdf.

16. Kim TallBear, "Making Love and Relations Beyond Settler Sex and Family," in *Making Kin Not Population*, eds. Adele E. Clarke and Donna Jeanne Haraway (Chicago: Prickly Paradigm Press, 2018), 152.

17. Sharon A. Holland, *The Erotic Life of Racism* (Durham: Duke University Press, 2012), 3.

18. While Srinivasan poses this question most explicitly in her conversation with Ezra Klein, its exploration is the premise of her book *The Right to Sex: Feminism in the Twenty-First Century* (New York: Farrar, Straus and Giroux, 2021). See also Amia Srinivasan and Ezra Klein. "Can We Change Our Sexual Desires? Should We?" *The Ezra Klein Show*. Podcast Audio, September 7, 2021.

19. Tiffany Lethabo King, *The Black Shoals: Offshore Formations of Black and Native Studies* (Durham: Duke University Press, 2019), 142.

20. For more on the relationship between race, sexuality, and nation, see Aliyyah I. Abdur-Rahman, "'Simply a Menaced Boy': Analogizing Color, Undoing Dominance in James Baldwin's *Giovanni's Room*," *African American Review*, 41.3 (2007): 477–86; Mae G. Henderson, "James Baldwin's *Giovanni's Room*: Expatriation, 'Racial Drag,' and Homosexual Panic," in *Black Queer Studies: A Critical Anthology*, ed. E. Patrick Johnson and Mae G. Henderson (Durham: Duke University Press, 2005), 298–322; Meg Wesling, "Sexuality and Statelessness: Queer Migrations and National Identity in *Giovanni's Room*," *Journal of Postcolonial Writing* 55.3 (2019): 323–36.

21. James Baldwin, *Giovanni's Room* (New York: Vintage International, 2013), 3.

22. Baldwin, *Giovanni's Room*, 6, 8.

23. Baldwin, *Giovanni's Room*, 28.

24. Josep M. Armangol, "In the Dark Room: Homosexuality and/as Blackness in James Baldwin's *Giovanni's Room*," *Signs* 37.3 (2012): 671–93.

25. Baldwin, *Giovanni's Room*, 20.

26. Baldwin, *Giovanni's Room*, 27.

27. Roderick A. Ferguson, "The Parvenu Baldwin and the Other Side of Redemption: Modernity, Race, Sexuality, and the Cold War," in *James Baldwin Now*, ed. Dwight A. McBride (New York: New York University Press, 1999), 233–61; and Robert Genter. *Late Modernism: Art, Culture, and Politics in Cold War America* (Philadelphia: University of Pennsylvania Press, 2010).

28. Baldwin, *Giovanni's Room*, 20.

29. James Baldwin, "Princes and Powers" *Collected Essays* (New York: Library of America, 1998), 145.

30. For example, President Eisenhower's Executive Order 10450, signed in 1953, added "sexual perversion" to the list of behaviors that could prohibit someone from holding a position in the federal government. David K. Johnson has argued that the accusations so veiled, the paranoia so pervasive that "security risk" became synonymous with "homosexual" during the so-called Lavender Scare. See David K. Johnson, *The Lavender Scare: The Cold War Persecution of Gays and Lesbians in the Federal Government* (Chicago: University of Chicago Press, 2004) as well as Robert Corber, *Homosexuality in Cold War America: Resistance and the Crisis of Masculinity* (Durham: Duke University Press, 1997) and Mary Dudziak, *Cold War Civil Rights: Race and the Image of American Democracy* (Princeton: Princeton University Press, 2000).

31. Baldwin, *Giovanni's Room*, 81.

32. Baldwin, *Giovanni's Room*, 94. For an insightful analysis of Cold War paranoia and Baldwin's affective style, see Marlon B. Ross, "Baldwin's Sissy Heroics," *African American Review*, 46.4, 2013: 633–51.

33. Baldwin, *Giovanni's Room*, 149.

34. Baldwin, *Giovanni's Room*, 150.

35. See Ari Adut, "A Theory of Scandal: Victorians, Homosexuality, and the Fall of Oscar Wilde," *American Journal of Sociology* 111.1 (2005): 213–48;

Lisa Duggan, *Sapphic Slasher: Sex, Violence, and American Modernity* (Durham: Duke University Press, 2000).

36. Baldwin, *Giovanni's Room*, 150.
37. Baldwin, *Giovanni's Room*,149.
38. Baldwin, *Giovanni's Room*, 161.
39. Ocean Vuong, *On Earth We're Briefly Gorgeous* (New York: Penguin, 2019), 3.
40. Vuong, *On Earth We're Briefly Gorgeous*, 52.
41. Vuong, *On Earth We're Briefly Gorgeous*, 24.
42. Vuong, *On Earth We're Briefly Gorgeous*, 130.
43. Vuong, *On Earth We're Briefly Gorgeous*, 14.
44. Vuong, *On Earth We're Briefly Gorgeous*, 119.
45. Vuong, *On Earth We're Briefly Gorgeous*, 102–3.
46. Vuong, *On Earth We're Briefly Gorgeous*, 143.
47. Vuong, *On Earth We're Briefly Gorgeous*, 111–12.
48. Vuong, *On Earth We're Briefly Gorgeous*, 120.
49. Vuong, *On Earth We're Briefly Gorgeous,* 15.
50. Carolyn Porter, "What We Know That We Don't Know: Remapping American Literary Studies," *American Literary History* 6 (Fall 1994): 467–526.
51. Valery Rohy, *Lost Causes: Narrative, Etiology, and Queer Theory* (New York: Oxford University Press, 2015), 14.
52. Judith Butler, "Imitation and Gender Insubordination," in *The Lesbian and Gay Studies Reader*, eds. Henry Abelove, Michele Aina Barale, and David Halperin (New York: Routledge, 1993), 310.

Transpacific Entanglements

Korean Immigrant Writers and the Militarized Modernity of American Literature

Jeehyun Lim

Wars and militarism are a constitutive part of US imperialism. They are not coterminous with imperialism, but how one understands a war affects one's view of US imperialism, just as how one understands US imperialism shades one's view of US military interventions abroad. This chapter engages with the rise of militarized modernity during the second half of the twentieth century, the post–World War II period that saw the waning of formal European colonialism as well as the rise of the US as a superpower with dominion reaching well beyond its national borders: the age of the Pax Americana or "American peace." The Korean immigrant writers discussed in this chapter – Richard E. Kim, Ty Pak, and Heinz Insu Fenkl – expose the underside of this "violent peace" by writing from their experiences of Korean partition, the Korean War, and the Cold War.[1] In doing so, these writers shape a strand of American literature that explores the embeddedness of South Korean history within a larger transpacific system of US economic and military dominance – an emergent American literary corpus that resists the prevailing national narrative of exceptionalism by insisting upon the militarized modernity of the United States itself.

Militarized modernity is a term I borrow from sociologist Seungsook Moon's study of South Korean modernization in the decades of military dictatorships (1960s–1980s).[2] Her study focuses on the impact of the state deployment of mass mobilization programs to serve the twofold aim of industrializing the economy and of building a strong military with political membership. Within the milieu of militarized modernity, Moon argues, men and women in South Korea had differentiated paths to a limited notion of citizenship. As the state crafted "the Korean nation as the anticommunist self at war with the communist other," this gendered and limited citizenship was primarily about turning individuals into dutiful subjects of the state, oftentimes through resort to military violence and state surveillance.[3] While the bulk of her study concerns the particular circumstances of South Korean state-building and citizenship, Moon suggests that her examination of South Korean militarized modernity echoes other sites of military violence in political modernity, such as fascist movements in Germany and Japan in the first half of the twentieth century, and corresponds to forms of economic development that take place under tight military control in numerous postcolonial states in the developing world.[4]

I borrow the term militarized modernity based on this idea that the term has broader implications for seeing and understanding the forces of militarism and militarization as they impact the making of the diasporic subject and the circulation of ideas, goods, and people between South Korea and the United States. In this chapter I use the term with an eye to exploring its applicability and significance for the culture of the migratory circuit between South Korea and the United States. If South Korea exists within a political economy of US hegemony, can South Korean state violence simply be viewed as exterior to the United States? What happens if we see it as embedded in a transpacific system of power and domination? The works of Kim, Pak, and Fenkl are an exemplary site for examining the circulation of narratives of militarized modernity. The figure of the citizen-subject that appears in these narratives exists in the interstices of South Korean state violence and the US exercise of military power and influence in South Korea.

Interstitiality also characterizes these writers' position in American literature. In terms of content, their writings look back on the writers' experiences of South Korean militarized modernity. But they also write in English for a primarily English-speaking audience, which positions their work right on the borders of Korean and American literatures. Their books thus fit well with the past quarter-century of US literary studies and the critical currents of transnationalism that have challenged the conventional view of a national literature as an imagined community written for an audience in the national language.[5] As these writers vividly attest, the fictiveness of a national community is too often constructed at the expense of histories and lives that do not comfortably fit into the prevailing narrative of the nation. This holds true for South Korean national self-imagining as much as the US one. As the literary critic Jin-Kyung Lee observes, while postwar South Korean ethnonationalism was "born of a confluence of transnational forces, such as the new US imperialist impulse, the global cold war conflict, and the South's ideological confrontation with the communist North," such ethnonationalism ironically fails to include considerations of these transnational forces in its ideas of the nation.[6] The "militarization of South Korean society" does not appear in isolation, she explains, but in a web of relations with "South Korean submilitarism in Vietnam, and the US Cold War militarism that involved greater Southeast Asia."[7]

In their disparate ways, Kim, Pak, and Fenkl draw attention to such transpacific entanglements, which I define as the web of relations between South Korea and the US under a Cold War climate. The interweaving of national, regional, and global interests during the Pax Americana created circuits of exchange for peoples, goods, and ideas between South Korea and the US, circuits which were defined by the market and the military. The experience of modernity to which Kim, Pak, and Fenkl testify in their writings helps to illuminate these circuits of exchange – and to clarify the unpeaceful effects of the American peace.[8] Indeed, their writings both exist within and seek to describe the space created and cultivated by Cold War transpacific entanglements, revealing South Korean modernization as indelibly marked by militarism, global capitalism, and the exigencies of US empire. By virtue of the space they inhabit, they also reveal the pressure points in these circuits of exchange, points where the logic of Cold War militarization breaks down and disruptions to the circulation of ideology can potentially occur.

While fully acknowledging the transnational qualities of their writings, I also emphasize them as belonging to American literature. On the surface, this may seem like an argument for inclusion, a common critical move for Asian American literary criticism in the 1980s.[9] For this critical model, arguing for the inclusion of Asian American writers in the American literary tradition was tantamount to correcting racial exclusion and marginalization. My purpose in emphasizing Kim's, Pak's, and Fenkl's works as American literature is less concerned with their identities or their standing in American literature. Rather my critical aim is to bring to light the Americanness of a militarized modernity that is all too often understood to be quintessentially un-American. Read as American literature, these writers' works help us to understand the ideological work by which militarized modernity is foreign-ized and rendered external to the US nation, to American society, and indeed to American literature. These texts, and the transnational readings they demand, explicitly counter the tendency to isolate certain modernities as exclusively belonging to the Third World or to developing countries. Instead, these works foreground the traces of their own context of produc-tion: their transpacific entanglements or the web of relations and ongoing back-and-forth flows between South Korea and the US that register both US imperialism and the ambiguous, changing status of South Korea, transition-ing from protectorate, to occupied country, to ally, and finally sub-empire.

Tuning into the Americanness of militarized modernity in Kim's, Pak's, and Fenkl's texts thus allows us to access an under-studied dimension of the cultures of US imperialism as they took shape in and through Cold War Asia.

This chapter turns to Richard Kim's *The Innocent* (1968), the sequel to his debut novel, *The Martyred* (1964), Ty Pak's short story collection, *Guilt Payment* (1983), and Heinz Fenkl's autobiographical novel *Skull Water* (2023) to assemble a picture of militarized modernity at the heart of their writings. Kim follows his depiction of the Korean War in *The Martyred* with the subject of postwar nation building in *The Innocent*. While Kim himself has denied any direct relationship between the May 16 coup of 1961 in South Korea and the events described in his novel, that historical shadow evidently informs his imagination. Meanwhile, Ty Pak's *Guilt Payment* – arguably his only publication released by a recognized publisher, the independent press Bamboo Ridge – contains a number of short stories on postwar Korean immigrants in Hawai'i, showing the effects of the Korean War through the lives and memories of these characters living in a Pacific island that was formally incorporated into the United States in 1959. Finally, Heinz Fenkl's *Skull Water* returns readers to the social space of the camptown that the writer portrayed in his first autobiographical novel, *Memories of My Ghost Brother* (1996). Through the main character Insu, now a teenager, Fenkl attempts a more sustained look at the camptown as an aftermath of the Korean War, interweaving the violence of the war with that of the camptown through temporal shifts in the narrative. The Korean War casts a long shadow over all these texts as familial, social, and institutional relations are cast and recast within the culture of militarized modernity. A future for South Korea and Korean America outside militarized modernity emerges as a longing but not as a viability in these texts. Moreover, the queries posed by these texts on the liberal values of freedom, the rule of law, and justice are not limited to South Korean modernity but point to militarized modernity as a constitutive element of US liberalism and its Pax Americana.

Imagining a Liberal Society through Military Power in Richard E. Kim's *The Innocent*

The Innocent follows a group of military officers planning a coup in postwar South Korea. Its narrator, Major Lee, turns out to be the lone voice in the group that resists the assassination of the few generals who stand in their way. From beginning to end, the novel is pervaded by the judgment that the Korean War has failed to usher in a liberal society despite bringing much suffering and devastation. A reverend cries out early in the novel, "The rich are getting richer, the poor are getting poorer. The police are nothing more than a one man's terrorist gang, spies are snooping around everywhere, extortions and tortures are rampant. Where is justice, where is democracy, where is freedom? Tell me, is this what the people have suffered through the war for?"[10] This failure of postwar state-building explains and ambiguously justifies the military coup depicted in *The Innocent*. Major Lee claims that the military is "the single largest, most efficiently organized and coherent establishment in the country," one that attracts the nation's best young men, a view that is sometimes attributed to Richard Kim himself.[11]

The novel presents political killings in the context of a military coup as a moral dilemma – one that creates some strange internal contradictions in a work that also emphasizes the value of the rule of law. Narrator Lee presents the coup as a necessary evil to ensure a new beginning to the rule of law. In his words, "[t]he vicious circle has got to be broken somewhere . . . We've got to make a clean break somewhere, sometime, now!"[12] From this point of view, the coup needs procedural legitimacy almost as much as a successful outcome. Hence Lee's consistent and repeated argument that the scheming generals should be court martialed and that the coup leaders should follow the decision of the military court. For the other members of the coup, Lee's view is idealistic at best and self-defeating at worst. These conflicting views illuminate a larger context: the moral dilemma raised by the political assassinations in *The Innocent* is also, at the same time, the inherent contradiction of building a liberal government out of the illiberalism of war and the society left in its wake.

The novel's moral reflections are dramatized most elaborately, and also strangely hollowed out, in the relationship between Lee and Colonel Min, his foil and the charismatic leader of the coup. Min's itinerant and chaotic past maps his story onto modern Korean history. Born in North Korea, Min studies abroad in Japan before returning home to evade being drafted into the Japanese imperial army. His efforts to stay out of military conflict, however, fail, and he is rumored to have been seen in multiple uniforms representing the different military forces that have converged in modern Korea: the Japanese army, the North Korean army, and finally the South Korean army. As Lee repeatedly calls for a legal and procedural accounting of the plotting generals, Kim creates an existential drama in *The Innocent* about what kind of man Min really is. Is he, like Lee, a believer that "the good in man . . . will ultimately destroy the evil in the world," or does he, as his silence in response to Lee's exhortations suggests, believe that "the evil in man can be destroyed only by the evil in man"?[13]

Complicating these seemingly abstract ideas of good and evil is a more historically based context for this narrative preoccupation with individual morals. Against the members of the coup who scorn his opposition to assassinating the scheming generals as a fantastic desire for a "lily-white revolution," Major Lee retorts that their drive to eliminate their opponents will only spur "bloodstained vengeance."[14] "We are trying," he insists, "to create an opportunity for the country and the people to correct the past wrongs but not an opportunity to drink blood and dance to the tune of vengeance."[15] The vengeance Lee fears reminds the readers that the Korean War was a civil war – if also a global proxy war – in which personal grievances and longstanding village politics combined with the fratricidal character of civil war to turn families and neighbors against each other. While the conflict may have ceased, the legacy of vindictive politics lives on, and Lee seems to believe that having a moral man, someone who is above the politics of vengeance, as a leader can lead a society away from the cycles of hatred and destruction.

So the narrative uncovers Min's past bit by bit, asking after each revelation of killings Min was involved in whether he is merely another "rotten murderer," an "evil beast," or, as James Lee puts it, a "salvific figure of Korean postcoloniality."[16] None of the revelations decisively answers the question of whether Min is a good or evil man, blurring the lines of the moral binary. Finally, as the coup succeeds and as the country is on the brink of a new government, the writer attempts an explanation of the dynamic between his two main characters. In a long dialogue, Min explains that he sees Lee as a check on his power. Lee was the "one, final reminder that a man like me . . . is a simple murderer and must not be called by any other name."[17] Lee, in other words, helped Min from devolving into a dictator, "from the intoxicating temptation of a self-styled godlike lawgiver, from the tantalizing delusion and illusion of omnipotence."[18] Something like a lesson on the separation of powers emerges as it turns out that Lee and Min share the tasks of the "judge" and the "executioner."[19]

Despite the narrative balancing of Lee and Min as the twin poles of the coup, there is no political future envisioned for South Korea at the end of the novel when Min is assassinated and Lee leaves the country for the United States. Why does Richard Kim resist an ending where Min and Lee work together to usher in an era of liberal democracy? Literary critic James Lee attributes Min's death to "the realism of the Korea of [the writer's] moment: corrupt, dictatorial, still subject to US influence."[20] Yet behind the novel's failure to imagine a liberal political future for South Korea is a limitation that goes beyond South Korean political reality: the dilemma of presenting the military as the institution of political change for a liberal democracy. On the fringes of the coup, behind the scenes of the South Korean generals' plotting, there is a more powerful military presence hinted at throughout the narrative: the US military. Appearing at various moments during the coup's execution and often in relation to Lee's place in the coup, the influence of the US can be seen in the generals' wariness about American reactions to their plans, the appearance of an American colonel of ambiguous title at crucial moments, and, most significantly, in the insulation Lee experiences from the stages of the coup he questions. These moments of American incursions into the narrative of a South Korean military coup show the continuing sway of the United States over South Korea. More concretely, such incursions index the contemporary milieu of the Vietnam War in which *The Innocent* was conceived, written, and received. The Vietnam War, Kim's novel suggests, significantly limits the potential for imagining a political future through a coup in South Korea.

Most immediately, the military unrest in South Vietnam becomes the context for the South Korean coup attempt. In *The Innocent*, the members of the coup realize that those who want to sabotage it will seek out Americans with the story that "a Communist-inspired and -led coup is in the making," a convenient resort to a Cold War alibi for prompting US military action.[21] The Vietnam War, though, makes this alibi ineffective. One coup member points to the "American policies behind those coups in Viet Nam" as evidence that Americans will actually side with the instigators of the coup rather than its saboteurs, a likely reference to the Kennedy administration's lukewarm support for Ngo Dinh Diem's government.[22] In another reference to the Vietnam War, a South Korean general uses the American perspective on political killings to dissuade other members from killing the saboteurs. "[A] melancholy precedent in Viet Nam," Min agrees, makes them particularly averse to the prospect of political killings in South Korea, a possible reference to the assassination of Ngo Dinh Diem in 1963.[23] As both the planners of the coup and their opponents try to anticipate the American response and to negotiate with the Americans, their options are limited to what the United States would find permissible and acceptable. Identifying the military as the driver of political change entails a recognition of the realpolitik that the party with the strongest military always has the upper hand. Military, if not brute, force, ends up setting the terms of the rule of law. This is the fundamental irony of *The*

Innocent's attempt to imagine a liberal society through a military coup: South Korean sovereignty is curtailed, as long as the US has a bigger, stronger military.

Richard Kim's *The Innocent* evokes a broad literary investment in the morality of political assassinations in post-World War II French existentialism. Jean-Paul Sartre's *Dirty Hands* (first staged in 1948) and Albert Camus's *The Just Assassins* (first staged in 1949) both dwell on the moral dilemma of political assassinations in revolutionary politics. If *The Innocent* is thematically similar to these plays, Kim's turn to postwar South Korea as the theater of this moral dilemma, perhaps unwittingly, shows the challenges of exploring ideals such as freedom, justice, and rule of law in a country where the histories of colonialism, trusteeship, war, militarization, and US imperial force bear down on these ideals.

Korean Immigrant Men and Militarized Modernity in Ty Pak's *Guilt Payment*

Told from multiple perspectives that are often seen as fragmented and disordered, Ty Pak's stories engage with an issue overlooked in American literature on the Korean War: the war's pressure on bonds of family and kin among its survivors. Pak's 1983 short story collection, *Guilt Payment*, is full of broken, fractured, and strained relationships among Korean immigrants in Hawai'i. Pak's stories speak unexpectedly to the effects of militarized modernity not on public institutions but rather in intimate realms of private life. Husbands turn against wives and children, friends betray friends, neighbors spy and inform on neighbors, and there are countless acts of physical violence among kin and friends. Pak points to Korean American male survivors as simultaneously victims and perpetrators in the violence of militarized modernity. Even as they attempt to repair broken relationships or redress past wrongs, Pak's characters struggle in the aftermath of war to find meaningful ways of doing so while their lives are still constrained by militarized modernity.

In many of Pak's stories, the veneer of ordinary immigrant life gives way to deeply buried secrets from the Old World. These secrets often involve conflicts in intimate relationships, such as that of husband and wife. In the title story, "Guilt Payment," the narrator is a middle-aged professor at the University of Hawai'i and single father who cannot say no to requests from his teenage daughter. To persuade her father Mira calls on her absent mother, who passed when she was still an infant, and when the narrator acquiesces without fail, Mira often wonders in jest "what wicked thing [the narrator has] done to her mother" to be so immediately and palpably affected.[24] The reader soon finds out that it is not the single father's sympathy for his daughter's loss that moves the narrator, and the rest of the story is an account of the narrator's past secret that holds him hostage to the mention of his dead wife. Newly married with an expecting wife when the North Korean army occupied Seoul within the first month of the war's outbreak, the narrator had to go into hiding in his own house in order to evade the North Korean soldiers. His wife, Yoomi, gives birth to Mira at home alone while searching for food and keeping the narrator hidden. The narrator, unlike his wife, shows no affection for the infant, seeing her instead as a "little vampire" "leeching" on his wife.[25] Soon the tides of the war turn, and as the US air bombings burn the city, the narrator tries to flee with Yoomi and Mira. Finding the infant an impediment to avoiding the retreating North Korean soldiers and finding a way out of the city, the narrator suggests to his wife that they leave Mira. Yoomi rebuffs his suggestion in horror, recoiling from him, and the narrator sets off by himself only to be hit by gunfire. When he regains consciousness, US soldiers, who have now taken back Seoul, help him dig out the wailing Mira from a mound of rubble, but Yoomi has been killed by a falling beam. The "wicked thing" the narrator has done is to forsake his child and wife in pursuit of his own life. A similar type of desperate husband also appears in "Nostalgia." The male narrators in these stories weigh the increased odds of their survival against their ties to their wives before choosing in favor of the former.

While the circumstances of war lead these men to act against peacetime morals and customs, their private pain is also accompanied by a callousness that continues to mark the survivors of the war. Economic concerns quickly take the place of remorse or regret in the narrator's recollection of his wife's death in "Guilt Payment." As his thoughts move onto how he would pay for his daughter's request for private voice lessons in Italy, the narrator is quick to deplore what he feels as the comparatively weaker value of the dollar in the global economy. "[W]hy do things have to be so tough for Americans now?" he asks, "I remember the times when an average American income commanded princely accommodations abroad. It is quite the other way around now. Damn Arabs, damn Japanese, damn Italians, damn Koreans with their exports and favorable trade balances!"[26] Clearly, remembering the loss of his wife and the horrors of the Korean War does not make the narrator more sympathetic to the plights of others. His identification as an American in the present makes him oblivious to his past self as Korean. It is as if in the race to escape the poverty of war and reconstruction, he has won by becoming American. The callousness of the male survivors of the Korean War in Pak's stories is not only a result of the violence of the war they experienced but also occasioned by their continued embeddedness in a culture of militarized modernity which prioritizes economic productivity and growth over other areas of life.

In "Steady Hands," Pak shows militarized modernity on a continuum between South Korea and the United States through the Vietnam War.[27] The only story in *Guilt Payment* that engages with the Vietnam War, "Steady Hands," features Stephen Gong, a Korean immigrant surgeon in Hawai'i who had been a medic in the Vietnam War as part of the Korean military before immigrating. After the war Stephen develops a condition where he experiences uncontrollable shakes and trembles in his hands, a condition which he hides from everyone else. Through Carl Sommers, an American veteran of the Vietnam War who feels an affinity with Stephen as allies in and survivors of the same war, Stephen visits a local Vietnamese bar, "Club Saigon," where he meets a woman, May Lee, who appears to be the sister of the Vietnamese woman who saved his life during wartime. He also learns for the first time that the woman, Lap Sing, had given birth to his son. Back home Stephen is struck with anxiety over his early-morning surgery the next day when he notices the aggravated shakes in his hands. He calls Carl that night to ask his veterans' association to sponsor Lap Sing and her son from the refugee camp in Malaysia where they are living.

Stephen's unsteady hands are an explicit symbol of his war-induced trauma and guilt. They index his contradictory position as both perpetrator of violence on the Vietnamese and victim of US and South Korean militarism. The gendered quality of his guilt, in particular, illuminates the sexual economy of militarized modernity. Stephen's guilt toward Lap Sing is based on the position he occupied in the past as part of a military force aligned with the United States as well as his position in the present as a successful immigrant. As Vietnamese women who become sexually available to American and Korean men in Vietnam and in Hawai'i, May Lee and Lap Sing take the place of the Korean bar girls that appear in Pak's other stories. Brenda Kwon notes that the "predominant stereotype of Korean women in Hawai'i" is that of the Korean bar girl, but in "Steady Hands," Vietnamese women substitute for Korean women as representative bar girls.[28] Superficially, Stephen's guilt may be about having abandoned a past lover. More importantly, though, it is about his active participation in the developmentalist paradigm of militarized modernity in which his ascent on the social and economic hierarchy exists in tandem with the victimization of another Asian ethnic group of women. Stephen's guilt is that of the "subimperial" agent, to adapt the concept of sub-empire that critics such as Jin-Kyung Lee and Simeon Man use to describe South Korean participation in the Vietnam War and which can generally be defined as "a semiperipheral nation-state that functions on behalf of a core hegemonic power."[29]

The characters in Pak's short stories are trapped in the system and culture of militarized modernity. They may have left behind the Korean War, but the effects of the war persist and are experienced in their lives long after the ceasefire. The Korean immigrant community as it is envisioned in Pak's stories is replete with private pain, which is not only felt by the individual but also poisons relationships and fractures kinship and friendship. The stories themselves do not offer any hope of an outside to militarized modernity. The narrator of "Guilt Payment" in the present has a seemingly strong commitment to his daughter, but his economically oriented mindset prevents him from seeking meaningful restoration or atonement. Stephen in "Steady Hands" takes the first step to find and help Lap Sing and their child, but he fails to act on his own behalf, which limits the kind of relationship he could have with her and their child after they arrive in the United States. Even when they engage in small acts of contrition and compensation, Pak's male characters live under the assumption that militarized modernity is the default condition of their existence.

Camptown and the Afterlife of the Korean War in Heinz Insu Fenkl's *Skull Water*

In his recently published autobiographical novel, *Skull Water* (2023), Heinz Insu Fenkl continues his literary exploration of the camptown, begun in *Memories of My Ghost Brother* (1996), through the writer's namesake protagonist, Insu. The novel opens with the fourteen-year-old Insu returning to camptown, the military base in Pupyong, as his military father receives another assignment in South Korea. Mainly a coming-of-age narrative, the novel is set in the close-knit community of camptown friends, all sharing similar family backgrounds to Insu's: an American soldier father and a Korean mother. Through this community, the novel explores the multiple afterlives of the Korean War well beyond the years of open conflict.

Camptown is a paradigmatic site of militarized modernity in Fenkl's writings. A reminder of Cold War militarization as historical fact and ongoing process in South Korea, camptown is also the site of convergence, conflict, and hybridity. Koreans and Americans are connected through camptown's economy, both the black market of stolen goods from the Post Exchange and the sex industry that caters to American soldiers. While these connections can evolve into enduring relationships – such as the biracial military families in the novel – the traffic in goods and people exists within the shadow of what is respectable and legal. The vulnerability of the Korean participants in this economy becomes most obvious when the trafficking goes wayward. Mixed-race children of camptown liaisons like himself, Insu suggests, are a forgotten byproduct of militarized modernity. While Fenkl's 1996 *Memories of My Ghost Brother* explores militarized modernity through an exclusive focus on the geographical and spatial specificities of camptown, his second novel extends his literary examination of camptown by locating it within a longer Cold War temporality spanning 1950 to 1975 and by spatially linking camptown to other sites of postwar violence in South Korea. Fenkl toggles back and forth between chapters set in 1974–75, narrated in the first person by Insu, and those set in 1950 that tell the story of Big Uncle during the Korean War from a third-person perspective. While the chapters on the narrative present by far outnumber those set in 1950, this organization effectively ties Insu's narrative present to the past of the Korean War.

The interweaving of the two temporalities demonstrates a spiritual kinship between Insu and Big Uncle. Early on in the novel, Insu visits the ailing Big Uncle, who has been banished from his village in Sambongni to a remote part of the woods across the river from the village. A geomancer connected to the spiritual world and the tradition of the folk, namely shamanism, Big Uncle is an outcast. The ostensible reason for his banishment is the stench from his rotting foot and his cries of pain which the villagers identify as noise, but behind these complaints is a greater discomfort with Big Uncle's closeness to the spiritual world. For the villagers, his physical ailment suggests he is "someone at a *kut* possessed by ghosts," touched by spirits that spell bad luck.[30] In contrast, Insu actively pursues Big Uncle's worldview, embarking on a quest for skull water – the cure-all of folk remedies – and for the last of the arrows Big Uncle shot into the woods in fulfillment of his wish when he passes. The spiritual kinship between Insu and Big Uncle traverses two worlds, the prewar space–time of tradition and the postwar militarized modernity, ultimately creating a lineage to the Korean folk that survives the rupture brought on by the Korean War.

The transmission of the folk, however, is hardly a salve for the violence of militarized modernity in *Skull Water*. In fact, the threat of violence is a constant undercurrent in both parts of the novel set in 1950 and in 1974–75. The kinds of violence Big Uncle and Insu face may at first appear quite different. In the chapters set in 1950, the primary source of violence is unambivalently military conflict. Big Uncle becomes a refugee as he flees southward from his village away from the encroaching North Korean army. As he develops an unlikely friendship with a Korean woman shunned by other refugees for being a "GI prostitute," it briefly seems that he would be placed under the protection of the US army.[31] The idea of the US army as any kind of protection for Big Uncle quickly turns out to be illusory, however, and the novel's last chapter set in 1950, "Three Days That Summer – 1950," features Big Uncle leaving his temporary refuge to become witness to a massacre, the Taejon massacre. In the novel's narrative of the Korean War, the scene of the Taejon massacre is a culmination of the violence of the Korean War.

A massacre of civil and political prisoners in the city of Taejon in July 1950, the Taejon massacre is an event in Korean War historiography that reveals how ideologized the writing of history was and how American complicity in the war atrocities was largely overlooked in the Cold War episteme.[32] While the current historical scholarship of the massacre views it as a case in which the South Korean police slaughtered the prisoners held in the city of Taejon soon after the North Korean army captured Seoul "as a preventive measure against collaboration with North Korean troops," the official account until the 1990s held the North Korean army as responsible for the majority of the deaths.[33] How the story of the Taejon massacre was told in history, in brief, shows the unresolved contestations over accountability and the unaccounted for grief of those who became doubly victimized by war violence and the violence of history. In the novel, Big Uncle is already somewhat privy to the egregious killings going in Taejon before he stumbles on a hastily dug grave site filled with corpses by the South Korean military police. He had heard the rumors among local farmers who in the novel are well aware of the politics of atrocities. The locals realize that, in the twin context of US militarism and South Korean authoritarianism, the killings at Taejon will go unaccounted for. Yet the senselessness of the violence prompts them to lament: "The Reds are already all over the place – why did you have to go and kill your own countrymen? Why?!"[34] Poignant as the question is, it went unheard for a long time in official accounts of the Korean War, as Fenkl suggests. By weaving into his narrative of the Korean War a tragedy that was subject to misrepresentation in historical narratives, Fenkl draws attention to the complex and often competing ways in which narratives shore up or challenge the culture of militarized modernity.

The threat of violence that Insu faces is on the surface at a remove from the threat of military violence Big Uncle experiences. Here it is instructive to focus on the chapter that immediately follows "Three Days That Summer – 1950," "The Dog Market – 1975." In this chapter, Insu and his friend Paulie reluctantly attend a dog fight in Incheon prompted by another friend, Miklos, who has been pulled into the enterprise. Just as Big Uncle is stunned by the senseless wartime massacre, so is Insu over- whelmed by the violence he witnesses at the dog fight. Gradually Insu comes to a vague understanding of the dog fight as part of a larger network of illicit market operations involving gambling and dog meat. While the dogs are the first target of a monetized form of violence, Fenkl also suggests a parallel between the mixed-race youths of camptown and the dogs. It is when he is faced with the prospect of getting caught in the violent network of illegal gambling and dog meat trade that Insu clearly sees his and his friends' social vulnerability: "who would miss a couple of *t'wigi* [mixed- race] kids whose whereabouts were unknown to begin with."[35]

The military violence of Big Uncle's narrative mutates into social violence in Insu's narrative. Yet Fenkl presents the two kinds of violence as existing on a continuum in wartime and post-armistice Korea. Insu's rumination on the unending timeline of the Korean War from an earlier moment in the novel is helpful here in understanding this continuum. Upon observing the fact that his and his camptown friends' mothers "were technically criminals" because of their dealings in the black market, Insu directs attention to how this criminality is created out of conditions of dependency and subordination that mark the relationship of the camp- town residents to the US army.[36] "[W]hat could we expect," he ponders, "living in a military dictatorship in Korea under the umbrella of the US Eighth Army, where everything was a SNAFU and every other GI was out to make a buck at Uncle Sam's expense, where the war was mostly over but the casualties kept mounting and usually turned out to be people like us?"[37] Individual relations of dependency and subordination are linked to larger scale relations of dependency and subordination between South Korea and the United States in Insu's observation. Within the terms of such relations, the social vulnerability borne by camptown youths like Insu can only be understood as the effect of the Korean War, even if "the war was mostly over."

It is important to note that *Skull Water* does not offer a historical cause- and-effect relationship between the violence of the Korean War and the violence of the 1970s South Korea. A causal relationship that holds the dehumanization effected by the Korean War as the cause of the brutality and disregard for life decades later would confer a narrative logic on militarized modernity. Fenkl's novel resists this view of causality; in its stead it offers juxtaposition. Arguably a weaker form of connection, juxtaposition suggests that the violence of militarized modernity defies a straightforward, linear narrative logic. By unfolding a narrative of juxtaposition in which wartime Korea of 1950 and South Korea under military dictatorship in 1974–75 coexist, *Skull Water* offers a way of comprehending the culture of militarized modernity as a continuum in narrative form.

In the above I have tried to show militarized modernity as a continuum in Cold War Korea with no certain beginning or ending through the works of Korean immigrant writers. The picture of militarized modernity in *The Innocent, Guilt Payment*, and *Skull Water* shows lives constrained by the forces of the military and the market as they work in tandem to create the conditions for living and dying. None of the main characters in the three texts – Colonel Lee in *The Innocent*, Pak's Korean immigrant men in *Guilt Payment*, and the fourteen-year-old Insu in *Skull Water* – can be fully apprehended when one tries to understand the formative influence of state violence through a single-country lens. These characters become citizen-subjects within the crosscurrents of South Korean and US participation in a culture of militarized modernity. Instead of offering any easy path out of militarized modernity, these writers ask readers to vicariously experience its continuity in the fictional worlds of 1961 Seoul, 1970s Hawai'I and 1970s camptown. While an exit from militarized modernity may not be in sight for their characters, these writings insistently probe where the logic of militarized modernity breaks down, asking where the continuing Cold War rationale of the market and the military may give way to other ways of imagining life.

Notes

1. I adopt the phrase from Carl and Shelley Mydans's book, *The Violent Peace*. In this book the phrase refers to the character of military conflicts after the end of World War II where limited wars replace total war due to the fear of "world destruction." Carl Mydans and Shelley Mydans, *The Violent Peace* (New York: Atheneum, 1968), 5.
2. Seungsook Moon, *Militarized Modernity and Gendered Citizenship in South Korea* (Durham: Duke University Press, 2005).
3. *Militarized Modernity*, 24.
4. *Militarized Modernity*, 19.
5. Jingqi Ling suggests that "a transnational Asian American literary discourse" "became fully established by mid- or late 1990s." See his chapter "The

Transnational Turn" in *Asian American Literature* for a succinct summary of the development of transnationalism in Asian American literature and the critical stakes. *Asian American Literature* (London: Bloomsbury, 2022), 75. In the Introduction to *The Cambridge Companion to Transnational American Literature*, Yogita Goyal suggests that "[i]t is conceivable to look back at the last three decades and claim that transnational frames have now become normative rather than insurgent in American literary studies." "Introduction: The Transnational Turn," in *The Cambridge Companion to Transnational American Literature*, ed. Yogita Goyal (Cambridge: Cambridge University Press, 2017), 5.

6. Jin-Kyung Lee, *Service Economies: Militarism, Sex Works, and Migrant Labor in South Korea* (Minneapolis: University of Minnesota Press, 2010), 16.

7. *Service Economies*, 28.

8. Christine Hong notes that "In Asia and the Pacific, where the Cold War immediately turned hot, the task of keeping the peace would thus prove hard to differentiate from the waging of war." *A Violent Peace: Race, US Militarism, and Cultures of Democratization in Cold War Asia and the Pacific* (Stanford: Stanford University Press, 2020), 2.

9. Elaine Kim's groundbreaking study, *Asian American Literature*, is exemplary of this inclusion model. Lisa Lowe's 1991 article, "Heterogeneity, Hybridity, Multiplicity," marked a significant departure from approaching Asian American difference through an inclusionary model. *Asian American Literature: An Introduction to the Writings and Their Social Context* (Philadelphia: Temple University Press, 1982); Lisa Lowe, "Heterogeneity, Hybridity, Multiplicity: Marking Asian American Differences," *Diaspora: A Journal of Transnational Studies* 1.1 (1991): 24–44. If one looks outside literary criticism, the Asian American argument for "claiming America" can be traced to the Asian American movement of the 1960s and the writings of Maxine Hong Kingston. See Viet Thanh Nguyen, "Pacific Rim and Asian American Literature," *The Cambridge Companion to Transnational American Literature*, ed. Yogita Goyal (Cambridge: Cambridge University Press, 2017), 190.

10. Richard E. Kim, *The Innocent* (Boston: Houghton Mifflin Company, 1968), 3.

11. *The Innocent*, 6. In a 1964 feature story on Richard Kim in *Life* magazine after the unexpected success of *The Martyred*, Kim suggests that had he not accepted the scholarship from Middlebury College, he would have remained an officer in the South Korean army because he "sensed the future power the army would have in Korea." "Best-selling Korean," *Life*, 56.12, March 20, 1964, 126.

12. Kim, *The Innocent*, 123.

13. Kim, *The Innocent*, 71.

14. Kim, *The Innocent*, 66.

15. Kim, *The Innocent*, 66.

16. Kim, *The Innocent*, 63, 68; James Kyung-Jin Lee, "Richard Eun-kook Kim," in *Asian American Literature in Transition* vol. 2, ed. Victor Bascara and Josephine Park (New York: Cambridge University Press, 2021), 345.
17. Kim, *The Innocent*, 368.
18. Kim, *The Innocent*, 368.
19. Kim, *The Innocent*, 75.
20. Lee, "Richard Eun-kook Kim," 345.
21. Kim, *The Innocent*, 142.
22. Kim, *The Innocent*, 368.
23. Kim, *The Innocent*, 179.
24. Ty Pak, *Guilt Payment* (Honolulu: Bamboo Ridge Press, 1983), 17.
25. Ty Pak, *Guilt Payment*, 9.
26. Ty Pak, *Guilt Payment*, 18.
27. For South Korean participation in the Vietnam War, see chapter 4 of Simeon Man's *Soldiering through Empire: Race and the Making of the Decolonizing Pacific* (Berkeley: University of California Press, 2018); *Service Economies*, 42–8; and *Militarized Modernity*, 26.
28. Brenda Kwon, *Beyond Keʻeaumoku: Koreans: Nationalism, and Local Culture in Hawaiʻi* (New York: Garland Publishing, Inc., 1999), 81.
29. Man, *Soldiering through Empire*, 105.
30. Heinz Insu Fenkl, *Skull Water: A Novel* (New York: Spiegel & Grau, 2023), 23.
31. Fenkl, *Skull Water*, 113.
32. Su-kyoung Hwang, *Korea's Grievous War* (Philadelphia: University of Pennsylvania Press, 2016), 118–35; Bruce Cumings, *The Korean War: A History* (New York: The Modern Library, 2010), 174–5.
33. Hwang, *Korea's Grievous War*, 120.
34. Fenkl, *Skull Water*, 181–2.
35. Fenkl, *Skull Water*, 214.
36. Fenkl, *Skull Water*, 137.
37. Fenkl, *Skull Water*, 137–8.

CHAPTER 13

Undocutime
Containment, Coloniality, and Childhood in Javier Zamora's Solito

Catherine S. Ramírez

Although children have migrated as long as people have, the figure of the child migrant – in particular, the unaccompanied child migrant – has come to prominence in the Global North in the twenty-first century. Images and sounds of child migrants locked in cages in south Texas in 2018 were preceded by the "child migrant crisis of 2014,"[1] a spike in the number of unaccompanied minors, mostly from Guatemala, Honduras, and El Salvador, apprehended at the US-Mexico border. Reports of Ukrainian children deported to Russia and the deracination of roughly one million Palestinian children in Gaza followed.[2] From the Darién Gap to the Mediterranean Sea, migrant routes and international borders have turned into sites of "mass child abuse."[3] "[O]ur epoch," literary and cultural theorist Claudia Milian observes, "is globally marked, in large scale, by the child migrant."[4]

Along with the figure of the child migrant comes the child migrant story, a story about and often by a child migrant or a former child migrant. How is that story told? By whom and for whom? And what can the child migrant protagonist tell us about the social construction of childhood and the relationship of this category to the coloniality of migration in the Americas? By coloniality of migration, I refer to the enduring impact of colonialism – specifically, the political and economic asymmetries it has wrought – on the mobility and immobility of people in our world, particularly between the Global South and Global North.[5]

To address these questions, I turn to Javier Zamora's *Solito*. Published in 2022, on the heels of the aforementioned "child migrant crises" and in the midst of yet another "migrant crisis" at the US-Mexico border, this memoir recounts Zamora's journey at the age of nine from his hometown of San Luis La Herradura, El Salvador, to the United States. From April 6 until June 11, 1999, he traveled by boat, truck, bus, and foot some 2,500 miles with five other Salvadorans and their Mexican coyotes. All were strangers to him before they set out. While his biological family had no idea where he was or even if he was dead or alive, three of his traveling companions, Patricia, Carla, and Chino, posed as his family and treated him as if he were kin. Zamora dedicates *Solito* to his "pretend"[6] family and "all the immigrants"[7] he met during his odyssey.

Solito has garnered praise because of its proximity to the undocumented, unaccompanied child migrant experience. Written primarily in English, Zamora's memoir is part of a twenty-first-century boom in life writing by former undocumented migrants.[8] However, unlike many other stories by writers who spent their childhood and/or adolescence undocumented in the United States, *Solito* is told from a small child's perspective. Its narrator-protagonist goes by two names. His biological family calls him Javiercito, while his migrant family – Patricia, Carla, and Chino – know him as Chepito. In a 2023 interview, Zamora explained his reason for taking on Javiercito's/Chepito's point of view: "Perhaps by describing things as a child it will open hearts more so that they accept that we are human beings."[9] Put another way, *Solito*'s child narrator-protagonist is a specific kind of literary figure, summoned to humanize the dehumanized: to evoke compassion for migrants from an Anglophone readership.

Javiercito's/Chepito's perspective and voice make his juvenility palpable and render *Solito* what literary critic Ana Patricia Rodríguez terms an "embodied story."[10] Here is a boy who talks to his friends during recess about getting to the United States and "eating our first pepperoni pizza like the Teenage Mutant Ninja Turtles" and "watching the new Star Wars inside a theater with air-conditioning."[11] Yet what he does *not* talk about, the social and political context of his migration, says just as much as what he does talk about. As a reviewer points out, "Zamora does very little to situate his story within the context of the mass emigration of Salvadorans in the wake of the US-funded Salvadoran Civil War (1979–1992)."[12] And, despite dedicating his book to the migrants he met on his journey, Zamora does not "overtly connect his plight to that of the thousands of other unaccompanied child migrants who have arrived in the United States from Central America in recent decades."[13] When *Solito* begins, Javiercito/Chepito has no idea that he will become a *migrante*, a word with which he is not yet familiar and that he will soon come to understand as pejorative. Instead, he believes that he is about to embark on a "trip," the innocuous – indeed, promising – word that opens chapter one: "*Trip.* My parents started using that word about a year ago – 'one day, you'll take a trip to be with us. Like an adventure. Like the one Simba goes on before he comes home.'"[14] His understanding of migration as an adventure accentuates his naïveté and points to what he does not know and cannot yet understand. "A child doesn't understand what immigration is," Zamora stressed in an interview, "you don't understand how close to death you are."[15]

At the same time that child migrants have been thrust into the media spotlight, a growing body of work in migration studies has approached hard international borders and the clandestine routes those borders force migrants to take as sites of "sanctioned maiming," "attenuated life," and "necropolitical abandonment."[16] As enduring symbols of vitality in literature and culture, children are supposed to be the antithesis of death. However, as the present essay shows, Javiercito's/Chepito's juvenility calls attention instead to the necropolitics of migration – in particular, to borders' deadly forms of biopower[17] – and to the "less-than-deadly aspects" that often structure captive waiting and psychological trauma.[18] To highlight this critical contribution of his memoir, I study not only Zamora's representation of his journey from El Salvador to the United States, but his descriptions of his body and language as well. I argue that efforts to contain this Salvadoran child physically, temporally, and linguistically bring into relief the coloniality of migration in the Americas – in particular, the United States' expansion of its southern border and the specific role of youth in its extractive relationship to Latin America.

In what follows, I begin by outlining theories of containment as "a series of strategies that operate to disrupt and hinder migrants' autonomous movements."[19] These strategies, however, are not simply spatial and physical; they are also linguistic, temporal, and psychic. Focusing on this multivalence alongside practices of deterrence and deferral, I show containment of migrants as a contemporary manifestation of a long colonial history. Then I turn to the role of containment – and the vitality that containment tries to capture and threatens to extinguish – in the unfolding of Javiercito's/Chepito's story in *Solito*.

Containment as a Hallmark of the US Immigration Apparatus

Migration has been essential to the United States' growth as a settler colonial society. That said, not all migrants have been welcomed in the so-called nation of immigrants. Containment has long served as a tool for keeping those deemed undesirable at bay, from the Chinese Exclusion Act of 1882 to Migrant Protection Protocols, a program first introduced by the Trump Administration in 2018 that forces asylum seekers who arrive at the United States' southern border to remain in Mexico for the duration of their immigration proceedings. In addition to being hemmed in by an increase in border security measures, such as fences, ground sensors, and surveillance cameras, migrants are held captive by a bureaucratic wall. The "precarious states of indeterminate waiting" to which migrants are subject and the intentional manipulation of their time in order to produce or exacerbate harm is what anthropologist Carlos Martinez calls "necrotemporality."[20] Drawing on this concept, I describe the prolonged waiting, permanent temporariness, enforced presentism, devaluation of time, and persistent patience of the undocumented as "undocutime" – a term that helps illuminate the different but intersecting temporal phenomena characterizing the enforced disposability of migrant lives.[21]

The terms *deterrence* and *deferral*, which point to spatial and physical as well as temporal containment, likewise help expose the logic and aims of US immigration policy in the late twentieth and early twenty-first centuries. Introduced by US Customs and Border Protection in 1994, and probably impacting Javiercito's/Chepito's own route into the United States, Prevention Through Deterrence is a series of policies that has diverted undocumented migrants from erstwhile high-traffic points of entry, such as the area around San Diego, California, to more remote and dangerous segments of the US-Mexico border. Meanwhile, Deferred Action for Childhood Arrivals (DACA) has granted certain undocumented migrants born on or after June 16, 1981, who have lived continuously in the United States since June 15, 2007, temporary permission to work and a temporary stay of deportation. Like the abortive Development, Relief and Education for Alien Minors (DREAM) Act, legislation that sought to provide undocumented migrants under a certain age with legal permanent residency or US citizenship, DACA is an executive order that has privileged youth. To qualify for DACA when it was introduced in 2012, a migrant had to have been under the age of thirty-one. More than a decade later, the DACAmented continue to wait for an adjustment of status or deportation. In the process of waiting, they defer – or submit – to the state. All the while, of course, they also age – thereby potentially aging out of the supposed privileges for which they first deferred. Similarly, since the DREAM Act's introduction in the US Congress in 2001, the bill itself has been perpetually deferred: no version has ever passed. Consequently, many migrants who would have qualified for it have now aged out of it. Ironically, the older prospective DREAMers and the DACAmented grow, the further away they move from the possibility of an adjustment of status under youth-centric legislation and policy like the DREAM Act and DACA. Deferral thus acts as a mechanism of containment and potential expulsion. Just as geography, in the words of a former US Immigration and Naturalization Service commissioner, has been transformed into "an ally" of the US immigration apparatus, so, too, has time.[22] Deterrence and deferral thus comprise the spatial and temporal containment of migrant lives: the death-dealing mechanisms by which their lives are rendered perpetually vulnerable.

Containment and Vitality in *Solito*

Geography and time conspire against Javiercito/Chepito. The distance that separates him from his parents and his impatience to reunite with them are evident from the outset. When *Solito* opens, he has just turned nine and is living with his grandparents and aunt Mali in La Herradura, a rural fishing village. Don Dago, the stern, elusive, and inscrutable Mexican broker arranging his migration to the United States, has a "'no one under ten' rule."[23] Foreshadowing and, at the same time, underestimating the "endurance test"[24] that is unauthorized overland and marine migration to the United States, Javiercito/Chepito insists that he is ready for the journey because he "can already jump the fence that separates [his grandparents'] house from the neighbors' pretty fast. And it's made of barbwire." "I've never gotten hurt," he boasts. "Not a single scratch."[25] His apprehension of the geography of migration is both all too knowing, as he anticipates galvanized fencing, and all too limited, as he knows only the world of his yard.

Like so many other nine-year-olds, Javiercito/Chepito is cocky, naïve, insecure, curious, anxious, hopeful, self-conscious, courageous, and vulnerable at once. Beginning in the first chapter, the reader learns about his talents, liabilities, fears, and desires. He can jump the aforementioned fence and is the best student in his class, but he does not know how to swim and has yet to learn how to tie his shoes. Nor can he sleep through the night without wetting himself, a consequence of his mother's departure to the United States when he was five. He is also "a good salesman; [he] learned from sitting on [his] Mom's lap" when she worked as a street vendor in La Herradura. She sold "the best horchata, ensalada, marañón, and chan," he boasts.[26] Above all, he admires his parents, misses them profoundly, and yearns to be with them. His desire is inherently and urgently spatial: to close the painful distance that separates them.

Zamora was born in 1990, in the midst of the Salvadoran civil war. In 1991, his father, the leftist head of a co-op, fled the country.[27] Three years later, Zamora's mother availed herself of Don Dago's services, entered the United States without papers near San Diego, and joined her husband in the San Francisco Bay Area. Zamora expected to follow in his parents' footsteps – indeed, to retrace his mother's by crossing the border near San

Diego – but had to remain with his grandparents and Mali in La Herradura until he was mature enough to make the journey. Javiercito's/Chepito's village has only one "pothole-filled asphalt road that ends at the pier," a concretization of the lack of mobility that forces many of its residents to emigrate.[28] The pocked road also contrasts sharply with the Golden Gate Bridge, "a huge bridge," the boy proclaims.[29] He cherishes a photo of his parents standing before the Bay Area landmark in which they embody the rights of mobility denied to the majority of people from the Global South.

Javiercito/Chepito dreads being stuck in La Herradura for the rest of his life, "selling pupusas to the same people Mom sold pupusas to."[30] He bemoans his hometown's poverty and the need for so many of its residents to leave, observing, "All my friends and I want to be with our parents, where everything is new, fresh, where garbage is collected by trucks, where water comes out of silver faucets, where it snows the whitest snow."[31] His grandparents' house is cozy, but humble and cramped. The door to the bedroom that he shares with his twenty-three-year-old aunt is a "bedsheet hanging from a wire."[32] Their room is so small, the smell of Mali's "pata chuca" (stinky feet) fills it when she removes her shoes after work every evening.[33] In contrast, he pictures "a huge door," along with a "huge TV," "a swimming pool, a lawn, fruit trees, a mini soccer field, [and] a white fence" at his parents' house in California.[34] At night, he lies next to Mali on her bed as she reports the day's *chambre* (gossip) and complains about "how bored" she is at work and the lack of viable suitors in their village.[35] The two of them "stare at the ceiling," a reminder that the house both envelops and traps them.[36] At bedtime, he wonders what kind of bed his parents sleep on. "¿Is it big? ¿Is it a waterbed like in the movies?" He imagines cuddling with them atop "[t]he comfiest white sheets" and beneath a mosquito net similar to the one that encloses his bed in La Herradura.[37]

Javiercito's/Chepito's naïve questions and musings about his parents' lives in the United States accentuate his youth. Meanwhile, his language accentuates his Salvadoran-ness. While Zamora wrote his memoir in English, inverted question marks and exclamation points indicate that the narrator and other characters are speaking Spanish. More specifically, they are speaking Salvadoran Spanish, as Salvadoranisms, like *pata chuca*, *chambre*, and *vos* (you), and references to Salvadoran foods, such as pupusas (the national dish of El Salvador), chan (a drink made with lemon, strawberry, and chia seeds), and marañón (cashew), make patent. For instance, in anticipation of his move to the United States, Javiercito/Chepito tells his friends, "Fíjate vos [Yo, check it out], one day I'm taking a trip. Like a real-real game of hide-and-seek."[38]

Before too long, Javiercito/Chepito finds himself in an all-too-real game of hide-and-seek as he traverses Mexico and the US-Mexico border as an unauthorized migrant. Yet, despite the perils he confronts, he retains a child's perspective. For example, he likens the small group of Salvadoran migrants with whom he travels to "the Power Rangers, Sailor Moon, or the kids with the rings that bring Captain Planet to life. We're a team. Our mission: get to La USA."[39] And he proudly keeps a checklist of firsts in his head. Before embarking on his journey, Javiercito/Chepito had never ventured farther than San Salvador. The house he grew up in lacked a bathroom and a phone. As he arrives in Guadalajara on May 1, 1999, he privately tallies his list of firsts: "Stay at a motel. Check. Use a fancy bathroom. Check. Shower with a showerhead. Check. Sleep in a two-story building. Check. Three-story building. Check. Stay at an aparta-mento. Check."[40] Migration expands his physical world and, at the same time, hems him in.

Javiercito's/Chepito's juvenility – his astonishment, fright, smallness, and vulnerability – are amplified when he is in grave danger. In a terrifying confrontation with Mexican soldiers at a checkpoint on the highway between Oaxaca and Mexico City, he and his companions – all Central Americans – are removed from a bus, verbally and physically assaulted, and robbed of their money. Lying face down on the hot pavement with his legs spread and his arms extended above his head, he pictures himself as

> Superman. Like I'm flying. Like I'm Goku . . . I close my eyes and fly far far very far away from here. Above the clouds. I'm flying over mountains, over lakes, over cities, all the way to the Golden Gate. I can't hear anything, I'm in California – until a small, dirt-colored lizard is close to my face, tan like me, blending in perfectly with the ground.[41]

Javiercito/Chepito further removes himself mentally from the violent scene in which he is caught by imagining a conversation with the lizard, whom he names Paula. She assures him that "[e]verything is going to be okay."[42] Similarly, weeks later, as he and his group make their way across the Sonoran Desert, he gives deceptively whimsical names, like "Lonelies," "Spikeys," and "Fuzzies," to the cactuses that pierce the migrants' flesh when they stumble into them.[43]

The run-in with the Mexican soldiers and the trek across the desert underscore the migrants' physical captivity and vulnerability. In addition to providing a petrified nine-year-old with the opportunity for flight, however imaginary, Paula is a site of identification for Javiercito/Chepito. Facedown on the asphalt, the boy sees himself in the small, brown lizard with "hands and legs sprawled like mine."[44] Both are at risk of being crushed by The Boots, the name he gives the soldiers who torment him and his companions. Not unlike the guileless names he gives the barbed desert plants, his language cuts these men down to mere parts and takes away a bit of their power. But the abstractions of the synecdoche also bespeak the violence he is simultaneously enduring as he leaves his body behind to be a superhero talking to a lizard named Paula.

Javiercito/Chepito admires Paula precisely because she is small and "blend[s] in perfectly with ground."[45] To pass through Mexico and the Sonoran Desert, he and his compatriots must also blend in. Indeed, they must disappear as *migrantes*, a word he quickly deduces is derogatory, especially when preceded by *pinches*, the distinctly Mexican approximation of *fucking* or *damn*. Slogging unseen through the desert entails wearing all black, speed walking at night, and seeking cover when a Border Patrol helicopter sweeps in. Passing unnoticed through Mexico as an unauthorized Central American migrant is also extremely difficult. Prior to setting out, the Salvadorans memorize not only the name on the fake Mexican passport their coyote gives each of them, but a fictitious Guadalajaran biography as well. Their performance as Mexicans hinges on a list of seemingly trivial imperatives, like knowing the number of soccer teams Guadalajara has in Liga Primera.

But if the knowledge required for passing as Mexican seems inconsequential, the consequences of even the most minor linguistic failure are not. Perceptive and impressionable, Javiercito/Chepito pays close attention to his Mexican coyotes' speech. He tries to copy their accents and to replace his Salvadoranisms with Mexicanisms. For example, he uses "*[p]opote* instead of *pajilla* [straw]. *Lana* instead of *pisto* [money]. *Carnal* instead of *chero* [buddy]." He vows, "When we land [in Mexico], I will be Mexican."[46] However, signs of his linguistic foreignness percolate up and brand him an undocumented migrant. After ordering a soda at a taco stand in Mazatlán, for instance, he inadvertently asks for a *pajilla* instead of a *popote*. The taco vendor snaps, "Pinches mojados [damn wetbacks], learn to speak," leaving Javiercito/Chepito wondering, "¿Are we gonna be ok? ¿Is [the taco vendor] gonna call the cops? She knows we're Salvadoran." Then he lists epithets used in Salvadoran Spanish: "Guanacos [literally an animal from South America, a nickname for someone from El Salvador]. Cerotes [turds]. Majes [morons]. Chambrosos [gossips]. Chiflados [crazies]. Cachimbones [simpletons]." Salvadoranizing *nopal en la frente* (prickly pear on the forehead), a Mexican phrase used to underscore a person's Mexican-ness, especially their indigeneity he is convinced that "[t]here's a pupusa on our foreheads." The straw's white wrapper becomes a manifestation of the shibboleth *pajilla*; it "glows too much in the dark – a bright sticker soldiers can see."[47] As a historically central instrument of empire, language plays a significant role in the contemporary coloniality of migration in the Americas as another medium of containment and racialization by state governments.

Similarly, the farther north he travels, the more Javiercito's/Chepito's brown skin marks him as an outsider and an "indio," a label his mother taught him to embrace, but that he comes to understand as a "bad word."[48] He fears getting "caught because of [his] skin," and "want[s] to blend in" like Paula.[49] However, on a bus in northern Mexico, he notices that "everyone around us is light-skinned."[50] Later, as he makes his way across the Sonoran Desert, he likens himself and the other migrants to the brown, furtive deer they encounter and the brown lizards he spies "pretending to be rocks."[51] "It's funny when [the lizards] run away, their small arms and legs paddling the dirt," he observes. "They look like me when I slide under fences."[52]

Javiercito's/Chepito's self-comparison to a scurrying lizard "the color of dirt" testifies not only to his entrapment and desire to flee, but to the dehumanization he endures as a dark-skinned, unauthorized Salvadoran migrant in Mexico.[53] His need to distance himself from his homeland and the epithets he imagines the Mexican taco vendor hurling at him and his Salvadoran companions is more than a survival tactic; it is also evidence of his internalization of the racialization – namely, the anti-Indigenous and anti-migrant sentiment – to which he is subject. Early in their journey, a Mexican coyote issues both a warning and a threat to him and the other migrants when he tells them that their lives do not matter and that all of Mexico, essentially, is a pen in which they are trapped. "'You're pinches migrantes,'" the coyote declares. "'Locals can call the cops, who will take you, rob you, or kill you.'"[54] *Solito* is riddled with insults, such as *pinches migrantes*, that speak to the migrants' debasement. Yet it also offers a glimpse of Javiercito's/Chepito's growing self-contempt. His fantasy of the United States as a place of safety, order, and cleanliness – of white snow, white fences, and white bedsheets – contrasts with the danger, disorientation, dirt, and darkness of the migrant route. By the time he is captured by the US Border Patrol, he is so beaten down, he describes the detention facility as a zoo, the detainees as monkeys, and their cell as a "cage. This silent and stinky room."[55]

The odors that figure prominently in *Solito* point to the convergence of spatial and physical captivity with embodiment and racialization. The

Border Patrol officers' uniforms "are clean and green, their boots black and shiny."[56] One wears cologne that "smells like firewood mixed with cypress."[57] In contrast, Javiercito/Chepito is acutely aware of his own and the other migrants' stench. "I know I stink," he admits. "I want to shower."[58] Along with dirt and grease, the smells of illegality mark and effectively confine the migrants' bodies.

But these same odors also point beyond to their vitality – in particular, their abilities to taste and smell. After a tumultuous journey by boat along the Pacific coast of Guatemala and southern Mexico, the stench of gasoline permeates Javiercito's/Chepito's senses and flesh: "I can taste it. I can smell it on my skin . . . Gasoline in my hair, inside my fingernails, between my legs, in my shirt, my pants, my underwear. Or maybe the smell is trapped in my nose, on my tongue."[59] Later, the Sonoran Desert "clings" to him and the other migrants and leaves them reeking of "[d]irt. Cactus. Sweat. Brush. Rocks. Blood. Spilled tuna juice. Piss. All of it on our skin."[60] The listing that structures Javiercito's/Chepito's language has a poetic quality, an aliveness, even as it bears witness to the humiliation of being filthy and malodorous. To maintain a semblance of dignity and control, Patricia, the only woman in the small group with which he travels, compulsively cleans the cramped spaces to which she and the other migrants are confined. "She's the Tasmanian Devil," the boy observes, "folding blankets, grabbing the broom, throwing trash away, whispering to herself . . . 'We're mojados, but we're clean.'"[61] Just as Javiercito/Chepito tries to scrub the Salvadoranisms from his vocabulary, Patricia tries to wipe away the markers of their inferior status in Mexico.

Javiercito/Chepito documents in vivid and excruciating detail the personal shame of his own embodiment – specifically, his growing body's uncontrollable excess, such as his "smelly feet,"[62] "chubby chest," "flabby belly," and "thick legs";[63] the "trail of poop" he sometimes leaves on his underwear;[64] and the "thick layer of . . . white stuff that" covers his tongue and "makes [his] breath stink in the morning."[65] At night, when he shares a bed with Patricia and Carla, his "pretend" mother and sister, he worries, "¿What if, when I'm sleeping, I fart and I wake both of them? ¿What if I drool?"[66] He attempts to minimize his physicality, an impossible task for a growing child. In detention, he struggles to hold his urine in because he does not want to relieve himself in front of other people. When he sees an adult male detainee urinate at the communal toilet in their cell, he is horrified by his "thing – so big," language that evokes his vulnerability to violation as a child.[67] Javiercito/Chepito also struggles to hold his tears in. Except when one of the migrants in his group dupes him into looking for "powdered gasoline," slang for cigarettes, the boy recounts the myriad ways he has restrained himself: "I haven't cried ... I've been good. Didn't cry when I saw the Mexican soldiers' guns. Didn't throw up on the boat. Didn't complain we walked far."[68] As he lists the moments of biting his tongue and suppressing his feelings, he also illuminates the ways in which restraining himself both physically and figuratively is part of the larger system of containment structuring the coloniality of migration.

Javiercito/Chepito personally witnesses the dire costs of failing at self-containment. A migrant he dubs The Screaming Man embodies unrestrained physical and emotional excess during a twenty-two-hour boat ride from Guatemala to Mexico. The Screaming Man has a panic attack, hallucinates, and wails "like he's a broken bone, like someone is beating him."[69] After begging the coyotes to stop the boat, he squats over the side so he can defecate – literalizing his inability to contain himself – then falls into the water. After he is pulled back on board, he lies wet and whimpering on the deck, where Javiercito/Chepito notices that The Screaming Man's pants are halfway down and that "[i]t's dark where his thingy should be."[70] Unlike the man who urinates at the communal toilet in detention, The Screaming Man does not have a big and terrifying "thing." Instead, there is a void where his diminutive "thingy" ought to be. Predictably, one of the coyotes mocks The Screaming Man as a "fucking pussy" and "a bitch."[71] Javiercito/Chepito records but does not employ such misogynistic terms himself. Instead, he likens The Screaming Man to "a dead fish": a horrifying figure for the state of mutilation and proximity to death that are one possible outcome of clandestine migration.[72] But if Javiercito/Chepito witnesses the death-like defeat of The Screaming Man, the boy himself does not die. Instead, he embodies a vitality that he is unable to stifle, despite his best efforts at embodying the work of containment instantiated and demanded by the state. As his two-week trip turns into a seven-week ordeal, his fingernails grow "thicker than crescent moons," evidence of his body's uncontrollable growth and the passage of time.[73] Despite the deadly forms of biopower that contain him on all sides, Javiercito/Chepito endures. But he endures in a state of undocutime: the collective temporal assaults of prolonged and captive waiting and endless temporariness that characterize his existence as a migrant.

Undocutime and the Capture of Youth

Where other child migrant stories – for example, Valeria Luiselli's 2019 novel, *Lost Children Archive*, and Marcelo Hernandez Castillo's 2020 memoir, *Children of the Land* – bring undocutime into focus via scattered events and non-linear narratives, *Solito* does so as a linear chronology, a sequence of diaristic episodes, each with a date and location.[74] Yet undocutime is evident from the outset. Before leaving La Herradura, Javiercito/Chepito must wait for Don Dago to decide that he is big, strong, fast, and independent enough to withstand undocumented migration to the United States. Don Dago even inspects the boy's teeth to ensure that they will not pose any problems during the arduous journey. As they wait, Mali reminds Javiercito/Chepito to "be patient."[75] "Coyotes take their time," she assures him, "like tortoises."[76] Meanwhile, the boy watches her and his grandparents "wilt like ferns in Abuelita's garden when she doesn't water them."[77] So eager is he to depart, he "feel[s] the trip in the soles of [his] feet . . . and see[s] it in [his] dreams."[78] Yet his journey is one of fits and starts. He leaves, only to get stuck over and over again in hotel rooms, migrant shelters, and so-called safe houses.

Captivity in one such "safe house," a bare, oppressive, smoke-filled apartment on the outskirts of Guadalajara, brings undocutime into focus. Before being locked in, Javiercito/Chepito and his companions are told to "stay hidden."[79] They must keep the curtains closed and the lights off. To kill time, they "watch TV all day."[80] When there is nothing left to look at or listen to, Javiercito/Chepito smells his surroundings; he gets on his hands and knees and pretends to be a dog. "I just watch TV, eat bad food, sniff," he reports.[81] He loses track of time, although a soccer game on TV signals that it is Sunday morning again. Between May 1 and May 21, the dates in this chronology of "eventlessness" are marked only with a question mark.[82] At the beginning of their journey, Patricia crosses out the days on a calendar in anticipation of what she believes will be their imminent arrival in the United States. However, after being stuck in the "safe house" in Guadalajara, she and her daughter grow listless and despondent. They sleep all day while Javiercito/Chepito "count[s] the tiny hairs above their lips" and "listen[s] to their snores." Reminiscent of his evenings with Mali in La Herradura, Patricia and Carla "stare at the ceiling in silence" when they are awake.[83] Not unlike Abuelita's ferns, the migrants wilt during these weeks of uncertainty and paralysis.

Indoor spaces like the "safe house" do not offer Javiercito/Chepito and his companions shelter. Rather, they stifle them. Yet the vast outdoor spaces into which they are flung are also oppressive. Time stands still inside and flies by with terrifying speed outdoors. When the migrants head into the Pacific Ocean off the coast of Ocós, Guatemala, before dawn, the boat that carries them "jolts" as dark waves "crash against" it. The anti-nausea pill a coyote gives Javiercito/Chepito does little to numb his senses. Rather, it heightens them: the boat's motor roars "*Rrrrrrr*," "the stench of gasoline" and vomit fills his nostrils, the cold wind lashes his face and chest, and his bottom is repeatedly hurled into the air and against the hard bench on deck.[84] Unable to swim and terrified of both sharks and the dark, he is "very close to death on that boat."[85] Still, his senses of hearing, smell, and touch signal how very alive he is. They overwhelm him and leave him feeling "dizzy" and as if his head "is spinning."[86] Similarly, after a coyote gives Javiercito/Chepito an amphetamine so he can keep up with the group as they march across the Sonoran Desert, the boy's mind and heart race and he feels as if "[a]nts crawl inside [his] head" and his "eyes want to pop out."[87] Trapped, ironically, by the expansiveness of the desert and in his own growing body, he feels that he is about to burst. Yet Javiercito/Chepito survives the worst exigencies of undocutime – in large part because he is young and vital.

On June 11, 1999, more than nine weeks after leaving his home in El Salvador, Zamora reunited with his parents in Tucson, Arizona. Over the following nine years, he navigated life in the United States as an undocumented migrant. He learned English, graduated from college, earned an MFA in poetry, helped launch a campaign to eliminate the US citizenship requirement for literary prizes, published a volume of poetry, and garnered multiple accolades, among them, fellowships from the National Endowment for the Arts, the Bread Loaf Writers' Conference, and Harvard University.[88] He also underwent decades of psychological therapy.[89] In 2018, US Citizenship and Immigration Services granted him an EB-1 visa.[90] Also known as an "Einstein" visa, this document is awarded to noncitizens with "extraordinary ability."[91]

Notwithstanding his special visa, Zamora is one of hundreds of thousands of bright, talented, hardworking, and overachieving undocumented migrants to come of age in the United States in the first decades of the twenty-first century. And while Zamora eventually naturalized as a US citizen, many of his youthful contemporaries – among them, DACA participants and prospective DREAMers – have continued to wait – for regularization, for reunion with loved ones, and for stability, certainty, acceptance, or deportation.[92] Unlike migrants in detention, the DACAmented are not incarcerated. Still, at the time of this writing, they remain tethered to a system that monitors them closely, limits their movement, threatens to expel them, and denies them permanent legal status. Differences notwithstanding, both detained migrants and DACA participants are unfree: held captive by a migration apparatus organized around spatial/physical and temporal forms of captivity. Moreover, the technologies of containment that underwrite this captivity operate "not through the logic of the border – demarcating, sealing, controlling, but rather through the expansive logic of the frontier."[93] While the contemporary US government deploys the language of a so-called "border crisis," it continues to develop the expansionist and extractive policies of an imperial nation bent on enlarging its territory and resources.

The United States' past and present in Central America, the formal and informal labor compact between it and its Global South neighbors, and its outsize impact on migration policy in the Western Hemisphere and throughout the world – in particular, the effective extension of its southern border into and beyond Mexico – speak to this expansive logic of the US frontier. Zamora was part of an historical exodus compelled by US intervention in El Salvador. Likewise, his unanticipated rerouting from San Diego to Arizona was, in all likelihood, a consequence of Prevention Through Deterrence, a program that was put into place five years before he left La Herradura. These military events and government policies are both shaped by and continue to shape the ongoing coloniality of migration in the Americas.

In many ways, Javiercito/Chepito and other unaccompanied child migrants trouble the longstanding, asymmetrical relationship between the United States and Latin America, a relationship based on the extraction of labor and other resources and "colonial legacies of the construction of the racialized Other."[94] Notwithstanding their debasement in popular and political discourse, migrants from Latin America have always had value to the US economy as cheap and/or disposable racialized workers. This was the case for Mexican braceros in the twentieth century and remains so for DACA participants, the majority of whom are Latinx.[95] But while braceros sold their arms, a metonym for their toiling bodies, DACA participants' capital has been their youth. Like braceros before them, DACA participants have productive bodies. Along with deportability, fitness for labor – "unskilled" in the case of braceros and often "skilled" in the case of the DACAmented – characterizes both groups. In contrast, unaccompanied child migrants are not supposed to be fit for labor. As asylum seekers, historian Laura Briggs maintains, they are not "part of a labor migration" and "refuse . . . to just be the bodies that do hard, dirty jobs for starvation wages."[96] Yet, as a 2023–24 *New York Times* investigation about child migrants toiling in factories and on construction sites has driven home, youth and vitality remain part of the US settler colony and racial capitalism.[97]

In 1963, labor activist Henry Pope Anderson observed, "You rent a bracero for six weeks or six months, and if he gets damaged, you don't care. You'll never see him again. You get next year's model – a newer, younger, healthier one."[98] In the twenty-first century, child migrants are all "next year's model." Zamora's story, while autobiographical, is thus by no means singular. If Javiercito's/Chepito's perspective and voice, by emphasizing his juvenility, bring needed attention to the plight of child migrants, this narrative quality is also the marker of his and other child migrants' vitality and extractable value. Indeed, the intertwinement of child vulnerability and value continue to characterize the coloniality of migration in the Americas across the centuries. By telling the story of migration as an experience of spatial and temporal captivity, Zamora's *Solito* points to yet another kind of extraction: the capture of youth itself from the undocumented, unaccompanied child migrant.

Notes

1. Dara Lind, "The Child Migrant Crisis Seems to Be Over. What Happened?" *Vox*, September 19, 2014, www.vox.com/2014/9/19/6433867/border-crisis-central-american-children-coming-over-why.
2. United Nations, "World News in Brief: Nearly a Million Children Displaced in Gaza, Guatemala 'Coup' Concerns, 'Enduring Menace' of Genocide." UN News, December 9, 2023, https://news.un.org/en/story/2023/12/1144607.
3. Thom Davies, Arshad Isakjee, and Jelena Obradovic-Wochnik, "The Politics of Injury: Debilitation and the Right to Maim at the EU Border," *Geopolitics* 1–29 (2024): 12.
4. Claudia Milian, *LatinX* (Minneapolis: University of Minnesota Press, 2020), 37.
5. Aníbal Quijano coined *coloniality* to shed light on the aftermath of "a process that began with the constitution of America and world capitalism as a Euro-centered colonial/modern world power. One of the foundations of that pattern of power was the social classification of the world population upon the base of the idea of race." See Aníbal Quijano, "Coloniality of Power and Eurocentricism in Latin America." *International Sociology* 15.2 (2000): 215. Building on Quijano's work, Encarnación Gutiérrez Rodríguez defines coloniality of migration as the "conjuncture" of "colonial legacies of the construction of the racialized Other" and "migration control." See Encarnación Gutiérrez Rodríguez, "The Coloniality of Migration and the 'Refugee Crisis': On the Asylum-Migration Nexus, the Transatlantic White European Settler Colonialism-Migration and Racial Capitalism," *Refuge* 34.1 (2018): 17–18.
6. Javier Zamora, *Solito* (New York: Hogarth, 2022), 245.
7. Zamora, *Solito*, n.p.

8. Regarding the body of life writing by formerly undocumented migrants, see Marta Caminero-Santangelo, *Documenting the Undocumented: Latino/a Narratives and Social Justice in the Era of Operation Gatekeeper* (Gainesville: University of Florida Press, 2016); Glenda R. Carpio, *Migrant Aesthetics: Contemporary Fiction, Global Migration, and the Limits of Empathy* (New York: Columbia University Press, 2023); Debbie M. Duarte, "How to Undocument a Narrative," *Public Books*, September 14, 2022, www.publicbooks.org/undocu mented-immigrants-narratives/; Sujatha Fernandes, *Curated Stories: The Uses and Misuses of Storytelling* (New York: Oxford University Press, 2017); Catherine S. Ramírez, "Undocutime: DREAMers, *Lost Children Archive*, and the Politics of Waiting and Storytelling in Twenty-first-century Migration Narratives," *Latino Studies* (2024): 533–51; and Ana Patricia Rodríguez, "The Art of (Un)Accompaniment: Salvadoran Child Refugee Narratives in the Twenty-first Century," *Studies in 20th and 21st Century Literature* 49.1 (2025): 1–21.

9. Albinson Linares, "'Migrant Children Survive the Horror': Javier Zamora Details his 3,000-mile Journey to the US in the Award-winning 'Solito,'" NBC News, February 27, 2023, www.nbcnews.com/news/latino/migrant-ch ildren-survive-horror-javier-zamora-details-3000-mile-journe-rcna72084.

10. Rodríguez, "The Art of (Un)Accompaniment," 7.

11. Zamora, *Solito*, 4–5.

12. Julia G. Young, "A Boy at the Border," *Commonweal*, December 8, 2022, w ww.commonwealmagazine.org/solito-young-migration-children-border-el-s alvador#:~:text=Zamora%20does%20very%20little%20to,that%20have%2 0plagued%20the%20country.

13. Young, "A Boy at the Border."

14. Zamora, *Solito*, 3 (italics original).

15. Linares, "'Migrant Children Survive the Horror'."

16. "Sanctioned maiming" and "attenuated life" are from Jasbir K. Puar, *The Right to Maim: Debility, Capacity, Disability* (Durham: Duke University Press, 2017), 141 and 139. "Necropolitical abandonment" is from Davies, Isakjee, and Obradovic-Wochnik, "The Politics of Inquiry," 6.

17. Biopower, the management of bodies and populations and the wholesale elimination of life, does not just foster life. It also eliminates some lives in order to preserve others.

18. Davies, Isakjee, and Obradovic-Wochnik, "The Politics of Injury," 5.

19. Patrisia Macías Rojas and M. Tazzioli, "Detention/Confinement/ Containment," *Politics and Space* 40.4 (2021): 70.

20. Carlos Martinez, "Waiting in Captivity: Slow Borders, Predatory Bureaucracies, and the Necrotemporality of Asylum Deterrence," *Refuge* 39.2 (2023): 2.

21. Ramírez, "Undocutime," 535.

22. Timothy Dunn, "Hardline US Border Policing Is a Failed Approach," *NACLA*, September 21, 2016, https://nacla.org/blog/2016/09/21/hardline-us-border-policing-failed-approach.

23. Zamora, *Solito*, 33.
24. Nicholas De Genova, "Anonymous Brown Bodies: The Productive Power of the Deadly US-Mexico Border," *From the European South* 9 (2021): 69.
25. Zamora, *Solito*, 10–11.
26. Zamora, *Solito*, 9.
27. *Democracy Now!* "'Solito': Salvadoran Writer Javier Zamora Details His Solo 4,000-Mile Journey to US as a 9-Year-Old," May 10, 2023, www.democracy now.org/2023/5/10/end_of_title_42_immigration.
28. Zamora, *Solito*, 12.
29. Zamora, *Solito*, 11.
30. Zamora, *Solito*, 10.
31. Zamora, *Solito*, 5.
32. Zamora, *Solito*, 7.
33. Zamora, *Solito*, 8.
34. Zamora, *Solito*, 4.
35. Zamora, *Solito*, 8.
36. Zamora, *Solito*, 10.
37. Zamora, *Solito*, 4.
38. Zamora, *Solito*, 4. I am grateful to Cecilia M. Rivas for helping me translate the Salvadoranisms in *Solito*.
39. Zamora, *Solito*, 82.
40. Zamora, *Solito*, 159.
41. Zamora, *Solito*, 125–6.
42. Zamora, *Solito*, 126.
43. Zamora, *Solito*, 304.
44. Zamora, *Solito*, 126.
45. Zamora, *Solito*,
46. Zamora, *Solito*, 93.
47. Zamora, *Solito*, 181.
48. Zamora, *Solito*, 126.
49. Zamora, *Solito*, 115.
50. Zamora, *Solito*, 188.
51. Zamora, *Solito*, 303.
52. Zamora, *Solito*, 304.
53. Zamora, *Solito*, 304.
54. Zamora, *Solito*, 110.
55. Zamora, *Solito*, 248.
56. Zamora, *Solito*, 248.
57. Zamora, *Solito*, 340.
58. Zamora, *Solito*, 255.
59. Zamora, *Solito*, 110.
60. Zamora, *Solito*, 248.
61. Zamora, *Solito*, 149.
62. Zamora, *Solito*, 141.
63. Zamora, *Solito*, 140.

64. Zamora, *Solito*, 143.
65. Zamora, *Solito*, 255.
66. Zamora, *Solito*, 142.
67. Zamora, *Solito*, 247–8.
68. Zamora, *Solito*, 166–7.
69. Zamora, *Solito*, 94.
70. Zamora, *Solito*, 97.
71. Zamora, *Solito*, 97.
72. Zamora, *Solito*, 98.
73. Zamora, *Solito*, 146.
74. See Valeria Luiselli, *Lost Children Archive* (New York: Vintage Books, 2019) and Marcelo Hernandez Castillo, *Children of the Land: A Memoir* (New York: Harper Perennial, 2020).
75. Zamora, *Solito*, 10.
76. Zamora, *Solito*, 33.
77. Zamora, *Solito*, 35.
78. Zamora, *Solito*, 3.
79. Zamora, *Solito*, 162.
80. Zamora, *Solito*, 163.
81. Zamora, *Solito*, 165.
82. "Eventlessness" is from Ruben Andersson, "Time and the Migrant Other: European Border Controls and the Temporal Economics of Illegality," *American Anthropologist* 116.4 (2014): 802.
83. Zamora, *Solito*, 166.
84. Zamora, *Solito*, 87.
85. *Democracy Now!*
86. Zamora, *Solito*, 89.
87. Zamora, *Solito*, 216.
88. Javier Zamora, "About," www.javierzamora.net/bio.
89. Javier Zamora, "My Journey to the US at Age 9 Nearly Killed Me. As an Adult, I Had to Face the Trauma," Today.com, September 9, 2022, www .today.com/news/essay/solito-author-javier-zamora-trauma-rcna46846. Anita Felicelli, "Event Recap: Javier Zamora and 'Solito,'" Alta, June 21, 2024, www.altaonline.com/california-book-club/a61176332/javier-zamora-solito-ev ent-recap-video-ingrid-rojas-contreras-john-freeman/.
90. Leah Worthington, "He Left El Salvador as a Boy. He Returned Home a Poet," *California*, October 19, 2018, https://alumni.berkeley.edu/califor nia-magazine/fall-2018-culture-shift/qa-javier-zamora-salvadoran-poet/.
91. US Citizenship and Immigration Services, Employment-Based Immigration: First Preference EB-1, /www.uscis.gov/working-in-the-united-states/perman ent-workers/employment-based-immigration-first-preference-eb-1.
92. Linares, "'Migrant Children Survive the Horror'."
93. Ruben Andersson, "The Bioeconomy and the Birth of a 'New Anthropology,'" *Cultural Anthropology* 37.1 (2022): 39.
94. Encarnación Gutiérrez Rodríguez, "The Coloniality of Migration," 17–18.

95. Migration Policy Institute, "Deferred Action for Childhood Arrivals (DACA) Data Tools," March 31, 2023, www.migrationpolicy.org/programs/data-hub/deferred-action-childhood-arrivals-daca-profiles.

96. Laura Briggs, *Taking Children: A History of American Terror* (Berkeley: University of California Press, 2020), 178.

97. Hannah Dreier, "They're Paid Billions to Root Out Child Labor in the US? Why Do They Fail?" *New York Times*, December 28, 2023, www.nytimes.com/2023/12/28/us/migrant-child-labor-audits.html.

98. This quote is from Lori A. Flores, "A Town Full of Dead Mexicans: The Salinas Valley Bracero Tragedy of 1963, the End of the Bracero Program, and the Evolution of California's Chicano Movement," *Western Historical Quarterly* 44.2 (2013): 125.

CHAPTER 14

Speculative Fiction as Anti-Colonial Theory
Indigenous and Latinx Film and Literature

María Josefina Saldaña-Portillo

This chapter considers speculative film and fiction by Indigenous and Latinx directors and writers as a mode of anti-colonial thought. If in the mid-twentieth-century anti-colonial theories were blueprints for analyzing and overthrowing imperial social relations of political domination and cultural representation, then contemporary speculative film and fiction provides a similar hermeneutic for transforming continuing relations of inequality and unfreedom. Latinx and Indigenous authors and directors of science fiction, neo-gothic, time-travel adventure, and dystopic/utopic genres explore the legacies and ongoing practices of colonialism, neocolonialism, dispossession, and extractivism by creating shared public visions of these histories for their audiences, as well as visions of future worlds yet to come. In the spirit of the Anna Brickhouse and Susan Gillman introduction to this edition of *The Cambridge Companion to American Literature and Empire*, I consider the genre of speculative fiction expansively, within the context of North American cultural production, inclusive of Mexican, Central American, US, and Canadian literature and film.[1] Any consideration of Indigenous and Latinx speculative film and fiction as modes of anti-colonial analysis of ongoing exploitation would necessarily pluralize empire in the Americas to include, at the very least, the Spanish and French. At the same time, these speculative forms also provide alternative Indigenous theories of liberation for the land itself: for what the Kuna people of Panama and Colombia call "Abya Yala" or "living land," and for what is known as "Turtle Island" in Lenape cosmology. Even these now decolonial nomenclatures – "Abya Yala" and "Turtle Island" – indicate a multiplicity of Indigenous peoples in North America, each with specific languages, cultures, and origin stories. Moreover, the relation between Indigenous history and Latinx history is itself constituted by empire. As Brickhouse and Gillman underscore, the experience of Indigenous and Latinx subjects in the United States is subjected to multiple, sequential, and overlapping imperial projects and racial regimes. The majority of Latinx peoples in the United States – including Indigenous Latinx people whose mother tongue is a Native one – are here because of a continuing history of US military and covert intervention in Latin America. We are here because you were there.

Explaining the migration of Guatemalan Indigenous youths to the United States today, for example, requires knowledge of racial protocols put in place by the imperial Spanish Casta system; of how this system subsequently enabled the dispossession of Indigenous peoples by creole national elites, as well as their exploitation in enclave economies of bananas and coffee; and of the culmination of this history in a genocidal Civil War orchestrated by the CIA and funded by the US Congress. In the latest chapter of the United States' neocolonial entanglement with Central America, the 1996 Illegal Immigration Reform and Immigration Responsibility Act facilitated the deportation of thousands back to Guatemala. These convicted gang members were the children of refugees from the 1980s Central American civil wars, who fled to the US but were only able to obtain temporary protection status for themselves and their children. This provisional status made their teenage and adult children deportable. Guatemalan convicted felons, with deported gang members in El Salvador and Honduras, established the deadliest regional network of drug trafficking in the history of Central America, threatening Guatemalan Indigenous youth with death, torture, and rape if they refuse to join their gangs, paradoxically setting in motion refugees in search of US asylum. This layered and ongoing colonial entanglement indelibly shapes several of the key texts explored here: the neogothic ghost tales of Guatemalan-American author Sabrina Vourvoulias' "Sin Embargo" (2012) and Guatemalan filmmaker Jayro Bustamante's *La Llorona* (2020) as well as Mexican filmmaker Issa López' *Vuelven* (*Tigers Are Not Afraid*, 2017).[2]

As Brickhouse and Gillman remind us, via Jane Radway's 1998 ASA address, the history of the formation of the "American" literary canon is itself indicative of a sublimated imperial vision. Thinking of the speculative genre *across* North America, under an expansive application of the concept of "American literature," allows us to observe connections otherwise occluded. This is especially true for Latinx literature which is too often contained within a US tradition because it is often written in English. While Latinx authors actively place themselves within a US literary canon through intertextuality, content, and form, thinking genres across national boundaries enables us to trace the lineage of Latinx speculative fiction to Latin American classics like Carlos Fuentes' *Aura* (Mexican, 1965), more contemporary neogothic films like Guillermo del Toro's *Cronos* (Spanish-Mexican, 1992), or contemporary science fiction like Alison Spedding's *De cuando en cuando Saturina: Una historia oral del futoro* (*Saturnina from Time to Time: An Oral History of the Future*) (British-Bolivian, 2004).[3]

Understanding Latinx authors and filmmakers as in conversation with their Latin American counterparts places the prevalence of blood thematics within a larger interrogation of Spain's colonial legacy of mestizaje. Mestizaje (mixed blood/culture) – imaginatively refigured as inheritance, contagion, cure, degeneration, fountain of youth – features prominently in Alejandro Morales *The Ragdoll Plagues* (Mexican American, 1992), in Junot Díaz's "Monstro" (Dominican-American Latinx, 2012), and in Silvia Moreno-García's *Mexican Gothic* (Canadian Mexican, 2022).[4] Meanwhile Daína Chaviano's "Accursed Linage" (Cuban American, 2020) uses the ingestion of blood less as a metaphor for mestizaje, and more as commentary on vampiric existence under dictatorship, though whether of Batista's or Castro's remains purposefully obscured. Chaviano's use of allegory mirrors that of the Argentine writer Angélica Gorodisher, whose science fiction has been interpreted as thinly masked critique of torture, disappearance, murder, and sheer madness in Argentina's Dirty War.[5]

Speculative fiction by US and Canadian Native American writers may center mixed-bloods or métis as protagonists, but to different effect than their Latinx counterparts. Again, only by considering the plurality of empires that colonized America can we assess the distinct meanings of their literary figurations of miscegenation. Under the racial logic of US white settler colonialism, miscegenation often entailed the loss of tribal membership, with mixed-race children absorbed into whiteness or blackness.[6] Recuperation of "lost" Indigenous heritage figures prominently in Sherman Alexie's *Flight* (Spokane Tribe, 2007) and Louise Erdrich's *Future Home of a Living God* (Ojibwe Tribe, 2017).[7] Mixed-raced/métis Indigenous identity is often the site of metaphoric possibility for queering futuristic societies in Native American short stories like Kai Minosh Pyle's "How to Survive the Apocalypse for Native Girls" (Red River Métis/Ojibwe/Polish American, 2020). Meanwhile, in "The Ark of the Turtle's Back," jaye simpson (Oji-Cree Saulteaux/Canadian, 2020), like their Latinx counterparts, uses mixed-race figuration to explore the transculturation of Western and Indigenous knowledge systems, the lure of heteronormativity, and its impact on queer kinship.[8]

Not all Latinx and Indigenous authors and directors working within the speculative genre analyze colonial relations, critique racial formations, or speculate about postcolonial futures. Likewise, not all speculative fiction, minoritarian or otherwise, concerns itself with liberation. Authors and directors are curated herein for the purpose of broadening the concepts of "American literature" and "empire," on the one hand, and thinking about the speculative genre in the aftermath of twentieth-century revolutionary movements.

Latinx Speculative Fiction and Film

By the last decade of the twentieth century, revolutionary movements in North America were stymied in their efforts to deliver on their decolonial agendas. While due in part to a failure of political vision, the determinant cause of revolutionary failure was the massive violence unleashed upon movements by counterinsurgency repression orchestrated and funded by the US across Latin America and the United States. In the face of horrendous violence unleashed on revolutionaries and subalterns – the unmitigated cruelty of modernity – is it any wonder that anti-colonial critique should go underground, absconding itself into speculative fiction?[9] Its aesthetic conventions are particularly apropo for understanding the fantastical horrors unleashed by colonial and neocolonial social relations of power across North America, for reanimating visions of future worlds under the ruse of mere speculation.

Critic James E. Gunn suggests speculative fiction takes an event that appears fantastical and treats it not as outlandish, but as a rational outgrowth of a current context.[10] Gunn differentiates science fiction from other forms of the genre, arguing for science fiction's pride of place among speculative fiction. Nevertheless, he elaborates that *all* speculative fiction – in contradistinction to realist, naturalist, or historical fiction – is uninterested in the psychological interiority and growth of a protagonist. Rather, it focuses on the global import of a change event for humanity (often scientific or technological), where the "race itself is in danger."[11] That Gunn refers here to the human race underscores the links between racialization and the very category of the human itself; indeed, early speculative fiction in the United States concerned itself with saving the white race from Asian, African, or Indigenous contagion.[12] Latinx and Indigenous authors revise the genre to address precisely this racial reasoning, especially when racial reasoning is promulgated as "scientific." Instead, in such corrective speculative texts the fantastical event of racism is rendered as the rational outgrowth of colonialism.

Darko Suvin, another foundational critic of science fiction, defines it succinctly as "the literature of cognitive estrangement": "The aliens – utopians, monsters, or simply differing strangers – are a mirror to man just as the differing country is a mirror for his world. But the mirror is not only a reflecting one, it is also a *transforming one.*"[13] Like Gunn, Suvin anxiously differentiates sci fi from nonfictional utopianism and naturalist literature, but also from other kinds of "non-naturalist fiction."[14] Sci-fi creates a literary world "with totalizing ('scientific') rigor," such that Columbus' letter concerning the Eden beyond the Orinoco River, or Swift's Laputan Island qualify, but "the *fantasy* (ghost, horror, Gothic, weird) tale" does not (1.3, 2.2).[15] Scientific rigor for Suvin enables an estrangement of cognition that is similar to Brechtian theater: "SF sees the norms of any age, including emphatically its own, as unique, changeable and therefore subject to a cognitive view," that is an interrogative view.[16] I would suggest, contra Suvin and Gunn's uneasy defense of the science in science fiction, that the speculative genres examined herein – ghost, neogothic, and the weird – all enable estrangement for the opposite reason: in the interest of questioning scientific rigor, especially in its modernizing and developmentalist guises. Indeed, these authors and directors question the foundations of Enlightenment thought, enabling the estrangement of its norms, by framing it as cause and effect of colonialism.

Carlos Fuentes, Alejandro Morales, and Silvia Moreno-García examine fantastical events as rational outgrowths of the neocolonial contexts their protagonists inhabit, staging occasions to interrogate cognition and knowledge production. Their works – respectively *Aura, The Rag Doll Plagues* [*TRDP*] and *Mexican Gothic* [*MG*]— critique an Enlightenment rooted in a racial animus against Indigeneity.[17] Moreover, Fuentes and Moreno-García create a shared vision Mexico's colonial past, using the trope of haunting to diagnose historiography's blind spots, whereas in Morales's text, time-traveling scribes traverse the borders of empires to stem the ongoing plague of conquest and racial reasoning. Where Fuentes and Moreno-García champion Indigenous agency and knowledge, Morales questions all forms of imperial epistemology, including Indigenous knowledge of empire.

Aura was published in 1962, the start of Central American revolutions that culminated in the 1994 Zapatista insurrection. However, 1962 also marks the beginning of the end of a Mexican revolution that *had* delivered goods and services to subalterns and transformed class relations. With prescience, *Aura* critiques the political contradictions in the PRI's revolutionary vision, which burst into the public sphere in anti-dictatorial protests of 1968. Young historian Felipe Montero is lured to a colonial-era house in downtown, mid-twentieth century Mexico City by a widow who offers the protagonist the job of compiling her husband's nineteenth -century papers. Entranced by the beautiful Aura, the widow Consuelo Llorente's niece, Felipe accepts the job. Lifted out of subaltern poverty by a free university education curtesy of the Mexico revolution, Felipe is nonetheless seduced by the positivism of European paradigms. Instead of producing a syncretic Mexican history, joining Indigenous and European knowledge systems (the purported intent of revolutionary mestizaje), Felipe dreams of producing an opus on "the Spanish discover-[ies] and conquests in the New World," evidence of the great "adventures of Spain's Golden age."[18] Felipe, educated by the revolution yet enthralled by Europe, is handmaiden to foreign paradigms. His imperial historiography is thwarted by the ghostly Aura, who is but a beautiful projection of Consuelo.

Aura addresses Mexico's continuing obsession with Europe, with the Enlightenment's disciplinary categorizations of hierarchical human proto-types. If Consuelo represents the specter of European colonialism – hiring Felipe to compile the memoir of her husband's allegiance to French annexation – Aura stands in for revolutionary Mexico, still unable to free itself from colonial paradigms. Felipe observes Aura mimic Consuelo's actions exactly, and mistakenly believes she is victim of Consuelo's tyranny. He desires to save Aura/Mexico from Consuelo/colonial tyranny, unaware of the ironic colonial mimicry haunting his own historiography.

Felipe describes Aura as "[e]mbrutecida"/"*made* brute-like" by Consuelo, indexing a key derogatory term used by colonial authorities to deride Indigenous reason and science.[19] If Aura represents the nation, then Fuentes hails Mexico's Indigenous peoples as its authentic public, invisi-blized yet refusing to leave the scene of Mexican historiography. The alienation of the Mexican nation from itself is due to the ghosting of Indigenous peoples from the revolutionary present. Consuelo/Aura will haunt Mexican historiography until Indigenous people are at the center of any revolution, rather than marginalized by a supremacist mestizaje that subordinates Indigenous peoples to European knowledge production.

The protagonist of *MG* is mestiza Noemí Taboada, a thoroughly mod-ern socialite from mid-twentieth century Mexico City, sent by her father to check on her cousin Catalina, his ward. Catalina claims that her husband, British mining heir Virgil Doyle, has poisoned and imprisoned her in a haunted mansion. Virgil's father Howard built "High Place" near a mining town, "El Triunfo," after dictator Porfirio Díaz (1876–1911) invited foreign capitalists to re-open colonial mines. The revolution may have ended neocolonial profiteering, but the Doyle's linger on thanks to a mushroom imported from Britain whose spores give the Doyles eternal life, turning their domestic help and Indigenous miners into laboring zombies. The mushrooms are losing effectiveness because Howard's eugenicism required family inbreeding. Catalina and Noemí are captive breeding stock, but Noemí's mother is Mazatec, so Howard worries her miscegenation will lead to degeneracy. Noemí counters Howard's eugenicist arguments by citing José Vasconcelos and Manuel Gamio on the virtues of mestizaje. For several pages, Howard and Noemí rehearse debates between prominent US social Darwinists on degeneracy from racial mixing, and Vasconcelos and Gamio on its genetic advantages. This exegesis, folded didactically into the novel, shows the continuing exploitation of Indigenous peoples as predicated on scientific racism, with extractive racial capitalism generating zombified ex-mining towns in conditions of underdevelopment: "There were many hamlets like El Triunfo where one could peek at fine chapels built when money and people were plentiful; places where the earth would never again spill wealth from its womb."[20]

MG is a revision of *Aura*, with several intertextual references to it. In both, representatives of modern revolutionary Mexico enter a house controlled by malevolent forces, hoping to free female captives. Whereas Felipe is eventually entombed in the house by Consuelo/Aura, Noemí not only escapes with Catalina, she burns the dystopic edifice to the ground. She is able to escape thanks to her Indigenous knowledge of the sacred uses of Mexican mushrooms, with which she contravenes the stupefying British one. As a Mexican-Canadian, Moreno-García said she felt compelled to write about Mexico's mining history because extractive racial capitalism in Mexico continues today under Canadian mining companies. She offers an alternative vision of mestizaje *and* development, one privileging Indigenous knowledge production, intellectual miscegenation, and the protection of the earth from the neocolonialism of extractive, racial capitalism.

Morales' *TRDP*, a novel in three parts, takes place in 18th-century Mexico City and Tepozotlán; twentieth-century Orange County and Tepozotlán; and the twenty-first-century "Lamex Pacific Coastal Region," encompassing the entire Pacific Coast and deserts from Mexico City to Los Angeles as part of a vast, futuristic "Triple Alliance" empire. The protagonist of each book is Dr. Gregorio/ Gregory Revueltas, direct descendant of his predecessor in Books I and II. Time travelers, appearing only to the Drs. Revueltas, assiduously record events, accompany the dead and dying, and intervene in treatments for a devastating plague. The time travelers are Gregory from Book II and his Indigenous grandfather Papá

Damián, a curandero. We also discover in Book III that the novel is Gregory II's diary. Structurally, as in *Aura*, we are reading a protagonist's unfolding journal.[21]

Dr. Revueltas of Book I, the Protometicato of Mexico City, has been sent by the Crown to cure a blood plague, *La Mona* (doll), ravaging New Spain. Revueltas, revolted by the filth and decay of city streets, attributes it entirely to the Indigenous population. Over the course of Book I, he recognizes the plague as the horrendous effect of colonial exploitation and is transformed from racist Spanish scientist into proto-nationalist defender of Mexico's Indigenous and mestizo population. The Drs. Revueltas of Books II and III, though mestizos, also begin as devotees to Western medicine who must be coaxed into Indigenous medical practices by female lovers and Indigenous or mestizo curanderos. In Book II, set in the 1990s, the blood plague is HIV/AIDS. In Book III, set in the 2050s, it is caused by a living mass of human garbage floating in the Pacific that vigilant Mexican and Filipino warriors keep from reaching shore. While the Triple Alliance references the Aztec Empire, the inclusion of the Philippines references New Spain's empire. It is a technology-driven amalgamation of empires. Dr. Revueltas discovers that only the blood of Mexico City mestizos, "MCM," can cure the plague, and its commercialization ensues.

If the MCM blood suggests that "mestizaje emerges . . . as a discourse of contact, contamination, and immunization" (as in *Aura* and *MG*), in *TRDP* mestizo blood is neither essentialist nor triumphalist.[22] Published at the height of anti-Mexican sentiment in California, the novel presents the dependence of the LAMEX region on MCM blood as a stand-in for the addiction of US agroindustry on the demonized documented and undocumented Mexican laborers who produce the nation's food stuffs, as María Herrera-Sobek has argued. It is also a cautionary tale about Chicanismo's romanticization of past Indigenous empires as potential revolutionary futures. The Triple Alliance has recuperated the Mexican territory annexed by the US in 1848, thanks to a warrior-class of *guerreros*, but it is still viciously segregated by class and race. The populace lives in Low, Middle, or High Life Experience enclaves. Meanwhile, the salutary elements in MCM blood are developed in response to the once-again toxic conditions of filth and contamination in Mexico City. Moreover, after Revueltas' discovery, the MCMers are effectively purchased by High Life Experience vampiric people, kept as blood slaves in gilded cages.

In a similar vein, Alex Rivera's film *Sleep Dealer* and Ricardo Bracho's play *Puto* – both from 2008 – offer a sci fi future premised on a profound racial animus against essential Mexican laborers.²³ In Bracho's dystopic parallel universe we live under a Bush imperial monarchy; the border wall has been finished, with Mexico and the US in complete accord over the maximal exploitation of the working classes on both sides of the border; and the Apache continue their anti-imperial war against both nations. The play is set in various locations in Los Angeles-county where working people live and labor in heavily policed "catchment zones," while the "agricultural prison industrial complex" captures the unfree labor of minorities, the poor, and political prisoners for food production. The front matter informs the us that "the illegal immigrant, the felon and certain aligned artist-intellectual/poet-philosophers have been decitizened ... form[ing] a permanent, generational servant class."²⁴

The protagonist, nicknamed Puto because of his sexual proclivities, specializes in pornographic, nationalist art featuring scantily clad dark-skinned Mexican boys coveted by the uber-wealthy in both countries. As he is free to cross all catchment zones as well as the border between the two countries, socializing with high powered folks, the action of this comedic play revolves around a "[c]ast of cast offs" tricking Puto into joining CREW, Communist Revolution Every Weekend.²⁵ CREW's revolutionary vision centers around returning agricultural sustainability to the people, and thus, the character Knees, a butch dyke and ex-con bee keeper, is also central to the action of the play. With sly and irreverent humor, Bracho makes queer sexual desire and kinship central to the successful execution of any revolutionary praxis. And while the principal revolutionaries are Mexican-Americans, CREW, like the Tristero in Pynchon's *Crying of Lot 49*, is made up of subalterns of all races and sexual orientations.²⁶

In *Sleep Dealer*'s dystopic future, transnational corporations own all the water in North America, charging Indigenous Mexican farmers exorbitant amounts to irrigate their crops from reservoirs of damned rivers on their communal lands. Meanwhile, under the auspices of wiping out "eco-terrorists" and "water-warriors," the US military uses drones to bomb targets in protection of transnational corporate interests. Rudy Ramirez, a Chicano drone pilot, bombs the house of an Indigenous farmer because his son, Memo Cruz, accidentally hacks into a covert military broadcast and is mistaken for a terrorist. Haunted by the memory of an old man crawling out of a hut to die, Rudy heads to Mexico to find this family, while the son Memo heads to the border in search for work. Thanks to virtual technology, factories along the border harness the labor of millions of Mexicans who implant cybernetic nodes into their bodies, allowing them to interface with millions of robots that work as agricultural laborers, construction workers, domestic servants, etc., across the US. *Sleep Dealer* literalizes a dystopia in which the US's insatiable desire for Mexican labor without the presence of actual Mexicans is finally quenched. Meanwhile, the wealthy, alienated from their bodies, crave authentic experience, creating a thriving virtual market for the consumption of uploads of subaltern memories, including Memo's. When Memo and Rudy inevitably meet in Tijuana, Memo convinces Rudy to bomb the damn on his father's farm, allowing the communal farmers to use the river water freely once again. Rudy, now a fugitive, joins a neo-Zapatista eco-revolutionary group in southern Mexico, while Memo plants a small milpa in his back yard, his commitment to Indigenous agriculture.[27]

Sleep Dealer and *Puto*'s sci fi universes are prescient about the logical outcome of the rational contradictions of neoliberal economics after the North American Free Trade Accords (1994). Canada, Mexico and the US conspired to drive down wages across the continent by permitting the free flow of capital and goods, but not labor. As displaced workers and peasants across Mexico fled to the US, industries with unionized labor forces in the US relocated to Mexico. Now, with US agricultural, meat, domestic, care, and service economies addicted to the hyper-exploitable labor of a permanent undocumented class, racial animus enables supremacists to target essential workers as the cause of US labor's demise. *Puto*'s catchment zones literalize an undocumented "generational servant class," while *Sleep Dealer*'s cyborg workers literalize the brutal repetitiveness of jobs consigned to this underclass.

In a related speculative trajectory, Latina writer Sabrina Vourvoulais and Guatemalan filmmaker Jayro Bustamante concentrate on the continuing injustice of the present, confronting the genocide perpetrated by the Guatemalan National Guard against the Mayan population through the cognitive estrangement of the gothic ghost story. Under the direction of General Efraín Ríos Montt and the CIA, the National Guard assassinated 200,000 Indigenous Guatemalans and razed more than 200 Indigenous villages during the civil war. Though found guilty of genocide by several tribunals, Ríos Montt was never jailed for his crimes, nor were any other officers. Vourvoulais' short story "Sin Embargo" (2017) and Bustamante's *La Llorona* (2022) invert genre conventions to haunt the present with this unending history.

In Mexican folklore, la Llorona haunts bodies of water in search of her children. The ghost of an Indigenous woman whose lover was a Spanish conquistador, she drowned their children in revenge for his unfaithfulness.

In contrast, for Lake Xochimilco Nahuas, la Llorona is a deity who, foreseeing the devastation of Spanish Conquest, wails in warning and grief for her lost children. The action of Bustamente's *La Llorona* stages the 2013 trail of Gen. Enrique Monteverde (a thinly veiled Ríos Montt) before Guatemala's Constitution Court for crimes against humanity, including reenacted testimony by Ixil women who had testified to the massacre of their villages, gang rape, and forced prostitution at barracks under Ríos Montt. Upon hearing this testimony, Carmen, Monteverde's wife, insists the women are lying, that her husband generously hired them to clean the barracks but they chose prostitution due to their Indigenous proclivities. Alma, the film's protagonist and ghost of one such Mayan woman, is hired during the trial to clean the General's house, which he shares with his wife, daughter, granddaughter, and staff.[28]

Alma haunts Enrique's and Carmen's dreams, getting him to sleep walk into her shower, exposing his lust for Indigenous women to the household. In a series of dreams, Carmen is transformed into an Indigenous woman witnessing the decimation of her village by soldiers. In a final dream/ trance, Carmen is on the banks of a river littered with half-naked women's corpses. While soldiers hold her two children under water, Monteverde demands to know where the guerrillas are hiding. She cannot answer what she doesn't know, so Monteverde has his soldiers drown her children before her eyes, then shoots her in the head. Only then do we see that Alma is the woman whose torture and assassination Carmen relives. When Carmen wakes from the trance, she has strangled Monteverde, bringing him to justice. Until this denouement, the audience perceives Alma as malevolent, repeatedly holding the granddaughter's head under water as if to drown her. By the end of the film, in a narrative inversion of the ghost genre, we learn that rather than trying to drown the granddaughter, Alma was teaching her to hold her breath so that she might survive what her own children could not.

In "Sin Embargo," the first-person narrator is a Philadelphia trans psychologist working with torture victims at a support center for immigrants seeking asylum. "Marijoe," her name anglicized after decades in the US, is a Tz'utijil Mayan who has a vulture perched on her shoulder, though only the narrator and Marijoe can see it. After years of searching, the psychologist has located Marijoe's brother, Rolando. The siblings became separated while fleeing a massacre. Rolando found refuge in Juchitan, Oaxaca, among the Zapotec community. After thirty years, the siblings are reunited via video-conference, recognizing each other at once. For a few minutes the screen blacks out, to display a filmic memory of six-year-old

Rolando standing terrified before a pile of charred corpses. Marijoe reaches into the computer screen, touching the boy's shoulder, instructing him, as she did then, to hide. He buries himself under the bodies.[29]

The video-call drops and the psychologist witnesses Marijoe sprout feathers on her face and neck, as she and the vulture become one. After Marijoe misses several therapy appointments, the psychologist visits her apartment where the new tenant gives him a box containing one vulture feather, $1000, and a matchbook cover with the numerical series "b52:b122:b13:b211:b215:b501:d150:e234," coordinates for Marijoe's razed village.[30] Each lettered sequence is also a catalog entry for magical birds in the Aarne-Thompson-Uther Index of folktales: truth-telling birds, vengeful birds, bird talismans, and finally, birds that take human form. Rolando informs his sister that a vulture guided his escape from his village, while a vulture has also sustained Marijoe's ghost until she found out that Rolando was alive and safe. Vourvoulais and Bustamante revise the gothic genre by populating the supernatural world with Mesoamerican deities and demons who personify justice and guidance for Indigenous Guatemalans, but also reanimate memory of Indigenous genocide for Western audiences. In "Sin Embargo" and *La Llorona*, the mestizo author and director thus respectively bear witness against genocide on behalf of Guatemalan Mayans because international institutions failed them.

Indigenous Speculative Fiction: *Native Slipstream*

US Indigenous scholar and writer Gerald Vizenor defines slipstream fiction as "convey[ing] the ... psychological experience of slipping into various levels of awareness and consciousness."[31] In homage to Vizenor, the Spokane author Sherman Alexie offers in *Flight* (2007) a protagonist, Michael, who navigates time travel in this fashion, slipping in an out of the consciousness of others. Through the process, Michael recuperates his Indigenous identity and a true understanding of justice and history, while Alexie recuperates his own Indigenous voice to bear witness to catastrophes waged against Native peoples in the distant and recent past. Because Michael's Native father abandoned him, the protagonist becomes a ward of the state whose knowledge of Indigenous peoples comes from television stereotypes. Michael has bad acne, but embraces the nickname "Zits" as it manifests his shame over Indigenous ancestry: "I wonder if being Indian causes acne."[32] Growing up in foster homes where his abuse gets progressively worse with each placement, Zits turns to violence as vengeance at the insistence of a white friend ironically named Justice. Justice convinces Zits to rob a bank to compensate for colonialism's crimes against Indians and to rid the US of whites by bringing to fruition the nineteenth-century Ghost Dances. In the instant before Zits pulls the trigger on a guard, he is transported, sequentially, to five different historical moments of consequence for Native Americans. In each period, Zits embodies the consciousness, without losing his own, of a person on the brink of taking another's life. At times Zits embodies an Indigenous personage, at times a white one, in each case unable to take a human life, even when justified as in the events of Custer's Last Stand and COINTELPRO at Pine Ridge. At each juncture, ethical issues of colonial circumstances are made startingly clear. Yet, by occupying the consciousness of white and Indigenous historical actors alike, Zits understands the complexity of human emotions and motivations in making split-second decisions to inflict carnage and death. At the end of the novel, Zits returns to the bank and refuses to shoot the guard. He has become Michael. His reward – oddly – is placement in the loving and accepting home of the white police officer who, instead of arresting Michael, sets him free, suggesting that human acts of kindness and understanding – of living in the other's skin – can accomplish more than violence. This individualist and normative resolution of Michael's psychic distress suggests a corrective to revolutionary theories that too often ignored the effect of genocidal violence on the psyche in favor of anti-colonial violence against oppressors. Instead, Michael's experiences on the slipstream are the fictional embodiment of political activist and philosopher Erica "Ricky" Sherover-Marcuse's theory of "unlearning racism." For Sherover-Marcuse, racist thinking is a form of "mystified consciousness . . . a disturbance in the learning process . . . which itself is the consequence of social oppression . . . and which in turn serves to perpetuate it."[33] For Sherover-Marcuse, true revolutionary transformation required addressing colonial violence at the psychic level. Unlearning racism is a mode of decolonial practice, in other words, with greater implications than the development and health of the individual psyche.

Louise Erdrich uses her Indigenous voice to foresee tomorrow's imperial catastrophes in *Future Home of a Living God* (FHLG 2018).[34] *FHLG* returns to a favorite trope in the genre of science fiction – the altering of the human genome, either through scientific experiment gone awry or genetic mutation. Erdrich thematizes learning and unlearning, particularly the need to unlearn our commitment to the teleological progress of Western modernity. *FHLG* is the personal diary of Cedar, a biracial Indigenous woman, pregnant in a near-future dystopia where human reproduction is so exceptional that the species is going extinct. Moreover, pregnant women are giving birth to post-human mutations whose births often kill their mothers. Cedar writes the diary to her unborn child as she is pursued by government agents in an Orwellian surveillance society. Scientists and government agents within the novel insist on reading the mutation of human embryos as valuable for the scientific knowledge their dissection will produce, such that the mothers of these children are entirely expendable. For Madhu Dubey the entire novel is an occasion for interrogating extant genetic and evolutionary science and "best read as a gesture against the racial teleology embedded in narratives of evolutionary development."[35] Erdrich is also invoking and critiquing the past use of women of color for scientific experiments.

Similar to García-Moreno in *MG*, Erdrich in *FHLG* makes Cedar a biology major in order to school the reader on theories of evolution, or more precisely on the racist distortion of evolutionary theory for imperialist purposes. Rather than relentless evolution forward, Cedar assures her unborn mutant child that the history of the human species is one of endless genetic redundancies and errors in DNA, such that the emergence of the human race is almost sheer accident. More importantly, she reassures her mutant baby that because of genetic doubles and errors, "Life might skip forward, sideways, in unforeseen directions ... Why? Because there was never a story moving forward and there wouldn't be one moving backward."[36]

Unlike *Flight*, *FHLG* is not a story about Cedar's recuperation of her Indigenous heritage. Happy with her white adoptive parents, Cedar seeks out her Ojibwe mother primarily because government agents can't go onto reservation land. Ironically, because of the diminution of the population, the Ojibwe are recuperating vast swaths of their original territory from the US and Canada – a reverse conquest-by-disease. Rather than a tragic story of abandonment, Cedar's Ojibwe mother and adoptive white mother, as well as her biological father and stepfather, conspire to protect her from government agents and to spring her from prison when she is captured. Like the possible evolutionary path of her mutant baby, this is a sideways Indigenous story, less invested in its Ojibwe-qua-Ojibwe protagonist than, as Dubey conclusively argues, in unraveling the narrative of a racist evolutionary science premised on the disappearance of a preliminary savage other, on the trope of what Lora Romero famously called the vanishing Indian.[37] Yet, *FHLG* is not a complete rejection of Western science as Cedar uses her own scientific training to debunk modernity's investment in evolution. Rather, *FHLG* is a travelogue of Cedar's cunning use of knowledge to evade the officials who are intent on imprisoning her; the novel writ large is a testament to Indigenous persistence as well as survivance, the cultural practices of Native creation and ongoingness.

The Creepy Kids of Speculative Film and Fiction

Demon children are a popular subgenre of neogothic film and fiction; in *The Children of Chicago* (2021), Puerto Rican author Cynthia Pelayo (Puerto Rican) explores the effects inner-city violence on Latinx and African American preteens, while in *Vuelven* (2017), Mexican director Issa López explores the cost that US drug use exacts on Mexican children.[38] Pelayo gives detective fiction a supernatural twist, as Detective Lauren Medina investigates the serial murder of Chicago's children of color. Medina discovers Latinx teens have summoned the Pied Piper to rid themselves of an annoying classmate. In exchange for drowning the classmate, the Pied Piper exacts payment: each teen must kill another, initiating a cycle of violence saturated in racial animus. Meanwhile, the reader discovers that Det. Medina – guilty of killing several Latinx and Black suspects – likewise entered such a pact with the Pied Piper as a child. This grim rendition of a Grimm's fairytale suggests that police violence and gang violence share a similar origin in internalized racism and the petty, misdirected hostility of ghettoized children with access to weapons of destruction.

In sharp contrast, the children of *Vuelven* are orphaned as collateral damage in a US-Mexican war on drugs that has claimed over 360,000 Mexican lives. These orphans ban together, forming a loving family that ekes out existence at the margins of the violence. The spirits of dead ancestors actively intervene to protect them from Tijuana's cartel leaders and their sicarios (assassins). Like Fuentes before her, director Issa López uses the Mexica concept of Mictlán – the underworld of departed souls – to facilitate justice for these children. In Mexica cosmology, those in Mictlán can and do cross into the world of the living. Using surrealist gothic aesthetics, where graffiti, photos, stuffed animals, and talismans all come to life to fight on behalf of these children, López exposes the collateral damage of a drug war we are all responsible for, while ensuring orphaned children retain their agency in the face of indominable odds.

The Speculative Short Story: *No nos queda más que reír*

Indigenous and Latinx speculative authors are prolific in the short-story genre, exploiting it to absurd and hilarious effect. In Gina Ruiz's "Chanclas and Aliens," "a night like any other night in Lincoln Park" ends with the entire Chicano neighborhood successfully fighting back an alien invasion with nothing but the perfect aim of chancla-wielding abuelas and of cholas wielding Aquanet hairspray as flame-throwers.[39] The LAPD arrives in the aftermath of battle, misinterpreting the purple alien goo splattered all over the park as graffiti and the whiff of Aquanaut as evidence of getting high due to obvious LAPD racial animus. Rather than receiving praise for saving the human race, these heroes are arrested and some deported. The story ends with heroine Rucas planning a trip to Tijuana to bring back boy-friends and baby-daddies, in a thinly veiled and highly entertaining allegory for the virulent disregard of the invisible and invaluable labor performed by documented and undocumented Mexican-Americans.

Richie Narvaez's "Room for Rent" (Puerto Rican, 2020) and Junot Díaz's "Monstro" each examine the complex racial relations in the Spanish-speaking Caribbean, a consequence of the mish-mash of humanity brought to the Islands through multiple colonialisms and imperial nationalisms.[40] With exquisite word-play in English and Puerto Rican Spanish, Narvaez also creates an allegory for colonialism out of alien invasion. The Cangri – invertebrates and slimy – invaded and conquered earth, but they introduce other alien species to do the hard work of pillaging its natural resources. Hala and Zangano are a Pava couple, a species brought to earth to do the hardest labor. Hala, who is pregnant, accepts a room for rent for her coming family, only to discover it is filled with "vermin" – a family of humans who previously owned the apartment. A tentative peace ensues after the tender-hearted Hala and the human father agree to share the space. Through a series of revealing exchanges, the reader learns the racial prejudices humans feel toward Pavas (the myth that Pavas eat their young) and Pavas toward humans (the belief that human frailty led to the forced migration of the Pava). Yet Hala empathizes with the plight of the humans because she sees their exploitation as related to her own. Prejudice ultimately wins the day, but the true story is the crucial role that racist representation and racial animus play in any imperial conquest. Through the well-worn trope of the lusty Dominican-American teenage boy, Díaz's "Monstro" parodies Dominican fears of being misrecognized as "black" in this parable of the Dominican Republic's historically discriminatory treatment of Haitians, where the whole island is eventually zombified due to the deplorable conditions in camps for Haitian refugees.

Artificial intelligence (AI) is also an ever-popular topic in Indigenous and Latinx short stories. In Darice Little Badger's "Story for a Bottle" (Lipan Apache, 2020), an AI runs a ship named "New America," equipped with every kind of imaginable luxury meant to sustain wealthy elites after an apocalyptic disaster.[41] With no humans onboard, a lonely AI tricks a young woman onto the ship. Little Badger adds a poignant twist to the AI theme. Rather than set the story in a dystopic future, this AI is a relic from a time when humans were on the brink of self-destruction, abandoned on a ship to wander the seas in search of company. After months on board, the protagonist tricks the AI by remembering and reliving all the games she played with her younger sister, eventually gaining control of the ship's navigation, steering it toward "New Houston." She swims to shore by following the light of a bonfire kept burning by her family. The epistolary form – a letter written to her younger sister and set adrift in a bottle – becomes an occasion for making amends for all the ways the protagonist purposefully hurt her sister. Yet the title's play on "message *in* a bottle" looks forward to a time when the need for AI to avert human-made disaster will be itself a relic, a story *for* a bottle.

Alex Hernandez (Cuban-American) in "Caridad" (2020) exploits the AI theme as a vehicle for exploring cultural difference, especially as it pertains to queer love within Latinx families.[42] "Cary," the story's protagonist, exists in a future where cybernetic implants enable family members throughout the globe to share a hivemind, thereby distributing wealth and opportunity equally to the entire clan. Cary has known since she was a child that she was to be the unifying consciousness. The snag? She has fallen in love with Ruth, a young white woman. The race or gender of Cary's choice of partner is not the dilemma. Rather, Cary must choose between a life of individuality – including her desire for Ruth—and a life of sacrifice to the family she loves, a sacrifice Ruth considers barbaric. Cary underscores that even before cybernetic implants, her family always func- tioned communally: "'The hive mind is how we've survived brutal Dictatorships and long exiles. We're like fucking bees, but it's a survival strategy that works.'"[43] Cybernetic technology literalizes the value placed upon and labor extracted from the educated few, those cultural translators in Latinx immigrant communities. After all, Cary's immigration to the US and her education is accomplished through her entire family's sacrifice; she must repay the debt. However, Cary queers the collective, insisting those under eighteen get to join (thereby updating family mores) and by includ- ing Ruth in the hivemind.

Queer kinship and its limits are at the heart of many Indigenous short stories as well. In "The Ark of the Turtle's Back" (TATB), the flexibility of Indigenous kinship allows for the flourishing of a queer family made up of an un-named Ojibwe trans narrator; Axil, the narrator's queer Métis lover; and their two Two-Spirit children, Giiweden and ashe.[44] Twenty-fourth century earth is a waterless hellscape dominated by an imperial US govern- ment that has terraformed Mars and the Moon for the exploitation of their resources by using forced labor. Reservations provide protection from labor recruitment, as well as for Two-Spirited people from anti-trans legislation. simpson makes it purposefully unclear if the two children are Indigenous or adopted white queer refugees. What is clear is that the Ojibwe reservation protects the queer family in their gender and sexual expression. The plot revolves around the need for the Ojibwe nation to flee because protections of Indigenous peoples from forced labor will soon be stripped away. The narrator's sister, Dakib, is the doctor-scientist who secretly designed vehicles for interstellar travel: "the Collective named it the Ark of the Turtle's Back. There are a hundred thousand pods [on the Ark] and an atrium system that can sustain us . . . and we're in a fleet of five Arks." Before leaving earth, Dakib arranges surgery for the narrator and Giiweden, implanting wombs to complete their transitions. They will arrive with the ability to bear children on their new planet. "TATB" offers multiple articulations of what it means to be Indigenous, emphasizing rituals that encapsulate Ojibwe cosmovisions and relations to place. Before entering a fifty-year cryogenic sleep, the narrator asks an attendant, "'How do we build a relationship with this new planet?'" The attendant laughs and answers, "'I would assume like all consensual relationships: we ask them out.'"[45]

Meanwhile, Pyle refuses to romanticize Indigenous peoples as universally accepting of Two-Spirited people or queer kinship. "How to Survive the Apocalypse for Native Girls" (HTSTA) is written as a set of enumerated rules for surviving the apocalypse. While some advice regards the transmission of tribal history, most specifically transmits the history of "2spirited" people within the Anishinaabe nation, from one Anishinaabe 2spirited girl to another. The apocalypse referenced in the title is a double entendre. A global apocalypse restored Anishinaabe sovereignty over an expanded territory governed by strict rules of kinship, but Nigig, the narrator, survives an apocalypse that occurs *within* her nation. As Nigig's queer mentor Migizi explains, "Kinship is a two-sided coin . . . You always have to ask yourself, who is being excluded here?"[46] Migizi, a militant activist for the rights of 2spirited people, is expelled from the nation, cast out into the wilderness to fend for herself for this transgression. To rid themselves of the troublesome advocate, the Anishinaabe Council falsely accuses Migizi of having burned down her village as a girl. In the course of the story, Nigig discovers Migizi's village caught fire because Migizi's parents and neighbors tried to burn Migizi at the stake for her queerness.

Nigig flees the village, abandoning her beloved bio-kin, when Anishinaabe kinship laws lead to the expulsion of her girlfriend Shanay.

Shanay's grandmother, Black and Anishinaabe, lacks proper documenta-tion of her tribal membership. This dubious status, combined with the fact that the grandmother is a doctor who insists on attending to the needs of non-Indigenous patients at the tribal hospital, leads to her expulsion as well as Shanay's. Nigig goes with Shanay in search of Migizi but also for all 2spirits, leaving her "rules for a girl" when she spots one in the crowd. "I don't know your name," Nigig writes, "But I know you're worth it, niijiikwe. And I know now that the only way to survive the apocalypse is to make your own world. So let's get started."[47]

Documented blood quantum and normative sexuality have both histor-ically served as tools of the US state to render Indigenous people inauthen-tically Indian and "American" respectively; lack of documented blood quantum and queerness have likewise often excluded or marginalized multiracial and Two-Spirit people from Native communities. Yet Pyle's story is itself the creation of and vehicle for the transmission of Indigenous knowledge production, as Nigig transcribes the truths she learns in her interactions with the elder's counsel, including the ongoing history of insidious violence against 2spirits. Nigig's rules are an example of queer Indigenous knowledge production that adapts, that realizes the importance of tradition but also of its transformation.

Conclusion

Latinx and Indigenous speculative fictions and films remind the reader that the horror of imperial and colonial history in Latin America and the US has never been speculative. Rather, through their craft, these authors and directors create a unifying public vision about a multifarious and nefarious US and European history of colonialism; of neocolonial filibustering, military intervention, and drug wars; of Native extermination; of genocidal counterinsurgency; of rape, assassination, and unimaginable forms of torture. Theirs is speculative body of fiction and film as historical record, as accounting, as the exaction of justice if only on the written page or on the screen. It is an indictment of the Enlightenment's will to mastery that has reduced everything, especially the racial other, to violence, exploit-ation, and disposability for the sake of progress.

For Indigenous authors like Little Badger, Pyle, and simpson, science fiction enables the recording and transformation of Indigenous know-ledges for the purpose of a queer futurity as well. In the hands of Latinx authors, speculative film and fiction can be an exuberant celebration of survival and survivance in the face of extreme violence. As Ruiz, Narvaez, and Díaz emphasize in their short stories, no nos queda más que reír y en esa riza quizás se encuentra la victoria. In one way or another, each of the authors and directors discussed here offers visions of decolonial futurity, a hard slap on the face to wake up, an "hasta la victoria siempre" in the face of our bleak collective present. A vision of a truly global postcolonial futurity lives on in these genres of speculative film and fiction, just as cries of "¡Viva, viva Palestina!" reverberate today from Madrid to Mexico City, from Buenos Aires to Cuzco, from Quito to San Francisco, from First Nations territories in Canada to the Patagonia, from Chiapas to Alaska and back again.

Notes

1. South America lies beyond my literary expertise.
2. Sabrina Vourvoulias, "Sin Embargo," in *Latinx Rising: An Anthology of Latinx Science Fiction and Fantasy*, ed. Matthew David Goodwin (Columbus: Ohio State University Press, 2017), 19–42; Jayro Bustamante, *La Llorona* (The Criterion Collection, 2022). Issa López, *Vuelven* (Filmadora Nacional Peligrosa, 2017).
3. Carlos Fuentes, *Aura* (New York: Farrar, Straus and Giroux, 1965 [1962]); Guillermo Del Toro Guillermo, *Cronos* (Producciones Iguana, 1992); Alison Spedding, *De cuando en cuando Saturnina: Una historia oral del futuro* (Editorial Mama Huaco, 2010).
4. Alejandro Morales, *The Rag Doll Plagues* (Houston: Arte Publico Press, 1992); Junot Díaz, "Monstro." *The New Yorker*, May 28, 2012. www.newyorker.com/magazine/2012/06/04/monstro; Silvia Moreno-García, *Mexican Gothic* (New York: Del Rey, Penguin Random House, 2022).
5. Liliana Colanzi advances this allegorical reading of Gorodisher's fiction in her essay "Speculative Fiction," trans. Jessica Sequeira, in *Latin American Literature in Transition, 1980–2018*, eds. Mónica Szurmuk and Debra A. Castillo (Cambridge: Cambridge University Press, 2022); Daína Chaviano, "Accursed Lineage," in *Latinx Rising*, 52–5.
6. This stands in contrast to the biopolitical uses of mestizaje, in which Indigeneity is preserved, if subordinated to whiteness, for nationalist ends.
7. Sherman Alexie, *Flight* (New York: Black Cat, 2007); Louise Erdrich, *Future Home of the Living God* (New York: Harper Perennial, 2018).
8. Kai Minosh Pyle, "How to Survive the Apocalypse for Native Girls," in *Love After the End: An Anthology of Two-Spirit and Indigiqueer Speculative Fiction.* Electronic, no pages (Vancouver: Arsenal Pulp Press, 2020); jaye simpson, "The Ark of the Turtle's Back," in *Love After the End*, n.p.
9. See Jean Franco, *Cruel Modernity* (Durham: Duke University Press, 2013), for a detailed discussion of this counterinsurgency violence and its function as deterrence.

10. James Gunn, "Toward a Definition of Science Fiction," in *Speculation on Speculations* (Lanham, MD: The Scarecrow Press, 2005), 5–12, at 5.

11. Gunn, "Toward a Definition of Science Fiction," 6.

12. See Jack London, *The Unparalleled Invasion*, about a dystopic future (1975) in which China rules despotically until the US unleashes a biological weapon targeting the entire population of China (1910); Charlotte Perkins Gilman, *Herland*, in which women build a utopia free of men through parthenogenic procreation determined by eugenics (1915); and Robert A. Heinlein, *Sixth Column*, in which "PanAsian" hordes take over the United States until biogenetic weapon isolates the Asian gnome for mass destruction (1941).

13. Darko Suvin, "Estrangement and Cognition," *Strange Horizons*, November 24, 2014. http://strangehorizons.com/non-fiction/articles/estrangement-and-cognition/, 1.1, emphasis added.

14. Suvin, "Estrangement and Cognition," 1.1.

15. Suvin, "Estrangement and Cognition," 1.3, 2.2.

16. Suvin, "Estrangement and Cognition," 2.1.

17. Suvin, "Estrangement and Cognition."

18. Fuentes, *Aura*, 65.

19. Fuentes, *Aura*, 72.

20. Moreno-García, *Mexican Gothic*, 17–18.

21. Morales, *The Rag Doll Plagues*.

22. Victoria Carroll, "Deforming and Transforming: Towards a Theory of 'Viral Mestizaje' in Chicano Literature," *Journal of Literary & Cultural Disability Studies* 10 (2016): 325.

23. Alex Rivera, *Sleep Dealer* (Likely Story and This Is That Productions, 2008); Ricardo Bracho, *Puto* (Los Angeles: Unpublished, 2014).

24. Bracho, *Puto*, n.p.

25. Bracho, *Puto*.

26. Thomas Pynchon, *Crying of Lot 49* (New York: J.B. Lippincott & Co., 1966).

27. Rivera, *Sleep Dealer*.

28. Bustamante, *La Llorona*.

29. Vourvoulias, "Sin Embargo."

30. Vourvoulias, "Sin Embargo." 33.

31. Gerald Vizenor, "Custer on the Slipstream," in *Walking the Clouds: An Anthology of Indigenous Science Fiction*, ed. Grace L. Dillon (Tucson: University of Arizona Press, 2012), 16–17.

32. Alexie, *Flight*, 4.

33. Erica Sherover-Marcuse, *Emancipation and Consciousness: Dogmatica and Dialectical Perspectives in the Early Marx* (Oxford: Blackwell, 1986), 145, n. 9.

34. Erdrich, *Future Home of the Living God*.

35. Madhu Dubey, "Ghost Genes and Genetic Doubles: Louise Erdrich's Counter-Narrative of Evolution and Extinction," unpublished manuscript, 2020; courtesy of the author, 11.

36. Erdrich, *Future Home of the Living God*, 54–5.

37. Lora Romero, "Vanishing Americans: Gender, Empire, and New Historicism," *American Literature* 63.3 (Sep. 1991): 5.
38. Cynthia Pelayo, *Children of Chicago* (New York: Agora Books, 2021); López, *Vuelven.*
39. Gina Ruiz, "Chanclas and Aliens." http://stories.ginaruiz.com/2023/07/20/chanclas-aliens/ 2023.
40. Ricky Narvaez, "Room for Rent," in *Latinx Rising,* 98–108. Díaz, "Monstro."
41. Darice Little Badger, "Story for a Bottle," in *Love After the End: An Anthology of Two-Spirit and Indigiqueer Speculative Fiction.* Electronic, no pages (Vancouver: Arsenal Pulp Press, 2020).
42. Alex Hernandez, "Caridad," in *Latinx Rising,* 115–27.
43. Hernandez, "Caridad."
44. simpson, "The Ark of the Turtle's Back," n.p.
45. simpson, "The Ark of the Turtle's Back," n.p.
46. Pyle, "How to Survive the Apocalypse for Native Girls," 36.
47. Pyle, "How to Survive the Apocalypse for Native Girls," 39.

Afterword

Anna Brickhouse and Susan Gillman

"On Imperialism"

Proxies—pertinent, prominent, proximate—
impose war, sustain it.

The Empire ever absent and seemingly elsewhere—
evasive, persuasive, pervasive. Things are

this complicated.

Raza Ali Hasan (2015, from *Sorrows of the Warrior Class*)

Amy Kaplan's enduring scholarship has been our touchstone since we first agreed to take on the project of editing this *Cambridge Companion*. We believed then, as we do now, in the special responsibility of Americanists to continue redressing the long "absence of empire," to borrow Kaplan's foundational phrase, in the study of US culture as well as national self-understanding. But we never imagined that we would be writing this afterword, in early January 2025, amid so much rhetorical resurgence of old-school US expansionism: in the last weeks alone, the incoming (past) president has vociferously contemplated the acquisition of Greenland, the return of the Panama Canal, and the annexation of Canada as a fifty-first state. An invasion of sovereign Mexican territory is also, apparently, not off the table of possibilities, nor is the renaming of the Gulf of Mexico as the "Gulf of America." The headlines that inform us of these potential rapacities are no less spectacular than the periodic pronouncements, across the last two decades, of the possible "decline of American empire" – predictions that seemed to begin nearly as soon as the very concept of "US imperialism" itself became a commonplace.[1]

The convenient shorthand of such phrases, whether in news headlines or academic titles, induces a certain calcification of thought, a stiffening and dulling that sets in once transformative work such as Kaplan's has become received wisdom, with all the reductionism and simplification this entails. The only way out is our collective continued attention, the ongoing work of trying to grasp the nature of the strange US present and its "pointillist

287

empire" – as bequeathed by past events that might have unfolded differently, and as shaped by contemporary events that may yet hold alternative futures.[2] These are the contingencies of what Ann Laura Stoler calls "imperial duress": "the hardened, tenacious qualities of colonial effects; their extended protracted temporalities; and, not least, their durable, if sometimes intangible constraints and confinements." But such "imperial duress" (or, to use Kaplan's formulation, the work of empire as "a way of life") can never be grasped or seen in its entirety and fullness. Which is why literary studies offers particularly apt critical resources: as Stoler puts it, "accounting for what duress looks like needs the poetics of thought to make its case."[3]

The poem we take as our epigraph – drawn from Raza Ali Hasan's 2015 collection *Sorrows of the Warrior Class* – aptly enlists this very problem of description as its poetic subject.[4] Its grandiose title – "On Imperialism" – seems to promise an explanation or organizing principle, at the very least a set of facts about the when and the where. But Hasan – a Pakistani-American poet whose collection touches on artifacts from multiple imperial cultures, from the early modern Mughal dynasty to US intervention in twentieth-century Guatemala and twenty-first-century Pakistan – offers no such specifics in this particular poem. Instead, its opening line spills an alliterative stream of substitutions ("Proxies – pertinent, prominent, proximate – ") that tell us nothing about the temporal or spatial coordinates of the poem's eponymous subject. Like all of empire's absences, though, as Kaplan has lucidly shown, this occlusion ironically suggests its own possible if unnamed specificity: the contemporary shadow zones of "black sites," private military contractors, and corporate empires. That imperial proxies "impose war/sustain it" is all we can know in a poem in which "Empire" and its catastrophic violence are "ever absent and seemingly elsewhere" for those with the luxury of time, safety, and access to this verse.

The idea that empire is seemingly but not specifically elsewhere adds another resonance to Hasan's elliptical description of imperialism. The poem nods at a broadly Western delusion that has special spatiotemporal traction in the US settler-national imagination: that "Empire" did not happen here and is not now happening here. And yet, as the poem suggests – and as the essays in this collection vividly testify – empire has been here all along: "evasive, persuasive, pervasive." The line's assonance lays claim to a sensorial truth insisted on by the poem but not, or perhaps yet to be, articulated: that imperialism slips through our attempts to name, to grasp it, and pervades all we experience by shaping how we see and know in both space and time. Indeed, "Empire" is "persuasive" enough to make us believe we *can* know it, whether as its architects and agents, its opponents and critics, or its participant observers.

Yes, "Things are/this complicated" – so much so that our language can hardly catch up, much less name and describe, the changing and sometimes illusory nature of empire, with its proliferating, and "pertinent, prominent, proximate" formations. This recognition, like the larger collection from which the poem is taken, begs for a certain epistemological modesty. The poem's meditation "On Imperialism" both fits into and exceeds the various disciplinary frames – American Studies, postcolonial theory, decolonial Américas studies – into which we might place Hasan's subjects in the book. It is in the poetics of thought, to recall Stoler's admonition, that we might avoid the rapid impoverishment of critical concepts once they begin to travel and lose their force: once they no longer require an active, dialectical relationship between a reader and a cultural work. Hasan's poem thus reminds us why empire continues to provoke literary attention to the vitiation and revivification of critical language over historical time.

What can we say today "On Imperialism" that wasn't or couldn't be said during the decade of Kaplan's *Cultures of US Imperialism*? The 1990s saw the unfolding of two great empire anniversaries: not just the much-debated 1992 quadricentennial of Columbus's first voyage but also the 1998 centennial of the Spanish-American War – the latter of which prompted many of the now best-known redefinitions of the major keywords in the field of American literary empire studies. Scholars inserted the third term "Cuba," for example, into the imperial nomenclature of the 1898 "Spanish-American" war, widening the chronology of events to embrace the elided Cuban War of Independence, which both preceded and coincided with the contest between the declining Spanish empire and an ascendant US one. Moreover, the three terms "America[n]," "literature," and "empire," discussed in our introduction to this volume, were all revised significantly during the decade of the empire centennials, yielding the hemispheric, transnational American Studies that is still with us today.

The 1990s era of American literary empire studies was also defined by the emerging additive logic of canon-expansion. As the literary canon grew with the addition of previously unknown or understudied texts, the texts themselves began to exceed traditional literary forms and represent a variety of related genres, including film and performance, legal documents, visual arts, and culture. Plurals dominated, replaced singular forms: to take the most foundational example, the "Americas" were recognized as the proper purview of the misused term "America," which itself yielded to the (also plural) "United States" to refer to the singular nation. The additive math driving the new American empire studies created an ever-expanding literary field – indeed, an expansionist field, as some critics charged, driven by the very imperial impulse it was meant to analyze. At the same time, the revisionist 1990s scholarship also sometimes tended to produce finite, definitive outcomes, all boiling down to the same unvaried mode of critique.

Today, by contrast, the literary and cultural study of American empire, broadly defined, working in concert with allied studies in popular culture, tends toward the open-ended, toward speculation and the speculative. Our volume, accordingly, both responds to and moves beyond the longstanding scholarly calls since the 1990s to diversify "American" literature and make it more inclusive of what's absent, missing, disavowed, or withheld – elided by the changing logics of American empire. But our volume's aim is not, as it was in the expansionist, boom-and-bust 1980s and 1990s, to permanently fill gaps with an ever-expanding literary canon. While we hope to intro-duce *Cambridge Companion* readers to some texts that are new to the field of American literary empire studies – including several in translation, reflecting their origins in languages other than English – there is no implied canon at stake for the scholars who contribute to this volume. As their chapters collectively remind us, the point is, to the contrary, that these little-known works were never completely silenced or unknown in their own historical contexts. And translational thinking provides a special medium, conduit to the uneven and open-ended entanglement of race, slavery, migration, and language in the context of Américas empires.

At the same time, as we reread the chapters gathered in this volume, we note that they end repeatedly on a speculative note, on a shout-out to the as-yet uncertainty of a collective future defined by the history of US empire, from contemporary environmental and immigration crisis to the unfinished work of racial, class, gender, sexuality, and ecological justice. We also note how much these chapters vividly resist the oversimplification process that inheres in the formation of concepts and their attendant phrases, including (to reiterate the point one last time) those that consti-tute our volume's title. With their insistent specificity and provisionality, their speculative historicism, and their historically grounded imagination and conjecture, these chapters testify that critique remains indispensable in the imperial present. Yet they also point to how critique's now-acknowledged limits have in turn inspired new forms of critical and political imagining, broadly associated with world-making and with rep-arative, speculative attention to the future. If critique's focus on the

ongoingness of empire can sometimes feel relentlessly bleak, our contributors remind us of literature's capacity to develop aesthetic and affective
modes that make new solidarities possible, and that foster new ways of
seeing and imagining our connections to others, those of the present, but
also of the past and the future. "Things are/this complicated" – but as these
chapters collectively attest and as Amy Kaplan made indelibly clear, such
complexity has always been with us and continues to require, even inspire,
literary attention to empire's history in the present.

Notes

1. See the subtitle to Amy Kaplan's Introduction, "Left Alone with America," in
   Cultures of United States Imperialism, ed. Amy Kaplan and Donald E. Pease
   (Durham and London: Duke University Press, 1994). On the surge of US
   expansionist rhetoric in January 2025, see "At a News Conference, President
   Refuses to Rule Out Using Force to Take Greenland," *NYT* (January 7) www
   .nytimes.com/2025/01/07/us/politics/trump-greenland.html; "Trump Floats
   Using Force to Take Greenland and the Panama Canal," *NYT* (January 7)
   www.nytimes.com/2025/01/07/us/politics/trump-panama-canal-greenland.html;
   "Trump Suggests US Expansion Into Greenland and Canada," *NYT* (January 7)
   www.nytimes.com/video/us/politics/100000009912859/trump-panama-green
   land-canada.html; "51st State? Canadians Say No Thanks," *NYT* (January 8)
   www.nytimes.com/2025/01/08/opinion/canada-51st-state-trump.html; "Trump
   Dreams of a New American Empire," *NYT* (January 21) www.nytimes.com/202
   5/01/21/opinion/trump-american-empire-panama.html. On the purported decline
   of American empire, see, e.g., "The American Empire in Retreat," *NYT*
   (September 4, 2021) www.nytimes.com/2021/09/04/opinion/afghanistan-with
   drawal-america.html; and "America Is an Empire in Decline. That Doesn't
   Mean It Has to Fall," *NYT* (September 4, 2024) www.nytimes.com/2023/09/04/
   opinion/america-rome-empire.html.
2. The term "pointillist empire" comes from Daniel Immerwahr, *How to Hide an
   Empire: A History of the Greater United States* (New York: Farrar, Straus and
   Giroux, 2019).
3. Ann Laura Stoler, *Duress: Imperial Durabilities in Our Times* (Durham: Duke
   University Press, 2016), 7 and 36.
4. Raza Ali Hasan, *Sorrows of the Warrior Class* (Rhinebeck: Sheep Meadow Press,
   2015), 19.

Further Reading

Introduction

Getachew, Adom. *Worldmaking after Empire: The Rise and Fall of Self-Determination*. Princeton: Princeton University Press, 2019.

Immerwahr, Daniel. *How to Hide an Empire: A History of the Greater United States*. New York: Farrar, Straus and Giroux, 2019.

Lowe, Lisa. *The Intimacies of Four Continents*. Durham and London: Duke University Press, 2015.

Nguyen, Viet Thanh. "Most American Literature is the Literature of Empire." *Literary Hub*, April 11, 2025. https://lithub.com/viet-thanh-nguyen-most-american-literature-is-the-literature-of-empire/ Accessed May 24, 2025.

Singh, Nikhil Pal. *Race and America's Long War*. Berkeley: University of California Press, 2019.

Vine, David. *United States of War: A Global History of America's Endless Conflicts, from Columbus to the Islamic State*. Berkeley: University of California Press, 2020.

Part I: Reimagining "Early American" Literature

Empire and the Hemisphere

Bauer, Ralph. *The Cultural Geography of Colonial American Literatures: Empire, Travel, Modernity*. Cambridge: Cambridge University Press, 2003.

Benton, Lauren, and Benjamin Straumann. "Acquiring Empire by Law: From Roman Doctrine to Early Modern European Practice." *Law and History Review* 28 (2010): 20–9.

Brickhouse, Anna. *Transamerican Literary Relations and the Nineteenth-Century Public Sphere*. Cambridge: Cambridge University Press, 2004.

The Unsettlement of America. Oxford and New York: Oxford University Press, 2014.

Elliott, John H. *Empires of the Atlantic World: Britain and Spain, 1492–1830*. New Haven: Yale University Press, 2006.

Hulme, Peter. *Colonial Encounters: Europe and the Native Caribbean*. New York: Routledge, 1992.

Langley, Lester. *The Americas in the Age of Revolution, 1750–1850*. New Haven: Yale University Press, 1997.

Pagden, Anthony. *Spanish Imperialism and the Political Imagination*. New Haven: Yale University Press, 2000.

Sayre, Gordon. *Les Sauvages Américains: Representations of Native Americans in French and English Colonial Literature*. Chapel Hill: University of North Carolina Press, 2000.

Seed, Patricia. *Ceremonies of Possession in Europe's Conquest of the New World, 1492–1640*. Cambridge: Cambridge University Press, 1995.

Williams, Robert. *The American Indian in Western Legal Thought: The Discourses of Conquest*. New York: Oxford University Press, 1990.

Against Imperial Nature: Hérard-Dumesle and the Making of Haitian Revolutionary Eloquence

Bhambra, Gurminder and Peter Newell. "More than a Metaphor: Climate Colonialism in Perspective." *Global Social Challenges Journal* 2 (2023): 179–87.

Daut, Marlene. *Awakening the Ashes: An Intellectual History of the Haitian Revolution*. Chapel Hill: University of North Carolina Press, 2023.

Dayan, Colin (Joan). *Haiti, History, and the Gods*. Oakland: University of California Press, 1998.

DuBois, Laurent. *Haiti: The Aftershocks of History*. New York: Picador, 2013.

Grove, Richard. *Green Imperialism: Colonial Expansion, Tropical Island Edens and the Origins of Environmentalism*. Cambridge: Cambridge University Press, 1996.

Hérard-Dumesle. *L'Observateur*. Les Cayes: l'Impremerie du Gouvernement, 1819.

Jenson, Deborah. *Beyond the Slave Narrative: Politics, Sex, and Manuscripts in the Haitian Revolution*. Liverpool: Liverpool University Press, 2011.

King, Tiffany Lethabo. *The Black Shoals: Offshore Formations of Black and Native Studies*. Durham and London: Duke University Press, 2019.

Scheller, Mimi. *Democracy After Slavery*. Gainesville: University Press of Florida, 2001.

Steiber, Chelsea. *Haiti's Paper War: Post-Independence Writing, Civil War, and the Making of the Republic*. New York: New York University Press, 2020.

Apocalypse and Native American Literature: from Samson Occom to the Contemporary Moment

Archuleta, Margaret, Brenda J. Child, and K. Tsianina Lomawaima. *Away from Home: American Indian Boarding School Experiences, 1879–2000*. Phoenix: Heard Museum, 2000.

Carr, Ryan. *Samson Occom: Radical Hospitality in the Native Northeast*. New York: Columbia University Press, 2023.

Child, Brenda J. *Boarding School Seasons: American Indian Families, 1900–1940*. Lincoln: University of Nebraska Press, 1998.

Fear-Segal, Jacqueline and Susan D. Rose. *Carlisle Indian Industrial School: Indigenous Histories: Memories, and Reclamation*. Lincoln: University of Nebraska Press, 2016.

Hooley, Matthew. *On Extraction: Indigenous Modernism in the Twin Cities*. Durham and London: Duke University Press, 2024.

Love, William DeLoss. *Samson Occom and the Christian Indians of New England*. Pilgrim Press, 1899. Reprinted Syracus: Syracuse University Press, 2000.

Miller, Douglas K. *Indians on the Move: Native American Mobility and Urbanization in the Twentieth Century*. Chapel Hill: University of North Carolina Press, 2019.

Witgen, Michael. *Seeing Red: Indigenous Land, American Expansion, and the Political Economy of Plunder in North America*. Chapel Hill: University of North Carolina Press, 2021.

Part II: Imperial Nation

Conquest and Compost: James Fenimore Cooper and the Literature of Ecological Empire

Calloway Colin G. *Pen and Ink Witchcraft: Treaties and Treaty Making in American Indian History*. Oxford: Oxford University Press, 2013.

Goode, Abby L. *Agrotopias. An American Literary History of Sustainability*. Chapel Hill: University of North Carolina Press, 2022.

Greer, Allan. *Property and Dispossession: Natives, Empires, and Land in Early Modern North America*. Cambridge: Cambridge University Press, 2018.

Huston, Reeve. *Land and Freedom: Rural Society, Popular Protest, and Party Politics in Antebellum New York*. Oxford and New York: Oxford University Press, 2000.

Justice, Daniel Heath, and Jean O'Brien, eds. *Allotment Stories: Indigenous Land Relations Under Settler Siege*. Minneapolis: University of Minnesota Press, 2021.

Ortiz, Roxanne Dunbar. *An Indigenous Peoples' History of the United States*. Boston: Beacon Press, 2015.

Seaver, James E. *A Narrative of the Life of Mrs. Mary Jemison*. 1824. Ed. June Namias. Norman: Oklahoma University Press, 1992.

Sundquist, Eric J. *Empire and Slavery in American Literature, 1825–1865*. Jackson, MS: University Press of Mississippi, 2006.

Waterman, Adam John. *Enclosure, Extraction, and the Afterlives of the Black Hawk War*. New York: Fordham University Press, 2022.

Manifestly Queer Domesticity: Empire and Nineteenth-Century Queer Fiction

Butler, Judith. *Gender Trouble: Feminism and the Subversion of Identity*. New York and London: Routledge, 1990.

D'Emilio, John and Estelle B. Freedman. *Intimate Matters: A History of Sexuality in America*, 3rd ed. Chicago: University of Chicago Press, 2012.

Faderman, Lillian. *Surpassing the Love of Men: Romantic Friendship and Love between Women from the Renaissance to the Present*. New York: William Morrow & Co., 1981.

Kahan, Benjamin. *The Cambridge History of Queer American Literature*. Cambridge: Cambridge University Press, 2024.

Kahan, Benjamin. *The Book of Minor Perverts: Sexology, Etiology, and the Emergences of Sexuality*. University of Chicago Press, 2019.

Looby, Christopher. "The Gay Novel in the United States 1900–1950." In *A Companion to the Modern American Novel*. Ed. John T. Matthews. London: Blackwell, 2009. 414–36.

Sedgwick, Eve Kosofsky. *Epistemology of the Closet*. Berkeley: University of California Press, 1990.

Snediker, Michael D. *Queer Optimism: Lyric Personhood and Other Felicitous Persuasions*. Minneapolis: University of Minnesota Press, 2009.

Snyder, Katherine V. *Bachelors, Manhood, and the Novel, 1850–1925*. Cambridge: Cambridge University Press, 1999.

Herman, or the Ambiguities: Melville, US Imperialism, and the Participant Critic

Cordery, Lindsey, and Beatriz Vegh, eds. *Melville, Conrad: Imaginarios y Américas. Reflexiones desde Montevideo*. Universidad de la República, 2006.

Cortiel, Jeanne. *With a Barbarous Din: Race and Ethnic Encounter in Mid-Nineteenth-Century American Literature*. Heidelberg: L Universitätsverlag Winter, 2016.

Giles, Paul. *The Global Remapping of American Literature*. Princeton: Princeton University Press, 2011.

Havard, John C. *Hispanicism and Early US Literature: Spain, Mexico, Cuba, and the Origins of US National Identity*. Tuscaloosa: University of Alabama Press, 2018.

Kelley, Wyn, and Christopher Ohge, eds. *A New Companion to Herman Melville*. Hoboken, NJ: Wiley & Sons, 2022.

Levine, Robert S., ed. *The New Cambridge Companion to Herman Melville*. Cambridge: Cambridge University Press, 2014.

"Melville and Spanish America." Special issue of *Leviathan: A Journal of Melville Studies* 23.3 (2021).

Spanos, William V. *Herman Melville and the American Calling: The Fiction after Moby-Dick, 1851–1857*. Albany: State University of New York Press, 2008.

Cultures of US Torture: Entertainment and Clandestine Spectacle

Anderson, Scott A. and Martha C. Nussbaum, eds. *Confronting Torture: Essays on the Ethics, Legality, History, and Psychology of Torture Today*. Chicago: University of Chicago Press, 2018.

Alemán, Jesse and Shelley Streeby, eds. *Empire and the Literature of Sensation: An Anthology of Nineteenth-Century Popular Fiction*. New Brunswick: Rutgers University Press, 2007.

Carson, Julie A. and Elisabeth Weber, eds. *Speaking About Torture*. New York: Fordham University Press, 2012.

Goldstein, Jeffrey. *Why We Watch: The Attractions of Violent Entertainment*. New York: Oxford University Press, 1998.

Holsinger, Bruce. *Neomedievalism, Neoconservatism, and the War on Terror*. Chicago: Prickly Paradigm, 2007.

Kundani, Arun. *The Muslims are Coming! Islamophobia, Extremism, and the Domestic War on Terror*. New York: Verso, 2014.

Lazo, Rodrigo. *Writing to Cuba: Filibustering and Cuban Exiles in the United States*. Chapel Hill: University of North Carolina Press, 2005.

Lazreg, Marnia. *Torture and the Twilight of Empire*. Princeton: Princeton University Press, 2008.

Levinson, Stanford, ed. *Torture: A Collection*. New York: Oxford University Press, 2004.

Ryan, John. *America's Trial: Torture and the 9/11 Case on Guantanamo Bay*. New York: Skyhorse, 2025.

Part III: Ongoing Empire and Speculative Worlds

The Du Bois Genealogy: Three Worlds and Three Writers on Black Anti-Imperialism

Bloom, Joshua and Waldo E. Martin Jr. *Black Against Empire: The History and Politics of the Black Panther Party*. Berkeley: University of California Press, 2016.

Boyce Davies, Carol. *Left of Karl Marx: The Political Life of Communist Claudia Jones*. Durham and London: Duke University Press, 2008.

Farmer, Ashley. *Remaking Black Power: How Black Women Transformed an Era*. Chapel Hill: University of North Carolina Press, 2019.

Higashida, Cheryl. *Black Internationalist Feminism: Women Writers of the Black Left 1945–1995*. Urbana: University of Illinois Press, 2011.

Horne, Gerald. *Race Woman: The Lives of Shirley Graham Du Bois*. New York: New York University Press, 2002.

James, C. L. R. *History of Pan-African Revolt*. Chicago: Charles H. Kerr Library, 2012.

Levering Lewis, David. *W.E.B. Du Bois: The Fight for Equality and the American Century, 1919–1963*. New York: Henry Holt and Co., 2000.

Plummer, Brenda Gail. *In Search of Power: African Americans in the Era of Decolonization, 1956–1974*. Cambridge: Cambridge University Press, 2013.

Rasberry, Vaughn. *Race and the Totalitarian Century: Geopolitics in the Black Literary Imagination*. Cambridge: Harvard University Press, 2016.

Harry Dean Foster and the Project of Black Maritime Empire

Bandele, Ramla M. *Black Star: African American Activism in the International Political Economy*. Urbana: University of Illinois Press, 2008.

Bolster, W. Jeffrey. *Black Jacks: African American Seamen in the Age of Sail*. Cambridge: Harvard University Press, 1997.

Dean, Harry Foster, and Sterling North. *The Pedro Gorino*. Ed. Nadia Nurhussein. New York: Broadview, 2024.

Ewing, Adam. *The Age of Garvey: How a Jamaican Activist Created a Mass Movement and Changed Global Black Politics*. Princeton: Princeton University Press, 2014.

Garvey, Marcus. *The Marcus Garvey and Universal Negro Improvement Association Papers* Ed. Robert A. Hill. 9 vols. Berkeley: University of California Press, 1983–2006.

Grant, Colin. *Negro with a Hat: The Rise and Fall of Marcus Garvey and His Dream of Mother Africa*. New York and Oxford: Oxford University Press, 2008.

Horne, Gerald. *Red Seas: Ferdinand Smith and Radical Black Sailors in the United States and Jamaica*. New York: New York University Press, 2005.

Stephens, Ronald J., and Adam Ewing, eds. *Global Garveyism*. Gainesville: University Press of Florida, 2019.

Stevens, Michelle Ann, *Black Empire: The Masculine Global Imaginary of Caribbean Intellectuals in the United States, 1914–1962*. Durham: Duke University Press, 2005.

Elusive "Sun-Bright Hardness": The Caribbean Horizons of Black Renaissance Fiction in an Age of Rising US Empire

Primary Texts

Johnson, Charles. S. *Ebony and Topaz: A Collectanea. Opportunity, Journal of Negro Life*. New York: National Urban League, 1925.

Secondary Texts

Baldwin, Davarian L., and Minkah Makalani, eds. *Escape from New York: The New Negro Renaissance beyond Harlem*. Minneapolis: University of Minnesota Press, 2013.

Edwards, Brent Hayes. *The Practice of Diaspora: Literature, Translation, and the Rise of Black Internationalism*. Cambridge: Harvard University Press, 2003.

James, Winston. *Holding Aloft the Banner of Ethiopia: Caribbean Radicalism in Early Twentieth-Century America*. London: Verso, 1998.

Karem, Jeff. *The Purloined Islands: Caribbean-US Crosscurrents in Literature and Culture, 1880–1959*. Charlottesville: University of Virginia Press, 2011.

Lowney, John. *Jazz Internationalism: Literary Afro-Modernism and the Cultural Politics of Black Music*. Urbana: University of Illinois Press, 2017.

Luis-Brown, David, *Waves of Decolonization: Discourses of Race and Hemispheric Citizenship in Cuba, Mexico, and the United States*. Durham: Duke University Press, 2008.

Murray, Joshua M., and Ross K. Tangedal, eds. *Editing the Harlem Renaissance*. Clemson, SC: Clemson University Press, 2021.

Stephens Michelle Ann, *Black Empire: The Masculine Global Imaginary of Caribbean Intellectuals in the United States, 1914–1962*. Durham: Duke University Press, 2005.

White, Eric. *Transatlantic Avant-Gardes: Little Magazines and Localist Modernism*. Edinburgh: Edinburgh University Press, 2013.

What We Know That We Don't Know: Nella Larsen, James Baldwin, and Ocean Vuong on US Empire and Desire

Canaday, Margot. *The Straight State: Sexuality and Citizenship in Twentieth-Century America*. Princeton: Princeton University Press, 2009.

Ferguson, Roderick A., *Aberrations in Black: Toward a Queer of Color Critique*. Minneapolis: University of Minnesota Press, 2004.

Hernández, Bernadine Marie. *Border Bodies: Racialized Sexuality, Sexual Capital, and Violence in the Nineteenth-Century Borderlands*. Chapel Hill: University of North Carolina Press, 2022.

Macharia, Keguro. *Frottage: Frictions of Intimacy across the Black Diaspora*. New York: New York University Press, 2019.

Ordover, Nancy. *American Eugenics: Race, Queer Anatomy, and the Science of Nationalism*. Minneapolis: University of Minnesota Press, 2003.

Snorton, C. Riley. *Black on Both Sides: A Racial History of Trans Identity*. 1st ed. Minneapolis: University of Minnesota Press, 2017.

Somerville, Siobhan B. *Queering the Color Line: Race and the Invention of Homosexuality in American Culture*. Durham: Duke University Press, 2000.

Spillers, Hortense J. *Black, White, and in Color: Essays on American Literature and Culture*. Chicago: University of Chicago Press, 2003.

Walkiewicz, Kathryn. *Reading Territory: Indigenous and Black Freedom, Removal, and the Nineteenth-Century State*. Chapel Hill: University of North Carolina Press, 2023.

Wong, Edlie L. *Racial Reconstruction: Black Inclusion, Chinese Exclusion, and the Fictions of Citizenship*. New York: New York University Press, 2015.

Transpacific Entanglements: Korean Immigrant Writers and Militarized Modernity in American Literature

Baik, Crystal Mun-hye. *Reencounters: On the Korean War and Diasporic Memory Critique*. Philadelphia: Temple University Press, 2020.

Cho, Grace M. *Haunting the Korean Diaspora: Shame, Secrecy, and the Forgotten War*. Minneapolis: University of Minnesota Press, 2008.

Höhn, Maria and Seungsook Moon, eds. *Over There: Living with the US Military Empire from World War Two to the Present.* Durham: Duke University Press, 2010.

Kim, Daniel Y. *The Intimacies of Conflict: Cultural Memory and the Korean War.* New York: New York University Press, 2020.

Kim, Jodi. *Ends of Empire: Asian American Critique and the Cold War.* Minneapolis: University of Minnesota Press, 2010.

Palumbo-Liu, David. *Asian/American: Historical Crossings of a Racial Frontier.* Stanford: Stanford University Press, 1999.

Park, Josephine N. *Cold War Friendships: Korea, Vietnam, and Asian American Literature.* Oxford: Oxford University Press, 2016.

Yuh, Ji-Yeon. *Beyond the Shadow of Camptown: Korean Military Brides in America.* New York: New York University Press, 2002.

Undocutime: Containment, Coloniality, and Childhood in Javier Zamora's Solito

Abrego, Leisy. *Sacrificing Families: Navigating Laws, Labor, and Love across Borders.* Stanford: Stanford University Press, 2014.

Blitzer, Jonathan. *Everyone Who Is Gone Is Here: The United States, Central America, and the Making of a Crisis.* New York: Penguin, 2024.

Bradford, Anita Casavantes. *Suffer the Little Children: Child Migration and the Geopolitics of Compassion in the United States.* Chapel Hill: University of North Carolina Press, 2022.

Caminero-Santangelo, Marta. "Undocumented Immigration in Latina/o Literature." In *The Cambridge History of Latina/o American Literature*, ed. John Morán González and Laura Lomas, 469–87. New York: Cambridge University Press, 2018.

Chomsky, Aviva. *Central America's Forgotten History: Revolution, Violence, and the Roots of Migration.* Boston: Beacon, 2021.

Martínez, Óscar. *The Beast: Riding the Rails and Dodging Narcos on the Migrant Trail.* New York: Verso, 2014.

Menjívar, Cecilia and Krista Perreira, eds. *Undocumented and Unaccompanied: Children of Migration in the European Union and the United States.* New York: Routledge, 2021.

Rivas, Cecilia M. *Salvadoran Imaginaries: Mediated Identities and Cultures of Consumption.* New Brunswick: Rutgers University Press, 2014.

Saldaña-Portillo, Maria Josefina. "The Violence of Citizenship in the Making of Refugees: The United States and Central America." *Social Text* 37.4, no. 141 (2019): 1–21.

Zamora, Javier. *Unaccompanied.* Port Townsend: Copper Canyon Press, 2017.

Speculative Fiction as Anti-Colonial Theory: Indigenous and Latinx Film and Literature

Allinson, Jamie, China Miélville, Richard Seymour and Rosie Warren. *The Tragedy of the Worker: Towards the Proletarocene*. New York: Verso, 2021.

Bolaño, Roberto. *The Spirit of Science Fiction: A Novel*. Translated by Natasha Wimmer. New York: Penguin Press, 2019.

Delaney, Samuel R. *The American Shore*. Middletown: Wesleyan University Press, 2014.

Shorter Views: Queer Thoughts & The Politics of the Paraliterary. Middletown: Wesleyan University Press, 2000.

Gunn, James E., Marleen Barr and Matthew Candelaria. *Reading Science Fiction*. New York: Palgrave Macmillan, 2009.

Herrera, Yuri. *Signs Preceding the End of the World*. Translated by Lisa Dillman. New York: And Other Stories Press, 2015.

Le Guin, Ursula K. *The Language of the Night: Essays on Fantasy and Science Fiction*. New York: Scribner, 1979 [revised edition 2024].

Dreams Must Explain Themselves: The Selected Non-Fiction of Ursula Le Guin. London: Gollancz, 2018.

Afterword

Cheyfitz, Eric. *The Poetics of Imperialism: Translation and Colonization from The Tempest to Tarzan*. Expanded ed., Philadelphia: University of Pennsylvania Press, 1997.

Edwards, Brent Hayes. *The Practice of Diaspora: Literature, Translation, and the Rise of Black Internationalism*. Cambridge: Harvard University Press, 2003.

Griffiths, James. *Speak Not: Empire, Identity and the Politics of Language*. New York: Bloomsbury, 2022.

Lomas, Laura. *Translating Empire: José Martí, Migrant Latino Subjects, and American Modernities*. Durham: Duke University Press, 2008.

McWhorter, John H. *The Missing Spanish Creoles: Recovering the Birth of Plantation Contact Languages*. Berkeley: University of California Press, 2000.

Defining Creole. London: Oxford University Press, 2005.

Rogers, Gayle. *Incomparable Empires: Modernism and the Translation of Spanish and American Literature*. New York: Columbia University Press, 2016.

Valdéon, Roberto A. *Translation and the Spanish Empire in the Americas*. Amsterdam and Philadelphia: John Benjamins, 1984 [rpt. 2014].

Index

Cambridge Companions to ...

AUTHORS

Edward Albee edited by Stephen J. Bottoms

Margaret Atwood edited by Coral Ann Howells (second edition)

W. H. Auden edited by Stan Smith

Jane Austen edited by Edward Copeland and Juliet McMaster (second edition)

James Baldwin edited by Michele Elam

Balzac edited by Owen Heathcote and Andrew Watts

Beckett edited by John Pilling

Bede edited by Scott DeGregorio

Aphra Behn edited by Derek Hughes and Janet Todd

Saul Bellow edited by Victoria Aarons

Walter Benjamin edited by David S. Ferris

William Blake edited by Morris Eaves

Boccaccio edited by Guyda Armstrong, Rhiannon Daniels, and Stephen J. Milner

Jorge Luis Borges edited by Edwin Williamson

Brecht edited by Peter Thomson and Glendyr Sacks (second edition)

The Brontës edited by Heather Glen

Bunyan edited by Anne Dunan-Page

Frances Burney edited by Peter Sabor

Byron edited by Drummond Bone (second edition)

Albert Camus edited by Edward J. Hughes

Willa Cather edited by Marilee Lindemann

Catullus edited by Ian Du Quesnay and Tony Woodman

Cervantes edited by Anthony J. Cascardi

Chaucer edited by Piero Boitani and Jill Mann (second edition)

Chekhov edited by Vera Gottlieb and Paul Allain

Kate Chopin edited by Janet Beer

Caryl Churchill edited by Elaine Aston and Elin Diamond

Cicero edited by Catherine Steel

John Clare edited by Sarah Houghton-Walker

J. M. Coetzee edited by Jarad Zimbler

Coleridge edited by Lucy Newlyn

Coleridge edited by Tim Fulford (new edition)

Wilkie Collins edited by Jenny Bourne Taylor

Joseph Conrad edited by J. H. Stape

H. D. edited by Nephie J. Christodoulides and Polina Mackay

Dante edited by Rachel Jacoff (second edition)

Daniel Defoe edited by John Richetti

Don DeLillo edited by John N. Duvall

Charles Dickens edited by John O. Jordan

Emily Dickinson edited by Wendy Martin

John Donne edited by Achsah Guibbory

Dostoevskii edited by W. J. Leatherbarrow

Theodore Dreiser edited by Leonard Cassuto and Claire Virginia Eby

John Dryden edited by Steven N. Zwicker

W. E. B. Du Bois edited by Shamoon Zamir

George Eliot edited by George Levine and Nancy Henry (second edition)

T. S. Eliot edited by A. David Moody

Ralph Ellison edited by Ross Posnock

Ralph Waldo Emerson edited by Joel Porte and Saundra Morris

Ralph Waldo Emerson edited by Michael Jonik (new edition)

William Faulkner edited by Philip M. Weinstein

Henry Fielding edited by Claude Rawson

F. Scott Fitzgerald edited by Ruth Prigozy

F. Scott Fitzgerald edited by Michael Nowlin (second edition)

Flaubert edited by Timothy Unwin

E. M. Forster edited by David Bradshaw

Benjamin Franklin edited by Carla Mulford

Brian Friel edited by Anthony Roche

Robert Frost edited by Robert Faggen

Gabriel García Márquez edited by Philip Swanson

Elizabeth Gaskell edited by Jill L. Matus

Edward Gibbon edited by Karen O'Brien and Brian Young

Goethe edited by Lesley Sharpe

Günter Grass edited by Stuart Taberner

Thomas Hardy edited by Dale Kramer

David Hare edited by Richard Boon

TOPICS

British Literature of the French Revolution edited by Pamela Clemit

British Postmodern Fiction edited by Bran Nicol

British Romantic Poetry edited by James Chandler and Maureen N. McLane

British Romanticism edited by Stuart Curran (second edition)

British Romanticism and Religion edited by Jeffrey Barbeau

British Theatre, 1730–1830 edited by Jane Moody and Daniel O'Quinn

British Utopian Literature and Culture since 1945 edited by Caroline Edwards

Canadian Literature edited by Eva-Marie Kröller (second edition)

The Canterbury Tales edited by Frank Grady

Children's Literature edited by M. O. Grenby and Andrea Immel

The City in World Literature edited by Ato Quayson and Jini Kim Watson

The Classic Russian Novel edited by Malcolm V. Jones and Robin Feuer Miller

Comics edited by Maaheen Ahmed

Contemporary African American Literature edited by Yogita Goyal

Contemporary Irish Poetry edited by Matthew Campbell

Creative Writing edited by David Morley and Philip Neilsen

Crime Fiction edited by Martin Priestman

Dante's 'Commedia' edited by Zygmunt G. Barański and Simon Gilson

Dracula edited by Roger Luckhurst

Early American Literature edited by Bryce Traister

Early Modern Women's Writing edited by Laura Lunger Knoppers

The Eighteenth-Century Novel edited by John Richetti

Eighteenth-Century Poetry edited by John Sitter

Eighteenth-Century Thought edited by Frans De Bruyn

Emma edited by Peter Sabor

English Dictionaries edited by Sarah Ogilvie

English Literature, 1500–1600 edited by Arthur F. Kinney

English Literature, 1650–1740 edited by Steven N. Zwicker

English Literature, 1740–1830 edited by Thomas Keymer and Jon Mee

English Literature, 1830–1914 edited by Joanne Shattock

English Melodrama edited by Carolyn Williams

English Novelists edited by Adrian Poole

English Poetry, Donne to Marvell edited by Thomas N. Corns

English Poets edited by Claude Rawson

English Renaissance Drama edited by A. R. Braunmuller and Michael Hattaway (second edition)

English Renaissance Tragedy edited by Emma Smith and Garrett A. Sullivan Jr.

English Restoration Theatre edited by Deborah C. Payne Fisk

Environmental Humanities edited by Jeffrey Cohen and Stephanie Foote

The Epic edited by Catherine Bates

Erotic Literature edited by Bradford Mudge

The Essay edited by Kara Wittman and Evan Kindley

European Modernism edited by Pericles Lewis

European Novelists edited by Michael Bell

Fairy Tales edited by Maria Tatar

Fantasy Literature edited by Edward James and Farah Mendlesohn

Feminist Literary Theory edited by Ellen Rooney

Fiction in the Romantic Period edited by Richard Maxwell and Katie Trumpener

The Fin de Siècle edited by Gail Marshall

Frankenstein edited by Andrew Smith

The French Enlightenment edited by Daniel Brewer

French Literature edited by John D. Lyons

The French Novel: from 1800 to the Present edited by Timothy Unwin

Gay and Lesbian Writing edited by Hugh Stevens

German Romanticism edited by Nicholas Saul

Global Literature and Slavery edited by Laura T. Murphy

Gothic Fiction edited by Jerrold E. Hogle

The Graphic Novel edited by Stephen Tabachnick

The Greek and Roman Novel edited by Tim Whitmarsh

Greek and Roman Theatre edited by Marianne McDonald and J. Michael Walton

For EU product safety concerns, contact us at Calle de José Abascal, 56–1°, 28003 Madrid, Spain or eugpsr@cambridge.org.